The Beauty
of
Inflections

THE BEAUTY OF INFLECTIONS

Literary Investigations in Historical Method and Theory

JEROME J. McGANN

Thinking involves not only the flow of thoughts,
but their arrest as well. Where thinking suddenly
stops in a configuration pregnant with tensions, it
gives that configuration a shock, by which it crystallizes into . . . the sign of a . . . revolutionary
chance in the fight for the oppressed past.

WALTER BENJAMIN

CLARENDON PRESS · OXFORD

1985

Oxford University Press, Walton Street, Oxford OX2 6DP

London New York Toronto
Delhi Bombay Calcutta Madras Karachi
Kuala Lumpur Singapore Hong Kong Tokyo
Nairobi Dar es Salaam Cape Town
Melbourne Auckland

and associated companies in
Beirut Berlin Ibadan Mexico City Nicosia

Oxford is a trade mark of Oxford University Press

Published in the United States
by Oxford University Press, New York

British Library Cataloguing in Publication Data

McGann, Jerome J.
The beauty of inflections: literary
investigations in historical method and theory.
1. Criticism
I. Title
801'.95   PN81

ISBN 0-19-811730-2

Library of Congress Cataloging in Publication Data
McGann, Jerome J.
The beauty of inflections.
Includes index.
1. Historical criticism (Literature)—Addresses,
essays, lectures. 2. Literature and history—
Addresses, essays, lectures. 3. English literature—
19th century—History and criticism—Addresses,
essays, lectures. I. Title.
PN98.H57M35 1985   801'.95   84-27303
ISBN 0-19-811730-2

Typeset by DMB (Typesetting), Oxford
Printed in Great Britain at
The University Press, Oxford,
by David Stanford,
Printer to the University

For

Lee and Leo

Preface

The essays in this book were all written between 1977 and 1983, and they began to appear in print in December 1979, when the Keats essay was published. They are not arranged here in the precise chronological sequence of their composition or publication because topical and eristic considerations sometimes forced me to adopt a different method of ordering. Nevertheless, the chronology of the essays has seemed important to preserve, so I have supplied the dates of composition and/or publication at the end of each essay. The essays are intimately connected with two books of mine which were conceived and written during the same period, and which were published in 1983: *The Romantic Ideology* and *A Critique of Modern Textual Criticism.* This body of work is the first part of a project to reintroduce a comprehensive socio-historical method into the study of literary texts.

In the case of the essays here which have already been published, I have kept my revisions to a minimum. Most of the alterations have been minor and stylistic. In a few cases, however, I have introduced larger changes. The opening pages of the essay on Keats and of 'The Text, the Poem, and the Problem of Historical Method' are reduced from their original form. I have not eliminated this material, however, but merely resituated it where—in this book—it more properly belongs: in the general Introduction. Two other essays have been expanded from their original form, 'The Anachronism of George Crabbe' and 'The Book of Byron and the Book of a World'. The latter has, in fact, nearly doubled its original length. The shorter version was written for a collection of essays by various hands, *Poems in Their Place*, edited by Neil Fraistat, a book which is scheduled to appear about the same time as the present volume.

Several of these essays were written for very particular academic occasions which have affected their style and form of presentation. 'Shall These Bones Live?' was delivered as a lecture at the inaugural meetings of the Society for Textual

Scholarship, in 1981 in New York. 'Tennyson and the Histories of Criticism' and 'Re-Evaluating Christina Rossetti' were originally written as review-essays; the former appeared in *Review* iv (1982), and the latter in *Victorian Studies* xxiii (1980) under a slightly different title. In all three of these essays, scholarship and its institutions are a central object of concern— at least as important as the more specialized literary subjects which focus the discussions. I have preserved the topical character of these pieces for the same reason that I have supplied dates for the essays. In a book which so emphasizes the importance of social context and history, these (sometimes small) details help to give a local habitation and a name to the arguments and the issues.

The other essays in the collection which have already been published are the following: 'Keats and the Historical Method in Literary Criticism', *Modern Language Notes* xciv (1979); 'The Text, the Poem, and the Problem of Historical Method', *New Literary History* xii (1981); 'The Meaning of the Ancient Mariner', *Critical Inquiry* viii (1981); 'The Religious Poetry of Christina Rossetti', *Critical Inquiry* x (1983); 'The Anachronism of George Crabbe', *English Literary History* xlviii (1981). As noted above, a version of 'The Book of Byron and the Book of a World' will appear shortly in a collection of essays by various hands, and the same is the case with 'The Monks and the Giants: Textual and Bibliographical Studies and the Interpretation of Literary Works' and 'Rome and Its Romantic Significance'.

For advice, encouragement, and help of various kinds I would like to thank Amy Barrett, Shelley Bennett, Marilyn Butler, James Chandler, Stephen Gill, Betty Hyland, Cecil Lang, Marjorie Levinson, Peter Manning, Annabel Patterson, Marjorie Perloff, Mac Pigman, Kim Scott Walwyn, and the editors of *Critical Inquiry, English Literary History, Modern Language Notes, New Literary History, Review, Text,* and *Victorian Studies.*

Contents

I do not know which to prefer,
The beauty of inflections
Or the beauty of innuendoes,
The blackbird whistling
Or just after.

WALLACE STEVENS, 'Thirteen
Ways of Looking at a
Blackbird'

Introduction

I

Early in his career, in 1874, Nietzsche wrote what has since become a classic attack upon philology and historical method. *Vom Nutzen und Nachtheil der Historie für das Leben*—or, in its common English translation, *On the Use and Abuse of History*—is the philologist's critique of his own education and tradition. The five specific charges which he brings against the historical view of human culture and its products resolve themselves into two inversely related moral criticisms. First, the historical critic's method engenders a type of smug superiority through which the past and its works are brought to ruin in the name of 'objective understanding', which Nietzsche sees as a licence taken in bad faith in order to make the past fit the triviality of the present. Second, the method reinforces an ironical sense of historical belatedness. Students who are taught human affairs in an historical perspective learn only that they are themselves 'the faded last shoots of mighty and cheerful generations . . . to whom Hesiod's prophecy applies that men would one day be born with grey hair and that Zeus would destroy that generation as soon as that sign [had] become visible. Historical education is really a kind of inborn greyheadedness, and those who bear its mark from childhood on surely must attain the instinctive belief in *the old age of mankind.*'[1]

Nietzsche's critique, as he remarks elsewhere in the essay, is itself a product and form of historical argument. He writes as a professional philologist. Moreover, his indictment is by no means a wholesale rejection of historical method; on the contrary, it is explicitly structured as an attack upon presently instituted forms of academic thinking and procedures in the field of the human sciences. Nietzsche's aim is to save (what he calls) 'youth', by which in part he means himself, from Dryasdust and its supercilious twins, the Critic and the Professor. Historical method, it turns out, is not the enemy. The

---

[1] My text for this essay is translated as *On the Advantage and Disadvantage of History for Life*, trans. with an Introduction by Peter Preuss, Indianapolis, 1980, pp. 43-4.

enemy are the ignorant inheritors of a past greatness whose most immediate names were Herder, Wolf, and Eichhorn.

At the end of his essay Nietzsche delivers a subtle parable which means to tell how the future will be rescued from the malaise of historicity. I will return to that parable shortly. For the moment, however, I would like to emphasize two fundamental implications of Nietzsche's essay. The first we have already remarked upon, that an attack upon historical method, after the eighteenth century, can only be mounted from an historically self-conscious perspective. This is explicitly borne out in Nietzsche's essay, but we see it repeated later in all the well-known critiques of historical method from Croce to Troeltsch and Popper, including the more narrowly focused attacks of the literary critics such as Tate, Brooks, and Wimsatt. The second implication is related to the first, and has also been glanced at above: that Nietzsche's critique of historicism is an effort to explore and renovate the ideological ground of his own critical tradition.

Had Nietzsche been able to survey the next one hundred years of historical criticism, in philological studies at any rate, he would have seen that his early attack had achieved a remarkable success. Classical and Biblical studies, with which Nietzsche was most directly concerned, remained firmly tied to historicist perspectives, despite the fact that source criticism gave way to a number of new formalistic methods which culminated in the frankly ahistorical programmes along structural and semiotic lines. The study of national and vernacular scriptures, on the other hand, especially those in the English language, took a more sharp and definitive turn from traditional philological procedures. When the history of this critical reaction is written, Matthew Arnold's influence will figure prominently.

In English language studies *per se*, the argument with historical procedures began in earnest early in the twentieth century. Several important ideologues of the Modernist movement— men like Babbitt, Hulme, Wyndham Lewis, and of course Leavis—helped to move English studies into directions which would culminate in a schism within the academy. Philological work was carried on by scholars of various kinds, but the final task of textual studies—the interpretation of literary works, their incorporation into the living world of culture—was removed from scholarly hands and given to the hermeneut and the literary critic. The aftermath of these changes is well known: 'scholarship' retreated from the fields of ideological turmoil, where issues of value and meaning were of paramount concern, and 'criticism' undertook responsibility for dealing with these matters.

In making these accommodations, the academy fostered the isolation of literary work from its social and historical contexts, including the originary context of the author and his world, the subsequent contexts which used and transmitted earlier works, and the immediate context of the critic and his culture, where all of the work's earlier contexts would be—whether knowingly or otherwise—recapitulated. The famous exegetical tactic of the New Criticism and its structural and post-structural aftermath—the concentration upon a 'close reading' of 'the text' —is precisely designed to generate meaning which will establish no self-conscious or systematic relations with any of these contexts. Hesiod's myth, which Nietzsche so feared, seemed at last to be evaded, and grey-haired generations banished forever from poetry and the coasts of light. The final displacement of historical methods from the centre of literary studies had been accomplished.

This initial victory over the philological tradition by the New Criticism turned out to be, however, a pyrrhic one, as the academy itself began to recognize about fifteen years ago. I shall not rehearse the recent and well-known history during which literary studies woke up to a crisis of their disciplines. This period is marked throughout by, on the one hand, a series of institutional self-investigations and indictments, and, on the other, a proliferation of new 'textual strategies' which seek to salvage, by subtle and sometimes ingenious modifications, the customary methods of close reading and analysis.

In this collection of essays I shall argue that literary studies today are experiencing the effects of certain internal divisions and contradictions, and that the disciplinary crisis will not be overcome until these contradictions are overcome. Most imperative is the need to reintegrate the entire range of sociohistorical and philological methods with an aesthetic and ideological criticism of individual works. These essays represent a series of initial and exploratory ventures toward such a programme of reintegration. I have already sketched the general historical context within which the issues taken up in these essays ought to be placed. To understand their particular objects and lines of argument, however, it will be necessary to place this book in the briefer context of its immediate origins.

II

These essays were all written between 1977 and 1983. When I began working on the earliest of them, 'Keats and the Historical Method in Literary Criticism', I had no programmatic goals in mind, and least of all did I plan to write a series of related studies in historical methodology. In the course of my work on Keats and the history of Keats criticism, however, I began to think that a general programme for the historical study of literary works might be usefully plotted out, if only to supplement the aggressively ahistorical procedures which had been dominating hermeneutics since the early 1930s. This appeared to me a particularly relevant project because the most recent types of stylistic, formal, 'readerly', and structural methods were themselves growing more and more autonomous and self-referential. Such a result, it now seems clear, is the natural consequence of our age's dominant concept of 'the literary work' as an integrated system of linguistic signs. The formulations are many and familiar: the poetic object, the Verbal Icon, the Poem Itself, and so forth. Our criticism has become a mirror, perhaps a parody, of the subject it defined as its own.

In this situation, the renascence of an historically based critical procedure, fully elaborated, assumed in my mind a positive necessity. I undertook the development of such a programme through a sequence of localized investigations of particular problems in historical method and theory. Several topics recur. The first and by far the most important of these centred in the pedagogical problem of how to integrate an historical method with the task of teaching specific poems and literary works. Whatever shortcomings beset a concept of the literary work as autonomous verbal object, this idea generated a powerful set of pedagogical techniques. Perhaps the greatest achievement of the New Criticism and its formal aftermath was the discovery of a way to teach individual literary works within the arbitrary limits of a classroom.

As a result, a number of these essays contain set-piece literary explications consciously modelled on the well-known techniques of 'close reading' which were developed in and through the New Criticism. The effort here—see in particular the explications embedded in the Keats essay, 'Shall These Bones Live?', 'The Text, the Poem, and the Problem of Historical Method', and 'Tennyson and the Histories of Criticism'—was to demonstrate that the preparation of a finished close reading was not incompatible with an historical procedure. The enabling principle is that if a literary work arrives to our view as a unique order of unique appearances, then a grid of the poem's social and historical filiations, both intra- and extra-textual, should help to elucidate the poem's orders of uniqueness. The poem, whether viewed as an experience or as an event, is a nexus of various concrete social determinations, and these can be critically specified as an aesthetic order. Indeed, if the poetic work is understood either as a cultural experience or a cultural event, its special structures of uniqueness must be consciously graphed, at some level, in socio-historical terms.

These early exegetical demonstrations—all but one were carried out before 1980—served to clarify several basic theoretical questions. The most pressing of these was the following: if a literary work is not to be conceived as an autonomous system of verbal signs, on the one hand, or on the other as the (free or determined) creation of reader and/or critic, then how *is* it to be conceived? It was my studies in the work of Mikhail Bakhtin that led to a conception of the literary work as a complex event in socio-historical space, the always particularized interchange of a present with a past. Poems at once locate a dialectical encounter between the past and the present, and they represent, through processes of reflection, a particular instance of dialectical exchange which is taken in the present as given from and through the past. The reflection of the art work is itself a doubled event, involving as it does the act of reflection on the part of the reader or critic as well as the fact of reflection which is preserved in the received work. This view of the poetical work proved especially useful for explaining a number of commonplace but untheorized critical practices which scholars have always pursued. In particular, it gave a theoretical ground to all the traditional disciplines of philology, from paleography, textual criticism, and all types of bibliographical work to the varieties of biographical, historical, and sociological investigations. Without an historically and socially founded hermeneutics, all the work of the *philologia perennis* would have to be seen —and was in fact seen throughout the modern period—as either anterior or peripheral to literary criticism: in the words of René Wellek, as either 'preliminary operations' to literary studies proper, or investigations of matters which were 'extrinsic' to the literary work of art.[2]

My view, on the contrary, was that these kinds of literary study had to be conceived as central to hermeneutics if literary studies were not to collapse in the schism which had developed between the traditional forms of scholarship and the new modes of interpretation. In practical terms this meant that the various traditional scholarly methods and preoccupations—from textual and bibliographical studies, on the one hand, to sociological analysis on the other—would have to have their inherent and structural relevance to criticism and interpretation firmly demonstrated.

The essays in this book represent part of my effort to carry through these demonstrations. Several of the essays are fully eclectic in that they attempt to make use of a variety of scholarly procedures and methods. Other essays concentrate on the hermeneutic relevance of certain key scholarly methods which have fallen into disuse. 'Tennyson and the Histories of Criticism' works toward an historically grounded revaluation of a famous poem, and it attempts to integrate this interpretation with several disparate yet related sets of historical materials, including different phases of the reception history of Tennyson's work. A similar preoccupation with reception history runs through both of the essays on Christina Rossetti, though in these instances the main topics being explored have to do with problems of canon and periodization. Rossetti is a peculiarly useful subject through which to explore how certain writers move in or out of critical attention. In addition, her religious poetry offers a testing ground in which to work out a method-

---

[2] See René Wellek and Austin Warren, *Theory of Literature*, New York, second edition, 1949.

ology of stylistic periodization. Because Christian poems, especially in the Anglican and Anglo-Catholic tradition, preserve a more or less stable ideology between the sixteenth and the early twentieth centuries, their period-specific characteristics can be more readily isolated and studied.

Throughout these essays, however, a recurrent methodological position is being argued: that all of the disciplines of philology (broadly conceived) resolve themselves into two general areas of work—the history of the text and the history of criticism. These two great worlds of scholarship incorporate many sub-disciplines, and they are, furthermore, only to be distinguished from each other for operational and practical purposes. A comprehensive act of interpretation will perforce be deeply involved in both, and will, in addition, make very clear how fundamentally related to each other are these material and ideological lines of historical development.

The hermeneutic relevance of a work's textual and reception histories used to be at the centre of academic consciousness. That the academy no longer thinks in this way helps to explain why two of the key essays in this collection are 'The Monks and the Giants' and 'The Ancient Mariner: the Meaning of the Meanings'. In the former I have tried to demonstrate the fundamental importance of textual studies (properly so called) to hermeneutics generally and to the specific act of criticism in particular. The essay has as its companion-piece the short book *A Critique of Modern Textual Criticism* (1983) where this large subject is taken up in greater and more technical detail.

The essay on Coleridge has two principal goals: first, to illustrate in a practical way the importance of *Rezeptionskritik* to the exposure of poetic meaning; and second, to show that Coleridge's poem constitutes a profound and conscious embodiment of the philological principles and procedures which the present book is arguing. The groundwork of such a view was laid in the late eighteenth century, principally in Germany, through the Classical and Biblical studies of men like Friedrich August Wolf and J.G. Eichhorn. The *fons et origo* of modern socio-historical criticism lies in their work, which Coleridge studied and was deeply influenced by. It is an irony of some magnitude that 'The Rime of the Ancient Mariner'—a *tour de force* of the new textual and philological methods—should have had its historicist meanings erased by the later intrinsic traditions of English and American literary criticism.

The final section of this book collects together a set of essays which explore the critical functions which literary works perform in the human world, as well as the relation in which these critical functions stand to the aesthetic character of the literary work. Modern aesthetic theory and criticism—even that carried out in a Marxist frame—generally assume the ideological innocence of poetic works: as one highly influential commentator has put the matter, 'I do not rank real art among the ideologies.'[3] But the truth in this conception has never been disentangled from the error, and in the final four essays I try to explore some of the ideological functions of literary work, both imaginative and critical. (These pieces all relate to a recent, more comprehensively argued study that I have made of the same kinds of topic: *The Romantic Ideology. A Critical Investigation* (1983).)

These last essays also bring into focus this book's recurrent preoccupation with Romanticism, the Romantic Period, and the critical representations of these phenomena. More than the other essays in the book, the last four operate with certain crucial working assumptions and definitions. Since these ideas lie behind so many of my arguments, I want to set them forth here as explicitly as I can.

In my view, 'literary period' is an historical and critical concept which enables the scholar to analyse, and therefore clarify, patterns of change and continuity within dynamic fields. Such concepts examine historical realities whose inherent processes— whose dynamism—has been defined, for critical purposes, to be complete. Nevertheless, because the significance, effect, and hence the full reality of the periods remain a perpetual human interest and endeavour, the analytic concepts undergo perpetual refinement and reformulation.

In the Crabbe essay, for example, I focus on his poetic theory and practice alike, in order to highlight the chief fault-line in current views of the Romantic Period, so-called: that is, the inability of our periodizations to provide an adequate critical account of the work of major figures like Austen, Scott, and Crabbe. In the critical terms which currently dominate dis-

---

[3] Louis Althusser, 'A Letter on Art in Reply to André Daspré', in *Lenin and Philosophy*, London, second edition, 1977, p. 203.

cussions of the period 1789-1824, these figures seem only marginally significant. Yet a periodization which is unable to place such writers at the very centre of its historical-critical analyses cannot be regarded as adequate.

Though I do not argue this explicitly in any of the essays, my view is that criticism must—if it is to deal with these kinds of problem—make a sharp distinction between *Romanticism*, on the one hand (which is a critical concept with a more or less concealed ideological component), and *The Romantic Period* on the other (which is a critical concept that defines an historic reality). Romanticism dominated the ideological debates during the Romantic Period, and Romanticism as a cultural movement continues to operate in mutant and peripheral ways down to the present day. The persistence of its authority, even in its later, indominant, and often debased forms, accounts for the difficulty we have in analysing it historically.

During the six years I was occupied with these essays I made two attempts to sketch a finished programme of historical studies in literature, the first in the essay on Keats, the second in the 1981 essay 'The Monks and the Giants'. The second is somewhat more comprehensive than the first, but neither offers anything beyond a schema of the relevant operations. A thoroughly elaborated methodology for a practical socio-historical hermeneutics is much needed. The truth is that one must return to August Boeckh's great *Encyklopädie und Methodologie der philogischen Wissenschaften* (1877, 1886) to find a study which exhibits both a dependable imagination and an adequate grounding and rigour. In addition, a great deal of work remains to be done on the tactics of an historical criticism. How one decides which parts of the strategic programme need to be emphasized in particular case studies is always a difficult question. I am not even sure that one can theorize these sorts of problem at all. More useful, perhaps, would be the accumulation of a large body of practical studies in criticism carried out from various sociological and historical points of vantage. What is possible for a developed theory and programme will only emerge through the adventures of an actual practice, where the powers and the limits of a socio-historical method will finally get revealed. My present suspicion, which I mean to test and interrogate in the next few years, is that one should only invoke a full repertory of programmatic procedures when the subject of study seems *not* to require such a programme for its elucidation; or, correlatively, when the critic cannot imagine what relevance or results will emerge through the inauguration of such a programme. In all other cases, to set in operation a presumptively complete investigative scheme is apt to produce only pre-arranged, uncritical results.

In the meantime, I believe that the basic principles of a general theory of historical criticism are reasonably clear. First, we must reconceive the literary 'text' as the literary 'work', i.e. as a related series of concretely determinable semiotic events that embody and represent processes of social and historical experience. Second, and following from this, is the concept of a critical methodology as embracing two large and related fields: the history of the literary work's textualizations and the history of its reception. Both of these histories occupy themselves with three important heuristic distinctions: between the work at its point of origin, the work through its subsequent transmissions, and the work situated in the immediate field of a present investigation. Third, these topics and focuses of critical work must be seen as moments in a dialectical investigation. They cannot be pursued in isolation; they must be integrated into a critical process which encourages various points of view to comment upon and critically illuminate each other. Finally, 'meaning' in the literary experience will also be reconceived as the process by which literary works are produced and reproduced. Meaning in poetry is neither the ideology of the poem nor the ideology of the critic; it is the process in which those ideologies have found their existence and expression. All the meanings which have ever been ascribed to poems will only be understood and comprehended when these meanings have been grasped as parts of the histories which poems reflect and reproduce.

III

At the conclusion of *On the Use and Abuse of History* Nietzsche offers what he calls 'a parable' for 'the hopeful ones' who look to gain a 'rescue from the historical malady'. It is a parable which illuminates that 'point in time at which they will again be well enough to engage in studying history anew and to use history under the dominion of life'. It is a parable delivered under the 'hard motto' of the Delphic oracle: know thyself. Finally, it is a parable drawn from that fundamental treasury of philological understanding, Greek history and culture.

Nietszche begins by calling attention to the 'centuries in which the Greeks found themselves in a danger similar to the one in which we find ourselves, namely of being swamped by what is alien and past, of perishing through "history"':

for a long time their culture was rather a chaos of foreign, Semitic, Babylonian, Lydian and Egyptian forms and concepts, and their religion a veritable battle of gods of the whole orient . . . And nevertheless Hellenic culture became no aggregate, thanks to that Appollonian motto. The Greeks learned gradually *to organize chaos* by reflecting on themselves in accordance with the Delphic teaching, that is, by reflecting on their genuine needs . . . Thus they took possession of themselves again; they did not long remain the overloaded heirs and epigoni of the whole orient; after a difficult struggle with themselves . . . they even became the happiest enrichers and increasers of the inherited treasure and the firstcomers and models of all coming cultured peoples. (p. 64)

This parable can only operate on someone possessed of an historical consciousness, and its deepest truths are directed at those who understand the relation of *Alterthumswissenschaft* to our knowledge of Greek culture. Nietzsche is here alluding to the historical elucidation of Greece by philological criticism, and he calls up the emergence of fifth-century Athens via a glancing reference to the early Greek historians, especially Herodotus. We are asked to understand that it is the work of these historians which helped to forge, through self-understanding, the powerful consciousness of fifth-century Greece. Because Nietszche represents the Greek achievement as a gradual process, however, he also seems to suggest that Homer initiated this cultural development in his two great poems. Following his own philological tradition, Nietzsche definitely views the Homeric epics as historically situated documents, moments in a Greek consciousness of its social and ideological mastery over the known world.

More important for the meaning of Nietzsche's parable, however, is the subtle analogy he draws between the early Greek works which epitomized the emergence of Greek consciousness, and the nineteenth-century German works which served to elucidate that achievement more clearly than had ever been done before. 'German culture', which Nietzsche's essay all but identifies with philology and the disciplines of historical understanding, is represented as undergoing a struggle similar to the struggle of the early Greeks. The wit of Nietzsche's analogy springs from the central place which the study of ancient Greece occupied in German philology, where the 'chaos . . . of all antiquity' is the object of study (*'Chaos . . . der gesammten Vorzeit'*). The implied argument in the parable is not that these historically grounded investigations should be abandoned, but that they should be carried out in terms of immediate interests and human needs.

Nietzsche argues that the primary goal of the German philologist ought to be self-understanding, which would include, on the one hand, ordering historical studies towards securing the 'genuine needs' of society; and, on the other, using these studies to develop a self-critical social awareness. In Nietzsche's mind, this double goal is what historical studies, of all the disciplines, is most capable of securing. Nevertheless, it is also the goal which philology, in Nietzsche's day, seemed least interested in.

The essays in the present book are part of an effort to reformulate an educational programme which answers to Nietzsche's call. My general argument, therefore, is the following: that we have to recover those traditional philological procedures for putting us in touch with worlds, people, and experiences from the past, and with the media in which these things embodied themselves; for putting us in touch with them in the full range of their pastness and differentials. The ultimate purpose of establishing a structure of such differentials is not to lose one's self in a displaced world, which is certainly a danger in pursuing such methods, but to gain a measure by which our own present interests and ideologies may be critically observed. Past worlds, in an historical consciousness, make up points of fixity and finishedness, but not in some permanent and absolute sense. The finished past is constantly being reformulated into new forms of finishedness, forms which answer to the changing needs of the immediate world. Nevertheless, whatever form of finishedness the past may take, it can be—must be—made into an (arbitrary) measure in terms of which the present may be understood and judged. Indeed, the past is the *only* fixed measure we can turn to and use in a critical and self-correcting way. For we do not have any agreeable absolutes, and the future—the other of our two eternities—is, while dependable, beyond our final control. It is the past alone which offers us a fixed but non-absolute standard of judgement which can be altered and modified according to changing circumstances and points of view. The past is the heuristic measure, re-erected in the present, for establishing the securities of a future. For this reason, more than any other, it must provide the ground of our studies.

(1983)

I

Keats and the Historical Method
in Literary Criticism

I

Conflicts between formal or stylistic analysis and historical scholarship are a traditional problem in literary studies. In the field of hermeneutics, where the lines of disagreement tend to sharpen, the best commentators—Lionel Trilling, for example —have generally aimed for, and achieved, various pragmatic agreements. Few critics would take seriously any suggestion that Byron's poetry could be adequately interpreted without bringing a fair amount of historical and biographical infor-mation to bear.[1] On the other hand, a text-only approach has been so vigorously promoted during the last thirty-five years that most historical critics have been driven from the field, and have raised the flag of their surrender by yielding the title 'critic' to the victor, and accepting the title 'scholar' for them-selves.

This division of labour has produced a fundamentally un-stable situation because it is based upon unresolved and, what is worse, unexamined tensions and conflicts. The problems appear, at first, in a purely practical form: for the student needs to know how he is to decide whether (or in what way) historical and biographical information is needed for interpre-tation. Confronted with a particular text, we cannot always tell at what points (if any) we ought to press for some particular 'extrinsic' material or approach.[2] Textual problems of these sorts are widespread, nor are they a function of a certain sort of poem (like a topical satire) or a certain type of writer (like, say, Byron). They exist because of general critical assumptions about 'the mode of existence of a literary work of art'.[3] The introductory remarks in Paul deMan's well-known essay on Keats amount to a literary consensus not only about that author, but about the nature of poetry itself: 'In reading Keats, we are . . . reading the work of a man whose experience is mainly

[1] Even an anti-historical critic like Northop Frye recognizes that this demand which Byron makes on criticism is an indication of a more widespread problem in literary studies. See his *Fables of Identity*, New York, 1963, p. 174. But Frye does not propose a method for coping with the problems he sees.

[2] I take the term 'extrinsic' from the heuristic distinction between 'extrinsic' and 'intrinsic' approaches to literature set forth in René Wellek and Austin Warren's widely circulated handbook *Theory of Literature*, New York, second edition, 1949.

[3] The formulation is Wellek and Warren's (see chap. xii).

literary . . . In this case, we are on very safe ground when we derive our understanding primarily from the work itself.'[4] DeMan is a brilliant critic, and he knows perfectly well that no reading of a poem—not even a poem by Keats—can take place in a bell jar. This is why he is so careful to say that we must 'derive our understanding primarily from the work itself', for with that 'primarily' he allows himself the option to invoke, when he feels that it is necessary, 'extrinsic' material of various sorts. The manoeuvre is a theoretical blind which sets free the insight of his shrewd practical criticism. But the problems of theory and of method only arise more insistently than ever: how are we to decide—even if we grant deMan's premises about Keats —when to admit 'extrinsic' materials and approaches?

Such practical decisions will always remain problematic so long as the critic agrees to accept the great commonplace of twentieth-century literary criticism: that a poem is fundamentally a word-construct, a special arrangement of linguistic units, or—as we now like to say—a 'text'.[5] Once that idea is accepted, the originally heuristic categories 'extrinsic' and 'intrinsic' are instantly reified, and the so-called poem becomes alienated from its social setting. Consequently, the practical problem I initially pointed toward—how does a person decide when to invoke historical materials or methods?—reveals itself as fundamentally a procedural question. A comprehensive theory will show that we need not doubt the relevance of 'extrinsic' methods and materials; rather, what the critic must weigh are the problems of how best and most fully to elucidate the poem's (presumed) networks of social relations.

II

A proper general theory of poetry ought to free one from the mare's nest of pseudo-problems created by those several generations of critics who agreed to enter the prison house of language. What follows is a summary and extrapolation of certain key ideas set forth by the so-called Bakhtin School of criticism, a

---

[4] 'Introduction', *John Keats: Selected Poetry*, New York, 1966, xi.

[5] This idea is so fundamental to modern English and American critics that one even finds it advanced by commentators who profess an historical, social, even Marxist orientation. See, for example, Evan Watkins, *The Critical Act*, New Haven, 1978, pp. 158-9.

small group of Marxist critics from the Soviet Union who made an early attack upon formalist approaches to poetry.[6] The Bakhtin School's socio-historical method approaches all language utterances—including poems—as phenomena marked with their concrete origins and history.

Every concrete utterance is a social Act. At the same time that it is an individual material complex, a phonetic, articulatory, visual complex, the utterance is also a part of social reality. It organizes communication oriented toward reciprocal action, and itself reacts; it is also inseparably enmeshed in the communication event. Its individual reality is already not that of a physical body, but the reality of a historical phenomenon. Not only the meaning of the utterance but also the very fact of its performance is of historical and social significance, as, in general, is the fact of its realization in the here and now, in given circumstances, at a certain historical moment, under the conditions of the given social situation.[7]

[6] M. M. Bakhtin is perhaps best known for his books *Problems of Dostoevsky's Poetics*, Ann Arbor, 1973, and *Rabelais and his World*, Cambridge, Mass., 1968. But so far the most important work to come out of this school, and to have been translated, is P. N. Medvedev and M. M. Bakhtin, *The Formal Method in Literary Scholarship*, Baltimore, 1978, a theoretical study of immense importance. For further material on Bakhtin and his 'school' see *The Dialogic Imagination: Four Essays*, ed. Michael Holquist and trans. Caryl Emerson and Holquist, Austin, 1981, especially the 'Introduction' by Holquist; also the 'Forum on Mikhail Bakhtin' in *Critical Inquiry* x (December 1983); the 'Introduction' to *The Formal Method* and 'Introduction' to V. N. Volosinov's *Freudianism: A Marxist Critique*, trans. I. R. Titunik and ed. in collaboration with Neal R. Bruss, New York, 1976; and see also the translator's 'Introduction' to V. N. Volosinov, *Marxism and the Philosophy of Language*, trans. Ladislav Matejka and I. R. Titunik, New York, 1973. Bakhtin's brilliant essay 'Discourse in Life and Discourse in Art' is reprinted in the *Freudianism* volume (Appendix I) and it anticipates many of the insights of *The Formal Method*, though the style of approaching the problems each takes up is quite different. On 'context', for example, Bakhtin says:

In life, verbal discourse is clearly not self-sufficient. It arises out of an extraverbal pragmatic situation and maintains the closest possible connection with that situation. Moreover, such discourse is directly informed by life itself and cannot be divorced from life without losing its import.

The kind of characterizations and evaluations of pragmatic, behavioural utterances we are likely to make are such things as: 'that's a lie', 'that's the truth', 'that's a daring thing to say', 'you can't say that', and so on and so forth.

 All these and similar evaluations, whatever the criteria that govern them (ethical, cognitive, political, or other), take in a good deal more than what is enclosed within the strictly verbal (linguistic) factors of the utterance. *Together with the verbal factors, they also take in the extraverbal situation of the utterance.* These judgements and evaluations refer to a certain whole wherein the verbal discourse directly engages an event in life and merges with that event, forming an indissoluble unity. The verbal discourse itself, taken in isolation as a purely linguistic phenomenon, cannot, of course, be true or false, daring or diffident.

[7] *The Formal Method*, p. 120.

Bakhtin goes on to specify methods for analysing contextualized language, and for defining more particularly the sociology of poetic utterance. By developing the concept of 'social evaluation' he lays the ground for a general theory of poetic construction.

> The material of poetry is not language understood as the aggregate or system of linguistic possibilities (phonetic, grammatical, lexical). The poet does not select linguistic forms, but rather the evaluations posited in them. All the linguistic characteristics of the word that remain after the abstraction of these evaluations are not only unable to be the material of poetry, but cannot even be examples of grammar.
>
> For instance, a linguistic example is a conditional utterance; a pure linguistic form only lends itself to symbolic designation. A linguistic form is only real in the concrete speech performance, in the social utterance.[8]

Or, in a still more concise formulation: 'The material of poetry is language . . . as a system of social evaluations, not as the aggregate of linguistic possibilities.'[9]

Nevertheless, to recognize these 'extrinsic' connections of the poetic utterance with its surrounding environment is to risk falling into a crudely reflective theory of poetry. Poetic utterances differ from every other form of language use in a special way which defines the character of poetic or literary form. Elaborating upon his analysis of poetry in terms of the concept of social evaluation, Bakhtin puts the matter this way.

> Every epoch has its sphere of objects for cognition, its own sphere of epistemological interests. The object enters the epistemological purview and becomes the focus of its social energy only to the extent that the actual needs of the given epoch and the given social group dictate. Social evaluation determines the choice of a theme. Social evaluation also organizes the scientific utterance on all stages of scientific work. But it does not do so for the sake of the utterance. It organizes the work of cognition itself, and the word only as a necessary but dependent aspect of this work. Here evaluation is not complete in the word.
>
> The poetic work is a different matter.
>
> Here the utterance is detached both from its object and from action. Here social evaluation is complete within the utterance itself. One might say its song is sung to the end. The reality of the utterance

---

[8] Ibid., p. 122.   [9] Ibid., p. 133.

serves no other reality. Social evaluation pours out and concludes in pure expression. Therefore, all aspects of the material, meaning, and concrete act of realization without exception become equally important and necessary.[10]

Poetry, that is to say, is a type of expression which forces its language to exhaust itself within the limits of the poetic experience as such. Poetic language, we say, is not directed to any extra-poetic use. But we must not take this correct idea to suggest that poetic experiences take place outside of history and specific social environments. To say that the forms of poetic language are exhausted in the particular poem would be correct, but to say that they are exhausted in the poetic experience could be misleading. The poetic language of specific poems has no extra-poetic use, but specific poetic utterances—specific poems—are human acts occupying social space; as such, they most certainly are involved with extra-poetic operations. For poetry is itself one form of social activity, and no proper understanding of the nature of poetry can be made if the poem is abstracted from the experience of the poem, either at its point of origin or at any subsequent period.[11] The special character of poetry and art—its universal or eternal aspect so-called—is that it permits its audience to encounter the human experience of the poem as finished, not only in respect to the poem's immediate, specified circumstances, but in terms of all human history (past and future). The poem, like all human utterances, is a social act which locates a complex of related human ideas and attitudes. Unlike non-aesthetic utterance, however, poetry's social evaluations are offered to the reader *under the sign of com-*

---

[10] Ibid., p. 126-7.

[11] Compare Bakhtin's 'Discourse in Life and Discourse in Art', op.cit., p. 98:
Aesthetic communication, fixed in a work of art, is, as we have already said, entirely unique and irreducible to other types of ideological communication such as the political, the juridical, the moral, and so on. If political communication establishes corresponding institutions and, at the same time, juridical forms, aesthetic communication organizes only a work of art. If the latter rejects this task and begins to aim at creating even the most transitory of political organizations or any other ideological form, then by that very fact it ceases to be aesthetic communication and relinquishes its unique character. *What characterizes aesthetic communication is the fact that it is wholly absorbed in the creation of a work of art, and in its continuous re-creations in the co-creation of contemplators, and does not require any other kind of objectification.* But, needless to say, this unique form of communication does not *exist in isolation*; it participates in the unitary flow of social life, it reflects the common economic basis, and it engages in interaction and exchange with other forms of communication.

pletion. That sign of completion is what formalists recognized as
their object of study; i.e. the integral language construction of
the poem, or what is called 'the text'. But this 'text' is not what
we should understand as 'a poem'. Rather, what we ought to
see is that 'text' is the linguistic state of the 'poem's' existence.
No poem can exist outside of a textual state any more than a
human being can exist outside of a human biological organism.
But just as a person is not identical to a particular human body,
so neither is a poem equal to its text.[12]

The special procedures which are appropriate for the study
of the poem's text are what literary critics—especially modern
ones—most often concentrate upon. An exclusive attention to
the poetic text, rather than to the entirety of the poetic event,
will necessarily produce a narrow critical focus. But this matter
is not my immediate concern. For the present what we need to
see is that the poetic text functions primarily as the sign of the
poem's completion. In every poem, we encounter a localized
and time-specific set of human circumstances which—because
of their placement in artistic space—enter our experience as if
their connections with all of human history were clearly present.
The poem seems aware of this historical totality—its integral
form is the sign of this seeming knowledge—and it persuades
its reader that such a totality is not just a poetic illusion, but
a truth. What is crucial to see, however, is that this experience
of finality and completion—of the poem as trans-historical—
fundamentally depends upon our initial experience of the
poem's complete, social particularity.

III

The Bakhtin School did not go on to develop, or even to outline, a methodological scheme for a proper historical criticism.[13]
Of course, such a scheme is implicit in all the practical historical criticism which different critics and scholars have produced

---

[12] The distinction here between 'poem' and 'text' seems to me related to what
Coleridge and Shelley were trying to articulate when they distinguished between
'poetry' and 'a poem'. See *Biographia Literaria*, chaps. xiii-xiv and *A Defence of Poetry*.

[13] The clear purpose of *The Formal Method* and the other theoretical works by
Bakhtin cited above is a critical rather than a synthetic one. Nevertheless, these works
repeatedly suggest, though never in a systematic way, various positive analytic procedures which a sociological poetics might follow.

(from the most particular bibliographical descriptions to the most broadly ranging studies in *Kulturgeschichte*). Generally speaking, historical critics acknowledge that such a scheme should emerge out of a dialectic between the work of art's point of origin, on the one hand, and its point of reception on the other.

The distinction between point of origin and point of reception is fundamental to any historical analysis. Without more precise distinctions, however, we will find that problems of definition arise at every juncture.[14] At this point, therefore, I want to describe—briefly, but as completely as I can—the basic procedural forms which should govern a complete historical project in literary criticism. These procedures are the practical derivatives, as I see them, of the theoretical formulations of the Bakhtin School.

Although writing verse is itself a social act, only when the poem enters circulation—in manuscript copies, in private printings, or by publication—does it begin its poetic career. Once begun, however, a poem opens itself to the widest possible variety of human experiences.

To determine the significance of a poem at its point of origin demands that we study its bibliography. That subject is the *sine qua non* of the field, for in the study of the poem's initial manuscript and printed constitutions we are trying to define the social relationships between author and audience which the poem has called into being. It makes a great difference if, for example, an author writes but does not print a poem; it also makes a difference whether such a poem is circulated by the author or not, just as it makes a very great difference indeed when (or if) such a poem is printed, and where, and by whom.

The expressed intentions, or purposes, of an author are also significant for understanding a poem. At the point of origin those intentions are codified in the author's choice of time, place, and form of publication—or none of the above, by which

---

[14] For example: what are we to understand as the point of origin? Is it the work's date of composition? The date of publication? And what difference would it make? Correspondingly, how do we distinguish current activity from the critical acts of the past? And is editorial work performed after a writer's death part of the work's critical history, or is it rather to be related to the work's point of origin? I believe that theoretical questions of these sorts—others will easily come to mind—begin to dissolve as soon as one develops a coherent methodology.

I mean his decision *not* to publish at all, or to circulate in manuscript, or to print privately. All such decisions take the form of
specific social acts of one sort or another, and those acts enter
as part of the larger social act which is the poem in its specific
(and quite various) human history.

What we call 'author intentions' all appear in his particular
statements about his own work. Those statements may be part
of a private or even a public circulation during his lifetime, but
as often as not they only appear later, when (for example) conversations or letters or other ephemeral writings are posthumously given to the world (an event that likewise occurs
under very specific circumstances). All publications of such
material are of course social events in their own right, and they
always modify, more or less seriously, the developing history of
the poem.

Once the poem passes entirely beyond the purposive control
of the author, it leaves the pole of its origin and establishes the
first phase of its later dialectical life (what we call its critical
history). Normally the poem's critical history—the moving
pole of its receptive life—dates from the first responses and
reviews it receives. These reactions to the poem modify the
author's purposes and intentions, sometimes drastically, and
they remain part of the processive life of the poem as it passes
on to future readers.

From any contemporary point of view, then, each poem we
read has—when read as a work which comes to us from the
past—two interlocking histories, one that derives from the
author's expressed decisions and purposes, and the other that
derives from the critical reactions of the poem's various
readers. When we say that every poem is a social event, we
mean to call attention to the dialectical relation which plays
itself out historically among these various human beings.

The traditional function of historical criticism has always
been taken to involve the study and analysis of these past sets of
relations. Roy Harvey Pearce's famous essay 'Historicism
Once More' shows this quite clearly. But the historical method
in criticism, to my view, involves much more, since every contemporary critic, myself at this moment included, focuses on
something besides a poem written, read, and reproduced in the
past. The critic focuses as well on the present and the future,

that is to say on the critic's audience, in whom he discerns the locus of his hopes for the project which his criticism *is*. Any reading of a poem that I make is a social act not primarily between myself and (say) Keats's work, but between myself and a particular audience.

Since this is always the case, the same sort of historical awareness which we would bring to bear on the past history of a poem must be introduced into every immediate analysis. In this case, the analysis must take careful account of all contextual factors that impinge on the critical act. Most crucially, this involves the need for precise definitions of the aims and the limits of the critical analysis. Like its own object of study ('literature'), criticism is necessarily 'tendentious' in its operations. The critic's focus upon history as constituted in what we call 'the past' only achieves its *critical* fulfilment when that study of the past reveals its significance in and for the present and the future.

I should add that everything I have noticed here is always involved in every critical act, whether the critic is aware or not that such matters are involved in his work, and whether the critic is an historical critic or not. (A person may, for example, give a reading of 'La Belle Dame Sans Merci' in total ignorance of the poem's bibliographic history. Students do it all the time, and so, alas, do some scholars. None the less, that history is always *present* to a person's critical activity despite his ignorance of that history, and even despite his ignorance *of* his ignorance. It is simply that the history is *not* present to his *individual* consciousness.) One of the principal functions of the socio-historical critic is to heighten the levels of social self-consciousness with which every critic carries out the act of literary criticism.

IV

Let me now illustrate how these procedures operate by looking at a few poems by Keats.[15] I want to start with a simple example

[15] Because the subjects of this discussion will necessarily appear to be material recovered from the past, I may seem to be setting aside the immediate context, and hence avoiding what I have called criticism's 'future project'. But in fact the present context and the future project are both self-consciously present in the rhetorical structure and aims of this essay. Keats has been deliberately chosen for obvious reasons,

of the way an historically oriented perspective can work from small details to open up for exploration large and significant literary matters. The first example, then, will try to demonstrate not historical *method* so much as the tactics one naturally employs when one operates *within* an historical method in literary analysis. This initial example is meant to prepare the ground for the subsequent more rigorous analyses. I should re-emphasize here that the illustrations are all taken from a poet for whom historical analysis—by the virtually unanimous decision of western literary critics—has no relevance whatsoever.

The following lines are from an early poem of Keats, 'To George Felton Mathew'.

> Too partial friend, fain would I follow thee
> Past each horizon of fine poesy . . .
> But 'tis impossible. Far different cares
> Beckon me sternly from soft 'Lydian airs',
> And hold my faculties so long in thrall
> That I am oft in doubt whether at all
> I shall again see Phoebus in the morning;
> Or flushed Aurora in the roseate dawning;
> Or a white naiad in a rippling stream;
> Or a rapt seraph in a moonlight beam;
> Or again witness what with thee I've seen—
> The dew by fairy feet swept from the green
> After a night of some quaint jubilee,
> Which every elf and fay had come to see,
> When bright processions took their airy march
> Beneath the curved moon's triumphal arch.
> (Lines 11-12, 17-30)[16]

The passage first drew my attention when I tried to understand, clearly, what scene Keats was trying to represent for his

and the poems to be discussed have not by any means been randomly selected (no one ever acts randomly). Were I to be discussing historical method with a different audience —undergraduates, say—I would probably choose different texts altogether and reorganize the entire structure of the paper. As I have already argued, all criticism seems to me, by definition, tendentious in character. A critic will be working within an historical method to the degree that he tries not merely to be personally self-conscious about his polemical aims, but to keep his audience aware of those aims at all times.

16 The lines here, and elsewhere, are quoted from Miriam Allott's fine edition, *The Poems of John Keats*, London, 1970. I have preferred this to Jack Stillinger's purely textual edition (*The Poems of John Keats*, Cambridge, Mass., 1978) because Allott's edition also gives useful historical annotation.

reader ('reader' in general, but also, specifically, George Felton Mathew). Who are those elves and fays, what is that jubilee, where are the bright processions, when were those nights? Is it some scene from mythology, from art? Is it purely imaginary and not to be specified beyond the poem?

None of Keats's editors or commentators answered these questions, or even raised them. But Miriam Allott, in her fine edition, implicitly acknowledged the relevance of such queries when she quoted George Felton Mathew's remark that 'when Keats wrote his epistle to me . . . he was walking the hospitals'.[17] That is, when Keats wrote his epistle, the lines 'far different cares / Beckon me sternly from soft "Lydian airs"' contained a specific and personal reference encoded within a more generalized remark. The generalized reference was for the public at large, whereas the personal reference would be available only to what Byron used to call the 'the knowing ones'.

Keats had begun his work at Guy's Hospital in London in October 1815, and he wrote these lines as part of a verse epistle to Mathew in November 1815, after Keats had read a poem Mathew had just published. In the passage at hand, Keats is telling Mathew that he is too busy at the hospital to write poetry, and he wistfully regrets the imaginative pleasures that he and Mathew shared together. These pleasures are objectified in those nymphs and fays and jubilees and processions — all commonplace examples of the artifices of poetry.

But this list of poetical paraphernalia is not a recollection of some 'fairy rings and moonlit groves of Mathew's verse';[18] it specifically recalls certain actual occurrences which Keats, his brother George, Mathew, and Mathew's cousins shared during the summer of 1815. Mathew could still remember, many years later, that it 'pleased me much to see [Keats] and his brother George enjoy themselves so much at our little domestic concerts and dances'[19] during that summer.

---

[17] Allott edition, p. 25, n. to lines 17-18.
[18] Aileen Ward, *John Keats. The Making of a Poet*, New York, Compass Books edition, 1967, p. 51.
[19] See *The Keats Circle: Letters and Papers 1816-1879*, ed. H. E. Rollins, Cambridge, Mass., 1965, ii. 184-8. Over thirty years later Mathew's cousin Caroline also remembered the revels quite clearly, but she had in the meantime developed some rather stern moral attitudes, so that she could not recall the scenes very fondly: see *The Keats Circle* ii. 189-91. See also J. M. Murry, *Studies in Keats*, London, 1930, chap. 1.

To see that the passage refers to specific historical events is perforce to be made aware of the extreme artificiality of the poetic style, and to be reminded as well how much of Keats's early verse typifies such a style. Throughout the poetry of 1814-17 the men and women Keats actually moves among are variously called 'fays', 'elves', 'nymphs', 'swains', and he employs as well a whole array of related Aesopian language to speak of other, equally ordinary matters. Later, under Hunt's influence, his artificial manner began to develop along a number of other lines, and the result we have come to call the Cockney style, which dominates both the 1817 volume and *Endymion*.

Of course, the general characteristics of Keats's early verse are well enough known to academics. I raise the matter again, in this context, only because the significance of this Cockney style—its specifically poetic significance—is not very widely recognized, even among specialists. Only by reading such poetry in a sharply specified historical frame of reference are we able to see, at this date, the aesthetic domain which Cockney verse attempted to conquer, and hence to describe precisely not merely the abstract *characteristics*, but the felt *qualities* of its poetic structure.

When critics today talk about Keats's Cockney poetry they dismiss it as some sort of aberrant juvenile necessity, one of those odd preludes to genius with which the history of art is generally marked. Here is a good critic's good summary of the technical characteristics of that 'precious, luscious, plaintively sentimental kind of verse' we call Cockney poetry:

As experiments in what he calls 'unaffected' or artless language, his verses sometimes degenerate into colloquial chatter; and adopting the manner of Spenser and seventeenth-century Spenserians, he writes a precious, luscious, plaintively sentimental kind of verse. There is no fusion, but just a queer juxtaposition of the natural and the archaic. The other characteristics of Hunt's poetry—especially of his vocabulary and versification—stem from his desire to secure a medium of expression which is both luxurious and lively, and have been noted in detail by De Selincourt, Claude Finney, W. J. Bate, and other critics and commentators: use of abstract nouns expressing a concrete thing or idea; abundance of present participles; predilection for adverbs formed from present participles, and delight in the use of —y adjectives; divergence from the closed couplet resulting in extreme looseness of structure; liberal use of double rhymes, trisyllabic feet, and

varied medial pauses; stress-failure; accentuation of final syllables of
polysyllabic rhyme words. Hunt apparently confused freedom with
laxity, and these stylistic devices—or aberrations—had undoubtedly
a pernicious influence on the young Keats who studied *A Feast of the
Poets* and the *Story of Rimini* with avidity.[20]

   If we return to the early reviewers who named and defined
the Cockneyism of Hunt and Keats, we find all of these qualities
enumerated, and most of them deplored. We also find, however, a pattern of negative remarks on the 'uncleanness of this
school'[21] as well as recurrent references to the 'slang' of its style
and its general effort at a casual and colloquial manner. Indeed,
the other recurrent charge, of vulgarity, is only explicable in
such a context. The reviewers who make this charge are cen-
suring not merely the erotic subjects in Keats's poetry but
Keats's peculiarly mannered treatment of sexual images and
subjects.

> Feed upon apples red and strawberries,
> And choose each pleasure that my fancy sees;
> Catch the white-handed nymphs in shady places
> To woo sweet kisses from averted faces,
> Play with their fingers, touch their shoulders white
> Into a pretty shrinking with a bite
> As hard as lips can make it . . .
>   ('Sleep and Poetry', lines 103-9)

> I stood tip-toe upon a little hill,
> The air was cooling, and so very still
> That the sweet buds which with a modest pride
> Pull droopingly, in slanting curve aside,
> Their scantly leaved and finely tapering stems,
> Had not yet lost those starry diadems . . .
>   ('I Stood Tip-Toe', lines 1-6)

'Vulgar' is a precise and accurate description of passages like
these. But we will not understand the *meaning* of that charge
unless we see that it is delivered from a certain perspective. The
reviewers who censure Keats's vulgarity consistently see him
from a class-conscious perspective. Keats is low-born and
ought not to be writing poetry in the first place; he lacks the

---

[20] Bhabatosh Chatterjee, *John Keats: His Mind and Work*, Bombay, 1971, p. 211.

[21] My discussion here is in debt to John O. Hayden's fine synthetic description of
contemporary reactions to 'The Cockney School' in his *The Romantic Reviewers*,
Chicago, 1968, pp. 176-215. Here see p. 189.

appropriate education for the office. That social judgement, as is well known, generates the notoriously *ad hominem* ridicule which some of the reviewers heaped upon Keats. But that social judgement also generates the related, and apparently 'technical' point: that Keats's style violates poetic propriety by treating a 'high' subject in a 'low' diction and colloquial manner. In fact, the attack upon the Cockney School is in many respects a repetition of the attack upon Wordsworth's programme in the Lyrical Ballads. In both cases the more traditional critics insist that a common lexicon and a colloquial style in poetry are only proper within certain prescribed—normally, comic—limits.

Against this background let us look at the following passage from the *Edinburgh Magazine*'s review of the 1817 volume:

He seems to have formed his poetical predilections in exactly the same direction as Mr. Hunt; and to write, from personal choice, as well as emulation, at all times, in that strain which can be most recommended to the favour of the general readers of poetry, only by the critical ingenuity and peculiar refinements of Mr. Hazlitt. That style is vivacious, smart, witty, changeful, sparkling, and learned—full of bright points and flashy expressions that strike and even seem to please by a sudden boldness of novelty,—rather abounding in familiarities of conception and oddnesses of manner which shew ingenuity, even though they be perverse, or common, or contemptuous. The writers themselves seem to be persons of considerable taste, and of comfortable pretensions, who really appear as much alive to the socialities and sensual enjoyments of life, as to the contemplative beauties of nature. In addition to their familiarity, though,—they appear to be too full of conceits and sparkling points, ever to excite any thing more than a cold approbation at the long-run—and too fond, even in their favourite descriptions of nature, of a reference to the factitious resemblances of society, ever to touch the heart. Their verse is straggling and uneven, without the lengthened flow of blank verse, or the pointed connection of couplets. They aim laudably enough at force and freshness, but are not so careful of the inlets of vulgarity, nor so self-denying to the temptations of indolence, as to make their force a merit.[22]

Certain phrases here are extremely interesting: the repeated comment on Keats's excessive 'familiarity' and poetic colloquialism, as well as the recurrent sense that the poetry is also—

---

[22] 'On the Cockney School of Poetry', *Edinburgh Magazine* (Oct. 1817), p. 256.

perhaps paradoxically?—marked by a smart mannerism. The general view is that Keats's work is a tissue of self-conscious artifice and poetic conceits.

Today we do not think of Keats's early poetry as 'vivacious, smart, witty, changeful, sparkling, and learned'. But the early reviewers—whether they praised, censured, or merely described Keats's work—did see the poetry in this way. Such descriptive terms necessarily offer an odd contrast to the views of twentieth-century critics, who customarily see Keats's early work as mawkish, self-indulgent, sentimental. The explanation of this notable difference of views is not my present concern, but it could be found through an analysis of the ideological structures of modern critical opinions.

For my present purposes, what I want to emphasize is this: that the Cockney style of Keats is sentimental to modern ears only *because* it is also self-consciously 'smart, witty . . . and learned'. As the reviewer notes, the style is marked by colloquialism and familiarity, and a lively, cosmopolitan chattiness. Indeed, this chattiness—recall the passage I quoted above from the verse epistle to Mathew—is directly, intimately related to the mannered and artificial style of the poetry. A close, modern analogue to the sort of work produced in Keats's early epistles, or in 'Sleep and Poetry' and 'I Stood Tip-toe', is the verse style recently cultivated by Frank O'Hara and the New York School in general.

V

The previous example illustrates the tactical procedures which typify an historical approach, as well as the way historical information tends to open up new dimensions for a more comprehensive and precise critical analysis. I now want to extend that discussion by showing, through a series of illustrative examples, how and why poetic analysis *requires* an historical method if it is to achieve either precision or comprehensiveness. This demonstration takes for its subject the idea of 'context' and tries to explain the special relevance of this for poetry, as well as the necessity of an historical method for elucidating the specifically pertinent contexts which penetrate every poem we read.

'La Belle Dame Sans Merci' is a great and famous poem, and has been much commented upon; yet for all that attention, its physical text has not been much analysed, nor ever satisfactorily. One is made especially aware of this problem because of Jack Stillinger's new edition of Keats, which Harvard Press announces as 'Definitive'.[23] In the Harvard edition the poem is printed in the physical form all of us, probably, have always read. The interesting thing is that this is not the text which Keats himself printed. Many questions arise in such a situation, but to an historical critic the bibliographical question will be the fundamental one; for in that question we begin to elucidate the poem's critical history. Astonishing as it may seem, that history remains to this day tangled and even mystified, despite the fact that the material for unravelling it is largely ready to hand.

Keats wrote his poem in April 1819. He did nothing with it immediately, but later published it, in May 1820, in Leigh Hunt's weekly literary periodical *The Indicator*. It appeared there signed simply 'Caviare', which was an allusion to the line in *Hamlet* ''twas caviare to the general' (Act II, Scene 2). This text is the only one Keats ever published, for he did not choose to print the poem in his 1820 collection, an interesting fact in its own right (the volume was published in June). The poem first entered Keats's collected works in 1848, in Richard Monckton Milnes's *Life, Letters, and Literary Remains, of John Keats*. In this 1848 printing, however, the text was taken from a copy of the poem made by Charles Brown. No one knows the source of Brown's text, though editors have conjectured, not implausibly, that it was made from a (now lost) holograph fair copy. This 1848 text, derived from Brown's copy, is the one we now read, and it differs greatly from the text printed by Keats himself. The new Harvard edition also prints the Brown/1848 text.[24]

Under the circumstances, the *prima facie* bibliographic facts would normally, and without any question, demand that an editor—especially an editor in 1978—print *The Indicator* text, not the Brown/1848 text, for it is *The Indicator* text which, so far

---

[23] *The Poems of John Keats*, Cambridge, Mass., 1978.

[24] For a good brief synopsis of the essential bibliographical data see Jack Stillinger, *The Texts of Keats's Poems*, Cambridge, Mass., 1964, pp. 232-4 and Stillinger's edition, pp. 643-4.

as we can tell, most closely corresponds to the author's final, active intentions. The question then naturally arises: why has the post-authorial critical tradition from 1848 to the present normally printed, read, and studied the poem in the Brown/ 1848 text? For a study of that tradition, particularly during its past fifty years or so, shows that editors and commentators are aware of the problem and have all along deliberately chosen not to print *The Indicator* text.

Arguments have been made to suggest that the Brown/1848 text more closely represents Keats's final intentions, but they are all suppositious, and have persuaded no one. The history of the criticism further shows that the choice was in fact made because certain key readers felt that *The Indicator* text was not so good a poem as the other. [25] An impressionistic argument was

[25] Sidney Colvin, in his *John Keats*, London, 1920, vehemently denounces *The Indicator* text on aesthetic grounds, and explicitly calls upon the Oxford University Press to revise its edition by removing *The Indicator* text. His argument (which is typical of this approach) deserves full quotation because it has been so influential (pp. 469-70):

> During those unhappy months at Kentish Town Keats's best work was given to the world. First, in Leigh Hunt's *Indicator* for May 20, *La Belle Dame sans Merci*, signed obviously in bitterness, 'Caviare' (Hamlet's 'caviare to the general'), and unluckily enfeebled by changes for which we find no warrent either in Keats's autograph or in extant copies made by his friends Woodhouse and Brown. Keats's judgment in revising his own work had evidently by this time become unsure. We have seen how in recasting *Hyperion* the previous autumn he changed some of the finest of his original lines for the worse: and it is conceivable that in the case of *La Belle Dame* he may have done so again of his own motion, but much more likely, I should say, that the changes, which are all in the direction of the slipshod and the commonplace, were made on Hunt's suggestion and that Keats acquiesced from fatigue or indifference, or perhaps even from that very sense of lack of sympathy in most readers which made him sign 'Caviare.' Hunt introduced the piece with some commendatory words, showing that he, at all events, felt nothing amiss with it in its new shape, and added a short account of the old French poem by Alain Chartier from which the title was taken. It is to be deplored that in some recent and what should be standard editions of Keats the poem stands as thus printed in the *Indicator*, instead of in the original form rightly given by Lord Houghton from Brown's transcript, in which it had become a classic of the language.
>
> It is surely a perversion in textual criticism to perpetuate the worse version merely because it happens to be the one printed in Keats's lifetime. No sensitive reader but must feel that 'wretched wight' is a vague and vapid substitute for the clear image of the 'knight-at-arms,' while 'sigh'd full sore' is ill replaced by 'sighèd deep,' and 'wild wild eyes' still worse by 'wild sad eyes': that the whimsical particularity of the 'kisses four,' removed in the new version, gives the poem an essential part of its savour (Keats was fond of these fanciful numberings; compare the damsels who stand 'by fives and sevens' in the Induction to Calidore, and the 'four laurell'd spirits' in the Epistle to George Felton Mathew): and again, that the loose, broken construction—'So kissed to sleep' is quite uncharacteristic of the poet: and yet

set off against a bibliographic one, and the former has prevailed. At this point I am not trying to make a case for restoring the authority of *The Indicator* text, but merely to understand the history which descends upon us, in a largely invisible form, whenever we read 'La Belle Dame Sans Merci'. In order to elucidate such material we would have to begin by studying both texts of the poem in relation, primarily, to their respective initiating contexts on the one hand (the literary and historical contexts 1819 and 1848), and to the people most involved in establishing both texts (that is, Keats, Fanny Brawne, Brown, Hunt, and Milnes).

Without attempting to develop an exhaustive analysis along these lines, let me merely indicate a few important matters. The first line of *The Indicator* text reads

> Ah what can ail thee, wretched wight . . .

rather than, as in Brown/1848:

> Oh what can ail thee, knight-at-arms . . . .

The difference is important, in the literary context of the period, for 'wretched wight' is a locution which had acquired—in the course of its belated Spenserian history through the late 18th and early 19th century—a distinctly ironic overtone.[26] The phrase is a consciously archaic signifier used by poets, in certain limited contexts, to tell the reader to stand at a critical dis-

---

again, that the phrase 'And there we slumbered on the moss,' is what any amateur rimester might write about any pair of afternoon picknickers, while the phrase which was cancelled for it, 'And there she lullèd me asleep,' falls with exactly the mystic cadence and hushing weight upon the spirit which was required.

[26] See 'wight' in the *OED*, where the word's history of two interlocked meanings is clearly set forth. Essentially, the two meanings are epitomized in Spenser's use of the term in *The Shepheardes Calender* on the one hand, and *The Faerie Queene* on the other. In the latter case the term develops through the literature of heroic romance and carries no ironic overtones. In the former, however, the word signifies a base individual and is used in mild contempt and derision. By the time the word reaches the nineteenth century, its archaic character is established, so that its romance meaning (as used in some of Walter Scott's poems, for example in *Marmion* VI. xx) is continually threatened by an ironic overtone. This situation occurs not simply because 'wight' is seen to be an archaic word, but because the word itself carries its own ironic history in its alternate tradition. The entire process emerges quite clearly in the influential opening stanzas of Byron's *Childe Harold*, Canto I, where the ironization of the romance usage is complete. That Keats was aware of these matters is plain enough from his treatment of romance materials in other poems written around the time of the ballad. See especially 'On the Character of C. B.'.

tance from the signified. When Keats opens his ballad with this phrase, then, he is also introducing a personal note into the poem by letting his reader glimpse the poet in his self-consciousness as an artist. More specifically, Keats shows his reader that he, as a poet, stands at a slightly critical distance from his subject.

In this respect, the 'wretched wight' usage supports the general tonal approach which characterizes *The Indicator* version of the poem. Unlike Hunt's *Examiner*, *The Indicator* was a non-political publication which devoted itself to literary and artistic matters.[27] Byron published in *The Examiner* and *The Liberal*, not in *The Indicator*. But if it was not a political publication as such, *The Indicator* was decidedly tendentious in its aims. Hunt established the magazine as an alternative to the more traditional periodicals of the day. Thus, when Keats signed his poem 'Caviare', he was, once again, adopting a self-conscious pose for the reader, only in this case he was glancing at his ballad in relation to the prevailing literary climate. The *Hamlet* allusion shows us that Keats means to share a mildly insolent attitude toward the literary establishment with his readers in *The Indicator*, who are presumed to represent an undebased literary sensibility.

Everyone would agree that these facts illuminate how the poem would have been originally received, and understood, by readers of *The Indicator*. The more important point, for the present, is that this history continues to affect the way people read the poem today. Our present text is the product of a long historical struggle, carried out in the Lilliputian land of bibliographers and literary critics, to suppress one form of the poem and to elevate another. Understanding this history helps to define the differences between the two physical texts, but it likewise helps to explain what the Brown/1848 text presently means by showing what meanings it has forbidden to us.

The Brown/1848 text shows many more variants than the one already mentioned, and their cumulative effect is pronounced. Perhaps the most important result of the Brown/1848

---

[27] On the significance of the 'Caviare' signature see Gittings, *John Keats*, p. 400, and Colvin, op. cit. n. 27. On the matter of *The Indicator*'s ideological function see Leigh Hunt, *Autobiography*, ed. J. E. Morpurgo, London, 1949, pp. 280, 489 n. 8.; and Edmund Blunden, *Leigh Hunt and His Circle*, New York, 1930, pp. 146-50.

changes was to make the character of the knight more sympathetic to the reader and the character of the elfin lady less so. In *The Indicator* the lady does not have 'wild, wild eyes' but 'wild sad eyes', and she does not lull the knight to sleep. The 'kisses four' with which he shuts her eyes in Brown/1848 are very different in *The Indicator*:

> And there I shut her wild sad eyes—
>   So kissed to sleep.
> And there we slumbered on the moss . . .

Here we see that *The Indicator*'s kisses are given in a mutual exchange, and that both fall asleep together after their love-making. This last fact seriously diminishes the demand made upon the reader by the Brown/1848 text to see the lady as a bewitching siren.

After 1848 readers of Keats characteristically saw the elfin lady as a sort of demon lover who had ensnared the unsuspecting knight. This is still an influential way of reading the poem, though with the coming of the ironies of the twentieth century the issue has sometimes been seen as more problematic than that. A persuasive case could be made showing that Brown and Milnes share the immediate responsibility—not merely in fact, but by ideological design—for giving us the idea that the elfin lady is simply demonic, a sort of uncomplicated lamia. (It was a commonplace of Victorian criticism that the lady of Keats's *Lamia* narrative was unambiguously evil.) Brown's attitudes toward women in general, and his crude behaviour to Fanny Brawne in particular, are notorious. For his part, Milnes had an enormous library of erotica and pornographic works, and he was the principal figure behind the introduction of Sade's books into English culture. It was Milnes who later specifically introduced the young Swinburne to Sade and other pornographic writers.[28]

Furthermore, Brown was one of a group of Keats's friends who strongly opposed Keats's inclination, which Keats shared with Hunt, of giving no quarter to his establishment enemies

---

[28] For Brown, see Aileen Ward, pp. 249-50, and Gittings, *ibid.*, pp. 285, 337, 363, 385. For Milnes and his library see *The Swinburne Letters*, ed. Cecil Y. Lang, New Haven 1959, I, xlvi.

(i.e. to those who controlled the publishing world of that day).[29] Both of the poems which Keats published in *The Indicator* were signed 'Caviare', and neither was printed in the 1820 volume, whose publication was overseen by Keats's conservative friends. The other poem was Keats's great Paolo and Francesca sonnet, whose bibliographical history is at least as interesting, and very similar to, the history we have been following.

This sonnet, written in mid April 1819, comes to us in two holograph copies, the draft (written on a blank leaf in Keats's copy of H.F. Cary's translation of Dante) and the fair copy (which Keats sent in his journal letter of 14 February-3 May 1819). Keats later published the poem in June 1820 in *The Indicator*, but he did not include it in the 1820 volume. The standard editions of Keats from Milnes to the present have always published the text which derives from Keats's early manuscripts or the copy Brown made from them.

The Indicator has three substantive variants which are unique to it, but these have usually been dismissed by Keats's editors.[30] Stillinger's recent commentary is both lucid and typical:

The *Indicator* text . . . has 'a' in 8, and unique variants that almost surely ought to be disregarded in 7 ('Not unto' for 'Not to pure') and 10 (''mid' for 'in' and 'world-wind' for 'whirlwind') . . . Keats presumably supplied copy for the *Indicator* version—he was living at Hunt's at the time the poem was published—and possibly by dictation, since the erroneous 'world-wind' sounds much like Keats's 'whirlwind.' The *Indicator's* variants in 7 and 10 are almost certainly corruptions (''mid' perhaps an editorial change by Hunt).[31]

The argument for refusing *The Indicator* reading in line 7 is a textual one: ' "Not unto Ida" in 7 looks like a copyist's or printer's mistake based on the similar wording in the next line.'[32] Although the point is a good one, Keats's situation at the time of publication makes it something less than conclusive,

---

[29] Brown was one of the principal people who encouraged Keats to try to make his way as a hack London journalist and dramatist. He also sought to separate Keats from Hunt.

[30] See immediately below. But this count does not include the poem's title and signature in *The Indicator*, though both are especially important elements of the poem and ought to be considered as important 'variants'.

[31] Stillinger, *The Texts of Keats's Poems*, pp. 226-7.

[32] Stillinger, *The Poems of John Keats*, p. 636.

especially since Keats almost certainly read a proof of the sonnet before it was printed.

In the case of line 10 we really have no good textual or bibliographical grounds for rejecting *The Indicator*'s readings as 'erroneous' or 'corruptions'. Stillinger's arguments against ''mid' are pure supposition; and even were it true that Hunt suggested the reading ''mid' we would have to conclude that Keats agreed to it. As for that most important variant of all, *The Indicator*'s 'world-wind', once again Stillinger must resort to supposition. For it is clear that no copyist or printer would be likely to misread 'whirlwind' as 'world-wind'. A copyist or a printer might conceivably read the unusual usage 'world-wind' as the more common word 'whirlwind', but an error occurring in the reverse order is, to say the least of it, unlikely. Stillinger's extraordinary suggestion that the poem was printed from a dictated copy is advanced because, as a skilled textual critic, Stillinger knows that *The Indicator's* 'world-wind' can hardly be a copyist's error.

Why, then, have editors continued to print 'whirlwind' instead of *The Indicator*'s reading? Three reasons suggest themselves immediately. First, Milnes printed the poem in 1848 from the Brown manuscript copy, and that printing exercised great authority over later editors. Second, *The Indicator*'s text of the sonnet lost some of its attraction when, in the twentieth-century, its text of 'La Belle Dame Sans Merci' fell out of favour. Third, our knowledge of Keats's debt to Cary's translation of Dante tends to support the 'whirlwind' reading. When Keats first wrote his sonnet he certainly borrowed this word, as well as other verbal usages, from Cary.[33] Under the circumstances, one can easily take 'world-wind' not for a deliberate change, but as a strange corruption.

I think we have to see, however, that 'world-wind' is not a textual error but a purposeful change. The 'Not unto Ida' in line 7 *may* be a corruption, but the whole of line 10 has to be presumed to be Keats's deliberate work.

The importance of these bibliographical issues for our understanding of Keats's sonnet appears very clearly when we make a full return to *The Indicator* text and read the poem in its

[33] See Robert Gittings, *The Mask of Keats*, Cambridge, Mass., 1956, esp. pp. 26-33.

original constitution. There the sonnet is titled 'A Dream, after Reading Dante's Episode of Paolo and Francesca', and it is signed 'Caviare'. Under the ideological circumstances which *The Indicator* localizes, and which I have already discussed, the reading 'world-wind' acquires a powerful significance which affects the whole sonnet. The word emphasizes the virtually allegorical meaning which the fate of Paolo and Francesca represented for Keats in 1819. They suffer not in a 'whirlwind' but in a 'world-wind', that is, in the storm of a 'world' antagonistic to everything which the lovers represent (recall, in this context, the end of 'The Eve of St. Agnes'). It is unnecessary to re-emphasize here what students of Keats have known and commented upon for a long time: that this theme is pervasive in Keats, and that it grows particularly obsessive after 1818, for reasons that are well known, and that have as much to do with his love for Fanny Brawne as they do with his literary career and his financial problems.[34]

VI

When we look at 'La Belle Dame Sans Merci' and the Paolo and Francesca sonnet in the light of the foregoing material, we are likely to feel, first, that the two poems have at least two important texts. In both cases one can show with a fair degree of conclusiveness that *The Indicator* texts represent Keats's last deliberate choices, and that later editors have returned to Keats's earlier versions of both poems. From a bibliographical point of view, this situation indicates that editors have been choosing the less authoritative texts of both poems. On the other hand, since all the texts in question derive pretty directly from Keats himself, the dominant editorial tradition has established its own bibliographical argument. We are not dealing here with textual errors, but with textual options.

But one must see as clearly as possible where these options take their origin, for in that information one begins to see the 'meaning' of the later editorial choices and hence the meaning of the poems as they have been constituted by various readers and critics. Colvin and others believe that 'wretched wight' is a poor substitute for 'knight-at-arms'. It seems to me,

[34] See Gittings, *John Keats*, chaps. 22-4 and Ward, chaps. 11-12.

however, that the issue is not a neutrally 'aesthetic' one, but rather that it involves a choice between a more and a less 'romantic' version of the ballad.[35]

As we have already seen, *The Indicator*'s ballad is slightly conscious of its romance materials. That consciousness arises directly from Keats's decision to *print* his poem, and hence to place it, and himself, in a specific relation to his audience. The Brown/1848 text, on the other hand, represents a poem which Keats gave to a very different audience (that is, to the circle of those close to him). Under those circumstances, Keats (originally) wrote a much less self-conscious ballad; but even then he felt called upon—when he sent the poem to his brother and sister-in-law—to append an ironic commentary:

Why four kisses—you will say—why four because I wish to restrain the headlong impetuosity of my Muse—she would have fain said 'score' without hurting the rhyme—but we must temper the Imagination as the Critics say with Judgement. I was obliged to choose an even number that both eyes might have fair play: and to speak truly I think two a piece quite sufficient—Suppose I had said seven; there would have been three and a half a piece—a very awkward affair—and well got out of on my side . . .[36]

This (private) communication shows us the sort of position into which Keats put himself, and his poem, in its early version. These comments are the 'private' equivalent of everything which Keats meant to imply when he signed his poem 'Caviare' in the version he chose to make 'public'. It would not be difficult to show that Keats's ironic remarks in his letter have helped to support the more complex readings of the poem developed in the twentieth century.[37]

From the outset, then, the ballad was written in such a way, and under such circumstances, that urged its readers to stand at a slightly critical distance from the poem's materials. The best criticism of the poem has always responded to those urgings. When Keats finally printed his poem, he behaved as any good

[35] By 'romantic' here I mean simply that the Brown/1848 text does not distance itself the way *The Indicator* text does. The former is a more self-absorbed and self-absorbing text, whereas the latter is more self-conscious and critical.

[36] *The Letters of John Keats*, ed. Hyder Rollins, Cambridge, Mass., 1958, ii. 97.

[37] See Colvin's remarks in the passage quoted in n. 27 above. See also Robert Gittings, *John Keats: The Living Year*, pp. 113-21, and Walter Jackson Bate, *John Keats*, Cambridge, Mass., 1963, p. 480.

artist does when he comes before the public: he revised the poem so as to define—through those public and conventional devices which readers of poetry at that time would recognize—the 'meaning' of the poem which he meant it to carry. That is to say, the poem's appearance in *The Indicator*—the event of it and the physique of it alike—was of a determinate character: from that printing Keats's audience was meant to recognize, and respond to, the poem's self-conscious and slightly critical treatment of its romance subject.

Though later readers of Keats did not usually have access to *The Indicator* version, the 'spirit' (as it were) of that version was kept alive in the critical tradition. This occurred partly because Keats's letters have always been of great interest to his readers, and partly because the bibliographic issue has remained a nagging scholarly problem. In the case of the Paolo and Francesca sonnet, however, *The Indicator*'s poem has not been nearly so accessible. As a result, that aspect of the poem which is defined by *The Indicator*'s 'world-wind' has not been strongly preserved in the critical tradition. This neglect has weakened the life of the sonnet.

A polemic for the stylistic superiority of 'world-wind' over 'whirlwind' can and ought to be made. Readers should be asked to consider whether 'world-wind' does not noticeably strengthen the sonnet by forcing it to operate in multiple ways even at its surface levels. 'World-wind' not only suggests everything contained in 'whirlwind', it adds the polemically allegorical dimension I have already noted. In addition, however, this portmanteau word allows the reader to experience Keats forcibly drawing a connection between Dante's 'whirlwind' and Keats's 'world'. This equation results in the startling critical re-evaluation which the sonnet contains: that Dante's lovers suffer, not in the misery of their sinful love, but in the cruel assaults of an indifferent and hostile world. Like Byron's fine translation of the Paolo and Francesca episode, this great sonnet represents a Romantic reinterpretation of Dante precisely analogous to the Romantic reinterpretation of Milton carried out by Blake and Shelley.

But the sonnet's power does not come simply from its illustration of a central concept of Romantic Love.[38] Rather, it

---

[38] See Frederick L. Beaty, *Light From Heaven*, DeKalb, 1971, chap. 7. Beaty does not, however, emphasize the social reflex of this attitude toward love.

appears (first) in the poem's ability to tell its audience that only the poetic imagination is able to understand the conflicts between a social existence and personal love. Keats's poem tells us that Dante saw these contradictions. But when Keats emphasizes the distance between his sonnet and the original passage in Dante—when, for example, he writes 'world-wind' for 'whirl-wind' and titles the sonnet 'A Dream' based on Dante—then he is telling his audience something Dante does not tell: that Dante understood the pathos of Paolo and Francesca because he was a poet, and that only poetry has the power to reach such insights.

This implicit assertion is, like the poem's idea of Love, deeply Romantic. Yet the poem has something further to say—a more grim assertion which emerges as a terrible function of the poem's ideas about love, the 'world', and poetry. For the sonnet's 'melancholy' tone also asserts that the conflicts between the World and Romantic Love cannot be resolved in the terms defined by the poem. Poetry itself is affected by these conflicts. The sonnet tells us—finally, desperately—that poetry's power to see these contradictions carries with it the fate of ineffectuality. Here, at all levels, we see a situation in which everything is to be endured, but nothing is to be done.

VII

The particular cases of 'La Belle Dame Sans Merci' and the Paolo and Francesca sonnet show how the general historical method, outlined earlier, might be applied to specific and current problems in criticism. Each part of the general method must be able to be uniformly invoked when any literary work is under study, but particular cases will always be demanding different critical emphases. In the case of the 'Ode on a Grecian Urn', for example, we do not have a problematic textual history comparable to the ones I have just been discussing. The ode does have a famous textual crux in the final two lines, as we know from the poem's critical history, and the crux seriously affects the poem's internal syntax. Nevertheless, the textual issues here are quite different because the two possible texts for lines 49-50 of the ode are both traceable directly to Keats. Moreover, careful bibliographical analysis will show, and has already shown, that the two readings are not, finally, incompatible at the level of textual criticism. The textual problems in the ballad and the sonnet, on the other hand, are not yet solvable at such a level—simply because the issues have not yet been so thoroughly discussed and analysed as have the comparable issues in the ode.[39]

Yet the ode has its own special problems, one of which appears in the contempt with which many twentieth-century critics look upon that great obsession of older Keats critics: I mean the quest for the 'original' urn of the poem. Even Walter Jackson Bate, perhaps the most distinguished living critic of Keat's life and work, patronizes the labours of those older scholar-adventurers: 'Attempts continue to be made to determine a particular vase or urn that Keats may have had in mind when he wrote the ode. Especially with a poem so distinguished for its universality, one thinks of Keat's own remark . . . that "they are very shallow people who take everything literal".'[40] But the 'universality' of the ode is surely no more extensive than the 'universality' of any great poem. Moreover, this 'universality' is a direct function of certain historical specifics. It makes a difference—a marked difference—that Keats decided to publish the poem first in *The Annals of the Fine Arts*. This small bibliographical point locates a set of contextual facts of the greatest relevance to any interpretation of the ode.

In the same way, it makes a great difference whether or not we see the ode as an attempt to describe a 'real' urn. Scholars now tend to agree with Ian Jack on this matter:[41] that the ode's urn is a composite imagining based upon Keats's knowledge of various artifacts (vases, sculptures, and paintings) which he saw either directly or in illustrated books of Greek antiquities. Nevertheless, two points must be insisted upon. First, Jack's widely accepted conclusions could never have been formulated at all had not older scholars spent so much labour searching after that 'original' urn. Second, the impetus for that scholarship was supplied by certain characteristics of the poem as Keats originally published it.

---

[39] See Stillinger, *The Texts of Keats's Poems*, pp. 246-7, and Allott, pp. 537-8n.
[40] Bate, pp. 510-11n.
[41] Ian Jack, *Keats and the Mirror of Art*, Oxford, 1967, chap. XIII.

The corollary of the first point is that all current interpretations of the ode which treat the urn as an imaginary object are
only justified on the basis of certain past historical research.
Nor is this merely a point in professional decorum, a request
that we pay our dues to our worthy scholarly forebears. The
crucial interpretive point is that the urn of the ode is an imaginary object in a very specific, historical sense. The ode's urn is
placed before its readers (both past and present) as an ideal example of such vases. Keats's urn—in the context alike of his
poem, its place of original publication, and the Romantic
Classicism which both represented—aims to be taken as both
a real concrete object *and* as an ideal, for it is central to the
Romantic understanding of Greek art that such art actually
produced, at its finest moments, perfect and complete embodi-
ments of a perfect and complete idea of The Beautiful. *The
Annals of the Fine Arts*, which printed Keats's poem, was one of
that age's chief ideological organs for disseminating such
ideas.[42]

Consequently, part of the poem's fiction—and this is why
scholars spent so much time trying to find the 'original' urn—is
that the urn it describes is an actual urn comparable to the
Townley, Borghese, or Sosibios vases. Not to grasp this fact
about the poem means that we do not see the importance of
when the poem was written, and by whom, and where it was
published. But the poem itself insists that we react to its historical dimensions, and in so doing it forbids that we understand its 'universality' outside of the ode's special historical
context. To see this elementary point more clearly all we need
do is imagine that the poem was written fifty years before or
after 1819. It would make a difference.

The poem's fiction—that its *ideal* subject is an *actual* urn—
asks its readers to try to visualize, in a concrete way, the urn of
the poet's imagining. Yielding to the poem's direction in this
way will profoundly alter how we read the ode, and may even
enrich our grasp of the poem's purely verbal art. Let me give
you an example.

Only one critic, so far as I am aware, has noticed that the

---

[42] See ibid., chap. III.

phrase 'leaf-fringed legend' involves a pun.[43] Furthermore, no critic has ever remarked on the fact that the urn has given a specific answer, in the poem itself, to the poet's initial question about that legend. When they were conducting their searches for the ode's original urn, those older scholars were attempting to answer many of the same questions which the poet raises in the poem: as if, should they be able to find that original urn, they might then be able to see *in fact* what men or gods Keats was speaking of. In any case, they did not have to search far to answer the question about the 'leaf-fringed legend'. The urn itself supplies the answer when it says to Keats: 'Beauty is truth, truth beauty'. A reader can easily fail to see these aspects of the poem if he is concentrating his attention on the verbal surface. But it all leaps to one's awareness as soon as a person looks past the words to the scene being described, and to the objects that occupy that scene; as soon as a person, that is to say, begins to read more in the spirit of those older scholars, with their deep (if excessively empiricist) historical awareness.

After the poet's initial address to the urn in the poem's first two lines, he quickly moves into his series of questions. At the moment my interest is only in the first of them, where the word 'legend' is employed in a typically Keatsian fashion: it means both a particular story from ancient myth or history, as well as an inscription. With the phrase 'leaf-fringed legend', then, Keats is in part asking the reader to see something typical of certain Greek funerary vases: that they carried inscriptions, or legends, characteristically surrounded by elaborate leaf decorations. Keats apparently asks his question of the urn because (according to the poem's fiction) he cannot clearly see the faded characters of the Greek inscription. Indeed, we are probably meant to take the poem's famous Beauty-Truth apothogem not as the urn's actual inscription (translated, perhaps?) but as Keats's substitute for an inscription which had grown too faded to be read any longer (as, according to the moral of the 'Ode to Psyche', all the ancient myths and legends of the Olympian hierarchy had faded). Those characters (in both senses) are illegible, yet Keats's poetic urn can still speak, as if it were some literalized example of the idea of a poem as a speaking picture.

[43] Ibid., p. 283 n.13.

VIII

These discussions of the ballad, the sonnet, and the ode have been chosen because they illustrate some of the critical powers which an historical method of criticism can supply. The examples are also meant to show that the general taxonomic structures of the historical method sketched earlier are not all equally useful or pertinent at different times. Changing circumstances alter the immediate relevance of particular methodological categories.

Furthermore, particular poems are defined in terms of certain relatively fixed structures (e.g. those of form and genre for the works themselves; or those of sex, nation, class, and geographical location for their authors and commentators). Because such forms are historically stable (some of these are more stable than others), they pre-exist the critical discussion and often determine the relative usefulness of different categories within the general taxonomy of the historical method.

For example, the sort of textual discussion which is presently relevant to the ballad and the sonnet and which has been, in the past, equally relevant to the ode, will never be relevant to the poem we now know as 'To Fanny' ('What can I do to drive away')—never, that is, unless the bibliography of the poem undergoes, in the future, some drastic alteration (e.g., if a manuscript of the poem were to be discovered, or if some hard evidence were to turn up which pinpointed the date of composition more specifically). On the other hand, although the poem has no textual problems to be sorted out, the textual history *is* important. Furthermore, 'To Fanny' raises all sorts of issues which are peculiarly relevant to it, and which have little relevance (for example) to either the ballad or the ode.

The special problems raised by 'To Fanny' begin to define themselves in the poem's early textual history.[44] No manuscript survives and Keats never printed the poem himself. It was first printed by Milnes in 1848 from a (now lost) transcript which he had from Charles Brown. This transcript Brown made from a holograph manuscript given by Keats to Fanny Brawne, who allowed Brown to copy it sometime before 1829. The poem

---

[44] Stillinger, *The Texts of Keats's Poems*, pp. 264-5.

seems to have been written late in 1819, probably around October.

When Milnes printed the poem in 1848, his prefatory remarks left no doubt as to the intimate nature of the work.[45] His printing, in other words, established the tradition of biographical criticism which has dominated the later critical commentary on this poem. But Milnes's edition was not forcing its readers to adopt some 'subjectively biassed' view of 'To Fanny'; on the contrary, Milnes took the most appropriate vantage possible on the poem, and the one most in the spirit of Keats's own purposes and intentions. This poem was written to and for Fanny Brawne, and was even given to her by Keats. It is not, in other words, a 'public' poem the way 'La Belle Dame Sans Merci' or the ode are, and always were, 'public'.

On the other hand, the poem is not, nor was it ever, a 'private' poem strictly speaking (by 'private' I mean a poem written but never deliberately communicated to anyone else: in Keats's case, for example, a poem like 'This living hand, now warm and capable'). 'To Fanny' is, rather, a 'personal' poem— by which I mean simply to distinguish it in a position between the other two categories, and to indicate thereby that its most immediate contextual range is defined in biographical terms, rather than in historical or psychological ones. Consequently, if a person were to read this poem without giving paramount attention to its biographical materials, he would be introducing a special bias into the critical act. In such a case, the criticism would be forcing upon the poem an 'extrinsic' approach precisely analogous to the sort of 'extrinsic' approach we recognize in biographical or Freudian readings of (say) *Lamia*. Special critical studies of these sorts are often important and useful, of course, but in relation to *Lamia* we have to see that they *are* specialized. In the case of 'To Fanny', it is the purely formal or stylistic reading which would constitute the specialized approach. Poems like this one are, by virtue of certain pre-emptive definitions created out of their historical circumstances, formally and, as it were 'by nature', biographical works.

A reading of 'To Fanny' therefore always begins, consciously or otherwise, at the biographical level; if it does not, we cannot

---

[45] See The World's Classics reprint of Milnes's work, Oxford, 1931, p. 229.

understand the simple lexical references of the poem's words. To read the poem—ultimately, to develop a full critical analysis —requires that we be aware of Keats's peculiar financial situation at the time; of the special circumstances of his love for Fanny Brawne (their relationship had just entered a new phase); and of the state of his physical health (the fact, in particular, that he had not yet suffered the haemorrhage of February 1820 which betrayed his fatal illness). It also requires that we be aware of his special feelings for his siblings, and especially for his brother George in America, who was on the verge of financial ruin. Finally, the poem demands our understanding of Keats's utter commitment to the life of imagination and a poetic career, and of the conflicts which these pursuits engendered both in his attitudes toward the quotidian world around him and in his feelings for Fanny Brawne.[46]

All of these details taken by themselves would be properly called 'biographical' in nature. But the total set of relations which these details establish when they are considered together constitute a biographical nexus which reveals the forceful presence of larger, socio-historical frames of reference. Keats's highly personal poem about Fanny Brawne localizes a set of tensions and conflicts which can only be adequately understood if we place the poem in a more comprehensive historical context. Why Keats, for example, should establish in his poem a dialectic between his erotic feelings for Fanny Brawne and his sublimated devotion to his (also feminine) 'Muse' is partly explicable in biographical terms, but finally requires the more comprehensive context of Romanticism to be understood. And that larger, predominating ideological context only acquires its analytic frame of reference within the still larger context of the history of the early nineteenth century. In short, biographical criticism only receives its complete set of analytic possibilities when it is placed in the controlling framework of a general socio-historical methodology.

IX

Biographical criticism is, taken by itself, a pseudo-historical method, though in our culture it is the critical path which still

---

[46] Allott's notes and commentary (pp. 686-9) on the poem bring together many of the pertinent biographical references.

seems most closely connected with actual human history. Formally oriented critics have been wary of the approach for precisely that reason. But the fundamental problem with a strictly biographical (or psychoanalytic) criticism is not that its method imports 'extrinsic' materials into the analysis. On the contrary, biographical analysis falters because it maintains the poem, and the poetic analysis, in the artificially restricted geography of the individual person. Such a criticism is aware that the artist writes in a dialectical relation to the objective world, but it often seems unaware that this relationship is fundamentally social rather than personal or psychological, and hence that objective history exerts a shaping influence upon the poetry.

Though biographical and psychoanalytic criticism remain in practice, a collateral type of pseudo-historical criticism dominates the field today, especially in the United States. In this case, the historical focus is upon literary history, which becomes the ultimate framing context for studying poems, poetic forms, and patterns of literary transmission. 'World' or 'epochal' history is deliberately removed from the analysis, or it is subordinated to literary categories, because of the premisses of the general approach: that history at large can only enter literature via a system of artistic mediations, and these mediations are the necessary and immediate focus of attention.

The premisses of this position—about the mediating function of literary categories—are strong, and they would be assented to by most historical critics. Literary mediations must indeed be the critic's focus of attention. Nevertheless, certain practical conclusions generally flow from this approach, and these conclusions expose a basic theoretical weakness. To hold a literary analysis within a purely poetic space is to ensure the conclusion —rampant in such criticism—that the subject of literature is— literature. Indeed, such conclusions are inevitable in a method which makes no serious attempt to analyse, and thereby explain, the special human significance of artistic mediations. Because the mediations are regarded as ultimate, they become mystified categories—indeed, fetishes.

A particularly apt example of this method is observable in Geoffrey Hartman's famous essay on Keats's 'To Autumn'.[47]

---

[47] 'Poem and Ideology: A Study of Keats's 'To Autumn''', in *The Fate of Reading*, Chicago, 1975, pp. 124-46.

The purpose of his essay, he says, is to examine a special sort of poem, one 'without explicit social context', and to explore 'its involvement in social and historical vision'. Hartman goes on to say that his 'use of the concept of ideology [in the essay] will seem half-way or uncritical to the Marxist thinker'. Nevertheless, he feels justified in using the term because, in his view, and contrary to more traditional readings of the poem, 'To Autumn' is a poem that 'has something to say: that it is an ideological poem whose very form expresses a national idea and a new stage of consciousness'. Hartman's method, then, will be both historical and non-historical: 'In uncovering Keats's ideology I remain as far as possible within terms provided by Keats himself, or furnished by the ongoing history of poetry . . . Keats's poem is indeed an event in history; not in world-history, however, but simply in the history of fiction . . .'[48]

One would want to argue with Hartman's essay on more fronts than I have opened up here through these selective quotations. I confine myself to these remarks in order to focus on Hartman's idea that 'To Autumn' is a poem 'without an explicit social context'. What Hartman means by this statement is that 'To Autumn' does not make the immediate factual context c. September 1819 an explicit part of his poem. It differs, in this respect, from the 'Ode to Psyche' and the 'Ode to a Nightingale', for example, or, even more obviously, from Shelley's 'The Mask of Anarchy' (which was written around the same time as 'To Autumn').

Hartman's engagement with 'To Autumn' is part of the poem's non-explicit social context, and one of the functions of criticism is to analyse the ideology of significant critical engagements like his. But I must pass by that subject here, interesting though it is, and return to Keats's poem. For if the social context of a poem achieves its first *visibility* in the immediate context of the reader of the poem, the poem's explicit social context achieves its first *constitution* at its point of origin. Let us turn now to that social context and examine what Keats has made explicit in his poem.

To understand the 'explicit social involvement' of 'To Autumn'—or of any literary work for that matter—demands that we reconstitute the initial stages of the poem's socializ-

---

[48] These quotations are taken from pp. 124-6.

ation. This means that we ask ourselves the question: when and where and by whom was the poem originally published? Defining these particulars allows us to see once again the initial historical moment of the poem's explicit and continuing social involvement, a moment that has often been removed from immediate consciousness by the passage of time. That initial moment of publication constitutes the first explicit appearance of the poem's meaning (a meaning that arises in the communication-event involving the author's expression and the reader's response). The special importance of this moment lies in its priority: whatever changes may occur in later readings of the poem, all subsequent responses derive in some way from the initial event.

'To Autumn' was first published in *Lamia, Isabella, The Eve of St. Agnes, and Other Poems*, the so-called 1820 volume (published 1 July 1820). The character of this book—widely and, generally speaking, very favourably reviewed[49]—is intimately related to the 'meaning' of 'To Autumn'. To elucidate the nature of this relationship we have to see the book, and its original context, very clearly.

The publishers of the 1820 volume were Taylor and Hessey, who also published *Endymion* in 1818. It was *Endymion* (not the 1817 volume, published by Ollier) that had been the immediate target of the hostile reviews of Keats, and the poet was not the only person who suffered in that literary world-wind. Consequently, when Keats approached Taylor and Hessey again, in the latter part of 1819, about publishing the new book of poems he had been planning, they were interested but wary. They had no intention of bringing out a volume that would call down again the sort of hostility and ridicule which greeted *Endymion*.[50]

Keats's struggles with his publishers over the 1820 volume are well known. At first it seemed that the poems would not be published at all, but a stroke of luck—the decision (later rescinded) by, the Drury Lane Theatre to stage *Otho the Great*—changed Taylor's mind about Keats's new poems. If the play were to be performed, a book of poems might just have a chance of succeeding, despite the apparently hostile predisposition of the periodical establishment.[51]

[49] Cf. Hayden, pp. 196-204.
[50] See Ward, pp. 315-16, 332-3.   [51] Ibid., p. 341.

The key fact in the pre-publication history of the 1820 poems is the insistence by Keats's publishers that the book not contain anything that would provoke the reviewers to attack (they were especially concerned about charges of indecency and political radicalism). Keats struggled with them over these issues, but he was eventually persuaded to follow their line. The two poems published in Leigh Hunt's *Indicator* did not find a place in the 1820 volume, and the reason for this is that Keats and his publishers did not want to give the reviewers any occasion for linking Keats's new work with the politically sensitive name of Leigh Hunt. For his part, Keats was also worried about the book's reception, but his concerns were slightly different. His principal interests were to show (*a*) the strength of his poetical technique, and (*b*) that he was not a 'sentimental' or 'weak-sided' poet.[52]

The 1820 volume, in other words, was constructed with a profoundly self-conscious attitude towards that climate of literary opinion which prevailed at the time. It was designed as a book that would not provoke the critics in the ways that *Endymion* had done earlier. Indeed, Keats reacted so explosively to the notorious 'Publisher's Advertisement' to the 1820 poems because he felt that the paragraph would call up the whole of that painful history surrounding *Endymion*'s public reception, and expose him once again to the same set of charges.[53]

This history is important because it reflects the set of dialectical relations which converge in Keats's book. All of the 1820 poems were written in the post-*Endymion* period and they show very clearly the depth of Keats's response to his earlier treatment at the hands of the reviewers. Many of the new poems were deliberately written with an eye to attracting the favourable attention of the public (this is especially apparent in the case of the three narrative poems in the book).[54] In the final event itself we see how successful Keats and his publishers were, for the book was received well, even warmly, in almost every quarter. Keats wrote, in his 1820 poems, what most readers at the time were quite pleased to hear.

[52] See *The Keats Circle*, i. 90-7 and *Letters* ii. 174.
[53] See Ward, p. 363, and Allott, p. 764.
[54] See the *Letters* ii. 139, 174; Allott, pp. 326-7, 450-1, 614-15; and Ward, pp. 289, 315, 333.

The special character of Keats's 1820 volume manifests itself
very clearly if we compare it to some other books published
around that time. Byron's *Don Juan* volumes—especially Cantos
I-II (1819) and Cantos VI-VIII (1823)—were deliberately written to provoke discussion and conflict, and the same is true of
all of Shelley's works published in 1819-20: *Rosalind and Helen*,
for example, or *Prometheus Unbound*, or *Oedipus Tyrannus* (the last
a work of such inflammatory character that its publication had
to be suppressed). Keats's 1820 poems, however, were issued
not to provoke but to allay conflict. In sharp contrast to a poem
like *Prometheus Unbound*, Keats's mythologically oriented works
in his new book presented their early readers with ideas about
art, myth, and imagination which did not open an explicit
ideological attack upon the book's audience. The *Lamia* volume
represented Keats's effort to show his readers how they might,
by entering his poetic space, step aside from the conflicts and
tensions which were so marked an aspect of that period. The
whole point of Keats's great and (politically) reactionary book
was not to enlist poetry in the service of social and political
causes—which is what Byron and Shelley were doing—but to
dissolve social and political conflicts in the mediations of art
and beauty. (I should note here that although the 1820 poems
were politically reactionary at the time of their publication,
they were deeply subversive at the time of their rediscovery by
the Pre-Raphaelite Circle).[55]

All of these matters constitute an 'explicit' part of a poem
like 'To Autumn' for they were (quite literally) *made* explicit in

[55] It is, I hope, unnecessary to point out that the 'reactionary' and the 'subversive'
character of Keats's poems is, in this context, a function of particular historical circumstances, and that the fundamentally *critical* aspect of the poetry persists through these
changes. In both cases we see that Keats's poems refuse to be reconciled with the
'actual world', though in each case the poems pass their critical judgements on the
world from differing points of vantage. For a fuller theoretical discussion of this point
see Theodore Adorno, 'Reconciliation Under Duress', in *Aesthetics and Politics*, London,
1977, especially pp. 159-60: 'Art and reality can only converge if art crystallizes out its
own formal laws, not by passively accepting objects as they come. In art knowledge is
aesthetically mediated through and through . . . In the form of an image the object is
absorbed into the subject instead of following the bidding of the alienated world and per-
sisting obdurately in a state of reification. The contradiction between the object reconciled in the subject . . . and the actual unreconciled object in the outside world, confers
on the work of art a vantage point from which it can criticize actuality. Art is the
negative knowledge of the actual world . . . Only by virtue of [aesthetic distance] can a
work of art become both work of art and valid consciousness'.

the event of the poem's publication. Today the explicit character of these subjects only reveals itself to an historical analysis,
since analysis alone can overcome the loss of memory which
necessarily occurs over a period of time. Yet such an analysis is
important not merely for recovering a lapsed memory of the
past. It reveals as well the dynamic relations which play themselves out at all points in the history of the poem's transmission.
Our present responses to 'To Autumn' are closely tied into this
entire historical development, whether we are aware of it or
not.

Having reconstituted the essential features of the ode's publication history, we are now in a position to move to the next
phase of the analysis. In this case—because of the prevailing
anti-historical climate of opinion epitomized in Hartman's
essay—what is needed is further exploration of the original circumstances surrounding Keats's poem.

X

Keats has, for example, chosen a slightly yet recognizably
archaic style for his poem about autumn. The season, that is to
say, is personified, even directly addressed in its personified
character. Furthermore, this personified figure is suggestively
related to mythic divinities like Ceres and Bacchus, thus rein-
forcing the poem's self-consciously assumed archaic quality.[56]
The poetical machinery is carried very lightly, however, and
the second stanza explicitly superimposes images of contemporary peasant labourers on the androgynous figure of the
pagan divinity. Finally, the agricultural labourers and the
mythic being assume highly stylized poses in the poem. They
are picturesque figures, that is to say, and the reason is that
they enter the poem via Keats's experience of them in the artis-
tically mediated forms of various eighteenth-century paintings
and engravings, and the landscapes of Poussin and Claude.[57]
The explicit fiction of the poem, then, is not to present a series
of 'natural' images of autumn, but rather to deliver autumn

---

[56] Ian Jack discusses the Ceres allusions in his essay on 'To Autumn' in *Keats and the
Mirror of Art*, Oxford, 1967, chap. XV. Bacchus he does not discuss, but that divinity's
history in art and poetry shows him frequently represented as a handsome youth with
fine, long-flowing hair.

[57] See Jack's discussion, ibid.

over to the reader's experience in a series of framed pictures—in forms, that is to say, which already emphasize the fact that art mediates human experience. Into the context of these poetic materials the ode introduces, with equal explicitness, the subject of the seasonal change from summer to winter with all its traditional thematic associations: living and dying, maturing and decaying, staying and leaving.

The significance of these themes in the poem must, however, remain at an inexplicit level without the application of an historical analysis. Indeed, the meaning of these thematic meanings is poetically defined by the historically specific ideological mediations invoked by the poem—in this case, by the specific materials Keats has drawn from the fine arts.

Let me explain this further. It is clearly important to know that 'To Autumn' contains allusions to pictures done in the tradition of Poussin and Claude. But it is equally important to know how Keats himself understood and interpreted this tradition of painting. In fact, Keats's ideas about these matters, as scholars have known for a long time, run parallel to Hazlitt's ideas—are, indeed, drawn from Hazlitt's writings, conversations, and public lectures. Keats's poem alludes at once to the historical tradition in the fine arts and to Hazlitt's Romantically interpretive extension of that tradition. 'To Autumn' makes explicit, in its verbal picture, what Hazlitt made explicit in discursive prose in another context. The landscapes of Poussin, he tells us, like those of Claude,

carry imagination back two or four thousand years at least, and bury it in the remote twilight of history. There is an opaqueness and solemnity in his colouring, assimilating with the tone of long-past events: his buildings are stiff with age; his implements of husbandry are such as would belong to the first rude stages of civilization; his harvests are such . . . as would yield to no modern sickle; his grapes . . . are a load on modern shoulders; there is a simplicity and undistinguishing breadth in the figures; and over all, the hand of time has drawn its veil.[58]

'To Autumn' draws its set of attitudes from the same ideological well which here serves Hazlitt. These attitudes have even been given a name by scholars: Romantic Classicism.

[58] Quoted in Jack, p. 69.

Let me return now to the problem of the meaning of 'To Autumn's' thematic meanings. The poem's special effect is to remove the fearful aspects of these themes, to make us receive what might otherwise be threatening ideas in the simpler truth of certain forms which the poet presents as images of The Beautiful. This effect is produced by so manipulating the mythological and artistic mediations that the reader agrees to look at autumn, and to contemplate change and death, under certain precise and explicitly ficitonal guises. The reader accepts the invitation because these mediations, though recognizably fictional, nevertheless promise a real, human benefit: the beauty of the mediations can transform one's felt response to the ideas of change, death, decay. Keats's poem is itself the proof that such historically generated fictions, self-consciously embraced, can have this consoling power.

Up to this point, the textual analysis has only attempted to bring to light some of the historical specifics latent in the traditional line of criticism which has received its most finished statement in Hartman's essay. But from the vantage of an historical methodology the analysis has only just begun, for what we now have to develop is an explanatory context for the analysis. Thomson's famous poem about autumn, for example, does not concern itself with the consolations of fictional mediations. Why does Keats's poem do so?

In Thomson's poetry, and eighteenth-century verse generally, when the theme of human mortality is taken up in the context of natural processes, human values emerge as a part of what have recently been called 'the sciences of the artificial'.[59] In *Windsor-Forest* and *The Seasons* we observe how human practical arts, including the art of politics, place Nature—including human nature—under control and regulation. But in 'To Autumn'—and here the poem is typical of its age—the factor of human control is not found in the practical arts, but in myth and in the illusions of the fine arts (both of which are made to stand for poetic artifice in general). In 'To Autumn', Beauty is not only Truth, it is Power. But what is it, we want to know, which drives Keats to place his faith in poetry as the most distinctively human achievement, rather than in the practical and the useful arts?

[59] Herbert A. Simon, *The Sciences of the Artificial*, Cambridge, Mass., 1969.

The most general and explicit answer to this question was formulated by Wordsworth in his 'Preface' to the *Lyrical Ballads*,
and by Shelley in his great *Defence of Poetry*. Both argued from
the current state of affairs, which they saw as destructive of a
truly human life. Science, or Natural Philosophy, as well as the
allied practical arts, did not seem to be ameliorating the conditions of human life; if anything, these forces only exacerbated
suffering and social injustice. The Romantic manœuvre—both
from the left- and from the right-wing—was to turn to poetry
and the fine arts as the only available instrument of human
melioration.

The Romantic programme developed along two distinct strategic lines. On the one hand, poetry was employed as a weapon
to be used in the context of an explicit, and accepted, audience
which the poet aimed to persuade, reinforce, or attack. Though
Blake consciously adopted this strategy, only his work between
1790 and 1795 shows consistently effective results. Shelley and
Byron use this strategy throughout their careers with repeated
success. The other strategy, which dominates the work of
Wordsworth, Coleridge, and Keats, received its most important formulation in Wordsworth's 'Essay Supplementary'
(1815) where he said that poets would now have to create their
own audiences.[60] Here Romanticism developed its patterns of
'internalization', as they have been so memorably called,
because it was unwilling to make contracts with the audiences
available to it. Keats, who is especially typical of this Romantic
line, showed how poetry could establish 'a world elsewhere'. In
that alternative geography, personal and social tensions could
be viewed with greater honesty and intellectual rigour.

'To Autumn' asks us to believe—to willingly suspend our
disbelief—that all autumns are the same. We must imagine
them to be, universally, the 'season of mists and mellow fruitfulness'. But Keats asks us to believe this because he knows, as
we know, that it is not true. Such an autumn of perfect harvests
and luxurious agricultural abundance is an autumn in the
mind. City people, industrialized communities, do not know of
these autumns except in the memories of art; and in the country

---

[60] Prof. James Chandler has pointed out to me that this idea was not originally
Wordsworth's; he first had it from Coleridge (see Wordsworth's letter to Lady Beaumont of 21 May 1807).

such abundance is rare indeed, particularly in the early nineteenth century. In fact, 1819 brought in a good harvest in
England, and the year was notable for its abundance precisely
because of the series of disastrous harvests which characterized
many of the years immediately preceding.

Keats encountered his imaginative autumn when he fled his
'little coffin of a room at Shanklin'[61] for the ease and tranquil
beauty of Winchester, where he wrote 'To Autumn' in the
middle of September. His letters from 12 August to the beginning of October—the period of his Winchester sojourn—recur
to his feelings of pleasure and relief. Winchester, and his time
there, are repeatedly seen as a respite from the tensions not
only of his own personal affairs, but of the contemporary social
scene at large. The massacre at St. Peter's Fields (Peterloo)
took place four days after Keats arrived in Winchester, and he
was glad to feel removed from the political turmoil which followed in its wake. 'We shall have another fall of Siege-arms',[62]
he wrote to Woodhouse, but even as he followed the events of
August and September in the *Examiner*'s radical reports, he
found Winchester a wonderful refuge: 'This Winchester is a
place tolerably well suited to me; there is a fine Cathedral, a
College, a Roman-Catholic Chapel, a Methodist do, an independent do,—and there is not one loom or any thing like
manufacturing beyond bread & butter in the place. It is a res-
pectable, ancient aristocratical place—and moreover it contains a nunnery'.[63] Winchester has for Keats an old world,
even a slightly archaic quality about it which he consistently
refers to in his letters. 'The abbottine Winchester',[64] he calls it
in a letter to his brother. The city and its environs are magical
in their ability to carry him away to a charmed world far
removed from the quotidian press of his money affairs and the
dangerous political tensions of his society.[65] 'The Eve of St.
Mark' begins as a tribute to this environment and 'To Autumn'
is its finished expression:

How beautiful the season is now—How fine the air. A temperate
sharpness about it. Really, without joking, chaste weather—Dian
skies—I never lik'd stubble fields so well as now—Aye better than the
chilly green of the spring. Somehow a stubble plain looks warm—in

---

[61] *Letters*, ii. 141.   [62] *Letters*, ii. 175.   [63] *Letters*, ii. 189.
[64] *Letters*, ii. 201.   [65] See, e.g. *Letters*, ii. 209.

the same way that some pictures look warm—this struck me so much
in my sunday's walk that I composed upon it.[66]

This well-known passage from the letters locates the ode's point
of origin. No one but Ian Jack has remarked on the important
reference to painting in the passage, and not even Jack notes
what Keats has in fact said here: that the subject of 'To
Autumn' is explicitly the relationship between natural scenes
and their expression in a certain tradition in the fine arts.

All of these biographical details illustrate Keats's special
point of engagement with a number of large cultural and political issues which bore upon his age, and which had equally
particular effects on everyone else, and which produced equally
particular responses. (Shelley, for example, wrote a whole
series of poems immediately after Peterloo in which he attacked
the terrorist policies of the government forces.) 'To Autumn' is
only *fictionally* a poem about 'any' autumn, or autumn 'in
general'. Such an autumn is, the poet tells us, a myth, or an
artistic reconstruction of a myth. Hartman discusses 'To
Autumn' as a poem about poetic fictions, and in this respect
much of the foregoing analysis can be seen as merely supplying
greater specificity to his sense of the ode. To study this work's
allusive use of the pictorial arts is to see more clearly the exact
form of the poem's chief fictionalizing devices. But in the specification of the poem's fictions we also acquire further explanatory powers. For now we can ask yet another question: why
does Keats resort to pictorial tradition for his poem's fictionalizing models? Why not depend more exclusively on, for example, literary models?

One way of answering this question is to recall briefly the
long critical tradition which has responded to the poem's 'impersonal' quality.[67] 'To Autumn's' words seem aspiring to the
condition of pictorial silence, where images present themselves
in arranged groupings and sequences. In such a work the poet
—as so many critics have said—seems almost to have achieved
a state of negative capability: to have removed himself from
his poem and to have erased his self-consciousness. Like the

---

[66] *Letters*, ii. 167.
[67] Hartman's essay explicitly builds on this tradition. See especially p. 146 of his
essay, where he concludes: 'Even fruitfulness is not a burden in "To Autumn". This, at
last, is true impersonality.'

Grecian urn, the images in 'To Autumn' are 'silent forms' which 'tease us out of thought'.

Although this does seem to me to be the poem's ideological argument, it is not the poem's artistic achievement. For the 'impersonality' achieved in the poem is an explicit function of a conscious desire, as one clearly sees in those great and famous lines which open the final stanza:

> Where are the songs of spring? Aye, where are they?
> Think not of them, thou hast thy music too . . .
> (Lines 23-4)[68]

Keats's autumn is the emblem of a condition freed from all weariness, fever, and fret, and his effort to describe such an autumn 'impersonally' is the sign of his own attempt to achieve such a condition himself. But these lines remind us that the poem has been born in a desire, and that Keats's ideal autumn is not an impersonal or even an abstract autumn, but the dream of a mind that recalls the lost promise of the spring. Keats imagines such an autumn—he writes this ode—because he needs to develop some means for silencing that melancholy question: 'Where are the songs of spring?' Instead of the songs of spring —the poems of desire and self-conscious thought—Keats offers the song of autumn—the poem of fruitfulness and picturesque sensation.[69] What is crucial to see, however—and this is what the above passage shows us—is that 'To Autumn' dramatizes Keats's self-conscious polemic for an art of sensations rather than an art of thought. The poem is not impersonal, it is tendentious and ideological in quite specific ways. Its message is that the fine arts, and by extension imagination generally, are more humanly productive than any of the other more practical sciences of the artificial. More even than this, 'To Autumn' argues for the power of a specific type of imaginative art, that is, for an art that can imagine the sufficiency of the imagination.

---

[68] The self-consciousness of these lines is anticipated in the poem at lines 9-11. There Keats suggests, by pathetic fallacy, a charming mood of querulousness in his poem's bees.

[69] One could easily develop here a (useful) biographical analysis by associating the 'songs of spring' with the great 'spring odes' Keats had written a few months before. In this analysis, 'To Autumn' would be seen not merely as an *acceptance* of the idea of 'fruitfulness', but also as the *resort* of that idea.

The poem tries to persuade its readers that human beings sometimes have need of its imaginings, that the poetic fictions of the fanciful (as opposed to the polemical) imagination can be as objectively real and socially functional as any more work-a-day realities. Criticism, for its part, turns upon such poems and tries to explain how and why poets and readers might be prepared to believe, early in industrialized nineteenth-century England (or at some later point in time and place), that such a myth—that such fantastic and 'romanticized' poetry—can be 'useful' and full of power.

The explanation necessarily asks us to see, very clearly, that the poem's autumn is an historically specified fiction dialectically called into being by John Keats as an active response to, and alteration of, the events which marked the late summer and early fall of a particular year in a particular place. Keats's poem is an attempt to 'escape' the period which provides the poem with its context, and to offer its readers the same opportunity of refreshment. By this I do not mean to derogate from Keats's poem, but to suggest what is involved in so illusive a work as 'To Autumn' and in all the so-called escapist poetry which so many readers have found so characteristic of Romanticism.[70] For the preoccupations of the Romantic style came to pass a fearful judgement upon the age which generated its various forms of artistic extremity. Already in Keats we begin to hear whispers of the motto of his great inheritor, D. G Rossetti: *'Fiat ars, pereat mundus'*. And why not? The viewless wings of poesy will carry one to the havens of intensity where pleasure and pain, life and even death, all seem to repossess some lost original value. This is the reflexive world of Romantic art, the very negation of the negation itself, wherein all events are far removed from the Terror, King Ludd, Peterloo, the Six Acts, and the recurrent financial crises of the Regency, and where humanity escapes the inconsequence of George III, the absurd

[70] That Romanticism is a reactionary and 'escapist' art movement is a critical commonplace. One can (and should) assent to this view, but only after one also sees that the 'reaction' of Romanticism is also an intense expression of critique. See above n. 55, and Arnold Hauser, *The Social History of Art*, New York, 1958, iii. 174-6, 196. Perhaps the most profound expression of this view of Romanticism can be found in the *first* detailed commentary on the subject in Heine's great essay on the Romantic Movement, *Die romantische Schule*: see my discussion of the essay in *The Romantic Ideology*, Chicago, 1983, pp. 33-9, 50-6.

Prince Regent, the contemptible Wellington. Here evil itself will appear heroic, Satanic, Byronic—not banal, like Castlereagh.

Without historical analysis we can at best—and this is what Hartman has achieved—see Keats's poem as an elaborately structured poetic artifice. The poem is, he says, an 'imagined picture . . . self-harvesting like the poet's own thoughts'.[71] And this is both a correct, and a traditional, view. But it is a view which agrees to read the poem simply, that is, wholly in terms of Keats's own artificially constructed fantasy. It takes the poem to be true, exclusively true, when in fact such a work—like all human works—is true only in the context of its field of social relations. The Romantic idea of imagination becomes, in Hartman's essay, a universal rather than an historical phenomenon. Hartman's is, then, a neo-Romantic reading of an old Romantic poem, and this fact itself tells us much about the judgement upon our own age which is implicit in Hartman's nostalgic commentary.

XI

I want to conclude with two sets of remarks. First, permit me to re-emphasize what, in my view, this sort of historical method undertakes to perform. Traditionally, literary criticism has been divided into three separate provinces: Analysis, Explanation, Evaluation. In the modern period, historical methods have been allowed to govern the second of these provinces (Explanation); formal (or intrinsic) criticism, on the other hand, is taken to govern the first province (Analysis). The third province, Evaluation, is currently ungoverned, and has been ever since the demolition of the classical science of Evaluation as it was embodied in the theory of decorum.

My argument here is that the historical method—and specifically a sociological poetics—must be recognized not only as relevant to the *analysis* of poetry, but in fact as central to analysis (that is, to the study of the so-called 'purely poetic' or 'intrinsic' aspects of literature). Though I have not argued here the necessary consequence of such a view, it should be evident that to establish the pertinence of historical method to the field

[71] Hartman, p. 143.

of literary analysis is tantamount to establishing the hegemony of historical method to literary studies in general. This is not to say that more specialized literary investigations should be discouraged; quite the contrary. But it is to say that the governing context of all literary investigations must ultimately be an historical one. Literature is a human product, a humane art. It cannot be carried on (created), understood (studied), or appreciated (experienced) outside of its definitive human context. The general science governing that human context is sociohistorical.

The second point I want to make is related to the first. I cannot develop here the arguments which would be needed to demonstrate, theoretically, the crucial significance of historical method for the analysis of the aesthetic effect of literature. But I would like to conclude with some directory remarks on that subject.

The *locus classicus* in Marxist aesthetics for a discussion of this matter is in Marx's *Introduction to the Critique of Political Economy*. In a famous passage Marx poses for himself the difficult problem of explaining why the great artistic products of Greece—an admittedly 'primitive . . . social order'—should 'still constitute with us a source of aesthetic enjoyment and in certain respects prevail as the standard and model beyond attainment'. His answer to this question has been something of an embarrassment to Marxist aesthetics ever since.

A man cannot become a child again unless he becomes childish. But does he not enjoy the artless ways of the child and must he not strive to reproduce its truth on a higher plane? Is not the character of every epoch revived perfectly true to nature in child nature? Why should the social childhood of mankind, where it had obtained its most beautiful development, not exert an eternal charm as an age that will never return? There are ill-bred children and precocious children. Many of the ancient nations belong to the latter class. The Greeks were normal children. The charm their art has for us does not conflict with the primitive character of the social order from which it had sprung. It is rather the product of the latter, and is rather due to the fact that the unripe social conditions under which the art arose and under which alone it could appear can never return.[72]

72 Quoted in Berel Lang and Forrest Williams, *Marxism and Art*, New York, 1972, p. 38.

Although Marx's comments are confused and wholly lacking in analytic rigour, his nostalgia for 'the glory that was Greece' is the emotional sign of an important, and characteristically Marxian, insight. This passage shows Marx's profound sense of the pastness of the past, and of the importance which this differential has for all aesthetic experiences.

Neither Marx nor his immediate followers were able to develop the necessary analysis which these insights called for. The next step toward such an analysis was not taken until certain Russian critics gave a name to what Marx naïvely saw as the charm of a childlike art. The name is 'estrangement'.[73]

The aesthetic effect of literature is profoundly related—paradoxical though it may seem—to the reader or viewer's sense of history. Aesthetic effect depends upon the distancing of the art work, the estrangement of it, its isolation from our immediacy. We say that it seems to occupy a place outside of time, as it were. But this is merely a way of saying that art works are forever placed *in* history, that is, in the vertical and horizontal circumstances which define human events. The apparent immobility of art, Bate's 'universality', is a function of the reader's historical sense, which registers the distance between the (past) object and the (present) experience.

This estrangement effect, however, cannot begin to be analysed without an historical method. Nor will a method that confines itself to *literary* history suffice, for art at all times is part of a human activity which transcends the limited materials and special history of art itself. Thus it has often, and properly, been said that poetry holds a mirror up to human life. But something more must be said. For poetry does not hold a mirror up to an immobilized 'Human Nature'; it reflects—and reflects upon—human nature in its social and historical reality. The celebrated estrangement effect of art is simply the sign of art's own inherent historical dimension *vis-à-vis* its audience. To analyse, in literature, this deeply felt distance between us and our pasts requires the precise specification of historical details—from the merest facts picked up in a gloss, to the most sharply defined general categories of ideological order.

---

[73] The concept of estrangement, as developed by the Russian Formalists and subsequent epigones, is used in a much more limited frame of reference than the one I am developing here. See also Bakhtin's trenchant critique of the concept in *The Formal Method, passim,* but especially pp. 60-2.

Literature focuses moments of intense feeling, of deep human sympathy, and these experiences occur because all readers of poems register in their feelings the social and historical gulfs which, even while they separate and define exact differences, ultimately join together by calling out human sympathy—that special feeling of a social union which, in our historical experience to this period has remained, like Wordsworth's cuckoo, something 'longed for, never seen'. What remains to be seen is the human limits which history imposes even on those famous words. Their meaning, their power— indeed, their ability to transcend their own historical limits—all depend upon the existence of those specific limits; and our appreciation of such power and transcendence equally depends on our ability to understand the fact of those limits, and to analyse it. Failing such things, I do not see how we can reciprocate the transcendence of Romantic verse, or feel anything but shame when we read such poetry.

(1977-9)

II

Textual Studies and
Practical Criticism

1. The Monks and the Giants: Textual and Bibliographical Studies and the Interpretation of Literary Works

I

What is the relevance of textual and bibliographical studies to literary interpretation? This is not a question which has been posed in a systematic way very often. Wellek and Warren, in their *Theory of Literature*,[1] saw clearly that 'merely bibliographical facts' could often 'have a relevance and value' (p. 47), and they explicitly concluded that textual and bibliographical studies were to be 'justified by the uses to which their results are put' in the interpretation and evaluation of literary works (p. 57). Nevertheless, their *Theory of Literature* made no attempt to set forth a programme, or even a schema, of such uses. Indeed, by calling textual and bibliographical studies 'Preliminary Operations' to literary study *per se* (whether the latter were to be 'intrinsic' or 'extrinsic'), the *Theory of Literature* effectively placed such work somewhere east of the Eden of literary interpretation and evaluation. The specific question of *how* textual and bibliographical studies were to be used in literary interpretation was set aside.

Still, the discussion of these matters in *Theory of Literature* is perhaps the most thoughtful to be found anywhere in the past fifty years, when we have witnessed, on one hand, a growing divorce between 'extrinsic' and 'intrinsic' literary work, and, on the other, a notable expansion—particularly in the past fifteen years—of highly idiosyncratic forms of literary appreciation. With the acceptance of 'free play' as both an operation and a standard in hermeneutics, the relation between extrinsic and intrinsic forms of criticism is further loosened; and textual/ bibliographical studies, already conceived as 'Preliminary Operations', are all but removed from the programme of literary studies. Nor is this merely a theoretical removal: today,

---

[1] René Wellek and Austin Warren, *Theory of Literature*, New York, second edition, 1955; see esp. pp. 26-34 and Part II ('Preliminary Operations') pp. 43-57.

courses in textual criticism and bibliography are no longer required in most graduate schools, and often they are not even available to the student.

In the event, the academy has ceded a privilege to textual scholars and bibliographers which allows them to live and move and have their being at the periphery of literary studies as such. It is a privilege that has been agreed to by all parties: the scholars have thereby gained a considerable freedom and autonomy to pursue their (often highly technical and specialized) work, and the critics have been released from the obligation to develop certain skills which are not easily or quickly acquired. As a result, the angels of hermeneutics have long feared to tread in the fields of textual/bibliographical studies, which are widely regarded, in fact, as a world well lost. Reciprocally, the bibliographers, editors, and textual critics have largely agreed to assume the bad eminence they have achieved, whence they may hurl defiance at the heavens of the interpreters.

Of course, textual critics and bibliographers can (and do) function quite well in their specializations. The difficulties of collecting and ordering a complex set of manuscripts, or of preparing a complete bibliographical record of a particular work, are often so complex that the operations have to be subdivided and further specialized if the work is to be performed correctly. Under such conditions, it is no wonder that 'the uses to which their results are put' are often left to the hermeneuts.

In recent years a few scholars have begun to reconsider the relations that do or might exist between textual/bibliographical studies and literary interpretation. In most cases these efforts have come from those who are knowledgeable in textual criticism and bibliography, and who thereby command the expertise necessary to begin serious inquiries into such matters.[2] Still, the efforts have been relatively scattered; only a handful of textual/bibliographical scholars have ventured into the field, while the literary critics have all but completely avoided these subjects. The latter indifference is perhaps to be expected: after all, the principal strains of literary criticism in the twenti-

---

[2] See the essays in *Textual Criticism and Literary Interpretation*, ed. Jerome J. McGann, Chicago, 1985; see also Randall McLeod's several essays, including 'UN *Editing* Shakspeare', *Sub-Stance* xxxiii/xxxiv (1982), pp. 26-55 and 'Unemending Shakespeare's Sonnet 111', *SEL* xxi (1981), pp. 75-96; John R. Sutherland, *Victorian Novelists and Publishers*, Chicago, 1976; and the work on William Blake by Morris Eaves and Robert Essick.

eth century developed in a conscious reaction against the philological and historical traditions which dominated the nineteenth.

It is the assumption of this essay that literary study surrendered some of its most powerful interpretive tools when it allowed textual criticism and bibliography to be regarded as 'preliminary' rather than integral to the study of literary work. I shall be arguing that the non-integral view of textual criticism and bibliography is historically explicable, that it derives from a particular understanding of the nature and goals of textual criticism and bibliography, and that this is an understanding which literary academics of all types now take for granted. Furthermore, in what follows I shall attempt both an exposition of this view of textual criticism and bibliography as well as a critique of its limits. I take it for granted that specialized studies in these fields—studies which are in fact 'preliminary' to critical interpretation—carry the justification that all specialized studies must be allowed, whatever the field. I shall argue, however, that textual criticism and bibliography are conceptually fundamental rather than preliminary to the study of literature, and that (consequently) their operations need to be reconceived along lines that are more comprehensive than the ones currently in force.

II

Fredson Bowers opens his discussion of *Bibliography and Textual Criticism* in the following way.

The general procedures of textual criticism as it deals with manuscript study have been formulated for some years. Differences of opinion may develop from time to time over the precise techniques for constructing a family tree from variant readings, and other matters of technical concern may occasionally come in dispute. But on the whole it is not unduly optimistic to suggest that when the editor of a classical or of a medieval text begins his task he can attack the problems from a position of strength. That is, he will be well aware that much drudgery lies ahead and that the difficult nature of the material may give him some bad hours; but he is seldom in doubt about the textual theories that guide him. Moreover, he can hopefully anticipate that if he follows these traditional methods for sorting out and arranging his texts, he will be left with few cruxes that cannot be solved by linguistic skill and ripe critical judgement.

In the halcyon days before the emergence of bibliography as a force, the textual critic of printed books could approach his task with something of the confidence of the manuscript scholar, fortified also by the comforting thought that, in comparison, the initial preparation of the text would be far less onerous. If he were the first adventurer, the number of early reprint editions to collate would not be large; and if he were a latecomer, he need only exercise his ingenuity in improving the edition of a predecessor, whose pages he could send to the printer with an occasional correction. The choice of copy-text was not a particularly acute question, for what are now called the 'accidentals' of a text would all be modernized, and literary judgement could mend the errors in the 'substantives'.[3]

I reproduce the whole of this passage because it fairly represents a number of ideas which remain current in the textual scholarship which focuses on modern national scriptures. Probably Bowers would no longer wish to stand by some of these ideas, and perhaps least of all the idea that textual critics of modern and classical works 'can attack [their problems] from a position of strength'.[4] Although it is true that classical and modern scholars are better armed for their tasks than they ever were, greater knowledge has only brought greater circumspection. Bowers speaks as he does here partly because he is a casual observer of the classical field, and partly because he is a methodist in the world of textual criticism.[5]

Bowers's views about the textual scholarship of classical works reflect an ignorance about the historical development of textual studies which is widespread among textual critics who work on national scriptures, especially in the modern periods. This lack of attention to the textual criticism of ancient literatures, both biblical and classical, has caused serious damage to the criticism and scholarship of our more recent and national literatures, and I will return to this problem in a moment. For now

3 Oxford, 1964, pp. 1-2.

4 Perhaps the best indication of Bowers's scholarly strength is to be seen in his flexibility. In the past ten years he has seemed anxious to alter and revise his views when the work of others suggested that he should do so. See his 'Multiple Authority: New Problems and Concepts of Copy-Text', *Library* 5th ser. xxvii (1972), pp. 81-115 and 'Greg's 'Rationale of Copy-Text' Revisited', *SB* xxxi (1978), pp. 90-161.

5 The textual problems in the fields of classical and biblical studies remain exceedingly vexed, and in many cases insoluble, given the current state of our documentary knowledge. In medieval studies the problems are often only slightly less difficult.

I want to concentrate on another, closely related problem which also appears in the passage I have quoted: its underlying and fundamental assumption that the disciplines of textual criticism have as their aim, their *raison d'être* even, the editing of texts.

When Bowers conceives textual criticism in editorial terms, he is of course following the common view. Indeed, many— perhaps even most—textual critics would argue that the editorial function of their discipline fairly *defines* its method and purposes.[6] Such a view of textual studies appears transparent, and hence goes unexamined, largely because of the actual historical development of textual studies in the early modern period. In point of historical fact, textual criticism as we know it today developed because Renaissance scholars of antiquity felt the need to find ways of establishing reliable texts.

Nevertheless, the historical conditions which initiated the development of modern textual studies could not—and, in fact, have not—permanently defined the nature of this discipline. Changed historical circumstances may modify or even alter one's conception (and practice) of a discipline. Textual studies in the late eighteenth and early nineteenth centuries underwent a radical shift, largely because they were carried out under the influence of the new biblical scholarship on one hand, and the widespread development of various historicist studies on the other. This was the period in which the grand conception of a *philologia perennis*, imagined and sought after by men like Petrarch and Politian, finally achieved operational form in what F. A. Wolf called *Alterthumswissenschaft*. With this philological ideal textual criticism had been so reconceived that the period saw the emergence of a conservative reaction within classical studies. Scholars like Gottfried Hermann, aware of the limits which textual criticism would always have to face when dealing with classical texts, determined to pursue a relatively narrow course of textual work. Others, like August Boeckh, resisted the line of specialization.[7] To the degree that we think of textual

---

[6] The view is commonplace; James Thorpe, for example, speaks of 'Textual study —or, to use a more enveloping term, editorial work', and he states that 'the goal of textual criticism is to determine the text of what we are to read as the work of literary art'. See *Principles of Textual Criticism*, San Marino, Ca., 1972, p. vii; and the *Oxford Classical Dictionary* entry: '*Textual Criticism*, the technique and art of restoring a text to its original state, as far as possible, in the editing of Greek and Latin authors'.

[for n. 7 see next page]

criticism in terms of its editorial function, to that extent we are following the line of Hermann's thought rather than Boeckh's.

In all these cases, of course, we are dealing with a textual criticism which is being theorized in terms of the works of antiquity. With the advent of *Alterthumswissenschaft*, however, emerged the professional study of national scriptures, or what we sometimes call Modern Philology, where radical changes of focus have to be made. These changes are most sharply defined in the field of textual criticism. The historical circumstances in which Renaissance and post-Renaissance works are transmitted into our hands differ sharply from those which surround classical and biblical works, and they also differ in crucial ways from the circumstantial field of medieval works. The textual problems which a scholar of ancient works has to face rarely find close analogues in modern national scriptures. Consequently, when textual critics of modern works assume an editorial function for their discipline, they also take over a methodology and structural focus which are normally not well adapted to the most pressing scholarly problems which they should be facing. (I should also say, in passing, that this assumption of editorial models drawn from the study of works of antiquity has had important conscquences for the theory of editing modern works, as well as for the theory of textual studies in general.)[8]

This larger context helps us to see why the textual and bibliographical study of modern national scriptures, and in particular English and American literary works, took the shape and course that it did. The tools developed for the study of biblical and classical texts from the late eighteenth to the early twentieth centuries were brought to bear upon English and American literatures. This in itself generated certain theoretical problems for students of modern philology. In addition, however, the classical tools were taken over at a particular period in the history of classical philology, that is to say at a time when classical studies had entered a specialized and even technocratic phase. The broad theoretical issues which had been the pre-

---

[7] Good discussions of these lines of development are available in John E. Sandys, *A History of Classical Scholarship*, reprinted New York, 1958, iii. 89 and Rudolf Pfeiffer, *History of Classical Scholarship from 1300 to 1850*, Oxford, 1976, pp. 179-82.

[8] Some of the problems in specialized textual studies are taken up in my study *A Critique of Modern Textual Criticism*, Chicago, 1983.

occupation of men like Wolf, Herder, and Eichhorn were no longer matters of imperative critical inquiry. Textual criticism had entered a phase of its modern life which Thomas Kuhn would later call 'ordinary science'. Also, because the classicist model presided over the development of the textual criticism of national literatures, our scholarship assumed that fundamental homologies existed between the problems of classical scholars and those of the moderns. This assumption is evident as early as the eighteenth century and is epitomized in Johnson's famous lament over the state of the Shakespearean texts.[9]

This historical context which I have been sketching should allow us to see why the textual criticism of our national scriptures became almost completely identified with an editorial function. When Paul Maas opens his classic work with the statement 'The business of textual criticism is to produce a text as close as possible to the original' he does so in a special context —the fields of biblical and especially classical scholarship— where the editorial function of textual criticism has to be emphasized. 'We have no autograph manuscripts of the Greek and Roman classical writers and no copies which have been collated with the originals,' Maas observes; and furthermore, 'the manuscripts we possess derive from the originals through an unknown number of intermediate copies . . . of questionable trustworthiness.'[10] In such circumstances textual criticism will and should concentrate on the task of producing reliable texts. Maas's statement on the business of textual criticism becomes a troubling one, however, when it is assumed as a premiss in the textual criticism of modern national scriptures, where the conditions faced by the biblical and classical scholar do not prevail.

Even in the context of classical scholarship, however, the editorial function ought to be seen as only one aspect of the aims of textual and bibliographical criticism. If we reflect upon the larger history of textual criticism, and in particular on the scholarship of men like Wolf, we are forced to remember that textual criticism has not always been identified with an editorial function.[11] When Teubner asked M. L. West to write

---

[9] See *Johnson on Shakespeare*, ed. Arthur Sherbo, New York, 1968, i. 51-2.

[10] *Textual Criticism*, trans. Barbara Flowers, Oxford, 1958, p. 1.

[11] For an excellent discussion of Wolf's significance see Anthony Grafton, '*Prolegomena* to Friedrich August Wolf', *Journal of the Warburg and Courtauld Institutes* xliv (1981), pp. 101-29.

a new book on textual criticism to replace the earlier works of
Maas and Stahlin, West approached his task with a more comprehensive view of 'the business of textual criticism'—largely,
I suspect, because his work had been influenced by the more
capacious views of Pasquali's *Storia della tradizione e critica del
testo*. For West, the business of textual criticism is not to produce a text as close as possible to the original, it is much more
comprehensive and—ultimately—hermeneutic.

Students have sometimes said to me that they recognize the necessity
of textual criticism, but they are content to leave it to the editor of the
text they are reading and to trust in his superior knowledge. Unfor-
tunately editors are not always people who can be trusted, and critical
apparatuses are provided so that readers are not dependent upon
them. Though the reader lacks the editor's long acquaintance with the
text and its problems, he may nevertheless surpass him in his feeling
for the language or in ordinary common sense, and he should be
prepared to consider the facts presented in the apparatus and exercise
his own judgement on them. He *must* do so in places where the text is
important to him for some further purpose. This book, therefore, is
not intended solely for editors, but for anyone who reads Greek and
Latin and desires some guidance on how to approach textual questions.[12]

This is a wise set of remarks which students of all literatures
ought to bear in mind at all times. The literary criticism of
English and American works has ceded to textual and bibliographical specialists almost total authority to pronounce upon
matters relating to their fields. In the process, the pursuit of
textual studies has been carried out by people whose practical
concerns are circumscribed by their editorial aims, or by that
subset of related, largely technical problems which bear upon
editorial method (e.g. the preoccupation in recent years with
the problem of copy-text). West's view takes it for granted,
however, that textual criticism is a field of inquiry which super-
venes the narrower issues that concern editors, and that textual
criticism is a pursuit incumbent upon anyone who works with
and teaches literary products. Textual criticism does not meet
its fate in the completion of a text or an edition of some particu-

<hr>

[12] M. L. West, *Textual Criticism and Editorial Technique*, Stuttgart, 1973, pp. 8-9.
West explicitly acknowledges his dept to Pasquali in his Preface, and he cites Pasquali's
second edition (Firenze, 1952).

lar work. Rather, it is a special method which students of literature must and should use when they examine, interpret, and
reproduce the works we inherit from the past.

When this more fundamental conception of textual criticism
loses its authority—when it is replaced by the more specialized
conception, that textual criticism is an editorial instrument—the
schism which characterizes current literary studies gets reified.
Whether textual scholars work with actual texts or whether they
comment, at a theoretical level, on the field of textual criticism
generally, they tend to conceive their operations almost wholly
in terms of the editorial functions of their discipline. The interpreters, for their part, either produce their work in the purest
state of scholarly innocence, or they agree to accept—quite
uncritically—the textual results of editorial scholars. In each
instance the practice of an informed and comprehensive literary
criticism is diminished.

Today, the editorial conception of textual studies remains
dominant, thanks largely to the profound influence of the work
of Fredson Bowers and his followers. Important consequences
have resulted from this dominance, for all fields of literary work.
Of course, shrewd scholars like Bowers are well aware that textual and bibliographical studies produce results which may be of
interest to many people besides editors. G. Thomas Tanselle
acknowledges this fact when he speaks of 'the effect which the
findings of bibliographical and textual research have on the
ultimate meaning of the work of literature as evaluated by the
[literary] critic.' Tanselle thinks that this relation of textual
studies to literary interpretation is so evident that it hardly
requires discussion.

That the establishment of texts is the basic task of literary scholarship,
a prerequisite to further critical study; that emendations which result
from textual research can significantly affect the critical interpretation of a work; and that detailed collation and bibliographical analysis
are necessary activities for the establishment of every text, even if
only to prove that no variants exist or that the variants are inconse-
quential—all these propositions are, to the scholarly mind, self-
evident, and they have all been buttressed by numerous concrete
examples in recent years.[13]

[13] G. Thomas Tanselle, 'Textual Study and Literary Judgment', reprinted in Vito
J. Brenni, ed., *Essays in Bibliography*, Metuchen, NJ, 1975, p. 355.

Of this passage two things must be said, at least initially. First, like Bowers, Tanselle accepts the editorial function of textual studies as fundamental. Indeed, this editorial function is presented as (literally) the Alpha and the Omega of all literary scholarship. This function appears so obvious to Tanselle that he sees no further need to inquire into the theoretical relation of textual studies and literary criticism; the relation is 'self-evident' and 'buttressed by numerous concrete examples'. What Tanselle means by this, as his note to the passage shows,[14] is that literary critics can, do, and should turn to textual critics and especially to editors for *specific facts* of verbal changes in the texts they study. This record of verbal variants, uncovered by the textual scholar and editor, supplies the interpreter with useful information which may affect his 'readings'. This is Tanselle's 'self-evident' relation of textual studies to literary criticism.

On the contrary, however, I think that this view of the relation is deeply misconceived, and that it springs directly from the assumption of an editorial approach to textual studies. From such an approach one can draw few connecting lines between a practical literary criticism and (say) a bibliographical record of early printings, or the history of a manuscript's provenance. Textual scholars must labour to elucidate the histories of a work's production, reproduction, and reception, and all aspects of these labours bear intimately and directly on the 'critical interpretation of a work'. To an editorial conception of textual studies, however, the bearing which these large fields of inquiry have upon interpretations of literary works is not merely *not* 'self-evident', it must remain positively invisible.

If we reconceive the projects of textual criticism along lines that are closer to those suggested by M.L. West, however, we will take a different view of this textual research, and will probably begin by putting the findings of the editorial textualists to very different uses. An analysis of the editorial history of a particular author's works may assume different forms, depending on the purposes to which the analysis is being put. If we wish to illuminate the reception history of an author—a matter of some consequence for the interpretation of the works—we shall have to be able to master and use, in a particular macro-

[14] Ibid., p. 363 n.9.

bibliographical field, various tools of micro-bibliography. Similarly, to study the verbal text of a particular work for its lexical or syntactic meaning is an operation which must employ the same historical resources of textual criticism that are used by editors when they prepare a critical text. The two operations, however, are conceptually different.

A proper theory of textual criticism ought to make it clear that we may perform a comprehensive textual and bibliographical study of a work with different ends in view: as part of an editorial operation which will result in the production of an edition; as part of a critical operation for studying the character of that edition; as part of an interpretive operation for incorporating the meaning of the (past) work into a present context. No one of these practical operations is more fundamental than another, and all three depend for their existence on a prior scholarly discipline: textual criticism. The practical direction which textual studies will take, under any given set of circumstances, will of course vary with the immediate requirements of the critic and the situation.

In any case, we might better start from the following ground: that the precise relation of textual scholarship to literary criticism is a good deal less evident than current theory suggests; and furthermore, that we cannot argue the relationship by an appeal to a series of concrete examples. Because the examples are produced out of a misconceived theory of textual criticism and its basic tasks, they do nothing to alter that conception; indeed, they merely reify it, as Tanselle's comment about self-evidence suggests. The examples which he cites all go to show how textual emendations and variants may affect the meaning of a certain work or passage. But the examples are congruent with an editorial theory of textual criticism and they are only as good as the theory which supports them.

If textual and bibliographical studies are to have a significant impact on literary interpretation, textual criticism will have to be reconceptualized along lines that transcend an editorial theory. Of course, an editorial perspective on the principles of textual criticism is imperative under certain circumstances. Nevertheless, such a perspective only tends to obscure matters when the central issue is the relation of textual scholarship to literary meaning.

For example, consider again Tanselle's comments on 'Textual Study and Literary Judgment'. In his view, 'the establishment of texts is the basic task of literary scholarship, a prerequisite to further critical study,' and he goes on to suggest the following as the model for how textual studies affect literary criticism: 'emendations which result from textual research can significantly affect the critical interpretation of a work.' But textual criticism does not ground its deepest relation to the 'critical interpretation of a [literary] work' on the textual emendations it may produce. Indeed, emendations are probably the least significant product of textual and bibliographical studies, from the point of view of literary criticism. Tanselle takes this position because he sees textual criticism as part of a comprehensive editorial programme, rather than as a key element in an even more comprehensive programme: the historical elucidation of texts, both ancient and modern. A text, from an editorial vantage, appears in its ultimate form as a linguistic or verbal event; and the act of interpreting texts, consequently, tends to appear as an operation we must perform on a definite and localized set of words. A more comprehensive socio-historical view of texts, however—for example, a view of texts as books, manuscripts, or otherwise materialized objects —forces us to approach the issues of criticism and interpretation in a very different way. For the language in which texts speak to us is not located merely in the verbal sign-system. Texts comprise elaborate arrangements of different and interrelated sign-systems. It makes a difference if the poem we read is printed in the *New Yorker*, the *New York Review of Books*, or the *New Republic*. Textual and bibliographical criticism generates, in relation to the works we read, a great deal more critical information than a calculus of variants or a record of emendations.

The interpretation of literary works, then, does take its ground in textual and bibliographical studies, as Tanselle has said, but not for the reasons or in the way that he has said. It does so because these studies are the only disciplines which can elucidate that complex network of people, materials, and events which have produced and which continue to reproduce the literary works which history delivers into our hands. Current interpretations of literary works only acquire a critical edge of significance when they are grounded in an exegesis of texts and meanings generated in the past—in an exegesis of texts and meanings gained, and perhaps also lost, over time. Such an exegesis depends for its existence on the tools and procedures of textual criticism. The current practice of hermeneutics does not ordinarily avail itself of these tools and procedures, largely because literary critics and interpreters have come to accept Hermann's specialized view of textual criticism. Nor is it to be expected that this part of the academic world will be able to rethink the limits of the editorial view of textual studies: literary criticism as currently instituted lacks the technical and historical knowledge to carry out, or even initiate, such a process of reconceptualization.

An immersion in textual and bibliographical studies presupposes and reciprocates an understanding of the entire developing process of a literary work's historical transmission, and this in turn creates, or ought to create, a profound sense of how many factors enter into the production of the literary work. Textual studies do not pursue emendations and corruptions (or their absence) as the justifying end of the discipline. The first obligation of textual studies is to elucidate the meaning of what has taken place, not to adjudicate between these events and their consequences. Of historical method in general Collingwood once said that it should not begin by asking the question 'Is this right or is this wrong?' but rather 'What does this mean?'[15] Collingwood's view is as applicable to the work of textual scholarship as it is to any other historically grounded discipline.

III

These general remarks will introduce the following methodological schema which I would propose as a model for a procedure in textual criticism. This programme is an analytic outline of the subjects and topics which are essential to textual criticism, whether it is viewed as a programme of study or as an operational (a practical) event. The specific subjects and topics placed under each of the general categorical headings call for an elucidation of their circumstantial character, i.e. a socio-historical analysis of each element in the heading. These specific analyses, related together, constitute an analytic presentation of the category, and the character as well as the adequacy of

[15] R. G. Collingwood, *The Idea of History*, Oxford, 1946, p. 260.

any act of textual criticism will be a function of the range of textual material which is critically examined.

My view is that a critical presentation of all the material ranged under categories A and B constitutes a finished programme of historicist textual criticism. Such a programme gains what I should call a properly historical character when the material ranged under category C begins to be brought into the critical analysis. The material in this category must of course be a part of any exercise in textual analysis; it need not be made a part of the *critical* (i.e. self-conscious) analysis, however, and in fact most of the material in this category is not material that is critically studied by textual scholars.

A. *The Originary Textual Moment*

1. Author
2. Other persons or groups involved in the initial process of production (e.g. collaborators; persons who may have commissioned the work; editors or amanuenses; etc.)
3. Phases or stages in the initial productive process (e.g. distinct personal, textual, or social states along with their defining causes, functions, and characteristics)
4. Materials, means, and modes of the initial productive process (physical, psychological, ideological)

B. *Secondary Moments of Textual Production and Reproduction* (*Individual and Related Sequences*)

This material should be ranged under two periodic subsets: a period of reproduction carried out during the author's lifetime; the periods of production and reproduction which begin with the author's death. The elements to be ranged under each of these subsets are the same as those set out under category A above.

In the critical study of this material certain shifts of emphasis take place. Most obviously, the author is studied as he or she is a critical and historical reconstruction. The heading 'Author', then, will comprise a range of ideas or concepts of the author which have emerged in the minds of various people and the ideologies of different classes, institutions, and groups. Reciprocally, the critic will necessarily bring to the centre of attention not the author himself, but those 'Other persons or groups' signalled in A.2.

Similarly, the influence of the work's own production history on the work itself grows more important with the passage of time. Works descend to our hands in certain concrete and specific forms, and along a series of equally concrete and specific avenues. The textual history of literary works reflects the influence of these factors even as the specific texts give a visible (if unanalysed) form to the meaning and significance of that history. The critical analysis of texts discovers one of its chief intellectual justifications in that set of circumstances. Certain patterns of history are literalized in complete and finished forms in such texts; consequently, the critical analysis of such forms is an invaluable key to understanding those most elusive types of human phenomena, social and historical patterns.

Categories A and B are chiefly to be studied under the historian's milder (and preliminary) rubric 'What does this mean?' rather than under the more severe polemical question 'Is this right or is this wrong?'

C. The Immediate Moment of Textual Criticism

This category calls for a critical analysis of the immediate critic's own programmatic goals and purposes. This is probably the most demanding of all critical tasks, since it involves a critical presentation of events which do not lie in a completed form of pastness, but which are coincident with the entire act of analysis itself.

This moment appears as a specific act of criticism—as a particular bibliography, edition, set of glosses, or critical commentary of one form or another. The particular bibliographers, editors, or commentators may approach the subject matter critically (categories A and B) without approaching their own work in a critical spirit. The heuristic model for such a case would perhaps be an edition undertaken by a technically skilled scholar as a set task.

The governing model for a criticism which fulfils the obligations of this categorical imperative might well be either Thucydides and his *History of the Peloponnesian War* or Trotsky and his *History of the Russian Revolution*, depending upon whether one wanted an experimental or a polemical model. In textual studies I would instance the Kane and Donaldson edition of *Piers Plowman* as a model of an experimental critical edition and

Bowers's edition of *The Dramatic Works of Thomas Dekker* as a model of a polemical sort; and I would set these beside F.A. Wolf's *Prolegomena ad Homerum* (1795) and Joseph Bédier's 'La Tradition Manuscrite du *Lai de L'Ombre*' as similar models of textual criticism carried out in the form of commentary.[16]

Works which exhibit a high degree of critical expertise in this aspect of their analysis will almost necessarily appear as controversial in their immediate scholarly context. Such works may display more or less serious deficiencies in their critical grasp of their subject matter (categories A and B). Whatever the case, they approach their own projects under the imperative query: 'Is this right or is this wrong?'

IV

This schema may be summarized in a brief set of instructions to the student of literary works. The elementary manœuvres for studying, understanding, and finally teaching such works involve, first, an elucidation of the textual history of the work, and second, an explication of the reception history. Neither of these operations can be performed independently of the other because the two historical processes are dialectically related. (This is why no textual criticism, however specialized, can be produced without at least an implicit reference to certain more broadly established social phenomena which impinge on a work's various textual constitutions.) None the less, in textual criticism the attention will focus, necessarily, on a work's shifting verbal forms on the one hand, and on its changing bibliographical states on the other.

The editorial function of textual criticism is to establish the reliability of the received texts and to determine whether a new edition is useful and what sort it might be. As I have argued, however, this is a specialized use of the method. A thorough study of the textual history of any work does not cease to be a *sine qua non* of literary criticism when readers are provided with good editions, even good critical editions: on the contrary, in

---

[16] George Kane and E. Talbot Donaldson, eds., *Piers Plowman: The B Version*, London, 1975; Bowers's edition was published by Cambridge University Press (1953-61); Bédier's essay was printed in two parts in *Romania* liv (1928), pp. 161-96, 321-56.

fact. Furthermore, the analysis of the textual history is crucial for a more broadly considered act of literary criticism not merely because such an analysis may turn up textual mistakes or interesting verbal variants. The analysis establishes its justification at more primitive levels altogether.

Let me give two sets of examples. The text of Byron's *Don Juan* Cantos I-II in the first authorized printing is identical in all essential verbal features with the text of the first pirated printings. When one examines authorized and pirated printings in their historical contexts, however, we discover that their 'meaning' was radically different. That difference in meaning is not simply a function of differences in verbal content, nor even of the acts of analysis and interpretation performed by later critics. It is an objective and original difference, and one which will only appear in our view if and when Byron's poem is analysed with the methods of textual criticism. Or consider a poem like Emily Dickinson's 'Because I could not stop for Death', which has an identical verbal text in Johnson's critical edition, in the *Norton Anthology of Modern Poetry* and in Franklin's recent *The Manuscript Books of Emily Dickinson*.[17] These three apparently 'identical' texts are in fact very different, for they exist in bibliographical environments (as it were) which enforce very different reading experiences. The analysis of these environments will only yield to an applied textual criticism.

There is as well the notorious case of Auden's 'September 1, 1939'. Its first printing in the *New Republic* established a text which Auden later grew to regret. He reprinted the poem in the 1945 *Collected Poems*, but in a revised text with the penultimate stanza removed. Later still he decided to suppress the poem altogether, and Auden's present editor, Edward Mendelson, has not printed the work in his posthumous edition of the *Collected Poems*.[18]

---

[17] I have discussed both of these examples at greater length below in chap. II. 3, 'The Text, the Poem, and the Problem of Historical Method'; see also the similar discussion of Edgar Allen Poe's 'Von Kempelen and His Discovery' and Byron's 'On This Day I Complete My Thirty-Sixth Year' in chap. II. 2 below, 'Shall These Bones Live?' The Dickinson editions cited are those of Thomas H. Johnson, *The Poems of Emily Dickinson* 3 vols., Cambridge, Mass., 1954 and R. W. Franklin's recent facsimile text in two volumes, Cambridge, Mass., 1981.

[18] New York, 1976. For a discussion of the textual history, see Joseph Warren Beach, *The Making of the Auden Canon*, Minneapolis, 1957, pp. 49-52.

That history is itself interesting. Equally interesting, however, is another, parallel history of the poem's textual fortunes. For this famous work remained in print—*in its original unrevised state*—throughout Auden's lifetime, and it continues to be printed to this day, in various anthologies of poetry, and especially in anthologies prepared for school use.[19] To read this poem now in one of those anthologies is to read a work which is very different from the first printed text (though they are verbally identical) as well as from the later revised text. Textual criticism is uniquely prepared to elucidate and explain these matters, to establish the ground for an advanced literary criticism; for these events will and do impinge upon the experience of Auden's poem in whatever textual state it is read, whether one is aware of the influence or not. The objective reality of these matters, along with their meaning and influence, may be changed by a reader's ignorance of them, but it will not be removed by such ignorance. It will merely assume a specific (and explicable) shape and significance, and one which will submit, in its turn, to the elucidation of textual criticism.

Furthermore, the example from Auden illustrates yet another important point: that when verbal changes and variations are revealed through a process of textual criticism, their significance may not lie merely in the (obvious) fact that two verbally different texts may have different meanings. More interesting, in the case of the Auden poem, is the conflict of meanings which the work necessarily incorporates in itself. The textual and bibliographical history of the poem from 1939 to the present reveals how and why, when we read any particular verbal text of this work, the other verbal texts are necessary poetic presences. No scholar can read this poem today, in any verbal constitution, without being aware of the conflicts and contradictions which are built into the poem, which have become part of it as a consequence of the work's peculiar historical life.

All literary works have their own special and peculiar histories, though some are more useful than others for illustrating this fact, and hence for demonstrating the theoretical and methodological point I am trying to make. The example from Auden might be supported by an analogous case from Marianne

---

[19] See, e.g. *Chief Modern Poets of England and America*, ed. G. D. Sanders *et al.*, London, 1970, i. 366-8.

Moore. In its first printing, her well-known poem 'Poetry' appeared as a work of thirty lines, and it was reprinted in this form several times by Moore herself, in the 1935 *Selected Poems* and in the 1951 *Collected Poems* as well. When she published the 1967 *Complete Poems*, however, the original work had disappeared in favour of a text which comprised only the first three lines of the original text. This three-line text is now accepted as the authorized version, and it appears alone in Moore's *Complete Poems*. Anthologies and school texts adopt varying approaches to this work, some printing the three-line text, some the original thirty-line version.

Whatever the choice, the significance of this history does not lie merely in the 'different meanings' which the two texts embody. What textual criticism also shows (and more significantly shows) is that no reading of either text of this work can remain innocent of the significance of the other text (though it may well remain ignorant or unconscious of that other text). To read the work called by Moore 'Poetry' entails something like a close encounter of a third kind: that is to say, an encounter in which the two texts are present to the reader's mind, an encounter in which the interplay of the two texts is at the centre of the reading experience.

Examples of the fundamental place which textual and bibliographical analysis occupy in literary interpretation are not difficult to multiply. The problem with such examples, in the current scholarly climate, is that they tend to obscure the essential theoretical point behind a screen of particulars. Many textual critics smile condescendingly on the innocence (or ignorance) of various literary interpreters who do not ground their work in a disciplined textual criticism. But textual criticism and its practitioners seem to me to labour under a corresponding sort of innocence which has only reinforced the schism which exists between hermeneutics and textual criticism. Bibliographers and textual critics tend to conceive their work today almost exclusively in terms of its editorial functions and application. This we have already seen. Equally significant, however, is the fact that contemporary textual work is dominated by a theory of literary production which is so author-centred that it has increasingly neglected the importance of non-authorial textual determinants. Establishing texts for editions too often begins and ends in the pursuit of the so-called 'author's intentions' or 'author's final intentions' (as if these were definitive matters, or as if the author could or even should exercise an exclusive authority over the use of his works). This pursuit has its corresponding consequences in the prevailing views of the relation of hermeneutics to textual studies. Readers look to the resources of textual criticism for emendations, corruptions, and textual variants, as if these were the contributions which literary criticism should expect from textual and bibliographical studies. The expectation seems to be shared by most textualists themselves, and the consequence of this state of affairs is only too apparent: the rich analytic resources of textual and bibliographical analysis have hardly begun to be recognized or used in the literary criticism which we observe today. That a different and much more fruitful relation might prevail is clear, if only because we know that it has prevailed, in the work of certain critics, in the past.

Earlier I mentioned Thucydides as a writer whose critical habits might well serve as a model for literary scholars, though he was himself neither grammarian nor critic nor philologue. But he had a profoundly critical mind—the *ne plus ultra* for textual or any kind of scholarship, as Housman once suggested.[20] And it so happens that in his great *History* he does make occasional forays into the field of textual criticism. These are always memorable events, and I want to recall one of them here to conclude this chapter.

After his narrative of the plague at Athens, Thucydides begins his summary with the following anecdote.

Such was the nature of the calamity which now fell on the Athenians; death raging within the city and devastation without. Among other things which they remembered in their distress was, very naturally, the following verse, which the old men said had been uttered long ago:
        A Dorian war shall come and with it death.
A dispute arose whether dearth and not death had not been the word in the verse; but at the present juncture it was of course decided in favour of the latter; for the people made their recollection fit in with their sufferings. I fancy, however, that if another Dorian war should

---

[20] In his famous essay 'The Application of Thought to Textual Criticism', *Proceedings of the Classical Association* xviii (1921), pp. 67-84.

ever afterwards come upon us, and a dearth should happen to accompany it, the verse will probably be read accordingly.[21]

The scholarship in this commentary does not lie in the recording of a textual dispute, and it clearly has nothing at all to do with adjudicating between the two received readings of the line, nor even with explaining what each version means. Thucydides' mordant eye is not directed toward the 'original version' of the line but toward the versions produced by later 'editors' and interpreters; and his interest lies in the meaning of scholarship and criticism rather than in the meaning of that line of ancient verse. To that extent the passage illustrates a textual criticism which has raised and answered Collingwood's historicist question: 'What does it mean?' But the passage pushes beyond that question in order to ask the further and more demanding one: 'Is this right or is this wrong?' Nor does Thucydides ask this question merely as a matter of technical accuracy, as editors today might perhaps ask such a question of the texts they will study. What is 'wrong' here is not a *textual* but a *critical* deficiency.

I think much the same kind of judgement might be passed on a good deal of the work we produce, whether as textual scholars or as literary interpreters. The weaknesses seem to me critical rather than technical, and they can often be traced to a failure of theory—a failure to begin the inquiry at fundamental levels. To the degree that this is true, to that extent does Thucydides' scholastic satire remain an important model and resource. It may be that we shall never know whether the original Greek word was *limos* or *loimos*, and that we shall fail forever to cross the boundary of the Greek New Testament or to pass beyond the Masoretic wall and the Alexandrian limits; it may be that we shall never hear the uncorrupted word of God, and that we shall not see Homer, or even Shelley, plain. If these are losses, and they are, they are losses which may be filled with meaning, in several senses—losses which bear fruit in a critical intelligence, losses over which we need grieve not but rather find 'Strength in what remains behind . . . In years that bring the philosophic mind.'

(1981-2)

---

[21] *Thucydides. The History of the Peloponnesian War*, ed. and trans. Sir Richard Livingstone, Oxford, 1960, p. 122 (Book II, sec. 54). The crux involves a choice between the Greek words *limos* and *loimos*.

2. Shall These Bones Live?

I

A professional society launches itself in 1981 under the aegis of 'textual studies' and proposes to issue scholarly papers in a journal called *Text*. These are notable events, all the more so because their initial impression belies their actual significance. For such a society and such a journal, in an academic world currently dominated by structuralist and post-structuralist theory and practice, necessarily suggest an interest in the semiological and Derridan 'text', and in the entire critical enterprise which goes under the heading of 'textuality'.

One has only to cast a glance at the editorial and advisory board of this society, however, to see that its interests must be very different indeed. Riffaterre, Said, Derrida, deMan: none of these famous men are part of this project. Instead we find other names—equally famous, perhaps, but residents of another planet—like Orgel, Litz, Vieth, and Tanselle. So an illumination begins. *Text*, and the Society for Textual Scholarship, is a revisionist action by philologists, scholars, and 'textual critics' in the traditional sense.

The creation of such a society and such a journal at this particular historical moment is, in other words, a bold—even an aggressive—move. It will bring not peace but a sword. Yet when the inevitable conflict is engaged, what will be the issues at stake? Is *Text* to be a sort of Vendéean Uprising, a centre of reaction where editors, bibliographers, and philologists can meet and agreeably deplore all that is new-fangled, French, and transitory?

I raise these matters here partly because I want to explain my own purpose in associating with this new venture, and partly because I want to make a polemic for a revisionist policy which will not be a reactionary one. In order to make my position clear, I shall have to rehearse some familiar matters relating to the present state of literary studies.

Textual criticism, in the traditional sense, is an analytic discipline separated into two provinces, the so-called Lower and Higher Criticism. Its practitioners are those guardians of our dry bones, the editors, bibliographers, and philologists of various sorts who are best known to the ordinary student of literature for the work they do *not* do: that is, interpretation and literary criticism.

It is an historical irony of some magnitude that twentieth-century stylistics and hermeneutics, or literary criticism and interpretation, emerged directly from the traditions of critical philology which developed over the course of the eighteenth and nineteenth centuries. From F.A. Wolf to Wilamowitz, philological analysis was intimately connected not merely to the elucidation of the text, but to what James Thorpe once (and forever) denominated 'the aesthetics of textual criticism'.[1] The New Criticism's devotion to 'the poem itself', as well as the more recent fascination with texts not as specific objects but as 'methodological fields'[2] (or *foci* for interpretive strategies), descend to us through the mediation of various form critics, linguists, and philologists, and most immediately through people like Saussure, Sapir, and Jakobson. In this descent, however, a gap opened up between the work of the scholar and the work of the critic. This gap confronts us today as almost unbridgeable, a gulf we locate by that ultimate sign of contradiction, The Text.

The problem with this polarization in literary studies is not at all that differences should exist between the methods and interests of scholars on the one hand and critics on the other, or between so-called extrinsic and intrinsic studies. One might well recall here those famous words of William Blake, for they seem especially pertinent: 'These two classes of men are always upon earth, & they should be enemies: whoever tries to reconcile them seeks to destroy existence.' Blake's view was that 'Without Contraries is no progression',[3] and his proverb holds equally well on our tight little island of literary studies. The problem is that these two classes of men (and women) tend to carry on their work in entire isolation from each other, and not

---

[1] James Thorpe, 'The Aesthetics of Textual Criticism', reprinted in *Bibliography and Textual Criticism*, ed. O. M. Brack, Jr. and Warner Barnes, Chicago, 1969, pp. 102-38.

[2] The phrase is Roland Barthes's. See below, n. 4.

[3] See *The Marriage of Heaven and Hell*, plates 16-17 and 3.

at all that they engage in those struggles and intellectual combats which Blake called 'Mental Fight'.

These struggles must begin, and I propose to aid the event here by examining some of the positions and fault-lines which appear on either side.

The enemies of traditional philology, from its early antagonists like Leavis to its most recent critics like Barthes, recurrently charge it with various sorts of dehumanization. Philologists murder to dissect, and where are the pleasures of the text for the editor and the bibliographer? Over and over again the literary critic struggles to tear the poetic work from the hands of the Casaubons of the world and to deliver it over to the Dorotheas.

One of the most eloquent, and influential, pleas for such a delivery was made in 1971 by Roland Barthes in his essay 'From Work to Text'.[4] In this exemplary paper Barthes distinguished sharply between the 'work' of traditional literary studies, both critical and scholarly, and the 'text' of a new type of hermeneutics. The distinction means to separate 'the work', which 'is concrete, occupying a portion of book-space', from 'the text', which, because 'it exists only as discourse' and never as concrete object, is in reality 'a methodological field', a locus for the continuous production of literary signification. Barthes spoke for a generation of new literary readers and interpreters when he said that *'the text is experienced only as an activity, a production'*. This famous dictum announces a renewed method for dealing with the polysemous aspects of literary productions. They are not 'works', which Barthes called 'objects of consumption', but 'texts', which 'ask the reader for an active collaboration'.[5] Those of us who have worked with the dead letters of our literary pasts, whether as editors, bibliographers, or whatever, understand all too well the force of Barthes's polemic. William Todd's essay 'On the Use of Advertisements in Bibliographical Studies'[6] is a model of its kind, even a brilliant work, but one does not value it—or consult it—because it generates textual pleasure, any more than Todd wrote it to collaborate in an

---

[4] The essay is reprinted in an excellent survey-anthology of post-structuralist criticism, *Textual Strategies*, ed. with an introduction by Josué Harari, Ithaca, NY, 1979, pp. 73-81.

[5] See Barthes, pp. 74, 75, 79, 80.

[6] The essay is reprinted in Brack and Barnes, pp. 154-72.

intertextual activity. Todd's essay treats literary works as concrete objects and—worse still—seems uninterested in aesthetic pleasures altogether. The essay merely (merely?) shows us a peculiarly reliable method for establishing accurate dates of publication.

Todd's is a piece of Dryasdust scholarship, then, sure enough, and those of us who—like myself—admire it, are faced with the need to justify that fine piece of work. Nor will it do merely to launch a tit-for-tat rejoinder, and ask how much pleasure gets generated through a Derridan text like *On Grammatology*, or through the turgid academese one repeatedly confronts in journals like *Glyph* and *Diacritics*. And indeed, such journals merely represent the tactical failures of an impressive general strategy; to locate these failures is, at the most, to uncover the symptoms of what ought to be our true objects of investigation.

In fact, these contemporary textual strategies have no more strength than their limits permit, and to use them well one must understand those limits. Barthes, for example, speaks for a large number of influential contemporary critics when he sets a premium upon literature as a process of production rather than consumption, and when he disvalues a critical method which tries to treat artistic works as objects. In each case he appeals to that powerful tradition of aesthetic criticism which emerges with Kant and Coleridge and continues into our own day. Coleridge declared that objects as objects are fixed and dead, and he elevated the activities of the so-called 'creative imagination'. Reason and what the Enlightenment termed 'the critical faculties' are suspect powers in this tradition, which has developed that ideology of process and production—'something evermore about to be'—that is perpetuated in post-structuralist criticism.

The great strength of this tradition lies in the freedom it can give to the critic-as-reader. Authority for literary creativity emerges from a dead past to a living present. In such a situation the function of criticism becomes, avowedly, to sustain its own productivity, and its object becomes the process of that productivity. But such a procedure will succeed only when it accepts the limits of its own method. One of those fundamental limits commands that such a method can generate literary experience only, not literary knowledge. Such criticism should not mean but be, and as it yearns to embrace its own aesthesis, it also tends to abandon knowledge and science.[7]

We must not mistake the character of this limitation, however. It is not a weakness or a fault in the method, it is simply one of its defining conditions. It appears in the method's lack of concern for historical studies, for philological pursuits of all sorts, for the *physique* and for the memory of artistic creations. These repudiations remind us that textual strategies carried out in a Barthesian mode occupy a definite, and antithetical, position throughout the modern periods. The function of such criticism is not to examine the newspaper advertisements of published books, or to assemble a bibliography of early printings, or to resurrect those historical references in a literary work which the passage of time has erased from our memories, or altered circumstances have concealed from view. This is a methodology which does not aim to study the text of the critic but to generate the text of the reader.

The post-structuralist text and the philological text represent, then, that fundamental opposition in the field of literary studies which used to be called 'criticism' *v.* 'appreciation', but which we now term analysis *v.* reading. The one aspires toward a science, the other toward an art, one toward knowledge, the other toward experience. These two classes of men are always upon the earth of humane letters, and whoever seeks to reconcile them seeks to destroy the existence of their shared world.

Blake's proverb does not mean to sanction peaceful co-existence, however. The refusal to seek reconciliation ought to entail a tension and struggle between these opposing interests, rather than an agreement to let each go its own way. This last option has been the road most often taken, and it has generally led to the even-handed excesses of Dryasdust and Skimpole— between whom there is, I think, little to choose.

Problems arise in each case when either method fails to take its own powers and methods into account. In the case of the critic-as-artist, this problem takes the form of an *anamnesis*, sometimes even a deliberate attempt to obliterate that aspect of

---

[7] Another limit has been explored by Jean Baudrillard in *The Mirror of Production*, trans. and with introduction by Mark Poster, St. Louis, 1975, where Baudrillard shows the capitalist and bourgeois ideological formations which are imbedded in every production-based approach to the study of social forms.

an immediate experience which has necessarily recuperated the past. For there can be no production process, no continuous act of generation, except within the limits of those specific means and relations of production which the present must accept as its continuing inheritance. This necessity exists because all literary products descend into immediate experience; that is, they come to the reader in determinate forms. The most elemental of these determinate forms is the physical object—normally, a bound and printed 'text' (in the traditional sense) which establishes the conditions for every particular experience of the 'text' (in the contemporary sense). Even the critical attempt to erase (or deconstruct) the traditional text depends upon an acknowledgment of its presence and relative authority. Such a text may come to us in forms that appear fairly well fixed, like *Mansfield Park*, or in forms that aspire to greater indeterminacy, like Cortazar's *Hopscotch*, or a play by Shakespeare. These differences are, of course, crucial both for the experience and for the understanding of literary products. In every case, however, we must deal with the specific determinations. The texts, in the traditional sense, of *Macbeth* are defined in very particular ways.[8]

Human beings are not angels. Part of what it means to be human is to have a body, to occupy physical space, and to move in real time. In the same way the products of literature, which are in all cases human products, are not disembodied processes. When Barthes says that literature 'exists only as discourse', we must forcefully remind ourselves that discourse always takes place in specific and·concrete forms, and that those forms are by no means comprehended by the limits of language. The aesthetic field of literary productions is neither an unheard melody nor a linguistic event, as one can (literally) *see* by merely glancing at Trollope's *The Way We Live Now* either in its first printing, or in some subsequent edition, like Robert Tracy's recent critical text.[9] If such productions are events in

---

[8] The texts of most plays are notoriously indeterminate and variable because they are written primarily for performance, and gain their printed forms in relation to that primary (unprinted) event.

[9] That is to say, the printed numbers of Trollope's novel—their size, their format, their schedule of appearance—are all relevant aesthetic matters, as are the physical characteristics of any edition. Books with decorated covers and bindings—like those we see in Hardy's *Wessex Poems* or in Rossetti's various early editions—forcibly remind us of this important aesthetic aspect of all literary works, even of those which are not

language, as of course they are, their eventualities are experienced in concrete and observable forms, and under specific circumstances of time and place. Nor are these concrete particulars merely 'accidental' aspects of literary productions. Just as the human body in its particular socio-historical environment establishes certain fundamental and defining human particulars, the concrete forms and specific moments in which literary works emerge and re-emerge are defining constituents of their modes of aesthetic existence.

Thus, if we are to understand how poems mean—if we are to gain knowledge of literary productions—we must pay attention to a variety of concrete historical particulars, and not merely to 'the poem itself' or its linguistic determination. Many literary critics, and even many post-structuralist critics, would not disagree with such a view. But I would urge a further proposition and say that an encounter with the concrete particulars of an aesthetic object—an experience of the objectivity of 'the text' in all its rich and various determinations—is fundamental to the *experience* of literary texts (or works) as well.

This proposition asks the critic-as-artist to understand that if the experience of art is an aesthetic process (i.e., a subjective encounter), the process gets carried through in specific sets of objective differentials. The generation of texts, whether philological or aesthetic, is a finite act which in every instance (and it is a process which takes place in particular instances) appears in some exemplary and specific case. It is crucial for the critic-as-artist to keep this in mind—to subject his or her acts to the interrogation and critique of that model of otherness which is the philologist's text—if the critic is not to lapse into ventriloquism. The generation of the text is, even for the aesthetic critic, a perpetually renewed historical process of specific and concrete events.

The 'discourse' of literature, then, is not an undifferentiated linguistic stream, but a continuing set of finite relationships that develop in a valley of Dry Bones between an author, printers, publishers, readers of various sorts, reviewers, academicians, and—ultimately—society at all its levels, and perhaps even

'beautiful', even mass-produced books. For an excellent discussion of these and related matters see Morris Eaves, 'What Is The "History of Publishing"?', *Publishing History* ii (1977), pp. 57-77.

international society. Every time a work of literature is encountered the reader places himself in a position where he is
able to experience, and join with, that complex human endeavour. Great literary works are valuable to us precisely because
they exist to foster and reproduce such discourse. Critics like
Barthes aim principally to put us into contact with the *idea* of
this discourse. The philologist, on the other hand, aims—or
should aim—to put us into contact with such a discourse in
a more concrete and experiential way. We can glimpse how
this aim is fulfilled even in a passage like the following, which
deals with its materials at a relatively high level of generality.

> Various forces are always at work thwarting or modifying the
> author's intentions. The process of preparing the work for dissemin-
> ation to a public (whether that process leads to publication in printed
> form or production in the theatre or preparation of scribal copies) puts
> the work in the hands of persons who are professionals in the execution
> of the process. Similarly, the effort to recover a work of the past puts it
> in the hands of professionals known as textual critics, or editors. In all
> of these cases, the process must be adapted to the work at hand, and
> the work to the process. Sometimes through misunderstanding and
> sometimes through an effort to improve the work, these professionals
> substitute their own intentions for those of the author, who is fre-
> quently ignorant of their craft. Sometimes the author objects and
> sometimes not, sometimes he is pleased, sometimes he acquiesces,
> and sometimes he does not notice what has happened. The work of
> art is thus always tending toward a collaborative status, and the task
> of the textual critic is always to recover and preserve its integrity at
> that point where the authorial intentions seem to have been fulfilled.[10]

In the field of literary production and reproduction, differentials are established through the elaboration of critical knowledge: specific details of (traditional) literary texts and their
interacting historical contexts. Such knowledge is furnished by
the normal 'methodological fields' of our discipline, that is, in
philological investigations carried out through the Lower and
Higher Criticisms.

It is not the possession of such knowledge—in Barthes's
terms, its 'consumption'—which the critic-as-scholar must
have as his object, however. It is the discovery, the repossession,
and the use of such knowledge which matters. For knowledge

---

[10] Thorpe, pp. 136-7.

in literary studies must be developed as a function of the aesthetic experience. If it is not, the knowledge is not literary knowledge; it is historical, and only potentially literary. Bilbliographers, philologists, literary historians, and traditional textual critics grow ridiculous figures in the eyes of many literate persons because of this passion they have for details that seem ancillary to the experience of literary works. This ridicule is understandable but it is also deeply misconceived; for the development and elucidation of a work's 'minute particulars' are, finally, the *sine qua non* of any aesthetic experience. This is so because all art, by its very character as a symbolic mode, operates in a medium of uniqueness.

A sure grasp of this fact is a distinctive mark of all the great textual critics of the eighteenth and nineteenth centuries, and it equally explains why their legacy continues to dominate their polarized inheritors in the twentieth. Their acts of revival, performed on classical, biblical, and national scriptures alike, were primarily attempts to define and sharpen the special character of the literary works they examined. The method entailed a massive programme of rigorous and creative antiquarianism: literary works were made distinctive in and for the present by an immediate act of alienation and distancing. Art, which Time seemed bent upon reducing to obscure ruins, or rendering invisible through familiarity, was led across the Red Sea of the past and the deserts of the present to the Promised Land of History. The Ruins of Time, past and present, were overcome by agreeing to co-operate with its passages. Time thereby became History, and Art seemed reborn out of its losses, its otherness, its very distance.

Eichhorn, writing on the book of Genesis, exemplifies such purposes and achievements very well. When you read this book, he tells us, you must

Read it as two historical works of high antiquity, and thus breathe the air of its age and land. Forget the century you are living in and the knowledge it offers you; if you cannot, do not dream that you are reading the book in the spirit of its origin. The youth of the world, which it describes, requires that one sink into its depths. The first beams of dawning intelligence will not bear the bright light of the intellect. The herdsman speaks only to the herdsman, and the Oriental of gray antiquity only to the Oriental. Without intimate acquaintance with the customs of pastoral life, without acquaintance with the manner of thinking and imagining among uncultivated peoples gained through the study of the ancient world, especially Greece of the earliest times, and of untutored nations of modern times, one easily becomes the betrayer of the Book, when one tries to be its rescuer and interpreter.[11]

This magnificent passage will not abide any irrelevant questions about intentionality, authority, or the general 'mode of existence of a literary work of art'. The passage shows us why Eichhorn's scholarly 'hours when the mind is watchful not to miss the slightest similarities or dissimilarities'[12] between the E and the J strands in Genesis, are an integral part of his aesthetic experience of that work.

Eichhorn's scholastic drudgery is not merely another part of the 'discourse' which the book of Genesis *is*; his scholarship defines the medium and the terms in which every aesthetic experience must take place. By specifying the distinctiveness of past forms of human life, the scholarship co-operates in and reduplicates the object (in both senses) of art, which can only exist in the media of its uniqueness. Reading Eichhorn we understand how the dead will live again.

II

So far this mild polemic has maintained itself at a rather cool and distanced level. It is time for specifics, illustrations, a few hard instances.

I mentioned earlier a celebrated paper by William Todd on the use of newspaper advertisements for establishing dates of publication. That paper focuses one of the recurrent preoccupations of bibliographers: their attempts to define precise details of place, date, and circumstances of publication, and even more the attempt to establish dependable methods for developing the information. The paper's fame rests on its procedural and methodological innovativeness.

His essay is not, of course, an act of immediate criticism. Its purposes are larger and more general—as, for example,

---

[11] Johann Gottfried Eichhorn, *Einleitung ins Alte Testament*, translated by Emery Neff in *The Poetry of History*, New York, 1947, p. 57.   [12] Ibid.

Barthes's purposes were in *his* paper, which is also not a piece of literary criticism as such. Nevertheless, what Todd does in his essay indicates the importance he attaches to precision in matters of publication facts. He makes no plea for the aesthetic importance of such facts—scholars rarely do any more—but he might and could have done so. For one can make that demonstration in the case of *all* literary works, whose bibliographical histories are always, and necessarily, crucial to their literary and artistic character.

It makes a great difference, for example, that Byron's noble lyric 'On This Day I Complete My Thirty-Sixth Year' first appeared posthumously. Moreover, the character of the poem is decisively marked by its early process of dissemination. The pathos of its heroism and its hopelessness is fixed and critically defined in the way he wrote it in his private journal on 22 January 1824, and in the way he then gave a copy of it, as an afterthought, to Pietro Gamba later that same day. 'You were complaining, the other day, that I never write any poetry now:— this is my birthday, and I have just finished something, which, I think, is better than what I usually write.'[13] The poem projects itself directly in the emotional conflict which these remarks also call attention to. For we must remember—as, in fact, the poem scarcely allows us to forget—that it was written shortly after Byron had arrived in Greece to support the latest Greek effort to throw off the Ottoman Empire. It is a peculiarly Byronic poem, fully conscious of its immediate circumstances and of its author's entire history in life and letters. Indeed, that history is the fundamental subject of the poem, which reflects upon its author's past under the clarifying pressure of Byron's special immediate circumstances. The poem fairly epitomizes how the emotional force of a literary work is a function of the most specific and precise matters of fact.

The artistic process which Byron had begun on 22 January only receives its complete definition in the early history of the poem's transmission and publication. Here are equally crucial matters of fact in the emotional nexus which the poem has called into being.

Byron wrote and forgot about his journal poem, and in a few months he was dead (19 April). When this news reached England

[13] See *The Works of Lord Byron*, ed. E. H. Coleridge, London, 1904, vii. 85-8 and nn.

in mid May it fell like a thunderbolt. Byron's body and his effects were brought back to England, along with his journal, and arrived early in July. Throughout this period, and for many months afterwards, the periodical press remained hypnotically fixed upon Byron, his career, and his final, haunting days in Greece.[14]

At the same time, some of those who were with Byron in Greece made copies of the poem given to Gamba, who also sent a transcript to Mary Shelley, at her request. One of these copies was used by the (unknown) author of 'Lord Byron in Greece', a long essay which appeared in the July 1824 *Westminster Review* and which contained a narrative of Byron's last months. Four lines of the poem were first printed in this essay. The complete poem finally appeared in the *Morning Chronicle* of 29 October 1824, printed from one of the many manuscript copies which were now at circulation. The poem was then reprinted in various other newspapers.

That the poem should have been transmitted and finally published in this way is in perfect keeping with every other aspect of its text and context. A poem about noble causes and the ephemeral, if willing, agents of those causes, 'On This Day' properly (we must say) makes its first public speech through the newspapers, and not through the devotion of those several intermediaries who were with him in Greece when he wrote the verses and met his immortal death. That the actual copy text for the *Morning Chronicle* printing should have disappeared in the complex network of the poem's early transmission history seems especially appropriate, for Byron's entire audience was in some way complicit in the process which brought this poem to be.

The more we pursue the poem's early bibliographical history, the more sharply do we experience the fragility of such a work, and the special human character of the circumstances which it defines and perpetuates. The scholarly reconstruction of that text and its context is no more than a correspondent effort to provide the work with a yet further range of response, and one that will eventually meet it on its own terms.

[14] For a good survey of these matters see Samuel C. Chew, *Byron in England*, London, 1924, pp. 194-219.

Or take another, less Romantic, but no less eloquent example: Poe's hoaxing tale 'Von Kempelen and His Discovery'.[15] In this case, if we reconstruct the context of the work's initial publication, we permit ourselves to regain access to the original, outrageous, and even highly significant wittiness of the narrative.

Poe published the work on 14 April 1849 in *The Flag of Our Union*. After his death, when his letters became generally available, readers learned from Poe's own words his initial intentions as he revealed them at the time in a letter to Evert A. Duyckinck, editor of *The Literary World*, the publication which was first offered, but which refused, Poe's narrative.

I mean it as a kind of 'exercise', or experiment, in the plausible or verisimilar style. Of course, there is *not one* word of truth in it from beginning to end. I thought that such a style, applied to the gold-excitement, could not fail of effect. My sincere opinion is that nine persons out of ten (even among the best-informed) will *believe* the quiz (provided the design does not leak out before publication) and that thus, acting as a sudden, although of course a very temporary, *check* to the gold-fever, it will create a *stir* to some purpose.[16]

A number of scholars, most notably Burton R. Pollin, have elaborated the specific relevance of 'Von Kempelen' in relation to the California Gold Rush, as well as its filiations with the hoax genre which emerged through the British magazine tradition in the nineteenth century, and they have also elucidated the tale's numerous coded references to more detailed topical matters of various sorts.[17] The development of this scholarly material lays bare the fundamental textual and contextual matrix of the narrative. Specifically, the scholarship reveals— though not all of the scholarship is aware of this revelation— that 'Von Kempelen' is a kind of witty demonstration of the old proverb 'All that glitters is not gold'.

Briefly, the narrative purports to correct and augment the pre-

15 All citations are from the text of *The Flag of Our Union* as reprinted in *The Science Fiction of Edgar Allen Poe*, ed. Harold Beaver, London, 1976, pp. 324-32.

16 *The Letters of Edgar Allen Poe*, ed. John Ward Ostrom, Cambridge, Mass., 1948, ii. 433.

17 See Burton R. Pollin, 'Poe's *Von Kempelen and His Discovery*: Sources and Significance', *Études Anglaises* xx (1967), pp. 12-23; Michael Allen, *Poe and the British Magazine Tradition*, New York, 1969; *The Collected Works of Edgar Allen Poe*, ed. Thomas Ollive Mabbott, Cambridge, Mass., 1978, iii. 1365-7.

valent accounts of the life and work of August Von Kempelen, the scientist who, according to Poe's narrative, developed a process for turning lead into gold. I do not wish to give a detailed commentary upon this, one of Poe's greatest tales, but to augment on my own part the important work of scholars like Pollin, Mabbott, and Allen. For whereas these men have developed all the necessary materials for revealing the secret of 'Von Kempelen'—which is, finally, the secret of how to turn lead into gold—they remain, like the police who broke into Von Kempelen's workshop, in possession of the facts but behindhand in their understanding of those facts.

Pollin, for example, performs a masterful elucidation of the story's many details, which constantly make reference to actual matters of significant fact in Poe's life. What Poe does is so to operate on these common and everyday facts that they emerge, transmuted, into the true 'realms of gold' which Keats and all literary persons are familiar with. The fundamental wit of the tale implies that the California Gold Rush is an idiotic quest after Fool's Gold, that Eldorado is a place existing in imagination, and that its treasures are works of art, like 'Von Kempelen'. 'I shall be a *littérateur*, at least, all my life', Poe told Frederick W. Thomas at the time he was writing 'Von Kempelen', 'nor would I abandon the hopes which still lead me on for all the gold in California.'[18]

Poe's letter to Duyckinck shows that he hoped his tale would produce a 'temporary check to the gold fever'. He wanted the hoax to work *in fact*, so that it would 'create a *stir*' among his readers—and, of course, lead eventually to the elucidation of the narrative's hidden secrets and treasures. The scholarly exploration of 'Von Kempelen' shows how the tale has transmuted certain important facts in his personal and literary life and turned them into gold. The narrative involves an extensive and elaborate send-up of contemporary journalism, which seems always to get its stories wrong (though it means to deal in 'matters of fact'), and to misunderstand what it reports (and especially what it reports about Poe).

When Poe says, in his tale, that he and Von Kempelen 'were fellow sojourners for a week, about six weeks ago, at Earl's Hotel', this is a coded reference to his public reading of 'The

Poetic Principle' at the Earl's House on 20 December 1848, just
'about six weeks' previous to the writing of 'Von Kempelen'.
The point of the reference in the fiction is to correct the journalistic 'misapprehensions' about Von Kempelen, which is to say
(in transmuted form) to correct the bad journalistic reports
about that notorious event. To correct the journalistic narrative
with this 'fictional' one is to substitute truth for error and reality for 'pure imagination'; it is to turn leaden accounts into
golden ones.

For the reader (or scholar) to decode such material is equally
to transmute something ordinary and apparently insignificant
into something valuable. Indeed, the act of decoding is a replic-
ation of the artist's original act of transmutation. In each case,
something leaden finds its golden echo. 'Von Kempelen' as a
fiction thus demonstrates, in actual historical fact, what Poe's
invented scientist revealed in the narrative. In the words of the
tale, quoted by Poe from an unrevealed source: *'pure gold can be
made at will, and very readily, from lead, in connection with certain other
substances, in kind and in proportions, unknown.'*[19] In the end the
narrative shows us (it does not tell us) how this is done: by
writing and then printing stories like 'Von Kempelen' in
specific journals like *The Flag of Our Union*. Imagination is not
enough, nor is the solitary artist. The artist needs the lead of
the printer's workshop 'in connection with certain other substances', like paper and all the materials and systems of printing and publication which allow a writer to bring his work into
being, that is, to bring it into its necessary contact with the
world of readers. That entire social nexus constitutes what Poe
called—in the poem he published in *The Flag of Our Union* a week
after 'Von Kempelen'—'Eldorado'. That Poe's entire career
as a writer was dominated by his longing for this Eldorado—
specifically, his desire to have, like Dickens, his own publication
resources so that his works would never lack for their necessary
social component—is a fact about his career which hardly needs
even to be mentioned.

I do not wish to derogate from Pollin's excellent work, but
his failure to grasp the significance of his own scholarship leads
him to certain important misconstructions, and especially to his

---

[19] Beaver text, p. 330.

general conclusion that 'Von Kempelen' is 'a "tired" kind of hoax, which defeats its purpose by presenting too much of the familiar from which readers could check on its authenticity.'[20] Pollin here misconstrues the nature of the narrative, and of hoaxes in general. For Poe certainly meant his tale to be decoded by his readers; its purpose is only fulfilled when such a decoding begins to operate. Of course, this purpose necessitates an initial secrecy or 'quizzing',[21] but the quizzing must be done in such a way that the reader is also encouraged to elucidate the story's hidden treasures. So Pollin calls the following reference to 'Presburg' a piece of 'inept humour': ' "The Literary World" speaks of him, confidently, as a *native* of Presburg (misled, perhaps, by the account in the "Home Journal"), but I am pleased to be able to state *positively*, since I have it from his own lips, that he was born in Utica . . . although both his parents, I believe, are of Presburg descent.'[22] The humour is called 'inept', presumably, because the pun on 'Presburg' seems so obvious—as indeed it is. But the wit of the passage turns on its second pun (which is by no means obvious), not this first one. The obviousness of the first play on words signals the reader to be alert to the possible presence of such devices; the second, on the other hand, is a test, an experiment to see if the reader is capable of reading Poe's story properly, of unlocking its secrets and transmuting its lead into gold.

The second pun involves the word 'Utica', Von Kempelen's birthplace, according to Poe's narrative. Poe's choice of this city is a cunning device for telling us that the narrative is a hoax. Von Kempelen is from a city whose verbal root is related to that famous Ulyssean self-characterization, *outis*, No Man. Utica is, in its Greek form, *outike*, and Poe is slyly telling those who have ears to hear that Von Kempelen is from No Man's Town.[23] In the end, the passage works its multiple-language puns in order to fashion a general indictment of the journalistic world of the day. It delivers an extremely witty slap at people like Duyckinck, the editor of *The Literary World* who was offered 'Von Kempelen' but whose editorial ineptitude brought him to

---

[20] Pollin, p. 14.

[21] See Poe's letter cited in n. 16 above.

[22] See Pollin, p. 15 and Beaver text, p. 327.

[23] See Pauly's *Realencyclopädie*, Stuttgart, 1962, Supplement ix, p. 1875: 'Man findet *outike* nur bei den Schriftstellern, die den Namen latinisieren'.

reject it, an act which only revealed (as Poe's story itself says) how little he understood about Von Kempelen (and 'Von Kempelen').

But if the artistic significance of Poe's wit has not always been fully grasped by scholars, I suspect that the full range of the story's tricks and surprises also remains to be explored. Too many of its passages have passed without scholarly comment, and seem to exist in the tale for no good aesthetic reason. Consider the following paragraph, for example:

> In the brief account of Von Kempelen which appeared in the 'Home Journal', and has since been extensively copied, several misapprehensions of the German original seem to have been made by the translator, who professes to have taken the passage from a late number of the Presburg 'Schnellpost'. '*Viele*' has evidently been misconceived (as it often is), and what the translator renders by 'sorrows', is probably '*Leiden*', which, in its true version, 'sufferings', would give a totally different complexion to the whole account; but, of course, much of this is merely guess, on my part.[24]

Pollin says that 'In relation to the gold-making achievement this insertion [about the 'Viele . . . Leiden'] makes no sense at all',[25] and he goes on to explain the passage in other (and quite relevant) terms. None the less, I think he goes wrong in his remarks quoted above, and I suspect he does so because he has not seen the general set of literary references in the basic alchemical metaphor. In this instance, Poe draws our attention to the clumsy way that Americans deal with passages from German by suggesting a mistranslation by the editors of the *Home Journal*, and an emendation on his own part. But the words he chooses to throw before us, and especially 'Leiden', may well lead us to suspect that it is this word, and not 'Viele', which 'has evidently been misconceived (as it often is)'. For 'Viele' is by no means a word that is often misconceived, whereas 'Leid' (sorrow, or suffering)—as anyone who has taught elementary German can attest—is frequently confused by the neophyte with 'Lied' (lyric, ballad, song). The passage seems to be an extremely clever and oblique witticism connecting Poe's Von Kempelen not with 'misanthropy'—which is the *Home Journal*'s construction, as Poe's next paragraph shows—but with poetic

---

creation. And once again we find ourselves at the heart of the story's principal subjects: the nature of poetry and the poetic principle, and the trials of a creative writer like Poe in a journalistic world (Presburg) whose ignorance threatens to destroy the entire social enterprise which we call artistic creation.

III

Poets and the guardians of poetry have always insisted that the products of imagination transcend time and circumstances. Art may appear in time, but its being's heart and home is with infinitude. It is a product of history, but an inhabitant of eternity. Yet we must sometimes wonder what such claims could possibly mean to Dryasdust, or to any scholar who repeatedly draws his transcendent subject back to its mortal and circumstantial condition.

As the passage from Eichhorn, quoted earlier, suggests, such claims can and should mean a great deal, even to the pedant digging patiently in his Valley of Dry Bones. Nevertheless, when we reflect upon the transcendent character of art, we do not normally find an image of that transcendence in the dead letters of the past, or in the scholar's obsession with what is ancient and completed. Rather, we are generally inclined to consider how ancient works find a contemporary relevance, a continuing ('general') application. In the Battle of the Books, the philologist, like Eichhorn, cries out, 'Make it old' whereas the Modernist cries out, after W. C. Williams, 'Make it new'.

It is time to remind ourselves that 'Making it new' can involve not the rebirth of art but its assassination, and the 'Making it old' may establish the essential conditions for the resurrection of past achievement. For the special privilege of past human products, especially artistic ones, is that they come to us in finished and completed forms which, by their very finishedness, are able to judge the incompleteness of our present lives and works. They speak to the present precisely because they speak in other tongues, saying what we cannot say, and criticizing what we can. Literary works transcend their historical alienation by virtue of their definitive otherness, by their sharp and peculiar differentials with their later audiences, including our own.

Because criticism must articulate a system of differentials, then, a special demand is placed upon it to elucidate literary works at their point of origin, where the initial and determining sets of differentials are permanently established. The concentration upon origins has been traditional in the field of criticism, and for good reason, but it should not be taken to mean that historical criticism fetishizes the archaic object. The purpose of an historical approach is to deal with the literary work as a dynamic event in human experience rather than as an object of analysis, linguistic or otherwise.[26] *Paradise Lost* as read in the seventeenth and eighteenth centuries succeeded to a very different event in the Romantic Age, especially with people like Blake, Shelley, and Byron. Our own experiences with that poem today have been indelibly marked by those earlier ones, and by our awareness of the differences between them. To remain ignorant of those human events which constitute literary works like *Paradise Lost* throughout their periodic and continuing lives is to immortalize the present. For all knowledge and experience is historical, including our present knowledge and experience of the literary works we inherit and pass on.

The analytic methodologies necessarily adopted by philologists have produced, even among historical critics, recurrent misconceptions about the aims and purposes of such a critical approach. Thus, in a lengthy, if sometimes naïve, recent attack upon philology, John H. Ellis argues that historical criticism is destructive because it pretends to offer the reader privileged and prepared solutions to the literary works we read: 'Since literary texts are inherently challenging and often even puzzling, the critic's pose of supplying essential information and the key to the text has proved as tempting to the reader as it has to the critic. It has given him the illusion of understanding complex works with minimum effort.'[27] Of course, one has only to pick up any of the great critical works from Wolf, Herder, and Eichhorn to our own day to see how far this characterization strays from the truth. Nevertheless, what Ellis argues seems to me an accurate picture of the work of the philologian who has failed to

---

[26] These remarks are made in the context of the recent scholarship which has emphasized litarary reception and the theory of literary reception.

[27] John M. Ellis, *The Theory of Literary Criticism*, Berkeley and Los Angeles, 1974, p. 154.

grasp the soul of his great method, the spirit of his life in letters.

I have tried in this essay to call that spirit back, to rouse it from its slumbers. Let me quote once again from John Ellis, since his challenge may recall to our minds the truth about historical criticism and scholarship which we have sometimes forgotten, and hence which Ellis, our contemporary, has never properly learned from those who should have taught him.

The context of a work of literature is that of the whole society for which it is a literary text, and which has made it such; its purpose is precisely that use; and its relation to life is to the life of the whole community. If we insist on relating the text primarily to the context of its composition and to the life and social context of its author, we are cutting it off from that relation to life which is the relevant one, and substituting for it another that is greatly restricted. Far from stressing the social importance of literature, this approach undervalues the social importance of literature by construing its relation to society in too limited a way. The result is a simplification of the issues of the text down to those relevant to one particular social situation only; but the literary value of the text resides precisely in the fact that this limited social situation was outgrown. Such a view of literature might with some justice be described as a 'static' one.[28]

When Ellis says that the context of literature is the use to which it is put by society at large, surely we all would agree. But when he speaks of one (originary) context of use being 'outgrown' by a later (present) one, we immediately recognize the poverty of his sense of 'society at large' and the root of his misconception about historical criticism. We do not, we must not, seek merely to reconstitute literary works in archaic forms; rather we try, in the full consciousness of our present circumstances, to raise up the past life of literary works in order to clarify and reveal the nature of our own present experience, including its dynamic relations of continuity and antithesis with all that has brought it to be.

We read literary works in present, but we have no way of judging such experiences—of testing their limits, their promises, and their ignorance—without an objective standard, a measure of absolute difference which will not submit to the absorption and manipulation of immediacy. That measure always, and necessarily, comes to us from the past. To study literature in

---

[28] Ibid., pp. 136-7.

the contexts of its origins and its later historical development is to free the reader from the ignorance of his presentness, to alienate him from himself and make him a pilgrim, if not *of* eternity, then at least *with* all 'the noble living and the noble dead'.

Shall these bones live? Surely if they do not—surely if we neglect the dynamic relation which exists between past and present—the dead will bury the dead. There can be no present or future, in life or in art, if the past is not a living reality *in its pastness*. Editors, bibliographers, textual critics, and pedants of all sorts hold the keys in their hands, the keys to the kingdom not merely of literature, but of all human culture.

(1980)

3. The Text, the Poem, and the Problem of Historical Method

I

At this point in academic time, the problem of historical method emerges most dramatically at the elementary levels of textual interpretation. The problem appears in two typical forms which are inversely related to each other. On the one hand, intrinsic critics cannot see that historical studies go to the heart of literary objects. Since the latter appear to address problems (and people) which are not historically limited, the 'problem' with historical studies is that they continue to be pursued at all. Why should works which transcend their originary moment require historical analysis and commentary?

On the other hand, historical method is also a problem for scholars and critics who work in any of the areas of extrinsic criticism: in bibilography and textual criticism, in philology, in biography and literary history, and so forth. In this case, the difficulty is that the scholar's work so often does seem irrelevant to the understanding and appreciation of poetry. What is most disturbing about this situation is that so few scholars even acknowledge that their methods require a theoretical grounding in hermeneutics.

These brief remarks will come as news to no one. We are all aware of the situation. Before I try to suggest how we might try to deal with these issues, however, permit me another brief essay into familiar territory. For I believe that we can best come to grips with these problems of historical method if we see more clearly how they came to assume their present form.

It is well known that the most advanced literary studies in the nineteenth century were those which developed and modified the enormous advances in theory and method made in classical and biblical philology and textual criticism. Wolf and Eichhorn are only the most familiar names among that group of brilliant, predominantly German, critics of the late eighteenth century who made the initial breakthrough in transforming literary studies into a modern scientific discipline. These are the scholars

who created both the Lower (or textual) Criticism and the
Higher (or philological) Criticism. Historical philology in the
nineteenth century brought analytic techniques to bear upon
previously synthesized material in order to see more clearly the
strokes of the tulip and the parts of the rainbow. The most
advanced of such critics—in England, men like Coleridge and
Arnold—hoped to enlist these analytic techniques in the service
of a new and higher synthesis: to adapt Coleridge's famous
declaration, by dissolving, diffusing, and dissipating, 'to re-
create . . . to idealize and to unify'.

In the twentieth century, however, the historical methods of
the Lower and Higher Criticism gave way before the advance
of several sorts of form criticism and structural analysis. As we
know, the principal impetus behind these critical movements
came from language study and especially from linguistics.
What Wolf, Lachmann, and Strauss were to nineteenth-century
literary criticism, Saussure and Hjelmslev have been to the
twentieth century. Hjelmslev's lucid *Prolegomena to a Theory of
Language* (1943) accurately describes the shift which took place
as a deliberate effort to break free of the descriptive, atomistic,
and empirical approaches which flourished in the nineteenth
century. 'The study of literature and the study of art', Hjelmslev
says, had been carried out under 'historically descriptive rather
than systematizing disciplines', and his project, which explicitly
follows Saussure, proposes a systematic rather than an empirical analytic of humanistic phenomena. '*A priori* it would seem
to be a generally valid thesis that for every *process* there is a corresponding *system*, by which the process can be analyzed and
described by means of a limited number of premises. It must be
assumed that any process can be analyzed into a limited number
of elements recurring in various combinations.'[1] In this passage
Hjelmslev prepares the ground for a systematic linguistics, but
his words clearly underwrite any number of other twentieth-
century programmes of a formal or structural sort (Bultmann
in biblical criticism, Lévi-Strauss in anthropology, Propp,
Greimas, and many others in literary studies). These new semiological methods can be applied in all humanistic disciplines, as
Hjelmslev well knew.

---

[1] Louis Hjelmslev, *Prolegomena to a Theory of Language*, trans. Francis J. Whitfield,
Madison, 1961, p. 9.

The shift from an empirical to a structural analytic has deeply influenced twentieth-century approaches to literary works, with far-reaching consequences. Before I turn to them, however, and thus reconnect with my initial two-handed 'problem of historical method', let me point out an interesting peripheral remark in Hjelmslev's book. When he attacks the empirical methods of the nineteenth century, its anti-systematic bias, he also explains the particular aesthetic position which underlies that

humanistic tradition which, in various dress, has till now predomi-
nated . . . According to this view, humanistic, as opposed to natural,
phenomena, are non-recurrent and for that very reason cannot, like
natural phenomena, be subjected to exact and generalizing treatment. In the field of the humanities, consequently, there would have
to be a different method—namely, mere description, which would be
nearer to poetry than to exact science—or, at any event, a method
that restricts itself to a discursive form of presentation, in which the
phenomena pass by, one by one, without being interpreted through
a system (pp. 8-9).

As far as the appreciation of poetry is concerned, the nineteenth-century's 'humanistic' methods sought to preserve and illuminate the uniqueness of the poetic object. We would do well to remember this fact about nineteenth-century philology, for in the modern period—as we survey those prelapsarian Germanic tomes of dryasdust scholarship—we do not always recall (indeed, their authors do not always recall) the aesthetic phenomena those critical procedures were designed to illuminate. Our preoccupation with the minute particularities of poetical works emerged from the philological traditions which gave us 'textual critic-ism'. The contemporary vulgarization of this philological term eloquently demonstrates the position that modern literary studies takes in relation to its immediate forebears.

The structural and semiological approaches to language and, in particular, to literature provided modern critics with operational procedures for analysing literature in a Kantian mode. In the *Critique of Judgement*, Kant offered a novel philosophy of art grounded in the notion that aesthetic works were integral phenomena whose finality was exhausted in the individual's experience of the work. The modern concept of 'the poem itself' as a self-referential linguistic system is fundamentally Kantian, though twentieth-century developments in linguistics provided this Kantian approach with its basic procedural rules for an actual critical practice.

These procedural rules operated under one fundamental premise: that literary works are special sorts of linguistic 'texts', that every poem is coextensive with its linguistic structure. Twentieth-century literary criticism contains a rich variety of schools and methods—analytical, structural, rhetorical, stylistic—but for all their important differences, they tend to share the conviction that poems are self-subsistent linguistic systems. The function of criticism is to illuminate the operations of those linguistic structures which we now like to call 'texts'. According to the classic formulation of Roman Jakobson: 'Poetics deals with problems of verbal structure . . . Since linguistics is the global science of verbal structure, poetics may be regarded as an integral part of linguistics.'[2]

This idea of the poem as verbal object is so commonplace in modern criticism that we may seem perverse to question it. Still we must do so, for the 'problem of historical method'— whether we approach it from an 'intrinsic' or an 'extrinsic' point of view—will never be opened to solutions until we see one of the signal failures of modern criticism: its inability to distinguish clearly between a concept of the *poem* and a concept of the *text*. Indeed, when we recover this essential analytic distinction, we will begin to reacquire some other, equally crucial distinctions which have fallen into disuse: for example, the distinction between concepts of *poem* and of *poetical work*. For the present I will concentrate on the first of these distinctions, and my analysis will proceed through a series of illustrative examples.[3]

[2] Roman Jakobson, 'Linguistics and Poetics', in *Style in Language*, ed. T. A. Sebeok, Cambridge, Mass., 1960, p. 350. In the latest, post-structural phase of these traditions the models are more generically semiological than linguistic. The shift in emphasis— from specific 'text' to the process of 'textuality'—marks the increased self-consciousness in this tradition, but not a departure from its fundamental premisses.

[3] Literary criticism in general would benefit if certain clear distinctions were preserved when using words (and concepts) like *text, poem*, and *poetical work*. In the present essay, the word *text* is used as a purely bibliographical concept which means to deal with the material of poetry in a purely physical or impersonal frame of reference. The term deliberately abstracts away the critic's or the reader's immediate (social) point of view. Poetry is a social phenomenon, but the concept of *text* withholds from consideration all matters that relate to the involvement of reader or audience in the reproduction of the work. It does so, of course, for analytic purposes, and *only provisionally*. I propose that we use the term *text* when we deal with poems as they are part of

II

When Byron sent the manuscript of *Don Juan* Cantos I and II to his publisher John Murray late in 1818, the poet was not only, with Goethe, the most famous writer in the Western world, his works were the most saleable products on the English literary market. He was not an author Murray wanted to lose. But this new work set Murray back on his heels. He was filled with wonder at its genius and with loathing at its immorality—at its obscenity, its blasphemy, its libellous attacks upon the poet laureate, and its seditious attitude toward the English government's policies at home and abroad.[4]

In the struggle that ensued, Murray and his London circle (which included some of Byron's best and oldest friends) pressed the poet either to withdraw the poem altogether or to revise it drastically and remove its objectionable parts. Byron agreed to some revisions, but his final line of retreat still seemed a fearful one to his publisher. When Byron threatened to take his poem elsewhere, Murray agreed to publish; he did not, however, tell his celebrated author precisely *how* he would publish.

For Murray, the problem was how to issue this inflammatory work without provoking a legal action against himself either by the government directly or by the notorious Society for the Suppression of Vice. His plan of action was ingenious but, in the end, self-defeating. Murray decided to issue a short run (1,500 copies) of the poem in a sumptuous quarto edition and to print it without either Byron's name as author or even his own as publisher. The price—£1 11*s*. 6*d*.—was set high in

a productive (or reproductive) process, but when we are withholding from consideration all matters that relate to the process of consumption. *Poem*, on the other hand, is the term I will use to refer to the work as it is the locus of a specific process of production (or reproduction) and consumption. *Poetical work* is my term for the global history of some particular work's process of production/reproduction and consumption. I use the term *poetry* to refer generically to imaginative literary works without respect to any specific social or historical factors. The terms *text* and *Ideal Text* also appear in this essay, and these refer to various (non-historical and non-sociological) twentieth-century critical concepts.

I hope it is clear that these distinctions mean to counter the semiological approach to the concepts of *text* and *textuality*. A paradigm example of the latter approach will be found in Roland Barthes's famous essay 'From Work to Text': see above, pp. 91-93.

[4] See *Don Juan: A Variorum Edition*, ed. T. G. Steffan and W. W. Pratt, Austin, 1957, i. 11-32 and iv. 293-308.

order to ensure a circulation limited alike in numbers and in social class.

The immediate effect of this manœuvre was successful, for *Don Juan* stole into the world without provoking any moral outcry. The earliest reviewers were generally quite favourable, even from entrenched conservative quarters like *The Literary Gazette.*

But Murray's plan for avoiding the censors failed, in the end, because it was, in the words of Hugh J. Luke, Jr., 'a contradictory one'.[5] Murray avoided prosecution for issuing *Don Juan*, but his method of publication ensured a widespread piratical printing of the poem in the radical press. Thousands of copies of *Don Juan* were issued in cheap pirated editions, and as the work received wider celebrity and distribution, so the moral outcry against it was raised, and spread.

The significance which this story holds for my present purposes—i.e. for my aim to elucidate the problematics of the 'text'—is neatly explained by an anonymous article (possibly by Southey) printed in the conservative *Quarterly Review* in April 1822. In its quarto form, the reviewer notes, *Don Juan*

would have been confined by its price to a class of readers with whom its faults might have been somewhat compensated by its merits; with whom the ridicule, which it endeavors to throw upon virtue, might have been partially balanced by that with which it covers vice, particularly the vice to which the class of readers to whom we are alluding are most subject—that which pleads romantic sensibility, or ungovernable passion; to readers, in short, who would have turned with disgust from its indecencies, and remembered only its poetry and its wit.[6]

But the poem was issued in numerous cheap piracies and therein lay the mischief, 'some publishing it with obscene engravings, others in weekly numbers, and all in a shape that brought it within the reach of purchasers on whom its poison would operate without mitigation—who would search its pages for images to pamper a depraved imagination, and for a sanction for the insensibility to the sufferings of others, which is often one of the most unhappy results of their own'. In short, as

5 'The Publishing of *Don Juan*', *PMLA* lxxx (June 1965), p. 200.
6 For the *Quarterly Review* quotations see ibid., p. 202.

the reviewer says so well: ' "Don Juan" in quarto and on hot-pressed paper would have been almost innocent—in a whity-brown duodecimo it was one of the worst of the mischievous publications that have made the press a snare.'

Several important conclusions follow from this eventful narrative. In this first place, the example illustrates how different texts, in the bibliographical sense, embody different poems (in the aesthetic sense) despite the fact that both are linguistically identical. In the second place, the example also suggests that the method of printing or publishing a literary work carries with it enormous cultural and aesthetic significance for the work itself. Finally, we can begin to see, through this example, that the essential character of a work of art is not determined *sui generis* but is, rather, the result of a process involving the actions and interactions of a specific and socially integrated group of people.[7]

The contemporary fashion of calling literary works 'texts' carries at least one unhappy critical result: it suggests that poems and works of fiction possess their integrity *as poems and works of fiction* totally aside from the events and materials describable in their bibliographies. In this usage we are dealing with 'texts' which transcend their concrete and actual textualities. This usage of the word *text* does not mean anything written or printed in an actual physical state; rather, it means the opposite: it points to an *Ur*-poem or meta-work whose existence is the Idea that can be abstracted out of all concrete and written texts which have ever existed or which ever will exist.[8] All these different texts are what can be called—Ideally—'The Text'.

---

[7] Cf. Levin Schüking, *The Sociology of Literary Taste*, London, 1966.

[8] Post-structural critiques of their own (formalist) tradition have been widespread during the past ten years and have contributed to the break-up of the academic consensus which developed between 1935 and 1965. See John Fekete, *The Critical Twilight*, London, 1978. The attacks upon the New Criticism have tended to accuse it of an arrogant and technocratic empiricism, with its insistence upon taking the poem as *sui generis*. These attacks—see Richard Palmer, *Hermeneutics* (Evanston, 1969), for example—charge the New Criticism with a crude theory of the poem as 'object' or 'thing'. This sort of attack is deeply misguided and misses entirely the fundamental Idealism of both the New Criticism in particular and its later formalist context in general. A revisionist commentator like Gerald Graff has been able to see the mistake in such critiques and to suggest what is in fact the case: that New Criticism and its academic inheritors (including many of its recent antagonists) are part of a single tradition (*Literature Against Itself*, Chicago, 1979, chap. 5). As Graff notes, New Criticism was marked throughout by contradictions along an Ideal/Empirical fault-line; nor could it have been otherwise with a fundamentally Idealist theory which was seeking to establish its

This Ideal Text is the object of almost all the critical scrutiny produced in the New Critical and post-New Critical traditions, whether formal, stylistic, or structural.[9] To arrive at such a Text, however, the critic normally obligates himself to make certain that his physical text is 'correct', which is to say that it corresponds, linguistically, to the author's final intentions about what editors call his work's substantive and accidental features. By meeting this obligation the critic pays his dues to the philological traditions of the last three hundred years. At the same time, the critic places himself in a position from which he can treat the literary work as if it were a timeless object, unconnected with history. The Text is viewed *sub specie aeternitatis*, and modern criticism approaches it much as the pre-critical scholar of Sacred Scripture approached the Word of God.

But in fact not even a linguistic uniformity sanctioned by philology can deliver over to us a final, definitive Text which will be the timeless object of critical interpretation and analysis. The example from Byron suggests this, clearly, but that case is merely paradigmatic. No literary work is definable purely in linguistic terms, and the illustration from Byron could easily be replaced by examples from any writer one might choose. It would not be very difficult to show, from the works of William Blake, that linguistic uniformity will hardly serve to establish a definitive Text. Of course everyone knows that Blake's *words* do not comprehend Blake's 'poetical works', so that (Ideally) critics recognize the necessity of 'reading' Blake in facsimile editions; and, in fact, facsimile editions do deliver more of Blake's work to the reader. But a Blake text comprising both words and illustrative matter still falls short of delivering this artist's work to an audience today.

Since Blake's work operates in an integrated verbal and visual medium, we are forced to see that the 'linguistic level' of this work corresponds to the entire mixed medium and not merely to the verbal one. But that Blake's 'poetical works' are

authority in a scientific, rational, and technological world. Graff's views have been anticipated by a number of trenchant critiques put out from relatively orthodox Marxist writers: see, e.g. Robert Weimann, 'Past Significance and Present Meaning in Literary History', in *New Directions in Literary History*, ed. Ralph Cohen, Baltimore, 1974, esp. pp. 43-50.

[9] That an Ideal Text is the object of contemporary 'textual' interpreters is patent; see also Tony Bennett, *Formalism and Marxism*, London, 1979, pp. 70-1.

not finished and complete in some Ideal mixed-medium Text is apparent if we simply recall the character of Blake's original methods of 'publication'. He is probably the most private and individualistic artist ever to emerge from England, and each of his engraved works was a unique publication by itself. It was part of Blake's artistic project that each of his works *be* unique, and he in fact achieved his purpose—most notoriously, I suppose, in his masterwork *Jerusalem*. Fewer than ten original copies of this work survive, and each is quite distinct. To speak of the Text of *Jerusalem*, then, as if that term comprehended some particular concrete reality rather than a heuristic idea, is manifestly to talk nonsense. One might as well try to speak of the Text of Emily Dickinson's verse. In reality, there is no such Text; there are only texts, of various kinds, prepared by various people (some by the author), at various periods, for particular and various purposes.

Yet the example of Blake carries a moral which takes us beyond the insight that an artist's work is not equivalent to an Ideal Text, nor even to some particular text or edition (say, an especially meticulous one prepared by a skilled editor). For every work of art is the product of an interaction between the artist, on the one hand, and a variety of social determinants on the other. Even the simplest textual problem—establishing a work's *linguistic* correctness—can involve other problems that are, quite literally, insoluble. Keats, we recall, wrote two distinct and finished versions of 'La Belle Dame Sans Merci'.[10] But even if one were to set aside these special problems and assume that we can establish 'the author's final intentions' toward the language or even the entire format of a work, we would still have, as readers, merely one text of the work, or—as scholars—the means for producing a number of possible editions, or texts.

The fact is that the works of an artist are produced, at various times and places, and by many different sorts of people, in a variety of different textual constitutions (some better than others). Each of these texts is the locus of a process of artistic production and consumption involving the originary author, other people (his audience[s], his publisher, etc.), and certain social institutions. Blake's special way of creating his works

---

[10] For a more thorough discussion see above, chap. I.

emphasizes the presence of these impinging social factors precisely because Blake strove so resolutely, even so obsessively, to produce work that was wholly his own. Each original copy of *Jerusalem is* unique, and in them Blake has achieved an extraordinary degree of artistic freedom. Had his work been reproduced through the procedures maintained by the ordinary publishing institutions of his day, it would have been a very different product altogether (it would have been reviewed, for example, and it would have fallen into many people's hands).[11] Nor are these differences merely accidental, and unimportant for the 'meaning' of Blake's work. Certainly to Blake they seemed immensely consequential; indeed—and he was quite right—they seemed definitive of the difference between one sort of art (free, creative) and another (commonplace, generalized).

In his own day Blake insisted upon having his artistic freedom, and the proper measure of his success in this aim—ironic though it seems—lies in his contemporary artistic anonymity. Yet the social life of an artist transcends his particular historical moment, and so Blake, lost to his own age, was 'discovered' by the Pre-Raphaelites, who initiated the process of full social integration which his work has since achieved. Blake's unique works, in consequence, would become mass-produced, and his fierce individuality would itself become deeply integrated into various ideologies and social institutions. We may well see an irony in this event. Even more, however, should we see how it illustrates a fundamental fact about all art: that it is a social product with various, and changing, social functions to perform.

The initial example from Byron and the general case of Blake illustrate very clearly, I think, that a work of art—a poem, in this case—is no more the isolate creation of an artist than 'the poem itself' is defined either by some particular text on the one hand, or by the Ideal Text on the other. Poems are artistic works produced, and maintained, under specific socialized conditions. It is the business of analytic criticism to isolate and categorize the various social factors which meet and interact in various works of art, and finally, to explain those interactions.

---

[11] As is well known, Blake purchased his artistic freedom at a fearful personal cost, for his conscious artistic policies ensured his contemporary isolation. Appealing to what Byron called 'the Avenger, Time', Blake's work had to wait for the justice of history. Cf. the discussion in J. W. Saunders, *The Profession of Letters*, London, 1964, pp. 146-73 *passim* and, on Blake particularly, pp. 164-6; see also Jerome J. McGann, *A Critique of Modern Textual Criticism*, Chicago, 1983, pp. 44-7.

In attempting to show how different poetical works have acquired different textual constitutions, I have drawn attention to certain physical characteristics of some texts of *Don Juan* and *Jerusalem*. The physical differences between the several texts stand as signs of a productive process which is different in each case, and which, consequently, produces several different artistic works. The first two cantos of *Don Juan*, as issued by Murray, are not the same work as the first two cantos as issued by the pirates. The fact that Byron's *Don Juan* should have called out these two sorts of edition is one sign of its creative power, just as the poem's long and complex bibliographical history has testified to its trans-historical character and relevance.

Let there be no confusion in this matter, however: when we see that an author's work exists in many different textual constitutions, we do not mean to suggest that, for example, there are as many poems called *Jerusalem* as there are texts or editions. We must resist the modern fashion of referring to poems as 'texts' precisely because this vulgar usage confuses the fundamental difference between a poem's *text*—which is one thing— and a poem—which is quite another. Preserving this distinction is crucial for purposes of critical method, since the distinction facilitates a clear view of a poem's changing life in human society. Speaking of poems as 'texts' implicitly affirms an idea of literary works which involves two contradictory propositions: (1) that a poem is equivalent to its linguistic constitution and (2) that the textual differences in a poem's bibliographical history have no necessary relation to issues of literary criticism as such. The poem-as-text, then, is a critical idea which at once reduces poetry to a verbal construct and inflates it to the level of an immaterial, non-particular pure Idea (the poem as Ideal Text). This result seems paradoxical, but in fact it is the necessary consequence of a view of literary works which is founded on a contradiction.

The example of *Don Juan* must not be taken to suggest, however, that a poetical work is the product of a social engagement entered into, voluntarily or otherwise, by author, printer, and publisher alone. Rather, the local publishing relationship among these three persons is itself a sign needing critical analysis. The fact that Blake deliberately avoided any involvement in this, the normal publishing relationship of his day, is of immense critical significance for his work and especially for a late work like *Jerusalem*. To know the publishing options taken (and refused) by Chaucer, or Donne, or Pope, or Blake, or Byron enables the critic to explain the often less visible, but more fundamental, social engagements which meet in and generate the work in question.

The illustration from Byron is especially illuminating because it brings to our attention another crucial productive figure (anterior to the audience of consumers) who participates in the artistic process initiated by the artist. I mean, of course, the reviewer (or critic), who is the final mediating force between author and audience. It is the function of the (contemporary) reviewer and (subsequent) critic to make explicit the lines of interpretation which exist *in potentia* in their respective audiences. Critics and reviewers—to adapt a phrase from Shelley— imagine what students and audiences already know about the works they are to read.

III

At this point in the analysis, though we have, I believe, established the generic functional usefulness of preserving distinctions among texts, poems, and poetical works, the specific value of such distinctions for literary criticism is still unclear. Are these the sort of distinctions which, in the end, make no difference?

In the example which follows I mean to illustrate two related points: first (on the negative side), that the failure to maintain these distinctions creates a procedural error which necessarily threatens any subsequent practical criticism with disaster; and second (on the positive side), that the pursuit and elucidation of such distinctions sharply increases our understanding of poetry and poems in both the theoretical and the practical spheres. This second aspect of the demonstration will return us to the 'problem of historical method' which was raised at the outset. By framing these historically self-conscious demonstrations along the traditional 'intrinsic' lines of formal and thematic analysis, I propose to show: (1) that poems are, by the nature of the case (or, as Kant might say, 'transcendentally'), time- and place-specific; (2) that historical analysis is, therefore, a necessary and essential function of any advanced practical criticism.

The case I propose to consider is Allen Tate's famous interpretation of Emily Dickinson's poem 'Because I could not Stop for Death'.[12] His discussion raises, once again, the whole range of unresolved problems which lie in wait for any critical method which cannot make serious distinctions between texts and poems.

Tate begins by quoting the poem in full and declaring it to be 'one of the greatest in the English language' and 'one of the perfect poems in English'. His argument for these judgements rests upon T. S. Eliot's famous discussion of the 'dissociation of sensibility'. Dickinson's poem is 'perfect' because it displays a perfect 'fusion of sensibility and thought': 'The framework of the poem is, in fact, the two abstractions, mortality and eternity, which are made to associate in equality with images: she sees the ideas, and thinks the perceptions. She did, of course, nothing of the sort; but we must use the logical distinctions, even to the extent of paradox, if we are to form any notion of this rare quality of mind' (p. 161). Tate argues for this general position by instancing what he sees as the poem's precision and tight structure of rhythm, image, and theme. The poem has nothing to excess; it is marked throughout by 'a restraint that keeps the poet from carrying' her dramatic images too far. As for the poem's ideas, they are something altogether different from 'the feeble poetry of moral ideals that flourished in New England in the eighties':

The terror of death is objectified through this figure of the genteel driver, who is made ironically to serve the end of Immortality. This is the heart of the poem: she has presented a typical Christian theme in its final irresolution, without making any final statements about it. There is no solution to the problem; there can be only a presentation of it in the full context of intellect and feeling. A construction of the human will, elaborated with all the abstracting powers of the mind, is put to the concrete test of experience: the idea of immortality is

[12] This is poem no. 172 in *The Poems of Emily Dickinson*, ed. Thomas H. Johnson, Cambridge, Mass., 1955, ii. 546-7. For Tate's discussion, see his 'New England Culture and Emily Dickinson', in *The Recognition of Emily Dickinson*, ed. C. E. Blake and C.F. Wells, Ann Arbor, 1968, pp. 153-67, esp. pp. 160-2, from which the quotations below are taken.

confronted with the fact of physical disintegration. We are not told what to think; we are told to look at the situation. (p. 161)

In evaluating this criticism we begin with the text quoted by Tate. When he calls the poem 'The Chariot', as he does at the beginning of his discussion, he tells us what his text shows: Tate is reading the work printed in 1890 by Todd and Higginson. But of course, 'The Chariot' is not what Dickinson wrote, at any time; rather, it is a text which her first editors produced when they carefully worked over the (untitled) text written by the author. Among other, less significant changes, an entire stanza was removed (the fourth) and several lines underwent major alteration.[13] Since Tate's argument for the greatness of the poem depends heavily upon his view of its linguistic perfection, we are faced with a rather awkward situation. Under the circumstances, one would not find it very difficult to embarrass Tate's reading by subjecting it to an ironical inquisition on the subject of textual criticism.

Of course, Tate had no access to the text Dickinson actually wrote. Nevertheless, his critical judgement ought to have been warned that textual problems existed since he did have available to him another—and, as it happens, more accurate—text of Dickinson's work. This text appeared in Martha Dickinson Bianchi's 1924 edition of The Complete Poems, and it is the one cited by Yvor Winters in the critique of Tate's essay first published by Winters in Maule's Curse.[14] But Tate's critical method could not prepare him to deal with problems in textual criticism. Indeed, he could not even see such problems, much less analyse their critical relevance. In this case, the impoverished historical sense of his general critical method appears as an inability to make critical judgements about poetic texts, to make distinctions between poems and their texts, and to relate those judgements and distinctions to the final business of literary criticism.

We have no call, nor any desire, to ridicule Tate's essay on this matter. Nevertheless, the issue must be faced squarely, for the problems raised by Tate's lack of textual scrupulousness

---

[13] See Poems by Emily Dickinson, ed. Mabel Loomis Todd and Thomas W. Higginson, Boston, 1890. Also see Johnson's edition, where the textual issues are succinctly presented.

[14] Winters's essay is reprinted in The Recognition of Emily Dickinson; see esp. pp. 192-3.

appear at other points, and in other forms, in his discussion, and his example typifies the sorts of problem that remain widespread in Western modes of formal, stylistic, structural, and post-structural procedures. We may observe the congruence of his critical practice—the symmetry between his lack of interest in textual matters and his general interpretive approach—by examining his remarks on the poem's thematic concerns. We shall notice two matters here: first, a tendency to overread the poem at the linguistic level; and second, a reluctance to take seriously, or even notice, either the fact or the importance of the poem's ideological attitudes. In each case we are dealing with something fundamental to Tate's literary criticism and to twentieth-century interpretive approaches generally: their attempt to lift the poem out of its original historical context and to erase the distance between that original context and the immediate context of the critical act.

In this next phase of my analysis, then, I am proposing to extend the discussion from its specific interest in 'the problem of the text' to the more general issue which that problem localizes. Critics who do not or cannot distinguish between the different concrete texts which a poem assumes in its historical passage are equally disinclined to study the aesthetic significance of a poem's topical dimensions, or its didactic, ethical, or ideological materials. Poems that have no textual histories have, at the thematic level, only those meanings and references which 'transcend' the particulars of time and place. The poetry of poems, in this view, is a function not of specific ideology or topical matters but of 'universal' themes and references—and the *most* universal of these universals are a poem's formal, stylistic, or structural excellences. The ultimate consequence of such approaches is that the present critic loses altogether his awareness that his own criticism is historically limited and time-bound in very specific ways. Losing a critical sense of the past, the interpreter necessarily loses his ability to see his own work in a critical light.

Let me return to Tate's analysis and the Dickinson poem, however, where we can study these problems as they emerge in concrete forms. When Tate says, for example, that the poem presents 'the problems of immortality . . . confronted with the fact of physical disintegration', we observe a critical move characteristic of twentieth-century criticism: that is, the habit of dealing with poetry's substantive concerns at the most abstract and generalized thematic levels. I will have more to say about this sort of critical abstraction in a moment. For now we want most to query Tate's interpretation of the thematic aspects of the Dickinson poem. When he argues, for example, that the poem does not treat 'moral ideas', and that it takes a non-committal ('unresolved') stance toward a serious intellectual problem, we are surely justified in demurring. The civil kindliness of Death is of course ironically presented, but the irony operates at the expense of those who—foolishly, the poem implies—regard Death as a fearful thing and who give all their attention to their mortal affairs ('My labor, and my leisure too') either because of their fear or as a consequence of it. Like the poem's speaker before Death 'stopped' for her, the readers of the poem are assumed to be fearful of Death and too busy with the affairs of their lives to 'stop' for him.[15] The poem does indeed have a 'a moral', and it appears in an unmistakable form in the final stanza:

> Since then—'tis Centuries—and yet
> Feels shorter than the Day
> I first surmised the Horses Heads
> Were toward Eternity—

'We are not told what to think' by the poem, Tate asserts, but his position is only technically correct. Of course the poem does not *tell* us what to think, but its message about the benevolence of Death is plain enough. This message, however, like the poem which carries it, is no simple-minded pronouncement; the message is rich and affecting because it is delivered in human rather than abstract space. Dickinson's poem locates a set of relationships in which Dickinson, her fictive speaker, and her invited readers engage with each other in various emotional and intellectual ways.[16] The focus of these engagements is the poem's

[15] This motif is an ancient one in the tradition of Christian art and poetry. For its biblical sources see Matt. 24:43 and 1 Thess. 5:2-4. An excellent contemporary example is to be found in Alan Dugan's 'Tribute to Kafka for Someone Taken'.

[16] See V. N. Volosinov (i.e. M. M. Bakhtin), 'Discourse in Life and Discourse in Art', in *Freudianism, A Marxist Critique*, trans. I. R. Titunik, New York, 1976, where Bakhtin distinguishes among the author, the reader, and the figure he calls 'the hero' or the 'third participant'.

commonplace Christian theme: that people who are too busily involved with their worldly affairs give little serious thought to Death and the Afterlife. Criticizing such thoughtlessness, the poem encourages its readers to ponder Death and the Afterlife in a positive way. Its procedure for doing so involves the assumption of another thematic commonplace—that people fear to think about Death—and then undermining its force by a play of wit.

The wit appears most plainly in the rhetorical structure of the poem, which pretends to be spoken by a person already dead. Like some Christian Blessed Damozel from New England, Dickinson's speaker addresses this world from the other side, as it were, and lets us know that Death leads us not to oblivion but to 'Eternity' and 'Immortality'.[17] But the wit goes deeper, for Dickinson does not present her fiction as anything *but* fiction. The playfulness of the poem—which is especially evident in the final stanza, whose quiet good humour has been remarked upon frequently—is the work's most persuasive argument that Death can be contemplated not merely without fear but—more positively—with feelings of civilized affection. The kindliness and civility of the carriage driver are qualities we recognize in the *voice* of the poem's speaker and in the *wit* of its maker.

When we speak of the poem's wit, however, we should not lose ourselves in a hypnotic fascination with its verbal reality alone. The wit is at least as much a function of Dickinson's perspicuous observations of, and comments upon, social reality as it is of her facility with language. We may see this more clearly if we recall the standard critical idea that the figure of Death in this poem is—in the words of a recent critic—a 'gentlemanly suitor'.[18] Tate seems to have initiated this reading when he spoke of the driver as 'a gentleman taking a lady out for a drive', and when he proceeded to notice the 'erotic motive' associated with 'this figure of the genteel driver'. His commentary shows an acute awareness of one of the poem's subtlest and least

[17] In adopting this rhetorical model, Dickinson was following a literary practice that had grown extremely popular in the nineteenth century. See Ann Douglas, 'Heaven Our Home: Consolation Literature in the Northern United States 1830-1880', in *Death in America*, ed. Daniel Stannard, Philadelphia, 1974; see esp. pp. 58-9, 61-2. But the procedure is deeply traditional: see also Rosemary Woolf, *English Religious Lyric in the Middle Ages*, Oxford, 1963, chap. 9 *passim*.

[18] Robert Weisbuch, *Emily Dickinson's Poetry*, Chicago, 1972, p. 114.

explicit aspects, but it also displays a failure to see a more obvious but no less important fact about the driver.

This man is not a suitor but an undertaker, as we see quite
clearly in the penultimate line's reference to 'Horses Heads'.[19]
This small matter of fact has considerable importance for
anyone wishing to develop an accurate critical account of the
poem. It forces us to see, for example, that the journey being
presented is not some unspecified drive in the country, but a
funeral ride which is located quite specifically in relation to
Emily Dickinson and her Amherst world. The hearse in the
poem is on its way out from Pleasant Street, past Emily Dickinson's house, to the cemetery located at the northern edge of the
town just beyond the Dickinson homestead.[20] Of course, these
details are not verbalized into the Dickinson poem as explicit
description. They are only present implicitly, as an originally
evoked context which we—at our historical remove—can (and
must) reconstitute if we wish to focus and explain the special
emotional character of the work.

Consider once again, for example, the undertaker who appears in the poem. The behaviour of this man—his correctness,
his rather stiff but kindly formality, his manner of driving the
carriage—defines a character-type well-known in nineteenth-
century culture, and a favourite one with contemporary cari-
caturists.[21] Behind the civility and kindly formal behaviour of

[19] That is to say, a suitor's carriage would have had only one horse.

[20] The hearse's journey to the Amherst cemetery—one of the new, so-called rural
cemeteries—must have been appallingly familiar to Emily Dickinson. The mortality ·
rate in Amherst was high, and Emily Dickinson's room overlooked the cemetery
route. See Millicent Todd Bingham, *Emily Dickinson's Home*, New York, 1955, the map
facing p. 62 and pp. 179-80; also Jay Leyda, *The Years and Hours of Emily Dickinson*,
New Haven, 1960, ii. 2-3. Emily Dickinson's bedroom was the best vantage in the
house for observing the stately procession of the funeral hearse as it moved out from
Pleasant Street to the cemetery. The special location of the Dickinson house meant
that the funeral hearse would always pass by, no matter where the deceased person
had lived in town. One should also note that the poem's references to the 'School' and
the 'Fields of Gazing Grain' are precise. In point of fact, 'Because I could not Stop for
Death' narrates the imagined (not imaginary) journey of the hearse from somewhere
in the central part of Amherst out along Pleasant Street, past the schoolhouse on the
left, and out to the beginning of the 'Fields of Gazing Grain', at which point the
undertaker would have turned to the right and driven past more fields to the gravesite.
For a general discussion of the rural cemetery see Neil Harris, 'The Cemetery
Beautiful', in *Passing: The Vision of Death in America*, ed. Charles O. Jackson, Westport,
1977, pp. 103-11.

[21] See Alfred Scott Warthen, 'The Period of Caricature' and 'The Modern Dance
of Death', in *The Physician of the Dance of Death*, New York, 1934. Twain was fond of

Emily Dickinson's undertaker lies a tradition which saw in this man a figure of grotesque obsequiousness, as we know from Mark Twain's memorable scene in *Huckleberry Finn*. Indeed, I do not see how one could fully appreciate the finesse of what Tate calls the 'erotic motive' without also seeing just how the poem plays with it, and how Dickinson's poetic style both *re*presents and quietly modifies the contemporary stereotype of this important social functionary so well known to the inhabitants of towns like Amherst. The poem's general ideology, as a work of Christian consolation, would be merely religious claptrap without these 'poetic'[22] elements; and such elements can only escape the critical method which does not seek to grasp the poem at a level more comprehensive than a merely linguistic one.

The power of the poem, then, rests in its ability to show us not merely the thoughts and feelings of Dickinson and her fictive speaker, but the attitudes of her implied readers as well. For all her notorious privacy, Emily Dickinson is, like every poet, a creator of those structures of social energy which we call poems. 'Because I could not Stop for Death' locates not merely an expressive lyrical act, but a significant relationship between the poet and her readers which we, as still later readers, are meant to recognize, enter into, and (finally) extend. Our sympathy with the poem may not be the same as that felt by a Christian reader, whether contemporary with the poem or not; nevertheless, it is *continuous* with the sympathy of such readers (who are consciously and explicitly assumed by the poem) because it takes those readers as seriously as it takes Emily Dickinson and her fictive speaker. Indeed, it must do this, for all are part of the poem in question. Later readers may not share the ideologies of the people represented by this poem, but they cannot read it without recognizing and respecting those ideologies—without, in fact, perpetuating them in a critical human memory whose sympathetic powers are drawn from a historical consciousness.

presenting the undertaker from a comic point of view. See *Huckleberry Finn*, chap. 27, and his essay 'The Undertaker's Chat'.

[22] What makes them 'poetic' is their ability to dramatize the relationships which exist between specific social realities and a complex set of related—and often antagonistic—ideological attitudes and formations.

Having discussed the 'ideological set' of this poem—its poetically rendered 'message'—let us return to Allen Tate's essay,
where an absence of ideological commitments is imputed to
Dickinson's work. We return to ask why Tate should insist upon
'misreading' the poem as he has done.

The reason emerges when we ponder carefully Tate's use of
T. S. Eliot. Tate's interpretation shows that he shares Eliot's
ideas about how moral concepts should appear in verse (not
'didactically' but dramatically); that he prizes Eliot's views on
Metaphysical verse and its excellences; and that he is anxious
to deliver his praise of Dickinson's poem in critical terms that
will draw her into the company of those poets who illustrate
Eliot's standards. In short, Tate reads Emily Dickinson in the
same spirit that Eliot read Donne and the Metaphysicals. *Why*
Tate, and Eliot before him, should have taken such a position
toward the moral aspects of poetry—and especially of Christian
poetry in its various forms—is beyond the scope of this analysis,
though scholars recognize that the answer lies in the historical
factors which generated modernism and its various ideologies.[23]

I have not dwelt upon Tate's discussion in order to debunk it,
but rather in order to show the consonance between his interpretation of the Dickinson poem and his ignorance of its textual
problems. Tate's eye is no more focused upon Dickinson's poem
than it is on the 1890 text of 'The Chariot'. Rather, Tate has
'taken "The Chariot" for his text', as we might say of one who
delivers a sermon or a moral lesson. 'The Chariot' is the occasion for his ideological polemic on behalf of certain aesthetic
criteria.

One important lesson to be drawn from this investigation of
Tate's essay is that literary criticism—and even the analysis of
poems—is not fundamentally a study of verbal structure *per se*.
The very existence of Tate's influential and justly admired essay
demonstrates that fact. Literary criticism must study poetic
texts—the 'verbal structures' of poems—but the analysis of
these verbal structures does not comprehend a poetic analysis.
This paradox of critical method emerges forcibly in Tate's

[23] See Richard Ohmann, 'Studying Literature at the End of Ideology' in *The Politics
of Literature*, ed. Louis Kampf and Paul Lauter, New York, 1973, esp. pp. 134-59;
Renato Poggioli, *The Theory of the Avant-Garde*, trans. Gerald Fitzgerald, New York,
1971; and see nn. 3 and 8 above, and below chap. IV.2 ('The Religious Poetry of
Christina Rossetti').

essay, which dramatizes, in its very limitations, the distinction between text and poem—a distinction, indeed, which Tate's analysis is incapable of making. Yet the distinction must be made—and textual criticism, in the traditional sense, must be revived among literary critics—if our received works of literature are to regain their full human resources—that is to say, if the entire history of poetry and all the potential of specific poems are to be made known and available to each new generation. Poetry and poems are, in this sense, trans-historical, but they acquire this perpetuity by virtue of the particular historical adventures which their texts undergo from their first appearance before their author's eyes through all their subsequent constitutions.

The textual histories of poems, in other words, are paradigm instances of the historically specific character of all poetry. By clarifying the distinction between a poem and its various texts, the examples from Byron and Blake illustrate the need for a systematic theory and method of historical criticism. On the other hand, the example from Dickinson argues, at the level of practical criticism, the specific critical powers inherent in a historical method. These powers appear as a special capacity for elucidating, in a systematic way, whatever in a poem is most concrete, local, and particular to it. Criticism cannot analyse poems, or reveal their special characteristics and values, if it abstracts away from their so-called accidental features. Attending merely to the formal or linguistic phenomena of poems constitutes an initial and massive act of abstraction from what are some of the most crucial particulars of all poems.

Facing the poem and its texts, then, historical criticism tries to define what is most peculiar and distinctive in specific poetical works. Moreover, in specifying these unique features and sets of relationships, it transcends the concept of the-poem-as-verbal-object to reveal the poem as a special sort of communication event. This new understanding of poems takes place precisely because the critical act, occurring in a self-conscious present, can turn to look upon poems created in the past not as fixed objects but as the locus of certain past human experiences. Some of these are dramatized *in* the poems, while others are preserved *through* the poetical works, which embody various human experiences *with* the poems, beginning with the author's own experiences. In this way does a historical criticism define poetry not as a formal structure or immediate event but as a continuing human process. That *act* of definition is the fundamental *fact* of literary criticism.

The new fact about *historical* criticism, however, is that it systematically opposes its own reification. Being first of all an *act* of definition rather than a *set* of definitions, historical criticism calls attention to the time-specific and heuristic character of its abstractions. Like the poetry it studies, criticism is always tendentious because it always seeks to define and preserve human values. One of the special values of historical criticism, to my view at any rate, lies in its eagerness to specify and examine its polemical positions. This self-critical aspect of an historical approach seems to be a direct function of its basic method, for in attempting to specify historical distinctions, we set a gulf between our past and our present. It is this gulf which enables us to judge and criticize the past, but it is equally this gulf which enables the past—so rich in its achievements—to judge and criticize us. Thus in our differences do we learn about, and create, a community.

(1980-1)

III

Interpretation and Critical History

1. The Ancient Mariner:
the Meaning of the Meanings

I

What does 'The Rime of the Ancient Mariner' mean? This question, in one form or another, has been asked of the poem from the beginning; indeed, so interesting and so dominant has this question been that Coleridge's poem now serves as one of our culture's standard texts for introducing students to poetic interpretation. The question has been, and still is, an important one, and I shall try to present here yet another answer to it. My approach, however, will differ slightly from the traditional ones, for I do not believe that we can arrive at a synthetic answer until we reflect upon the meaning of the question itself. I will begin, therefore, by reconsidering briefly the history of the poem's criticism.

1. The Critical History

From its first appearance in *Lyrical Ballads*, the 'Rime' was an arresting, if problematic, work. Though well known to readers during the first two decades of the nineteenth century, no early consensus about the meaning or value of the poem was reached. Readers might praise Coleridge's imitation of 'the elder poets'—which is what John Stoddart, Southey's and, later, Wordsworth's friend, had done—or they might, like Robert Southey, ridicule the act of imitation;[1] in either case, most early readers found the poem difficult to understand, mysterious, strange.[2] This response itself divided into two camps: on the one hand, those who, like Charles Lamb, valued

---

[1] Stoddart's review appeared in *The British Critic* xiv (October 1799), Southey's in *The Critical Review* xxiv (October 1798); both are quoted in *Wordsworth and Coleridge: The Lyrical Ballads*, ed. R.L. Brett and A.R. Jones, London, 1963, pp. 317-20, 313-14, where Stoddart's review is attributed to Francis Wrangam. For the attribution to Stoddart see R. S. Woolf, 'John Stoddart, "Michael", and *Lyrical Ballads*', *Ariel* i (1970), pp. 7-22. For a good selection of early reviews, see *Coleridge: The Critical Heritage*, ed. J.R. de J. Jackson, London, 1970.

[2] See Richard Haven, 'The Ancient Mariner in the Nineteenth Century', *Studies in Romanticism* xi (1972), esp. pp. 265-8.

the poem for its ability to keep 'the mind . . . in a placid state of wonderments'; and, on the other, those who, like the anonymous *Analytical* reviewer, compared it to 'the extravagance of a mad German poet'. Dr Charles Burney's conflicted set of remarks is entirely typical of the situation:

> The author's first piece, the *Rime of the Ancyent Marinere*, in imitation of the *Style* as well as the spirit of the elder poets, is the strangest story of a cock and a bull that we ever saw on paper: yet, though it seems a rhapsody of unintelligible wildness and incoherence, there are in it poetical touches of an exquisite kind.[3]

The 'Rime' was the opening poem in the first edition of *Lyrical Ballads*, and these troubled reactions of the book's first readers were a serious worry to Wordsworth:

> From what I can gather it seems that The Ancyent Marinere has upon the whole been an injury to the volume, I mean that the old words and the strangeness of it have deterred readers from going on. If the volume should come to a second edition I would put in its place some little things which would be more likely to suit the common taste.[4]

In the end the poem was not replaced, but its position was changed, its title was altered, and its archaic style was drastically modernized. All this was done at Wordsworth's insistence, but not every reader was pleased with the result. Lamb was dismayed because the alterations had the effect of rationalizing the strange beauty of the poem:

> I am sorry that Coleridge has christened his *Ancient Marinere*, a *Poet's Reverie*; it is as bad as Bottom the Weaver's declaration that he is not a lion, but only the scenical representation of a lion. What new idea is gained by this title but one subversive of all credit—which the tale should force upon us—of its truth.[5]

Lamb was right, of course, but then so was Wordsworth: each simply had a different way of responding to the poem's 'obscurity'. Coleridge, typically, had his own special reponse: to expound at length with 'metaphysical elucidations' the pro-

---

[3] *The Analytical Review* xxviii (December 1798); Burney's review was in *The Monthly Review* xxix (June 1799); see Brett and Jones, pp. 314-17.

[4] Wordsworth to Cottle, 24 June 1799, *The Letters of William and Dorothy Wordsworth*, ed. Ernest de Selincourt, rev. Chester Shaver, Oxford, 1967, i.264.

[5] *The Letters of Charles Lamb*, ed. E. V. Lucas, London, 1935, i.240.

found 'mysteries' of his ballad imitation. Coleridge's interlocutor on this occasion—in Germany, from 1798-9—was Clement Carlyon, who did not find Coleridge's commentary much more lucid than the ballad and who later poked fun at Coleridge's explanations when he was recollecting the events.[6]

During Coleridge's lifetime the poem was recognized to have an intellectual or allegorical import, even—witness the essay by J.G. Lockhart—a religious or visionary significance.[7] These impressions remained inchoate until the mid-century, however, when critics first began to develop explicitly symbolic and allegorical interpretations. Those mid-Victorian readings established the hermeneutic models which have dominated the subsequent history of the poem's interpretations. Though details and emphases have changed and shifted, and though the commentaries have become more extended, the fundamental interpretive approach has not altered significantly since that time.[8] Those who have veered away from such interpretations do so not by developing alternative hermeneutic methods but by rejecting the approach at more fundamental levels. Thus E.E. Stoll and Elisabeth Schneider deny that Coleridge ever 'intended' his poem to be read symbolically or allegorically; on the other hand, Irving Babbit, William Empson, and David Pirie reject the entire Christian-symbolic schema not because it is unintended but because it is trivial.[9] Rather than simply dismiss the poem, as Babbitt does, Empson and Pirie go on to solve the problem by substituting one (trivial) text with another (presumably important) one: that is to say, they argue the necessity of reading the poem in its 1798 rather in its 1817 version.

This brief analytic summary of the poem's interpretive tradition is necessary if we are to come to grips with the problem of the 'Rime' and its meaning; for meaning, in a literary event, is

[6] See Clement Carlyon's remarks quoted in Jackson, pp. 197-204.

[7] J.G. Lockhart, 'Essay on the Lake School', *Blackwood's Magazine* vi (1819); see also the anonymous reviews of *Sibylline Leaves* in *London Magazine* (July 1820) and *The Monthly Review* (January 1819).

[8] See Haven, pp. 370-4.

[9] See E.E. Stoll, 'Symbolism in Coleridge', *PMLA* lxiii (1948), 214-33; Elisabeth Schneider, *Coleridge, Opium, and 'Kubla Khan'*, Chicago, 1953, pp. 252-5; Irving Babbitt, 'Coleridge and Imagination', *On Being Creative and Other Essays*, Boston, 1932, pp. 116-20; and William Empson and David Pirie, eds., *Coleridge's Verse: A Selection*, New York, 1973.

a function not of 'the poem itself' but of the poem's historical relations with its readers and interpreters. As we shall see, when the history of the 'Rime''s hermeneutics is traced to the ballad's point of origin, we begin to understand how the work developed under the dominion of Coleridge's own hermeneutic models. To see this last point in its full historical particularity is to arrive, finally, at a *critical* vantage on the poem. For not until we see that our dominant interpretive tradition has been licensed and underwritten by Coleridge himself will we be able to understand the meaning of that tradition, and hence the meaning of the meanings of the 'Rime'. Richard Haven has said that the poem 'seems to rule out few of the interpretations which have been offered' during the past one hundred and eighty years; and his further argument—that modern interpretations represent variant rather than alternative versions of nineteenth-century commentaries—is a point equally well-taken.[10] The full significance of Haven's findings emerges when we come to see the relation of these facts to Coleridge himself and to the hermeneutic traditions which he helped to establish in the academy.

2. *Early Textual History: The Formal Significance*

Everyone knows that the 'Rime' underwent a series of major textual alterations between 1798, when it first appeared in *Lyrical Ballads*, and 1817, when Coleridge all but completed his revisions in the *Sibylline Leaves* collection of his verse. These revisions included additions, subtractions, and changes in the verse text; changes in the poem's title and prefatory material; and, most dramatic of all, the addition of the prose gloss in the textual margin.

Let me begin with the gloss, which to this day most readers take to represent at least one level of Coleridge's own interpretation of his poem. M. H. Abrams, for example, takes this view for granted: 'Coleridge added [the gloss] to assist the bewildered

---

[10] See Haven, p. 361. The general uniformity of approach to the poem's formal and thematic aspects is illustrated quite clearly in the various contemporary handbooks and student guides: see esp. *Twentieth-Century Interpretations of* 'The Rime of the Ancient Mariner', ed. James D. Boulger, Englewood Cliffs, NJ, 1969, and '*The Rime of the Ancient Mariner*': *A Handbook*, ed. Royal A. Gettmann, Belmont, Calif., 1966. The point is also nicely illustrated in John Beer's excellent *Coleridge the Visionary*, London, 1959, chap. 5.

readers of the first published version' in interpreting the poem's symbolic Christian narrative.[11] Even critics who, unlike Abrams, dislike the gloss share his view of its function and status. Pirie's comments, for instance, illustrate the sort of problems which arise when the status of the gloss is misconceived in this way. The following passage appears in Pirie's longer argument for taking the 1798 rather than 1817 version as the base-reading text:

The most serious attempt to distract the reader from the poem in the *Sibylline Leaves* version is of course the addition in the margin of the ageing Coleridge's own interpretation of his poem. Partly just a feeble literary joke, this must have always been intended to confuse the unwary as indeed it continues to do. Whether Coleridge was optimistic enough to hope that the marginalia would be regarded as much a part of the poem proper as they now are is debatable. But the marginalia are by their very nature perverting. They are a third-person, and thus by implication objectively true, account of a story whose essence is that it is a first-person narrative. Its full title, its narrative framework of the hypnotized listener, its disturbing vividness, all stress that it is at once event and account. The poem breaks through simplistic distinctions between 'subjective feeling' and 'objective reality'. It concentrates by its very form on the fact that the mariner is condemned to recurring moments of 'total recall' of which this is but a single example, condemned to experience again all that he felt alone on the wide, wide sea. The marginalia turn the speaker into a specimen. Worse, they lie. It is clearly not true, nor ever could be, that 'the curse is finally expiated' and the very real creature that the mariners fed on biscuit-worms cannot become 'a pious bird of good omen' without being ludicrous. To tell the reader in the margin that it is a good omen, when the succeeding stanzas demonstrate how impossible it is until too late to tell whether it is a good or bad omen, is to make nonsense of the poem at its very core. Coleridge claimed that Walter Scott's handling of superstition put the writer in a damagingly superior position to his story: 'that discrepance between the Narrator and the Narrative kills and deadens the Sympathy.' The narrator in the marginalia puts a similarly cold distance between the reader's sympathy and the story as experienced by the mariner.[12]

First, some preliminary explanations. Pirie speaks of the gloss as 'a feeble literary joke' because he recognizes its antique

[11] M. H. Abrams, *Natural Supernaturalism*, New York, 1971, p. 272.
[12] Empson and Pirie, pp. 214-15.

character. When he calls it a 'third-person' account, he points toward an important fact about the gloss, but he seems to miss the significance of that fact. Finally, his discussion of the gloss's 'lies' also registers an important fact whose function Pirie seems once again to overlook.

We may begin to unravel the problems raised by Pirie (and preserved as well in nearly all contemporary interpretations) if we return to the poem's initial publication. The 'Rime', as noted above, was the opening poem in Wordsworth and Coleridge's *Lyrical Ballads*. This 1798 version tries to adhere so closely to the conventions of ancient balladry, which Coleridge adapted from Thomas Percy, that the work sometimes approaches pastiche. This quality in the early 'Rime'—its status as an imitation or literary ballad—sets it quite apart from all the other ballad-influenced poems written for *Lyrical Ballads*. The others are not literary ballads but lyrical ballads, a very different thing altogether.

When a second edition of *Lyrical Ballads* was called for in 1800, Wordsworth, as we have seen, urged Coleridge to make some alterations. His views carried the day, and the result was a conscious attempt, acutely registered by Lamb, to make the 'Rime' appear less a literary ballad and more a lyrical ballad. Archaisms were removed from the verse text, but the most important alterations came at the beginning. The title was changed from 'The Rime of the Ancyent Marinere' to 'The Ancient Mariner: A Poet's Reverie', and the 1798 Argument, which was archaic and slightly mysterious,

How a Ship having passed the Line was driven by Storms to the cold Country towards the South Pole; and how from thence she made her course to the tropical Latitude of the Great Pacific Ocean; and of the strange things that befell; and in what manner the Ancyent Marinere came back to his own Country,

became more descriptively straightforward:

How a Ship, having first sailed to the Equator, was driven by Storms, to the cold Country towards the South Pole; how the Ancient Mariner cruelly and in contempt of the laws of hospitality, killed a Seabird; and how he was followed by many and strange Judgements; and in what manner he came back to his own Country.

The former, archaic in style, is appropriate to a literary ballad; the latter, on the other hand, remains in a contemporary idiom that perfectly marries with the new, self-conscious title. Lamb did not like the distance which the 1800 changes enforced between the 'mariner's ballad' and 'Coleridge's poem'. Changes like these broke the spell under which Lamb's belief, in 1798, had been willingly suspended.

Pirie's (and Empson's) discussion of the 'Rime' is fundamentally akin to Lamb's: all three prefer the work in its most primitive character and appearance. This is a poem in which Coleridge *in propria persona* seems most thoroughly removed from his own work. When Empson and Pirie object to the further changes introduced into the work in 1817—and principally to the addition of the gloss—they argue that these alterations represent a further, and even worse, modernization ('the ageing Coleridge's own interpretation of his poem'). In fact, however, Coleridge's 1817 additions were a complex effort to represent (if also to methodize) his poem as a literary ballad. In this he worked on two fronts especially: first, to strengthen the original archaic aspect of the work; and second, to carry even further the process, begun in 1800, of distinguishing as it were 'levels of authority' or points of view in terms of which the poetic events were to be experienced and narrated.

When Pirie called the gloss a third-person account, he drew attention to the distance between the attitude represented in the gloss and that represented in the verse text conceived as imitation archaic ballad. For the truth is that the verse narrative and the prose gloss present themselves in Coleridge's poem as the work of two distinct (fictional) personages. The verse narrative appears as one 'received text' of an early English ballad, a type that Percy called an 'old minstrel ballad' and that Scott, later, called a 'romantic ballad'.[13] When Coleridge printed his poem in 1817, however, he added the prose gloss, which is to say he added to his work a fictive editor of the (presumptively) ancient ballad text. In an important and much neglected article, Huntington Brown demonstrates very clearly the distinctive character of these two figures in Coleridge's poem, and he shows that (*a*) the minstrel's ballad is meant to be

[13] See Thomas Percy's *Reliques of Ancient English Poetry*, ed. J. V. Pritchard, London, 1905, I. xliii, and Walter Scott's Introduction to *Minstrelsy of the Scottish Border*, ed. Thomas Henderson, Edinburgh, 1902, i.168-73; see also Scott's 'Modern Imitations', Henderson, i.173-6, and his 'Essay on Imitations of the Ancient Ballad', ibid., iv.1—52.

seen as dating from the time of Henry VII or thereabouts—in any case, certainly after the voyage of Columbus but prior to the age of Shakespeare—and (*b*) the editor is a later figure still, a scholar and an antiquarian whose prose indicates that he lived some time between the late seventeenth and the early eighteenth centuries.[14]

As Brown has shown, this fundamental distinction between the verse text and the gloss has two principal effects. First, it 'serves to emphasize the remoteness of the story and its teller by setting them off at two removes' from the contemporary reader. Second, it calls attention to the multiple points of view which are embedded in the total work. Brown distinguishes 'the personality of the Mariner who reports [the voyage], . . . the Wedding-Guest who listens [to the story], . . . the minstrel [who authors the verse] and, finally . . . the pious antiquarian [who edits the ballad]'.[15] As we shall see, Coleridge's 'Rime' in fact presents yet another point of view—that is, Coleridge's, or the contemporary author's—who operates in a determining way, controlling all the others.

The textual changes which the 'Rime' underwent between 1798 and 1817 tell an important story about Coleridge's developing purposes toward his poem. These changes, in fact, highlight the formal poetic terms within which all interpretations of the poem must take place. Before we can take up the hermeneutical problem, however, we must elucidate more clearly the historical significance of the textual events. Empson and Pirie regard the process of revision as a reactionary movement in which a daring and radical poem is transformed into a relatively tame work of Christian symbolism. For them, the textual changes tell the story of Coleridge's scandalous ideological retreat from his radical views of the 1790s to his later Christian orthodoxy. Their position eventually places the poem's entire interpretive tradition of criticism under an inquisition;[16] for this tradition, in their view, has merely carried forward into

14 Huntington Brown, 'The Gloss to the Ancient Mariner', *Modern Language Quarterly* vi (1945), pp. 319-20.

15 Ibid., pp. 322, 324.

16 J.R. Ebbatson's 'Coleridge and the Rights of Man' (*Studies in Romanticism* xi [1972], pp. 171-206) contains an interesting discussion of some of the poem's historical intersections; it consciously follows the line opened by Empson in his 1964 *Critical Quarterly* essay, 'The Ancient Mariner', in which his view on the poem initially appeared.

our own day symbolic Christian interpretations sanctioned by 'the ageing Coleridge'.

As I shall try to show in the next section, Pirie and Empson have accurately represented the historical relation between Coleridge's developed theory of hermeneutics and the later, dominant tradition of interpretation. Important as it is, however, their attack upon the established critical tradition needs to be revised historically. That is to say, we must look again, much more carefully than Empson and Pirie have done, at the sorts of continuities which exist between the 'radical' Coleridge of the 1970s and the Sage of Highgate. Not only do Empson and Pirie misrepresent Coleridge when they characterize the history of his religious convictions; what is worse, they fail to see the relation of his religious ideas to the 'Rime' either at the poem's point of origin in the late 1790s or at its later stages of revision up to 1817.

3. Coleridge's Hermeneutic Models: 1792-1834

At his death in 1834, Coleridge left his manuscript treatise *Confessions of an Inquiring Spirit* in which he set forth his most mature and coherent thoughts 'on the Inspirations of the Scriptures'. Indeed, the essay sums up the developed state of Coleridge's ideas from their first emergence in the early 1790s to their latest—and in many ways most radical—form. Coleridge's marginal glosses on J.G. Eichhorn, Gotthold Lessing, and Johann Gottfried von Herder, his *Lay Sermons*, the *Aids to Reflection*, and all of Coleridge's scattered commentary on the issues of the Higher Criticism are gathered together and summed up in the *Confessions*.

In the *Aids to Reflection*, Coleridge condemned 'the pretended right of every individual competent and incompetent, to interpret Scripture in a sense of his own, in opposition to the judgement of the Church, without knowledge of the originals or of the languages, the history, the customs, opinions, and controversies of the age and country in which they were written.'[17] The *Confessions* explains Coleridge's view more clearly when he rejects the conservative theological position which insists upon

---

[17] Coleridge, *Aids to Reflection and The Confessions of an Inquiring Spirit*, London, 1893, p. 200n.; all further citations to this work, abbreviated as *AC*, will be included in the text.

the immediate divine authority for every word and line in the
Bible:

Why should I not believe the Scriptures throughout dictated, in word
and thought, by an infallible Intelligence? . . . *Why* should I not?—
Because the doctrine evacuates of all sense and efficacy the sure and
constant tradition, that all the several books bound up together in our
precious family Bible were composed in different and widely distant
ages, under the greatest diversity of circumstances, and degrees of
light and information, and yet that the composers, whether as utter-
ing or as recording what was uttered and what was done, were all
actuated by a pure and holy Spirit, one and the same—(for is there
any spirit pure and holy, and yet not proceeding from God—and yet
not proceeding in and with the Holy Spirit?)—one Spirit, working
diversely, now awakening strength, and now glorifying itself in weakness, now giving power and direction to knowledge, and now taking
away the sting from error! (*AC*, pp. 305-6)

Coleridge's view is that the Scriptures are, as it were, a living
and processive organism, one that comes into existence in
human time and continues to develop in that 'fallible' and
limited sphere. This view leads him to affirm that the Bible is
indeed the Word of God, but that its Word is uttered by God's
mortal creatures:

Every sentence found in a canonical Book, rightly interpreted, contains the *dictum* of an infallible Mind;—but what the right interpretation is,—or whether the very words now extant are corrupt or genuine
—must be determined by the industry and understanding of fallible,
and alas! more or less prejudiced theologians. (*AC*, p. 316)

Such a historical view of the Scriptures leads Coleridge along
a radical path to a relatively conservative stance as regards the
authority of the Church. Each new generation, and every new
reader of the Bible, must listen to the assembled 'panharmoni-
con' which is the Church's authority, that is, its recorded history
of those who read and interpreted the Scriptures in the enthusiasm and the faith that was peculiar to their age and circumstances. The faith of the historical Church must be the model
for the contemporary faithful. God's eternal Word is expressed
and later re-expressed through commentary, gloss, and interpretation by particular people at different times according to
their differing lights. The sting is taken out of whatever error
they may introduce by the existence of their faith, by their

enthusiasm for the Word and the diffusion of the Word and by their participation in the continuous historical process of incarnation.

As Elinor Shaffer has shown, these views represent Coleridge's particular reformulation of the Higher Critical approaches of men like C.G. Heyne, J.D. Michaelis, Alexander Geddes, Lessing, F.A. Wolf, Herder, and Eichhorn —that is, of the leading figures in the new approaches to textual criticism which were being most radically pursued in Germany. The theoretical foundations of this movement were laid by the mythographic, philological, and historical exegetes of the eighteenth century who studied various sorts of ancient texts and cultures—classical, oriental, biblical, and national. In her discussion of this movement, Shaffer has shown that Coleridge was not merely influenced by its work, he himself emerged as one of its principal and most important representatives.[18]

Like the other founders of the Higher Criticism, Coleridge was not trying to use its methods to destroy religion but to salvage it. The programme resulted in what Shaffer calls 'a new form of history' as well as a mythological hermeneutics which dominated Western thought for over a century and which continues, to this day, to exercise considerable authority, especially in the literary academy (p. 32). Shaffer describes very well the originary circumstances in terms of the famous problem of the 'authenticity' of the Scriptures:

Coleridge's argument reflects a long struggle of the new criticism with the idea that an eye-witness account must be of special value. If, by their own critical endeavour, it became clear that none of the Gospels was an eye-witness account, the status of the 'event' therein recounted must, on the old view, be diminished, its credibility undermined; but if there are no such privileged accounts, if all event is interpretation, than the Gospels need not suffer. Indeed, as we shall see, their value as literature is increased. For Coleridge, 'event' and 'mystery' must be expressed with equal delicacy, obliquity, and restraint. The miracle becomes the paradigm of reported historical event; the historical events reported by eye-witnesses represent

---

[18] See Elinor Shaffer, '*Kubla Khan' and The Fall of Jerusalem*, Cambridge, 1975, esp. chaps. 1-3; all further citations to this work will be included in the text. This is a work of real importance for students of Romanticism as well as for Coleridge scholars.

instantaneous mythmaking. 'Erkennen ist mythologisieren'. (Pp. 46-7)

Such a view of experience (it is to this day a prevalent one) carries with it a wholly revised sense of 'tradition' and 'authority':

It is neither the unquestioned authority of the Church nor the unquestioned authority of the Biblical text on which tradition rests, but the perpetually shifting sense within the Christian community of what has the power to persuade its members and strengthen them in the faith. Coleridge was to develop these two, still embryonic, approaches into one in his later writings: whatever the literal documentable truth might be found to be, the historical experience of conviction within the Christian community was in itself a form of validation, and this experience could be maintained and reawakened through an imaginative grasp of what that experience had been.

As Shaffer goes on to remark, 'These concerns were, of course, at the centre of romantic aesthetics' (pp. 85-6).

Coleridge's explicit, extended prose discussions of the leading figures and ideas dealt with by the Higher Critics were not made until after he went to Germany in 1798. Nevertheless, that he was earlier thoroughly familiar with the general approach and with the work of Heyne, Michaelis, Lessing, and Geddes, is absolutely certain.[19] Shaffer dates Coleridge's acquaintance with this critical tradition from the late 1780s, but her estimate may be too early. Still, by 1792 Coleridge was fully aware of these important scholarly developments, though his own views were, at that point, still fairly traditional. In 1795, for example, Coleridge was still arguing that Moses had authored the Pentateuch.[20] By 1796 his views had begun to show some considerable alterations, however, for in his 'Essay on Fasts' we find him arguing that the 'coincidence of the number of days [between Elijah's and Pythagoras' forty-days fastings] seems to cast a shade of doubt on the genuineness of the beginning of the fourth chapter of Matthew and Luke: in which the same miraculous circumstance is related of our Savior.' Coleridge's method of

---

[19] For Geddes, see ibid., pp. 24-34; Coleridge's 1795 'Lectures on Revealed Religion' were written with Michaelis in hand; and Coleridge refers to Heyne—who was, indeed, a giant figure in scholarly circles—in his *Notebooks* of 1796 (see *The Notebooks of Samuel Taylor Coleridge*, ed. Kathleen Coburn, New York, 1957, i, no. 278).

[20] See Coleridge's *Lectures 1795 on Politics and Religion*, ed. Lewis Patton and Peter Mann, Princeton, NJ, 1971, p. 118.

reasoning here plainly follows a Higher Critical line:

> It was the policy of the early Christians to assimilate their religion to that of the Heathens in all possible respects. The ceremonies of the Romish church have been traced to this source by Middleton; the miraculous conception is a palpable imitation of the story of Romulus, the son of a vestal virgin, by the descent of a Deity; and so, I suppose, because Pythagoras fasted forty days, the Interpolators of the Gospels must needs palm the same useless prodigy on Jesus. Indeed the conversion of the Heathens to Christianity, after the first century, does very much resemble Mahomet's miracle: as the mountain would not come over to him, he went over to the mountain.[21]

The set of Coleridge's mind revealed in this passage differs very little from what is to be found later in his annotations to Herder and Eichhorn, in the *Lay Sermons*, and in the *Aids* and *Confessions*. The only marked difference is a tonal one: for the later Coleridge would not have permitted even the suggestion of jocularity in his discussion of such weighty matters. Interpolations and glosses in the text of Scripture by later writers, redactors, and scribes were a matter for the most serious thought and analysis.

The plainest evidence for the continuity of Coleridge's thought lies, however, in the coincidence of ideas between his 1796 'The Destiny of Nations' (see especially lines 13-126) and his later prose writings. Coleridge says in his early poem, for example, that the highest form in which 'Freedom' appears is the following:

> But chiefly this, him First, him Last to view
> Through meaner powers and secondary things
> Effulgent, as through clouds that veil his blaze.
> For all that meets the bodily sense I deem
> Symbolical, one mighty alphabet
> For infant minds;
>
> (lines 15-20)

This theory of symbolism is well-known from 'The Aeolian Harp' and *The Statesman's Manual*.[22] In 'The Destiny of Nations', Coleridge develops his thought in some detail:

---

[21] Coleridge, *The Watchman*, ed. Lewis Patton, Princeton, NJ, 1970, p. 52.

[22] For *The Statesman's Manual*, see *Lay Sermons*, ed. R. J. White, Princeton, NJ, 1972, pp. 29-31 and 70-3.

> So by a strange and dim similitude
> Infinite myriads of self-conscious minds
> Are one all-conscious Spirit, which informs
> With absolute ubiquity of thought
> (His one eternal self-affirming act!)
> All his involved Monads, that yet seem
> With various province and apt agency
> Each to pursue its own self-catering end.
>
> (lines 42-9)

Implicit in both of these passages is Coleridge's further range of thought which he expands upon later in the poem: that God's self-revelation through the 'apt agency' of finite, historical beings is a processive event. When Coleridge presents his example from primitive Lapland culture (lines 60-126), his point is that the 'Wild phantasies' of Greenland's epic lore are full of deep import. Not only is such primitive lore symbolic, it illustrates the developing historical operation of the One Life:

> For Fancy is the power
> That first unsensualises the dark mind,
> Giving it new delights; and bids it swell
> With wild activity; and peopling air,
> By obscure fears of Beings invisible,
> Emancipates it from the grosser thrall
> Of the present impulse, teaching Self-control,
> Till Superstition with unconscious hand
> Seat Reason on her throne.
>
> (lines 80-8)

The 'legends terrible' (line 90) teach, immediately, certain fundamental human virtues, but ultimately they operate as part of a vast, worldwide, spiritualizing scheme:

> Till from Bethabra northward, heavenly Truth
> With gradual steps, winning her difficult way,
> Transfer their rude Faith perfected and pure.
>
> (lines 124-6)

The 'Beings of higher class than Man'—God and his angels—'choose their human ministers' (lines 127, 130) to carry out a providential economy; and each historical period raises up its ministers of this continuous revelation. When Coleridge writes 'The Destiny of Nations', he reveals himself to be an important functionary in the scheme he himself is articulating.

These ideas coincide fundamentally with what Coleridge says later in the works already cited. A repetition of this important point, however, is not out of order. In the *Confessions*, for example, Coleridge argues at length that the Scriptures are not an unmediated and fixed biblical text but an evolved and continuously evolving set of records which include the Church's later glosses on and interpretations of the earlier documents. The entire project of textual transmission and elucidation is a symbolic, revelatory act: 'all the intermediate applications and realizations of the words are but types and repetitions—translations, as it were, from the language of letters and articulate sounds into the language of events and symbolical persons' (*AC*, p. 303). As a result, Coleridge goes on to argue that every person should approach the Scriptures with a double understanding. First, readers must see that the received documents— primitive texts, interpolations, commentaries—report historically mediated materials and hence must be 'examined each in reference to the circumstances of the Writer or Speaker, the dispensation under which he lived, the purpose of the particular passage, and the intent and object of the Scriptures at large' (*AC*, p. 320). Second, the reader must also understand that he is, as a reader, equally subject to time-specific cultural limitations: 'the conflicts of grace and infirmity in your own soul, will enable you to discern and to know in and by what spirit they spake and acted,—as far at least as shall be needful for you, and in the times of your need' (*AC*, p. 320).

This is Coleridge's version of 'a man speaking to men'. Having a more explicitly historicized theoretical view than Wordsworth, however, Coleridge is able to see that the communication involves contact between what we would today call ideologically committed beings—between individuals whose humanness seems complete because they appear so thoroughly involved in their social and cultural milieux. As Coleridge had said earlier in *The Statesman's Manual*:

And in nothing is Scriptural history more strongly contrasted with the histories of highest note in the present age than in its freedom from the hollowness of abstractions. While the latter present a shadow-fight of Things and Quantities, the former gives us the history of Men, and balances the important influence of individual Minds with the previous state of the national morals and manners, in which, as constituting a specific susceptibility, it presents to us the true cause both of the Influence itself, and of the Weal or Woe that were its Consequents.[23]

This sure grasp that the concreteness and particularity of an individual is a function of his ideology ('national morals and manners') is an important aspect of Coleridge's thought to which I shall return later.

4. The 'Rime' and the Critical Tradition

As far as the 'Rime' is concerned, we have to note the special importance of certain aspects of this body of thinking. I refer specifically to the idea, which Coleridge explicitly endorsed, that the biblical narratives were originally bardic (oral) poetry which gradually evolved into a cycle of communal literary materials. Embedded in primitive and legendary saga, the Scriptures grew by accretion and interpolation over an extended period of time. They do not represent a 'true' narrative of certain fixed original events; rather, they are a collection of poetic materials which represent the changing form of 'witness' or testament of faith created by a religious community in the course of its history.[24] The function of the Higher Criticism, as a method, was to reveal the various 'layers' of this poetic work by distinguishing the Bible's different religious/poetic styles, or forms of expression, from the earliest and most primitive to the latest and most sophisticated.

This general approach toward historically transmitted texts produced two specific theories which bear particularly on the 'Rime'. Geddes' 'Fragment Hypothesis' argued that the Pentateuch 'was put together by an editor out of a collection of independent and often conflicting fragments'.[25] Coleridge accepted this interpretation but modified it by arguing that the conflation of the disparate fragments was a communal process rather than a unique event.

The second theory, put forth by Wolf in his *Prolegomena ad Homerum* (1795), argued that the *Iliad* was a redaction of different lays which had been passed down through a bardic tradition. Wolf's ballad theory of the epic partly drew its inspiration from the scholarship developed in the writings of the ballad revival. The argument in Percy's influential 'Essay on the

[23] Ibid., p. 28.   [24] See Shaffer, pp. 75-9.   [25] See Ibid., p. 78.

Ancient Minstrels of England', which introduced his *Reliques*, is paradigmatic. According to Percy, England's ancient poetic tradition from the pagan skalds to the old Christian minstrels was a continuous one; and although 'the Poet and the Minstrel early with us became two persons', 'the ancient minstrels' preserved in their ballad and song traditions a profound continuity with the old pagan skalds. Indeed, the common practice of the ancient minstrels—in contrast to the new, developing line of leisured poets—was not to compose new works but to adapt and extend the older ones which descended through the tradition from primitive pagan times.[26]

The foregoing is the ideological framework for the following remarkable passage. The quotation is Coleridge's marginal gloss in his copy of Eichhorn's *Einleitung in das alte Testament* and is itself a theory, or explanation, of the meaning of glosses and textual interpolation. Commenting on Genesis 36:31, Coleridge writes: 'But why *not* consider this as a gloss introduced by the Editors of the Pentateuch, or Preparers of the Copy that was to be layed up in the Temple of Solomon? The authenticity of the Books would be no more compromised by such glosses, than that of the Book before me by this marginal Note of mine'.[27] Coleridge means that, given a coherent cultural tradition, the text which exhibits marks of its historical passage (in the form of later interpolations, glosses, and other textual additions and 'impurities') retains its ideological coherence despite the process of apparent fragmentation. Such a text is, in truth, a Book of Revelation by itself, an apocalypse of its evolved and interconnected poetic/religious coherences.

When Coleridge applies these critical views to non-Scriptural texts, as he does in 'The Destiny of Nations', his idea is that the pagan bards of Greenland initiated a body of poetic material whose traditions culminated in the Christian revelation. Ancient 'superstition', in these poetic repositories, will eventually 'Seat Reason on her throne' through the processive movement of spiritual history. The textual history of primary epic and ballad materials exhibits in a concrete way the process of continuous spiritual revelation.

The 'Rime' is presented as just this sort of text, and its own

[26] See Percy, pp. xxiii-xxvi and nn.
[27] Coleridge quoted in Shaffer, p. 79.

bibliographical history illustrates *in fact* what Coleridge fictively represents his poem to be *in imagination*. The special significance of the gloss, as far as the 'Rime' is concerned, lies in its (imagined) historical relation to the ancient ballad which Coleridge has represented through his poem. By the time Coleridge has 'evolved' his 1817 text, we are able to distinguish four clear layers of development: (*a*) an original mariner's tale; (*b*) the ballad narrative of that story; (*c*) the editorial gloss added when the ballad was, we are to suppose, first printed; and (*d*) Coleridge's own point of view on his invented materials. This last represents Coleridge's special religious/symbolic theory of interpretation founded upon his own understanding of the Higher Critical analytic.

From Coleridge's viewpoint, the 'Rime' is a poem which illustrates a special theory of the historical interpretation of texts. In its earliest state (1798), the theory is not easy to deduce, though it is certainly in operation; when the glosses are added, however, Coleridge has extrapolated fully, and thereby made explicit, his religious theory of interpretation which has its roots in the Higher Critical tradition.

Like all literary ballads, the 'Rime' is a *tour de force*, for Coleridge built it according to theories of the ballad (and of other historically transmitted works) which he had studied and which he expected his readers to know and to recognize. Certain stylistic facts about the poem demonstrate—on the authority of Percy—that the text has material which 'dates back' to the early days of the ancient minstrels.[28] On the other hand, other stylistic aspects of the text, including the gloss, show that its 'date' is relatively late, certainly after Columbus, but perhaps before Magellan's voyage to the Pacific. In general, Coleridge means us to understand that the ballad narrative dates from the sixteenth century, that the gloss is a late seventeenth-century addition, and, of course, that Coleridge, at the turn of the nineteenth century, has provided yet another (and controlling) perspective upon the poetic material. Indeed, Coleridge certainly intended his more perspicuous readers—that is, those read in the theory and practice of the new historical criticism—to see that the 'Rime' was an imaginative presenta-

---

28 See the discussion in Percy, pp. xlii-xliii, of the diction of the ancient minstrels (e.g. the accentuation of words like Coleridge's 'countree', 1. 407).

tion of a work comprising textual layers of the most primitive, even pre-Christian, sort. No one schooled in the new German textual criticism could fail to 'see' that the opening portions of part 6 represented a textual survival of the most ancient kind of pagan lore.

Coleridge's final (Broad Church) grasp of the 'Rime' demonstrates his great theme of the One Life.[29] Like the Bible, the *Iliad*, and all great imaginative works possessed and transmitted by different cultures, the 'Rime' is Coleridge's imitation of a culturally redacted literary work. The special function of the poem was to illustrate a significant continuity of meaning between cultural phenomena that seemed as diverse as pagan superstitions, Catholic theology, Aristotelian science, and contemporary philological theory, to name only a few of the work's ostentatiously present materials. The 'Rime', in its 1798 or its 1817 form, reconciles many opposite and discordant qualities.

A well-known passage from *The Table Talk* sets out the structural and thematic foundation of the 'Rime' in its most general philosophic formulation:

My system, if I may venture to give it so fine a name, is the only attempt I know, ever made to reduce all knowledges into harmony. It opposes no other system, but shows what was true in each; and how that which was true in the particular, in each of them became error, *because* it was only half the truth. I have endeavoured to unite the insulated fragments of truth, and therewith to frame a perfect mirror. I show to each system that I fully understand and rightfully appreciate what that system means; but then I lift up that system to a higher point of view, from which I enable it to see its former position, where it was, indeed, but under another light and with different relation; so that the fragment of truth is not only acknowledged, but explained. Thus the old astronomers discovered and maintained much that was true; but, because they were placed on a false ground, and looked from a wrong point of view, they never did, they never could, discover the truth—that is, the whole truth. As soon as they left the earth, their false centre, and took their stand in the sun, immediately they saw the whole system in its true light, and their former station remaining, but remaining as a part of the prospect.[30]

The 'Rime' is structured around three fundamental ideologies:

[29] See Charles Sanders, *Coleridge and the Broad Church Movement*, Durham, NC, 1942, and James D. Boulger, *Coleridge as Religious Thinker*, New Haven, Conn., 1961.
[30] Coleridge, *The Table Talk and Omniana*, ed. T. Ashe, London, 1923, pp. 138-9.

pagan superstition and philosophy, Catholic legend and theology, and Broad Church Protestantism. As noted, the poem's formal layering reflects this material. The pre-Coleridgean 'fragments of truth' represent 'a wrong point of view' on the material of human experience. The 'events' treated in the poem actually represent interpretations of events carried out in terms of certain fragmentary 'systems' of human thought, and the purpose of the poem is to 'lift [these systems] to a higher point of view' whence they will be open to a critical, self-conscious, but sympathetic valuation. This 'higher point of view', which *The Table Talk* passage represents as a final (divine) one, is Coleridge's own 'system' where 'the whole truth' adumbrated by the (historically relative) fragments of truth is discovered. *What* that whole truth constitutes is (*a*) that there is a whole truth which justifies and is the ground of all the fragments of the truth; and (*b*) that this whole truth is in a perpetual process of becoming—indeed, that its being is *the process of its being.*

Coleridge's system, then, is justified in the continuous and developing history of human thought. In terms of the 'Rime', Coleridge's ideological commitment to a preconditioned ground of processive truth sanctions in its readers a diversity of interpretations based upon their particular lights. Because 'the whole truth', recognized or not, subsumes *a priori* all the interpretations, readers are encouraged to formulate their particular expressions of the truth. Coleridge's much-discussed symbolic method in the poem is nothing more (or less) than his rhetorical machinery for producing such interpretive results. In Coleridge's terms, the symbolically grounded interpretations are acts of witness rather than definitions, human events which dramatically testify to the desire to know and continuously create the truth that has always set men free.

In this context, when Haven shows the congruence between nineteenth- and twentieth-century interpretations of the 'Rime', we are able to extrapolate the significance of his research. The basic continuum of thought comprising the poem's many interpretations testifies to the power of Coleridge's own poetic project. Although a few critics have attempted to resist the tradition outlined by Haven—I will return to them in a moment—the vast majority follow the model set forth in Coleridge's own comprehensive hermeneutic system established through the poem itself. The interpretive tradition licensed by the 'Rime' corresponds to the network of ideological institutions (the Clerisy) which Coleridge's ideas helped to create. Before Coleridge, the Church for centuries had been the principal ideological state apparatus, but *On the Constitution of Church and State,* among other works, marks the change which Coleridge was promoting. With him we witness the retreat of the Church and the emergence of the educational system, the academy, as Western society's principal ideological institution. As John Colmer recently remarked, in referring to educators in today's secular world, 'We are the clerisy'.[31] To measure the influence of Coleridge's programme one need but recall the dominant ideologues in Anglo-American culture during the past one hundred and fifty years: from Coleridge, through Arnold, Emerson, Leavis, and Eliot, to Trilling, Abrams, and the contemporary apologists for English and American Romantic thought.

The complex cultural problems related to the hegemony of this tradition appear again, in miniature form, when we approach Coleridge's great literary ballad. The history of the poem's criticism reveals, for example, that readers have not found it easy to escape the power of Coleridge's hermeneutics. From Babbitt to Empson and Pirie, a few critics have struggled against the dominant tradition of readers. Their characteristic method is to attack either the Romantic-symbolical readings— ridiculed by Empson and Pirie, for example—or Coleridge himself and the entire project ('spilt religion') which generated such readings. Sometimes, as in Empson's case, a distinction is drawn between the 'early', 'secular' Coleridge—author of the 1798 'Rime'—and the late, Christian dodderer—author of the 1817 revisionist piece. This antithetical tradition is important chiefly because it corroborates, from a hostile position, the basic ideological uniformity which underlies the dominant symbolic tradition initiated by Coleridge.

The problem with such antithetical readings is that they are at war with the differentials they themselves emphasize and corroborate. Babbitt and Empson are married, by antithesis and anxiety, to the positions they are attacking. The rules for

---

[31] John Colmer, *Coleridge: Critic of Society,* Oxford, 1959, p. 32.

such relationships, which have been laid down in the theoretical works initiated by Harold Bloom's *The Anxiety of Influence*, produce what can well be called 'the fate of reading'. What this means—I merely state the basic problem in another form—is that a historical process begins to appear as a fatal one; specifically, the act of literary criticism comes to seem so repetitional that drastic evasive measures begin to be taken. Babbitt's and Empson's violence succeeds to the play of differences in post-structuralism because acts which make a difference, in the mind as well as in the world, begin to seem difficult if not impossible to achieve. When traditional human activities seem as unimportant as academic criticism has grown to seem in this period of our culture—when it appears to make no difference what, if any, literary criticism you read or write—movements begin (deconstructionism in this period, aestheticism and naturalism at the end of the nineteenth century) which throw into relief the crisis line of an ideological tradition.

In terms of the critical history of the 'Rime', antithetical critics like Babbitt and Empson seem to violate the past of its treasures, while the traditional line seems to have exhausted its future and left us with nothing to follow. At such moments a historical analysis becomes a cultural imperative, for it is through such an analysis that we can recover what the past has sent to us and redefine the future of our own work. Such a method demands that differences be sharpened and clarified historically. The resources made available through the 'Rime' and its critical history will not be recovered until we begin to specify clearly the ideological gulf which separates us from them both. A poem like the 'Rime' dramatizes a salvation story, but it is not the old story of our salvation *in* Christ; rather, it is the new story of our salvation *of* Christ. Coleridge would have us believe that the latter story is the latest expression of the former and hence that the former retains its cultural truth. To the critical view of a contemporary materialist and historical consciousness, however, the advanced Christian machinery of the 'Rime' represents a view of the world only qualitatively less alien to ourselves than the ideology which supports the *Iliad* or the writings of Confucius. These works, we must come to see, transcend their particular cultural circumstances not because they contain unchanging human truths but rather because their *particular* truthfulness has been so thoroughly—so materially—specified.

Like the *Iliad* or *Paradise Lost* or any great historical product, the 'Rime' is a work of transhistorical rather than so-called universal significance. This verbal distinction is important because it calls attention to a real one. Like the *Divine Comedy* or any other poem, the 'Rime' is not valued or used always or everywhere or by everyone in the same way or for the same reasons. Poetical and artistic works have chequered critical histories which testify to their discontinuous power and employment. The study of a work's critical history is imperative precisely for that reason: the analysis reveals to us, in yet another form, the special historical life which a work has been living in the dialectic of its processive career. Historical analysis uncovers, therefore, a paradox of thought which yet contains a fundamental human truth: that the universal or transhistorical significance of an ideological product is a function of the specific limits of place and circumstance which are inscribed, and therefore 'immortalized', in those works we call poems which are created and re-created over time. The importance of great art is that it has always made a difference.

Anyone who has taught ancient or culturally removed literature has experienced the difficulty of transmitting historically alienated material. Nor does it help much to assume or pretend that what Bacon says in 'Of Education', what Sophocles dramatizes in the *Oedipus*, or what the Jahwist has presented in his Genesis can be appreciated or even understood by an uneducated student or reader. Of course, the problem can be solved if the teacher avoids it altogether and asks the student to deal with the work in its present context only, that is, to supply it with a 'reading'. Alien works may be, as we say, 'interpreted'. But we must understand that such exercises, carried out in relative historical ignorance, are not *critical* operations. Rather, they are vehicles for recapitulating and objectifying the reader's particular ideological commitments.[32] To 'read' in

---

[32] This result lies in the nature of hermeneutics itself, at least as presently understood. See, for example, Heinrich Ott's 'Hermeneutics and Personhood', where he states the basic principle of this interpretive method: 'In my first knowledge of the subject matter I already know implicitly all that which I later learned in addition' (from *Interpretation: The Poetry of Meaning*, ed. S. R. Hopper and D. L. Miller, New York, 1967, p. 17).

this way is to confront Ahab's doubloon, to read self-reflexively. The danger in such a method is that it will not be able to provide the reader with a social differential that can illuminate the limits of that immediate interpretation. The importance of ancient or culturally removed works lies precisely in this fact: that they themselves, as culturally alienated products, confront present readers with ideological differentials that help to define the limits and special functions of those current ideological practices. Great works continue to have something to say because what they have to say is so peculiarly and specifically their own that we, who are different, can learn from them.

Though the 'Rime' is not nearly so removed from the present as the *Oedipus*, we must not allow its alienation to escape us. The force of a line like 'It is an ancient mariner' comes from one's sense that an ancient minstrel did not write it but that Coleridge did. This is an awareness which was, and was meant to be, available to audiences from the poem's first appearance. But with the passage of time other perspectives become both possible and necessary. *We* see, for example, that the minstrel represented to us here is *not* the figure known to Child or Gummere but the one specifically available to a reader and admirer of Percy. To see this fact, even in so small an event as that line, is to be able to read the line *in* its own terms but without being made *subject* to those terms. We willingly suspend our disbelief only when disbelief, or critical distance, is the ground of our response. Such critical scepticism (it is not an attitude but a method) is especially important for a work like the 'Rime', since the poem itself seeks to break down a sense of ultimate discontinuity through the structure of its artistic illusions. Criticism must penetrate those illusions and specify what is involved in the particular uses to which they have been put. The meaning of the 'Rime' emerges through the study of the history of its illusions.

5. The 'Rime' and the Meaning of Symbol

In his introduction to the *History of the Russian Revolution*, Trotsky defends himself against the charge that he is a biased reporter by attacking the concept of 'objective history'. No historian's presentation can ever be free of tendentious and ideological elements, Trotsky argues. His position is not, however, subjectively relativistic. On the contrary, one judges the adequacy of a historian's work by its value as an explanation of the phenomena, by its congruence and comprehensiveness in relation to the objective circumstances. But the explanation must be constructed, Trotsky says, from an ideological vantage of some sort, and in his own case Trotsky argues that he is both more objectively correct in his vantage and analysis and more subjectively honest and clear about his methods. Trotsky, that is to say, makes every effort not to disguise his ideological position behind a specious appeal to objectivity but instead builds and objectifies his bias into the very structure of the analysis and keeps the reader aware of it all the time. Trotsky does this because, in his view, the ideology is a crucial part of the analysis, as much a part of his historical subject as it is the basis of his historical method.

Trotsky's ideology corresponds to what Coleridge called 'first principles', except that the former is a structure of scientific thought and the latter a theological, or what Coleridge termed a metaphysical, system. The general argument in the *The Statesman's Manual*—that the Bible is the most reliable guide for secular statecraft—is based upon a view wholly analogous to Trotsky's: that history, whether lived or narrated, is not a sequence of atomized movements or facts but a structured phenomenon, the praxis of a living and related set of commitments. For Coleridge, the crucial importance of a work like the Bible lies in its continuous historical existence. Because it must be read through the mediation of its transmitters, that is, through the Church, readers cannot receive its words except through acts of faith or, as we should say, through tendentious interpretations, acts of conscious commitment to the received materials. The Bible comes to us bearing with it the history of its criticism; it is a writing which also contains its own readings and which generates the cumulative history of its own further retransmissions and reinterpretations.

As already seen, Coleridge's views on the Bible were merely paradigmatic of his views on all literary texts. A committed Christian, he necessarily saw the Bible as the world's central literary event; but, like his contemporaries, he understood very well that other non-Christian cultures had their equivalent of the Western Bible. Indeed, as Coleridge argued in 'The Destiny of Nations', the West's central pre-Christian documents, for example, the saga literature of the skaldic bards, were important scriptual events not merely in themselves but in relation to the general development of mankind's religious cultures. German biblical critics were revealing the non- and pre-Judaic strands in the Scriptures, and the new philologists of primitive and classical texts were at work on similar projects.

The 'Rime', as readers have known all along, is an imitation or literary ballad modelled on works like those contained in Percy's *Reliques*, or on translations of Gottfried Bürger's imitation ballads. What has not been so clear is Coleridge's ideological motive in producing the 'Rime'. The context of his religious and critical thought shows quite clearly, I believe, that the poem is, as it were, an English national Scripture; that is to say, the poem imitates a redacted literary text which comprises various material extending from early pre-Christian periods through a succession of later epochs of Christian culture, and the ultimate locus of these transmissions is England. We must also understand, however, that for Coleridge each redaction specifies and calls attention to the series of distinct epochal (that is, ideological) interpretations through which the poetic material has been evolving.

By re-presenting not merely a text but an evidently *mediated* text, Coleridge provided both a spur and a model for later readers, who have been encouraged to elucidate for themselves and their own special needs the meaning and significance of the poem's symbolic statements. Ultimately, however, although Coleridge's project aimed to generate an unlimited number of readings, it was equally committed, by its own hermeneutic ideology, to a certain sort of reading. These are the interpretations which Haven has synthesized for us. Coleridge's theory of symbolism is a Western and a Judeo-Christian theory, and the hermeneutics of the 'Rime' has always been governed by this general frame of reference and set of, what Coleridge called, 'facts':

Christianity is especially differenced from all other religions by being *grounded* on *facts* which all men alike have the means of ascertaining, the same means, with equal facility, and which no man can ascertain for another. Each person must be herein querist and respondent to himself; Am I sick, and therefore need a physician?—Am I in spiritual slavery, and therefore need a ransomer?—Have I given a pledge, which must be redeemed, and which I cannot redeem by my own resources?[33]

Such facts are, of course, what we call ideology. The important thing to see, however, is that Coleridge knew perfectly well that these facts were 'interpreted facts', faith-determined and faith-constitutive. To read the 'Rime' in such a 'redemptive' frame is, as Coleridge maintained (and as we must agree), to reduplicate its determinative, *a priori* ideology. In this way does the 'Rime' assume into itself its own critical tradition.

Through works like the 'Rime' Coleridge successfully sustained his theistic and Christian views about nature and human history in the institutions of Western education. Hence the literary criticism of the 'Rime' has never been, in the proper sense, *critical* of the poem but has merely recapitulated, in new and various ways, and not always very consciously, what Coleridge himself had polemically maintained. To a *critical* view, however, what Coleridge re-presents in the 'Rime' is a historically and culturally limited set of ideas. Readers have not always found it easy to see this fact when they interpret the poem's 'symbols' because they characteristically regard their interpretations as something which *they bring to* the pre-existent 'text'. The 'Rime' is one thing, and its interpretations are something else, separated by time, place, and person. But Coleridge's own poem, as well as his involvement in the German critical tradition, ought to remind us that an act of interpretation may be assumed *a priori* in the materials to be interpreted. In the case of a poem like the 'Rime', hermeneutics is criticism's grand illusion.

A properly critical view of the 'Rime' can only begin with the recognition that what needs criticism and interpretation is not simply the work's set of symbolic paraphernalia (albatross, mariner, spectre-bark, water snakes, rain, sun, moon, etc.); these are 'in' the poem and therefore the objects of our analysis, but they are only in the poem *as symbols*. That is to say, they enter the reader's horizon as objects-bearing-meaning, as already significant (or pre-interpreted) phenomena. A critical analysis of the poem's poetic materials, therefore, cannot be

---

[33] Coleridge, *Lay Sermons*, p. 55.

carried out by erecting a thematic elucidation of albatross, sun, moon, water, and so on but only by erecting an analysis of the *meaningful* albatross, the *significant* sun, moon, stars, water. The materials dealt with by the 'Rime' are not—indeed, never were—mere 'secular' or 'natural' facts; they are predesigned and pre-interpreted phenomena. We may, indeed must, read the poem's symbols, but what we must critically elucidate are the meanings of the symbols. Readers of the 'Rime' generate its meanings; critics set out and explain the meaning of its meanings.

The albatross, for example, is an interpreted phenomenon *ab initio*: the bird is part of the mariner's superstitious preconceptions. So too the mariner himself: by virtue of his association with the Wandering Jew, for example, he has been incorporated by the poem into a special structure of signification. In each case the reader is reading the meaning not of the bird or mariner in isolation but of bird and mariner as they represent or locate certain superstitious (and, ultimately, religious) forms of thought. Similarly, the terms 'Bridegroom' and 'Wedding-Guest' are delivered to and through the Western, nineteenth- and twentieth-century readers in terms of their Christian frame of reference. These are not words from an innocent, 'natural' language, as it were, but from a particular symbolic and religious context of discourse.

In general, what Coleridge does in his poem is to present us, via an imitation ballad, with a wide variety of culturally and historically mediated material; and he arranges this material, formally, according to philological rules which governed the constitution and transmission of ancient texts and which were just then being formulated in the circles of the Higher Critics. This formal procedure empowers Coleridge to produce a wide variety of poetic effects. It enables him, for example, to achieve the wit of lines like 'We were the first that ever burst/ Into that silent sea' (lines 105-6), where the contemporary reader encounters an 'explanation' for how the Pacific Ocean (*Mare Pacificum*) may originally have received its name (see also line 110). More significantly, the Higher Critical model gave Coleridge a structure in which various materials apparently alien to each other could be reconciled and harmonized. Different sorts of superstitious phenomena are held in a significant relation with various Christian ideologies. We are enabled to 'interpret', for example, the originally pagan Polar Spirit in terms of a redemptive Christian scheme because the philological model tells us that the two are historically related via the operation of processes of textual transmission and interpolation. One important function of Coleridge's Polar Spirit, therefore, is to remind us that such superstitious phenomena retain their power of signification in history even after their ideology has ceased to play a dominant role in the institutions of a culture; that they retain this power by virtue of their incorporation by later ideological systems; and, finally that they are available to such incorporation precisely because they are, originally, *interpreted* rather than merely natural phenomena.

Creating this sort of poem required Coleridge to imitate a transmitted ballad. He had to establish a text which displayed several textual 'layers', as we have already seen, and the poem's lexicon is the ultimate carrier of this set of textual layers. The 'Rime' cannot work if it does not contain words which the reader will associate with diverse historical periods. Attention has always been drawn to the archaic diction of the ballad, but equally important is the modern diction. 'Bassoon' and 'lighthouse' are seventeenth-century words, and their appearance in the text indicates (fictively, of course) 'late interpolated passages'. In general, the archaic diction is only significant in its relation to the more modern dictions; the poetic system that holds them together is using both as the formal foundation for its work of symbology.

Coleridge takes it for granted that an 'Enlightened' mind of his or a later period will not believe that the spectre-bark ever had a concrete and objective existence or that the creatures called Death and Life-in-Death ever did what the poem reports or ever existed in the ordinary sense. The Enlightened mind will recognize such phenomena to be mental projections of the mariner's delirium; indeed, he will see all the fabulous events in this way, that is, as phenomena mediated either by the mariner, or by the balladeer(s), or by some still later editor or scribe, like the writer of the gloss. All of these are pre-Enlightenment minds. But to Coleridge's (post- and anti-Enlightenment) mind, this Enlightened view is itself a limited one. The Enlightenment (Higher Critical) attitude sees (*a*) that all phenomena are mind-mediated and (*b*) that these mediations are culturally and historically determined. What it does not see, in Coleridge's view, is that the entire system (or history) of the mediations is organized *a priori* and that the history of the mediations is an evolving process whereby the original (God-instituted and redemptive) system is raised up into human consciousness by the processive acts of human consciousness itself.

This Coleridgean view of the poem is what has licensed its traditions of symbolic interpretation. But this view must itself finally be laid aside as a determinative one. Coleridge's appeal to historical process and his insistence that symbolic interpretation (the meaning of symbols) is a function of specific cultural and historical factors ultimately overtake his own poetic ideology. For his is a sacramental and Christian view of symbols in which history itself is revealed as a sacramental Christian symbol. The 'Rime' imitates or re-presents a process of textual evolution, and the symbolic meaning of that process—which is the poem's dominant symbolic event—is that the process *has* a symbolic value and meaning, that is, a religious, a Christian, and ultimately a redemptive meaning. In this we can see very clearly the living operation of processive historical events. At the outset of the nineteenth century and in reaction to the revolutionary intellectual developments of the Enlightenment, Christian ideas find a new birth of freedom, not in the *fact* of Christ's resurrection, which is the traditional Pauline view, but in the symbol of the resurrection, in its *meaning*.

6. Pre-Raphaelite Symbolism: A Critical Differential

We can specify the peculiar (historically determined) character of Coleridge's form of symbolism if we juxtapose it briefly with some alternative symbolic modes. The limits of the Coleridgean view would be quite apparent if we were to compare it with, for example, Mallarmé's or Rimbaud's *symboliste* programmes, which represent a very different set of cultural determinants and limitations. But this cross-cultural comparison will not illuminate Coleridge's position nearly so well as a comparison drawn from within the English poetic tradition. I have in mind here the programmatic symbolism developed through the Pre-Raphaelite movement, by Dante Gabriel Rossetti in particular.

M. H. Abrams has rightly said of High English Romanticism that it sought to reformulate and save the 'traditional concepts, schemes, and values' of the Christian heritage. Abrams
believes, wrongly I think, that this was the programme of all
forms of Romanticism; however that may be, his thesis is perfectly exemplified in Coleridge's work.

The Ancient Mariner is neither an allegorical fable nor a symbolist
poem. The persistent religious and moral allusions, however, both in
the text and in the glosses . . ., invite us to take the Mariner's experience as an instance of the Christian plot of moral error, the discipline
of suffering, and a consequent change of heart. The Mariner's literal
journey, then, is also a spiritual journey . . .[34]

The commentary is right on the mark, though one would wish
to add that Coleridge's glosses were a brilliant addition to his
poem because they emphasized a slight sense of historical discontinuity. Abrams is correct to say the poem is neither *symboliste* nor allegorical because this discontinuity exists. The
'Rime' presents us with an obviously 'Christian' plot, but it
insists that we 'read' the plot in a highly personal and unorthodox way. Though its meaning is not so extensive or open as the
meaning of a *symboliste* poem, the 'Rime' relaxes the allegorical
urgency of its materials just enough to permit 'personal' interpretations that will yet not violate the poem's essentially
Christian structure of concepts and values.

As we know, the Pre-Raphaelites and their circle were
devoted to the literary ballad, which in fact achieved the rank
of an important genre in the hands of the Romantics. The
'Rime' is the best early representation of this highly Romantic
form. But with the Pre-Raphaelites, verisimilitude of historical
detail, both substantive and formal, became so central an issue
that England produced, in the person of Swinburne, her greatest master of the literary ballad. Paradoxically, or so it might
seem, this demand for a literalness of imagination resulted in
poems which did not draw close continuities with the spirit of
the past and its traditional forms of order, but which rather
heightened one's feeling of the separation between past and

[34] Abrams, p. 272. The following section of the present essay is a revised portion of
a review essay, 'Romanticism and the Embarrassments of Critical Tradition', which
appeared in *Modern Philology* lxx (February 1973).

present. The medieval worlds evoked by Morris and Rossetti and Swinburne were interesting precisely because the famous Pre-Raphaelite detail distanced their material, made it appear remote and strange. The reader of 'The Blessed Damozel' is placed in a forest of symbolic detail so dense that correspondences become unmanageable. Yet the situation is neither symbolic (in the Coleridgean mode) nor *symboliste*. Pre-Raphaelite detail does not put the reader on the threshold of a fresh openness, of extensive new sets of possible relations, but shocks him with the realization that his traditional Romantic accommodations with past symbolic orders do not serve the actual truths of those orders, which are in fact much more mysterious than had been realized. The 'Rime' draws continuities with the past; Pre-Raphaelite ballads enforce separations.

The relevance of these observations for Coleridge's use of a Christian symbolic mode will become clearer if we extend this analysis into a few more Pre-Raphaelite commonplaces. Pre-Raphaelite art and literature reproduce Christian inconography in great quantity, but anyone familiar with this pivotal movement knows that, despite its religious substance and even the religious convictions of at least some of its practitioners, Pre-Raphaelitism is not a religious art. The inheritors of Pre-Raphaelitism—the Vienna Sezession and Art Nouveau—are the logical extensions of a Pre-Raphaelite attitude; and though a true religious mood is discernible in these later movements, it is a religious mentality doing conscious battle with forms of Romantic orthodoxy, as the work of Gustav Moreau and Stefan George makes very plain.

Pre-Raphaelitism, on the other hand, represents a return to certain basic Romantic principles. It is a movement which did not want so much to elaborate a revision upon traditional Romantic forms—which is what Tennyson ended up doing—as to return Romantic perception to its *raison d'être*. The Pre-Raphaelite insistence upon careful realistic detail, so apparrently un-Romantic, is in fact one of the two essential features of its Romanticism. The other is the inclination to deal with very traditional subjects, and in particular with Christian subjects. These two qualities, operating together, opened another revisionist phase wherein Pre-Raphaelite art at last discovered a usable aesthetic medium for the viewpoint of a wholly secularized, and therefore non-Coleridgean, form of the Higher Criticism.

But the whole matter is best discussed in an example. Rossetti fixed the following sonnet to his painting 'The Girlhood of Mary Virgin'.

> These are the symbols. On that cloth of red .
>   I' the centre is the Tripoint: perfect each,
> Except the second of its points, to teach
>   That Christ is not yet born. The books—whose head
> Is golden Charity, as Paul hath said—
>   Those virtues are wherein the soul is rich:
>   Therefore on them the lily standeth, which
> Is Innocence, being interpreted.
> The seven-thorn'd briar and the palm seven-leaved
>   Are her great sorrow and her great reward.
>   Until the end be full, the Holy One
> Abides without. She soon shall have achieved
> Her perfect purity: yea, God the Lord
>   Shall soon vouchsafe His Son to be her Son.

In an older context, this sonnet might not seem so strange. Its force here comes from the fact that, though the interpretation he gives to the details of the painting is quite traditionally grounded, it is an interpretation without any essential religious import precisely because it is so literal. The details of poem and painting are precise enough, and their Christian context is sufficiently complete to allow an allegorical action; yet the poem forbids a religious response. For if Rossetti's allegorical pattern is exact, it is also consciously recovered, and thus presents itself to us not as a religious insight but as an antiquarian discovery. The result is that all the details in the painting and the poem, though 'interpreted', have an even greater phenomenological innocence than they would have had in a medieval context. One is suddenly faced with a world (Christianity) which one thought one knew but whose spirit is in fact now seen to be profoundly remote.

Unlike the 'Rime', this poem is no vehicle back to the essential religious significance of the Christian myth. Rather, it transports us back further still, to the essentially secular, or aesthetic, significance of that myth. The poem shows us that Christian iconology can have a significance, its beauty, which

is even more radical than the most profound allegorical interpretation. It also tells us that allegorical interpretation can retain its own importance even after the withdrawal of the sea of
faith, for such interpretations still possess the beauty of their
design. The very details of Rossetti's 'Christian' interpretation
acquire a physique comparable to the details of the painting.
Rossetti forces the interpretation to stand apart from us, forces
us to view it as an object of delighted curiosity. What ought to
be a definitive interpretation of the picture is discovered to be
not an intellectual but a purely sensational, or perhaps anthro-
pological, experience.

When Pre-Raphelites return to an extremely detailed reproduction of traditional forms, it is always to work for effects like
this. Indeed, when Rossetti writes upon some work of a painter
from an earlier culture—one of his numerous sonnets for pictures—he not only repeats the technique of 'The Girlhood of
Mary Virgin' and its pendant sonnet; he tends to make his purposes even more explicit. His sonnet 'An Allegorical Dance of
Women', for example, is written on Mantegna's 'Parnassus',
in the Louvre, which seems to represent the triumph of Venus
over Mars. But Rossetti opens his sonnet with the observation:
'Scarcely, I think; yet it indeed *may* be/ The meaning [of his
own work] reached him'. Rossetti is doubtful that Mantegna
knew the full meaning of his own picture because Rossetti
knows that, while meaning and allegorical constructs multiply,
the essential character of art and life alike is their ability to
generate human creations which are forever escaping the ideologies which made them possible. Of the Mantegna 'Parnassus',
then, he concludes:

> Its meaning filleth it,
> A secret of the wells of Life: to wit:—
> The heart's each pulse shall keep the sense it had
> With all, though the mind's labour run to nought

That is, though the cultural gap between Mantegna and Rossetti
is complete—a situation which is distinctly *not* the case with the
historically diverse materials re-presented through Coleridge's
'Rime'—Rossetti is yet able to join hands with Mantegna across
the gulf of their differences. What the two share, according to
Rossetti, is not a mutual commitment, symbolically main-

tained, to a religious ideology but a common devotion to the practice of art. In this case symbolism is material and technological rather than conceptual. The atheist Rossetti keeps company with the Catholic Mantegna, and with Christian traditions generally, by seeing hermeneutics not as a process of interpretation but as a history of changing style. In the Pre-Raphaelite movement appears, for the first time unmistakably, the polemical deposition: no ideas but in things.

7. Conclusion

What, then, is the meaning of the 'Rime'? Coleridge tried to guide his early readers to an answer in his famous *Biographia Literaria* pronouncement on the poem and the entire *Lyrical Ballads* project:

> In this idea originated the plan of the *Lyrical Ballads*; in which it was agreed that my endeavours should be directed to persons and characters supernatural, or at least romantic; yet so as to transfer from our inward nature a human interest and a semblance of truth sufficient to procure for these shadows of imagination that willing suspension of disbelief for the moment, which constitutes poetic faith. (Chap. 14)

If we examine this passage carefully—assisted, perhaps, by our knowledge of its critical history—we will see that the famous dictum about the 'willing suspension of disbelief' is being used in two senses. In the first instance the phrase refers to Coleridge's use of legendary, 'supernatural', 'romantic' materials, that is, to what is 'contained' in the 'Rime' when we see it as an ancient tale or, as we might now say, as a 'myth'. This sort of material is recognized to be a 'delusion' by Coleridge, and his work shows that similar delusions can be found at the level of the ballad narrative as well as at the level of the gloss. The spectre-bark, Life-in-Death, the Polar Spirit, and the 'grace of the Holy Mother' are not, to use Coleridge's term, 'real' except under the deluded eye of the beholders of such phenomena. The art of the 'Rime' persuades us to suspend our disbelief in such matters; indeed, when Coleridge speaks of a '*willing* suspension of disbelief', we understand that he is presuming in his readers a shared consciousness of the superstitious character of his primitive (mainly pagan and Roman Catholic) materials.

But Coleridge intimates a more comprehensive understanding of the willing suspension of disbelief when he says that it 'constitutes poetic faith'. From this vantage the statement can be seen, and of course has been seen, as a *locus classicus* for the Romantic ideology of the creative imagination. 'To transfer from our inward nature a human interest and semblance of truth' to the 'Rime's' superstitious materials is to psychologize reality and to suggest that the 'true' reality of all external phenomena, whether 'real' or 'delusive', is inward and subjective. In this case, the willing suspension of disbelief does not apply to a poetic *tour de force* but to an imaginative construct which offers limitless opportunities for symbolic interpretation. In the first case the reader is willing to suspend his disbelief—which he none the less remains conscious of and attached to—whereas in the second he is willing to gain a poetic faith. When the latter occurs the 'Rime' enters upon its symbolic history and becomes the object of Romantic hermeneutics.

From our present vantage, what we must do is inaugurate our disbelief in Coleridge's 'poetic faith'. This Romantic ideology must be seen for what it is, a historical phenomenon of European culture, generated to save the 'traditional concepts, schemes, and values' of the Christian heritage. To interpret the 'Rime' at all, without a prior historical analytic, is necessarily to reify the Romantic concept of the creative imagination. But that concept must become for us the same sort of 'superstition' and 'delusion' which 'the grace of the Holy Mother' was to Coleridge. Only then will the poem become available once again to a (new) tradition of interpreters. Indeed, only then will Coleridge's own 'poetic faith' become possible, for such a faith depends upon the hypothetical suspension of a prior, and presumed, disbelief.

To inaugurate such a disbelief in the 'Rime's' ideology of symbolism, we must historicize every aspect of the work. This is a procedure which the poem's own method has initiated. The mariner interprets his experiences by his own lights, and each subsequent mediator—the ballad transmitters, the author of the gloss, and Coleridge himself—all represent their specific cultural views. In such a situation we must read the poem with the fullest possible consciousness of its poetically organized 'historical layerings'. The spectre-bark is seen as such by the mariner and is accepted *literatim* by the fictive textual transmitters. But if the poem assumes these superstitious attitudes into itself, it also presumes the presence of Enlightened readers. The latter will of course recognize the ship to be a hallucination, perhaps with no basis in physical reality at all, perhaps an imagined structure created by the mariner's fevered brain out of some wisps of sea fog. Because Coleridge has an Enlightened mind as well, he knows that 'In a distempered dream things & forms in themselves harmless inflict a terror of anguish.'[35] But his mind is also Christian and symbolist, so even as he asks us, in the 'Rime', to disbelieve in the phenomenal reality of the spectre-bark, he also asks us to suspend that disbelief:

The excellence aimed at was to consist in the interesting of the affections by the dramatic truth of such emotions, as would naturally accompany such situations, supposing them real. And real in this sense they have been to every human being who, from whatever source of delusion, has at any time believed himself under supernatural agency.

What may be seen as a 'delusion' in one point of view may be usefully regarded as a spiritual truth in another. Meaning replaces event, and word replaces fact as the real gives way to the symbolic.

When Newman watched Coleridge replace the Truth with the Imagination of the Truth, he concluded that Coleridge had 'indulged a liberty of speculation which no Christian can tolerate, and advanced conclusions which were often heathen rather than Christian'.[36] Newman's analysis, like his orthodox fears, were both correct and far-sighted, for Coleridge's own method would necessarily place his interpretive scheme beneath the critical razor he first employed. Interpretation of the spectre-bark is analogous to the interpretation of every facet of the poem, including its general theme and structure: interpretation, including the author's interpretation, falls subject to those historical limitations which critical analysis can explicate. The fictive writer of the gloss gives a long and beautiful commentary on the stars of line 266. The best gloss on such a gloss is a passage like the following from *The Statesman's Manual*:

The great PRINCIPLES of our religion, the sublime IDEAS spoken out

---

[35] Coleridge, *Notebooks*, 1 no. 205 (the entry is dated 1796-7).
[36] Newman, 'The Prospects of the Anglican Church', *Essays Critical and Historical*, London, 1897, p. 268.

everywhere in the Old and New Testament, resemble the fixed stars, which appear of the same size to the naked as to the armed eye; the magnitude of which the telescope may rather seem to diminish than to increase. At the annunciation of *principles*, of *ideas*, the soul of man awakes, and starts up, as an exile in a far distant land at the unexpected sounds of his native language, when after long years of absence, and almost of oblivion, he is suddenly addressed in his own mother-tongue. He weeps for joy, and embraces the speaker as his brother.[37]

This is not the meaning of the poem's text, but it is the meaning which perhaps best clarifies what kind of poem we are dealing with. Coleridge might associate the meaning of this passage with his text, but it is a special reading, peculiar to Coleridge. In such matters, as Coleridge had said, 'Each person must be . . . querist and respondent to himself.'[38]

A poem like the 'Rime' encourages, therefore, the most diverse readings and interpretations. Since this encouragement is made in terms of the Christian economy, the interpretations have generally remained within the broad spiritualist terms— 'heathen' terms, in Newman's view—which Coleridge's mind had allowed for. The historical method of the 'Rime', however, had also prepared the ground for a thoroughly revisionist view of the poem, in which the entire ideological structure of its symbolist procedures could finally be seen in their special historical terms. When this happens the meaning of the 'Rime' emerges as the 'dramatic truth' of Coleridge's intellectual and religious commitments. In the event the poem suffers no loss of power or significance; on the contrary, at that point we begin to see quite clearly the true extent of its power and the immense significance it has had, just as we also begin to see how these things came to pass. When the entire poetical work—including, perhaps especially, its verbal forms and its symbolic procedures—is scrutinized through the lens of a critical rather than a hermeneutic method, the 'Rime' will once again begin to discover its future. It will cease to be an object of faith—whether Romantic or Christian—and become, instead, a human—a social and a historical—resource.

(1980-1)

---

37 Coleridge, *Lay Sermons*, p. 24.   38 Ibid., p. 55.

2. Tennyson and the Histories of Criticism

I

In his 'Introduction' to *The Letters of Arthur Henry Hallam* Jack Kolb says that *In Memoriam* 'is not merely the most personal elegy in English, it is also the only major work in the genre in which specific details of its subject's life and character enter so largely into the process of the poem.'[1] This remark, which seems to me quite correct, points to the fundamental reason we wish to have a work such as the one that Kolb has produced. Hallam's letters help us to recover the significance of important details in Tennyson's poetry. They illuminate the aesthetic function of specific references and local fact. From our removed historical vantage, they supply the deficiencies which have developed through a lapse of time and shifts in cultural views.

Kolb's observation underscores the general critical significance which biographical and historical works have for poetry, including the documentary materials which these works depend upon and reproduce. An accurate transmission of facts is a *sine qua non* of criticism and scholarship, and a careful scholarly elucidation of obscure facts is only slightly less fundamental. All scholars accept these obligations, of course, though I am not entirely sure that they all understand equally well how such a concern for referential fact relates to the aesthetic operation of works of art, and hence to the pursuits and methodologies of literary criticism. I shall try to demonstrate these relationships at a later point in this essay, through a detailed examination of 'The Charge of the Light Brigade'.[2] Before we can turn to this

---

[1] Cambridge, Mass., 1981, p. 34.

[2] I shall mention here a small matter of fact which bears upon the circumstances surrounding 'The Charge of the Light Brigade'. In his biography of Tennyson, Robert Charles Martin says that the poem was based upon an account of the charge which Tennyson read in *The Times* of 14 Nov. 1854 in which the phrase 'a hideous blunder' appeared; and furthermore, that Tennyson wrote the poem on 2 Dec. and sent it off to John Forster for printing in the *Examiner* (see *Tennyson. The Unquiet Heart*, Oxford, 1980, p. 381). This account is based upon certain earlier accounts, on the one hand, and certain documentary evidence on the other—the most important of which

example, however, we must first reflect on some other matters which bear upon the subject of poetry, specific poems and the historical contexts which help to generate and support them.

I shall begin with a quotation from the 'Introduction' to Henry Kozicki's recent book *Tennyson and Clio*, a work which sets out to define Tennyson's 'philosophy of history' and explore its poetic operations.

The 'meaning and purpose' of the past cannot obtain without both a conceptual system and intense convictions. And we cannot interpret properly a poem in which we deem Clio's influence operational unless we are able to identify both idea and emotion. For example, the presence of the notion of historical cycles does not bring meaning to a poem unless we can discover what the poet felt about the notion. The intellectual order that is a philosophy of history in Tennyson's major poems is, thus, an inextricable compound of concepts and convictions that must be determined in its totality, as a lifelong development, before it may be used as a sounding board to enhance any note elicited from a particular poem. Lest this be taken as an intentionalist intent (and a disregard of everything we have learned from the new criticism) I can only say, with Cleanth Brooks, that 'my basic concern has been to read the poem,' but to note that, in order to do this, the critic must select 'from scholarship those things which will help him understand the poem *qua* poem'.[3]

This is a promising set of remarks, for Kozicki seems to understand the relationships which function between specific poems and their ideological materials. Facts, whether referential or ideational, are always interpreted facts, and in a poetical context the ideological formatting assumes a paramount impor-

---

are the notoriously problematic *Memoir* and the equally problematic *Journal* of Emily Tennyson. But there is no question that the account which Tennyson read was in *The Times* of 13 Nov. (the leader in the 14 Nov. issue is very different, though equally interesting) and that the poem itself was written and sent to Forster on 6 Dec., not the 2nd: see the discussion of the poem below, as well as *The Letters of Emily Tennyson*, ed. James O. Hoge, University Park, Pa., 1974, pp. 70-1, and Hoge's editions of *Lady Tennyson's Journal*, Charlottesville, Va., 1981, pp. 40-1. June Steffansen Hagen's *Tennyson and His Publishers*, (University Park, Pa., 1979) produces an even more garbled account of these events; indeed her book is excessively dependent for all its material not on an examination of original documents, but on secondary and hand-me-down narratives. Consequently, her entire project—which seems to me of central importance for the study of Tennyson's poetry—suffers in her treatment from its willingness to depend upon unreliable guides.

[3] *Tennyson and Clio. History in the Major Poems*, Baltimore, Md., 1979, p. xii.

tance. This happens because the concrete utterances of poems incorporate not merely linguistic terms and their referential 'objects', but a whole network of what has been called, at various times, 'belief' (Coleridge), 'ideology' (Marx), 'social evaluation' (Bakhtin).

Kozicki's work shows that he understands these matters only in a superficial way. For example, when he discusses the topic of the English Great House as its appears in Tennyson's work (pp. 56 ff.) he is unable to make critical distinctions between gothic and Neo-Gothic, or between the English Great House (which is one thing) and certain Victorian ideas about the English Great House (which are quite another matter). Kozicki sees these distinctions, it seems to me, but he does not understand them critically.

The weakness of his treatment—the source of its failure as criticism—emerges clearly when we turn to Robert Martin's biography, where the topic of Tennyson's lifelong obsession with the English Great House is a recurrent one. Martin's treatment of this subject—like his treatment of Tennyson's relations with women—is as strong as it is because he sees the fundamental contradictions which support Tennyson's attitudes. These contradictions are epitomized in Tennyson's early (and lifelong) contempt for his uncle Charles Tennyson d'Eyncourt, whose deep passion for the past appeared as an obsession with all the accoutrements of lineage and pedigree, as well as his single-minded commitment to the project of rebuilding Bayons Manor into the very image of his idea of the English Great House. A good deal of what Tennyson most heartily despised in his uncle were essential features of his own central ideas and imbedded attitudes.

Kozicki is not aware of these contradictions—many others could be instanced here—because he approaches Tennyson's 'philosophy of history' in an uncritical fashion and spirit. The problem appears early in his work and operates throughout. Speaking of Tennyson's Juvenilia, for example, Kozicki argues that their treatment of their subjects is not 'tendentious' but 'merely accurate' (p. 11). This remark might seem an odd one if we recall Kozicki's explicit comments on ideology in poetical works (some of which I have quoted above). But the remark explains itself in its immediate context, where Kozicki also says:

> In these early poems, Tennyson may be indicating that for him pageantry, high passion, and monumentality possess the brightest colors on the literary canvas. But he also takes pride in an exact knowledge of his subject matter and, further, looks without squeamishness or illusions upon the ordained ways of the world (unless Christian orthodoxy is taken for illusion). He wants to understand history. And in this understanding, as it is revealed in these early poems, we may see the basic characteristics of Tennyson's philosophy of history. A divinity of some sort is working out its nature in history. History is occurring in apocalyptic cycles. The hero, either as individual or as collective spirit, somehow is a 'free' agent of this divinity. (p. 11)

Kozicki's parenthetical observation is revealing: that is, we are dealing with a critic who shares Tennyson's views on these matters, whose own ideology (we must assume) merges with Tennyson's. Kozicki does not—apparently, cannot—seriously entertain the idea that 'Christian orthodoxy' might well embody a set of historic (and historical) illusions, or that Tennyson's so-called 'philosophy of history' is actually a theology of history, and hence—to a non-Christian or humanist intelligence— necessarily illusive and illusory.

The ideology which Kozicki observes in Tennyson's poems is one of the subjects which appear throughout Peter Allen's *The Cambridge Apostles. The Early Years* (Cambridge, 1978). This excellent book describes the social and intellectual context in which Tennyson and his poetry were so deeply and reciprocally involved. The 'philosophy of history' which Kozicki takes as his subject is traced through its nineteenth century development— which is to say, is traced from its (English) *fons* in the mind of Coleridge through its subsequent transformations and modifications in the work of various Apostles. Unlike Kozicki, however, Allen maintains his critical distance from his subject.

This comparison between Kozicki and Allen is not entirely fair, however, because Allen is not directly concerned with Tennyson's poems, whereas the poetry is the final point of reference for Kozicki's ideational discussions. A thorough criticism of poetry and poems must negotiate a difficult arrangement with its subject: on the one hand, it must remain sufficiently disinterested to see the work 'as in itself it really is'; on the other, it must, like the poet, 'bring the whole soul of man into activity'. Poems are the foci of significant acts or social evaluation and human experience, and one of the central elements in a poem's focus is the reader of the poem (both original and subsequent). Kozicki reads Tennyson ideologically, which is as it should be. The weakness of his critical discussion is that his ideological position permits him no critical vantage on his subject-matter. He cannot see the contradictions in Tennyson's poetry; by the same token, he cannot see that these contradictions are precisely the source of Tennyson's poetical strengths; and, finally, because Tennyson's work does not stand at a critical distance from his own ideas and ideologies, Kozicki's readings never have to bear the illuminating critique which Tennyson's (alien) views might have brought to light.

At this point one might reasonably object on the grounds that Tennyson's poetry does not involve contradictions in any ultimate way, that it is not a field in which tensions are promoted and maintained. In his book *Tennyson and Tradition* Robert Pattison says of *In Memoriam* that it 'is a poem of syntheses [where] pagan and Christian myth [are] united in a single sense'.[4] In this view Pattison stands with Kozicki and almost all Tennyson commentators, who in fact do no more than reproduce the ideological stance which *In Memoriam* itself is bent upon promoting. (Thus Kozicki denigrates 'Locksley Hall' as a poem full of 'contradictions', whereas *In Memoriam*— a poem of resolutions and processive syntheses—is pronounced a success.)

That Tennyson's poetry aimed for and in large measure achieved a poetic of syntheses and resolutions cannot really be doubted. The history of his relations with the publishing institutions of his day, including his deep concern for and interest in the views of his readers and reviewers, bears eloquent testimony to the presence of this factor in his work. What appears in the verse as poetic theme and artistic form is matched, in the social arena of Tennyson's work, as a concern to reach as large an audience as possible—to forge a sympathetic contact with the widest possible number of its class and interest groups. Tennyson's habits of composition, revision, and publication all testify to his interest in his audiences and their opinions. Indeed,

---

[4] Cambridge, Mass., 1979, p. 110.

many twentieth-century commentators have deplored this aspect of Tennyson's poetical work as a sign that he sacrificed his artistic integrity and authenticity in the pursuit of popularity.

I shall set aside for the moment any judgement on this matter and merely observe that Tennyson's verse style and form exhibit a genuine congruence and symmetry with his methods of production. Indeed, his *symboliste* poetical methods, which have so preoccupied the attention of recent criticism, involve a strategy whereby the poet is able to be, as it were, all things to all men. This is a strategy which traces its source to the philosophical, aesthetic, and theological ideas of S. T. Coleridge, whose impact in these areas, during the Victorian period, was profound— and not least profound on the Apostles. Tennyson's famous set of remarks, recorded in the *Memoir*, on the *symboliste*-allegorical method of his poetry, incorporate a rather clumsily expressed Coleridgean set of ideas:

'There is an allegorical or perhaps rather a parabolic drift in the poem' [Tennyson said]. 'Of course Camelot, for instance, a city of shadowy palaces, is everywhere symbolic of the gradual growth of human beliefs and institutions, and of the spiritual development of man. Yet there is no single fact or incident in the 'Idylls,' however seemingly mystical, which cannot be explained as without any mystery or allegory whatever.' The bishop of Ripon (Boyd Carpenter) once asked him whether they were right who interpreted the three Queens, who accompanied King Arthur on his last voyage, as Faith, Hope and Charity. He answered: 'They are right, and they are not right. They mean that and they do not. They are three of the noblest of women. They are also those three Graces, but they are much more. I hate to be tied down to say, '*This* means *that*,' because the thought within the image is much more than any one interpretation.'

As for the many meanings of the poem my father would affirm, 'Poetry is like shot-silk with many glancing colours. Every reader must find his own interpretation according to his ability, and according to his sympathy with the poet.' The general drift of the 'Idylls' is clear enough. 'The whole,' he said, 'is the dream of man coming into practical life and ruined by one sin. Birth is a mystery and death is a mystery, and in the midst lies the tableland of life, and its struggles and performances. It is not the history of one man or of one generation but of a whole cycle or generations.'[5]

[5] *Alfred Lord Tennyson. A Memoir by his Son*, London, 1897, ii. 1127. Tennyson told his son that he 'considered [the allegorical readings of his poems] the best' (ibid., p. 126).

Tennyson worked hard to fashion a poetic vehicle that was not merely designed to accomodate different views and alternate readings, but that actively anticipated these differences— that (as it were) called out to them, and that offered Victorian readers a place where they would find their differences reconciled. The whole project of *The Princess* illustrates Tennyson's aesthetic of reconciliations. It is a 'medley' of social, political, and sexual differentials which are held together in an equally heterogeneous poetical form. The accommodations which the poem makes—indeed, the ideology of accommodations which it promotes—are notably epitomized in the 'Conclusion'. Here Tennyson offers a series of tableaux marked by differences and differentials which are not characterized by serious strife or disruptions. More than anything else the 'Conclusion' manages an arrangement of variegated detail and accommodations of various people.

This ideology enters the style of Tennyson's poetry as a strategy of those unmistakable and Tennysonian ambiguities. *In Memoriam* offers a host of examples. The simplest type centres in Tennyson's use of the pun and associated forms of wordplay. For example, 'The shade by which my life was crost' (LXVI) works a pun in the word 'shade', and section LXV begins with an ambiguous address to a 'Sweet soul' whose identity, in the context, might be either Hallam or his own buried life. Or consider this final quatrain of section XVIII:

> Ah yet, even yet, if this might be,
>   I, falling on his faithful heart,
>   Would breathing thro' his lips impart
> The life that almost dies in me.

The third line here operates an ambiguous syntax to suggest both that Tennyson's life might be revivified by drawing on Hallam's breath, and also that Tennyson might ('o that 'twere possible') impart to the dead Hallam some of Tennyson's own life-breath, failing though it now seems to be. Indeed, these last two examples call to mind one of the poem's persistent and most fundamental motifs—that Hallam and Tennyson are 'incorporate' (see section II, l.16). The latter is a poetical term of some importance in Tennyson's poem, and another example of a Tennysonian pun: that is to say, it is a word which suggests almost diametric opposites—both incorporeality, on the one hand, and physical embodiment on the other. Tennyson manages to suggest through this word that he and his dead friend become at once two in one flesh as well as two in one spirit.[6]

In such verse the reader finds himself encouraged to read in many different ways, for many different meanings. 'Every reader must find his own interpretation according to his ability'; which is also to say that the poetry believes itself able to anticipate those multifarious readings and readers, believes itself ready to accommodate not so much all *levels* of reading as all the interests and ideologies of its readers.

Many of Tennyson's critics, and not least of all his recent critics, have devoted their attention to the study of these symbolic effects, and to the thematized forms which Tennyson's symbolic style was developed to support. Pattison's book on Tennyson's employment of the idyl is a good case in point. The strengths of this book rest in its accurate presentation of the tradition of the idyl, on the one hand, and in its careful descriptions of Tennyson's special idyllic employments on the other. The book's weakness lies in its uncritical methods of examination. Pattison's reading of *In Memoriam* thematizes the work as a poem of evolutionary syntheses, and his discussion of *The Idylls of the King* as a poem of 'process' follows similar lines. Form and style in both poems combine into a vision of 'a new, unified relation expressing the advance of civilization' (p. 151). This presentation is of course accurate enough, so far as it goes, but it does not go nearly far enough. Pattison's entire book offers these ideas not merely as Tennyson's ideology, but as the triumph of Tennyson's poetic discourse—ideas which we are expected to honour as if they offered us some elemental and unambiguous truth, some final solution (as it were) of the conflicts and contradictions which the poetry brings into focus.[7]

---

6 See Pattison, 169 n. 29 where this characteristic of Tennyson's verse style is nicely touched on.

7 The lack of a particularized historical sense weaken Pattison's book even at some of its best moments—e.g. in his excellent discussions of the tradition of idyl (see especially pp. 18-22, 29). Pattison discusses the idyl form in its various actual manifestations as if the form contained, in itself, certain poetic qualities and powers; and furthermore, as if the characteristics of these qualities and poems were uniform in all their historic incarnations.

This is not the way to approach the statements and themes of a poetical work. Like matters of referential fact, ideas operate in a poetical discourse as historically specific elements of the artistic event. The 'theme' of 'universal process' in Tennyson's poetry (see Pattison, pp. 135-6) is not a transcendental category or idea, it is a specifically Victorianized form of thought which operates in Tennyson's work in a specifically Victorian way (it is quite different from a Romantic concept of 'universal process', which is its most immediate source). More particularly, ideas enter a poetical medium as interpreted and polemicized ideas, as ideas which carry with them, into the poetry, various specific kinds of emotional attitudes and social valuations. This characteristic of the statement-level of all poetical works is crucial to bear in mind, for two reasons. In the first place, it is the source and ground of all the 'ambiguities' and 'contradictions' which poems are known to generate and promote. In the second place, it locates the gulf which eventually separates the author from the reader, which allows the reader to enter the poet's world *from a distance*, at a point of difference which encourages both sympathy and judgement.

Of course Tennyson's poetry explicitly sets out to short-circuit such differentials, to produce a poetry which builds a grammar of assent in order to solicit various agreements. His work is, in this respect, quite unlike (for example) the work of Blake, or Byron. The latter was, by his own admission and will, 'born for opposition', and his poetry was deliberately fashioned as a sign of contradiction. Blake's goals were somewhat different, but finally analogous. In *The Marriage of Heaven and Hell* Blake allied himself with the Jesus who came not to bring peace, but a sword (plate 17), and he explicitly wrote under the motto: 'Opposition is true Friendship' (plate 20). Or, as he observed of those two 'classes of men' the Prolific and the Devourer: 'These two classes of men are always upon earth, & they should be enemies: whoever seeks to reconcile them seeks to destroy existence.'

Needless to say, these are not Tennysonian ideas and attitudes. Where Blake and Byron seek to promote contradiction and conflict, Tennyson will always be aiming for reconciliations and syntheses. Nevertheless, because human experience in its historical passage is at all points marked by struggles, by blindness and self-deception, by contradictions—as well as by the continual effort to deal with these matters, to overcome whatever adversative forces one meets with; because this is so, and because poetry's subject is human experience in time, poetry inevitably reproduces the conflicts and contradictions which it is itself seeking to deal with, and even perhaps seeking to resolve. Tennyson's syntheses and resolutions are part of his subject-matter, part of his Victorian materials; they are not the 'answers' to the questions raised in his poetry, they are themselves a part of the problem, for this reason: that they bring into sharpest relief the conflicts and contradictions which the poetry has dared to call forth. At the heart of Tennyson's creative work lie a quest and polemic for a certain ideology whose subject is society and whose forms of thought are aristocratic, evolutionist, and synthetic. But precisely because this *is* an ideology, it remains subject to those (self-generated and unapparent) limitations which bring into focus the social and psychological conflicts which the poetry struggles with, and is itself a part of.

The ideological elements which operate in poems are not, however, an *aesthetic* problem for the works. Ideology functions in poetry not as generalized idea, abstract thought, reified concept, but as a specific and historically concrete manifestation of such things. Poetry, like art products generally, can only exist in a medium of uniqueness. Its value lies in the sharp edge of its particularity, in its ability to evoke the sense of a complete human world by focusing upon some salient and specific matters of time, place, and circumstance. Like the particular referential elements in poems—the so-called 'historical facts' which critics and editors will gloss for later readers—ideology in poems is a matrix of historical particularities: in this case, the particularities of belief and commitment, ideas written in a grammar of needs, feelings, and attitudes.

Ideology is not an aesthetic problem for poems, it is a critical problem. The fundamental uniqueness of a poetical work is threatened not by its own ideological commitments but by the ideological structures of literary criticism—and most particularly by the ahistorical structures of interpretation which have dominated criticism for the past fifty years. The threat arises because literary works are *parole* rather than *langue* structures. In contrast to art or music criticism, then, the critical medium which studies literary works employs (ideological) forms which are structurally congruent with the forms of literary works themselves. This structural congruence frequently betrays criticism into that characteristic pitfall of interpretive methods: the mirroring of the object of interest, the representation of the work of art. As a consequence, the unique and particular work comes to us in a more generalized form of thought, and we are often seduced into taking the reflection of the work for the thing itself. This is the process by which contemporary culture subjects literary works to an ideological consumption. Poems are made to speak what the consciousness industries of the moment desire them to say. And one of the things such industries (principally, the academic industry) most wants to find in the poetry of the past, in the Great Tradition of art which we inherit, is a Truth (or Truths) that may set one free (that has set one free, and that may be counted on to set one free again and again).

An authentic criticism must vigorously oppose these spurious forms which criticism itself sometimes assumes. The case of Tennyson is merely symptomatic—and an opportunity. The study of Tennyson's poetry must begin and conclude in a field of historical particulars. To do so requires, of course, that we be able to elucidate the specific socio-historical contexts of the originary works themselves. However, because those works are at all points mediated in time by a series of readers and audiences, we cannot make contact with the originary works except through the social mediations and mediators which have handed them over to us. Consequently, before I turn to a specific Tennysonian text, I want to fill out the reception history which stands behind his work, and which has so powerfully affected contemporary critical attitudes.

II

The first two reviews of Tennyson's poetry[8]—W.J. Fox's in the *Westminster*, and Arthur Henry Hallam's in *The Englishman's*

---

[8] For convenience of reference, the following discussion of the reception history of Tennyson's poetry will cite only texts which can be found in J.D. Jump's excellent *Tennyson. The Critical Heritage* London, 1967. The reader will also want to consult Edgar F. Shannon's standard, and indispensable, *Tennyson and the Reviewers,* Cambridge, Mass., 1952.

Magazine—are remarkable in several ways. Both are brilliant assessments, and both introduced Tennyson to the reading public in highly laudatory terms. In addition, although Fox and Hallam had only Tennyson's early volume *Poems, Chiefly Lyrical* (1830), to comment upon, their views can now be seen, from our privileged historical vantage, to have set the terms for the entire subsequent history of Tennyson criticism and interpretation.

Fox, a Radical and a Utilitarian, opened his review with a lengthy excursus on the moral and philosophical powers of poetry. 'Why is Shakespeare the greatest of poets?' Fox rhetorically asked. His answer was not long in coming, nor any surprise: 'Because he was the greatest of philosophers . . . Extent of observation, accuracy of thought, and depth of reflection, were the qualities which won the prize of sovereignty for his imagination.' And as for Tennyson's verse? 'Here is a little book . . . which shall beautifully illustrate our speculations, and convincingly prove their soundness.' Fox speaks for a whole tradition of Tennyson readers that extends from his early admirers among the Cambridge Apostles to several later generations of (predominantly) Victorian readers, including that dear and honoured Lady, Queen Victoria herself. In our own day this tradition has suffered an eclipse, though it preserves its authority in a variety of quarters which include such notable commentators as G. M. Young, Jerome Buckley, and A. J. Carr.

Hallam, a Cambridge Apostle himself, was a most reflective and philosophical young man with all the moral earnestness one could hope to find, even in a Victorian. His notice of Tennyson's early poems also opens with a long excursus on the general grounds of his criticism; but, unlike Fox, Hallam argues for a sensational and aesthetic view of art. 'It is not true', Hallam says, 'that the highest species of poetry is the reflective: it is a gross fallacy, that, because certain opinions are acute or profound, the expression of them by the imagination must be eminently beautiful. Whenever the mind of the artist suffers itself to be occupied, during its periods of creation, by any other predominant notice than the desire of beauty, the result is false in art.' His position is largely an extreme statement of views developed by Coleridge and extrapolated by the chief ideologues among the Apostles. Coleridge never separated the two traditional functions of poetry—to please and to instruct—so radically as Hallam did. In fact, the sharpness with which Hallam drew this division reflects the accuracy and importance of his criticism of Tennyson's poetry, which displaces its truth content and referential connections—especially in the early work—to a marked degree.

Hallam's views would eventually gain an all but complete academic ascendancy in the melancholy long withdrawing roar of the Victorian Period. To the degree that Tennyson's poetry is taken seriously today, it is read almost exclusively against the grain of what we take to be Tennyson's Victorian Frame of Mind. Harold Nicholson initiated this movement when he distinguished between the 'remarkable depth and originality of his poetical temperament and the shallowness and timidity of his practical intelligence'. Nicholson established the line that there are two Tennysons, and that only one of them is worth reading. The bard of Farringford and Aldworth—Tennyson Laureate, the Victorian Sage—was quietly stored away in the archives of Literary History so that the true poet could be permitted to emerge. No fact so dramatically illustrates this situation as the current status of a poem like 'The Charge of the Light Brigade'. Once a set-piece example of Tennyson's greatness—required reading and always anthologized—this great poem cannot be found in any of our currently standard collections of Victorian Poetry.

An additional fact about the history of Tennyson's critical reception needs to be emphasized. Along with the predominant distinction between Tennyson as sage and Tennyson as *symboliste* runs a related pattern of praise and critique. Today we generally value the symbolist Tennyson and denigrate the sage, and these two valuations tend to operate dialectically. In Tennyson's day, however, the approach was different. Fox and Hallam both praised Tennyson's early verse, though their critical grounds for doing so seem to us poles apart. Indeed, the history of Tennyson's Victorian reception shows very clearly that these same critical grounds were both employed to attack Tennyson's work. An extensive critical line, beginning with John Wilson's early assault upon Tennyson, denounced Tennyson's artificiality, aestheticism, and obscurity. This line included some of Tennyson's admirers as well, most notably R.C. Trench, who urged Tennyson to abandon the line which

Hallam was promoting. 'Tennyson,' he said, 'we cannot live in art.'[9]

Similarly, the grounds of Fox's praise were also the basis for the sharpest kinds of critique. Gladstone's and Goldwin Smith's famous remarks on *Maud* epitomize a line of Victorian criticism which attacked Tennyson's ideas and social attitudes. We know this line best through the banter of people like Swinburne, whose grounds of complaint were aesthetic. People like Gladstone and Smith, however, launched their criticisms from moral positions. Tennyson's poems seemed uninteresting or worse because of their social attitudes and intellectual positions, Lest we think that such an approach has fallen into disuse, we have merely to recall the recent critical history of *The Princess* and *Maud*.

The purpose of this brief survey of the history of Tennyson's reception is to provide us today with the basis for a critical perspective on our own views. Critics spend a great deal of time— properly so—trying to arrive at critical assessments of the works they inherit, but they sometimes neglect to place their own views under the microscope. Until Harold Nicholson's epochal work, critics generally argued about the relative merits of Tennyson as sage and Tennyson as symbolist. Since that time, however, Tennyson's ideas and social attitudes have not seemed especially interesting to the critics, and least of all to those who admire his work and are seeking to re-establish Tennyson's high reputation. Lionel Madden is the spokesman of our moment when he says: 'The modern reader who recognizes Tennyson's need to express social ideas may nevertheless feel considerable difficulty in accepting much of the official verse. Certainly many of the occasional poems are limited in significance by the specific nature of their themes.'[10] This is merely Hallam's position in a new key. As such, it seems to me a limited view of Tennyson's artistic significance—and all the more limited because it is a position that dominates the approach to Tennyson in a way that Hallam's view, in his period, never dominated the critical discussion.

[9] But see the discussion in A. Dwight Culler's *The Poetry of Tennyson*, New Haven, Conn., 1977, pp. 64-9.

[10] Lionel Madden, 'Tennyson. A Reader's Guide', in *Writers and Their Background. Tennyson*, ed. D.J. Palmer, Athens, Ohio, 1973, p. 18.

If it is true that the modern reader can accept Tennyson's 'need to express social ideas', then I would argue that this modern reader is obliged to deal with those social ideas in the critical analysis of Tennyson's works. The fact that we today may have 'considerable difficulty in accepting' many of Tennyson's works because we are uninterested in or hostile to the ideas they express seems to me as much a judgement upon our own ideas and their limitations as it is upon Tennyson's. More than this, I think such a view betrays a fundamental misconception of the function of ideas and ideology in poetical works.

I want to illustrate what I mean by looking closely at 'The Charge of the Light Brigade', one of those occasional poems which are thought to be 'limited in significance by the specific nature of their themes'. Madden's view on this matter, we should recall, is a commonplace of our received notions about the 'mode of existence of a literary work of art'. That is to say, most readers today would take it for granted that a poem like 'Tears, Idle Tears' is much less 'limited in significance' than a poem like 'The Charge of the Light Brigade'. This assumption operates in criticism because the latter work seems to be 'limited' by virtue of the explicit and specific character of its historical points of reference. 'Tears, Idle Tears', on the other hand, appears an altogether more 'universal' work because it takes up topics of so-called general human interest, because it does not display any explicitly 'occasional' elements.

I would argue, on the contrary, that such views about the nature of poetical works thoroughly mistake the relation between a poetical work and its historical contexts (whether its original context or its subsequent ones). This is not the occasion to take up such general issues of literary theory. Nevertheless, what I wish to say here about Tennyson's poetry is based upon certain general ideas on the relation between poetry and history, so that a few remarks on this broader subject are in order.

I take it that poems, like art products in general, can only operate in a medium of uniqueness. Their value is always a function of the sharp edge of their particularity. Because poems represent various sorts of human ideas, events, and attitudes, the character of their uniqueness is always socially and historically embedded. Consequently, if we are to appreciate or study, say, the religious verse of Christina Rossetti, we must find a way—either intuitively or with the self-consciousness of criticism—to grasp the unique religious character of Rossetti's poetry. Her Christian themes, and even her verse forms, are much in debt to the work of Herbert in particular, and they locate themselves within a recognizable and well-known tradition of religious verse. The business of literary criticism, however, is precisely to resist the impulse toward a general Christian (or even Anglican) thematics for her poetry, which is part of the context of her work, and to seek to formulate what *distinguishes* her work, what sets it apart from (say) Herbert's and within (say) the tradition of Anglican poetry. To perform these critical operations we must, I believe, find ways for defining the special historical and social terms within which her poetry emerged, and from which it drew its unique characteristics.

The same may be said of Tennyson's poetry (or of any poet's). In his famous essay on 'Tears, Idle Tears', Cleanth Brooks located the poem's strength in the fact that its tears are 'occasioned by no immediate grief [but] spring from a deeper, more universal cause'.[11] This is an interesting critical remark, for several reasons. Most noticeable is Brooks's idea that universal causes for grief are somehow deeper and more telling than merely occasional ones: in literal fact, that a cause of grief which springs from the region of ideas is deeper and more important than one that springs from a simple matter of fact (say, the death of one we love). I shall pass without comment why Brooks may have held such an idea and turn instead to Tennyson. For 'Tears, Idle Tears' does in fact express a consciousness which suffers under an existential malaise, which experiences an ideological grief rather than a concrete or 'occasional' one. This fact about the poem's subject is extremely important, for it gestures toward those qualities of the poem which specify and define its characteristics. 'Tears, Idle Tears' is not the good poem that it is because its grief springs from deeper and more universal causes rather than from more immediate and occasional ones. This is what Brooks believes about the poem because this is what Brooks seems to believe about human life in general: that there are universal causes and factors and that these are deeper and more important than

11 Cleanth Brooks, *The Well-Wrought Urn*, New York, 1947, pp. 153-4.

immediate and concrete ones. This thought is Brooks's thought. It is one with which I do not happen to sympathize very readily. But that is beside the point for the moment. What is not beside the point is this: that it is an idea which Tennyson himself finds troubling, an idea with which he can sympathize but not one which he wants to feel, least of all indulge. His poem shows that he has such an idea—'Tears from the depth of some divine despair'— but it also shows his perplexity at this 'strange' feeling: 'Tears, *idle* tears' he calls them.

Tennyson's poem, then, expresses an existential malaise all right, but it does not present that malaise as a 'deeper and more universal' phenomenon of the heart. Rather, the poem's presentation emphasizes something else altogether, emphasizes the *peculiar* character of Tennyson's feeling. In fact the grief expressed in this poem is moving and human in its special Tennysonian, in its peculiar mid-Victorian qualities and characteristics—just as Christina Rossetti's religious poetry draws its special character from the unique circumstances in which her faith had to live.

'Tears, Idle Tears' is not simply a poem which expresses an existential malaise. It is a poem which dramatizes, as it were, a person's discovery that he suffers from such a feeling. Further-more, it is a poem in which the feeling is consciously and meticu-lously detailed, but not as a drama in which Tennyson is seen to discover the meaning of the feeling. What he discovers is the strange relation in which feelings stand to experience: that they are mediated at all points by preformed concepts, interpreted images and memories, by ideology. This fact about the poem is what makes Leo Spitzer's critical analysis so much more telling than Brooks's.[12] For whereas the latter is able to describe fairly well the 'dramatic truth of the situation' which the poem evokes, Spitzer's account brings to the poem a degree of critical understanding which Brooks's does not. Spitzer examines the lyric in comparative relation to a number of similar works by Ovid, Quevedo, Hofmannsthal, and Hemingway, and his method has the virtue of being able to draw clear and concrete distinctions. Like Brooks, Spitzer confines his discussion to verbal stylistics; unlike Brooks, his analysis appeals to a method-

[12] Leo Spitzer, ''Tears, Idle 'Tears'' Again', reprinted in *Critical Essays on the Poetry of Tennyson*, ed. John Killham, New York, 1967, pp. 192-203.

ology which is based in an historical approach to cultural products. The appeal remains implicit, but it governs every aspect
of his paper.

One virtue of historical method in literary criticism lies in its
ability to set poems in contexts, and thereby to provide them
with an analytic structure that can reveal the unique features of
the poems themselves. Spitzer's approach to 'Tears, Idle Tears'
is one of several that might be taken. The fact that he does not
deal with the poem in terms of its immediate social context
means that his analysis does not attempt a self-conscious explanation of the meaning of this poem in and for mid-Victorian
England. The refusal to develop such an explanation—to set
forth a comprehensive social and ideological analysis of the
poem in terms of its originary context—is significant because
only that sort of analysis can provide a later reader—a reader in
late twentieth-century America, for example—with a critical
context for his (later) reading. To interpret 'Tears, Idle Tears',
to read it with sympathy and understanding, requires that we see
it as in itself it really is. We cannot have it on any terms, least
of all on our own terms, unless we understand the terms that
are and are not possible. We may have it on our own terms—we
may read the poem in terms of our own (implicit or explicit)
ideologies—only when we are clear about the differences that
separate us from the poem, and hence that permit us to sympathize with it.

In short, an historical method in criticism is always comparative and dialectical. To expose the mid-Victorian ideology
which informs every part of Tennyson's poem is to define critically the specific shape and special quality of its humanness.
The poem is moving and human *in its mid-Victorian* qualities.
Recognizing this fact about the poem's aesthetic mode of operation is important for later readers because it provides us with a
critical perspective upon our own ideologies. The peculiar
shape of our own forms of humanness are exposed in the light
of the past that appears before us through a poem like this.

Such an effect is especially salutary and dramatic when the
critic chooses to take up a poem like 'The Charge of the Light
Brigade'. We survey the reception history of this poem to find
that it has not merely fallen out of favour, as Byron's and Swinburne's works once fell out, but that it has come to seem mildly

ludicrous, slightly contemptible. Here is Tennyson at his most 'official' and most 'Victorian'—a period piece which even Tennyson's admirers are happy to have since it provides them with a contrast to those 'deeper, more universal' poems like 'Tears, Idle Tears'. In my view, however, the force of this poem derives from its resolute and human particularity. Its importance for criticism—for criticism at the present time in particular—lies, first, in the critical light which it throws upon 'deep' and 'universal' readings of poems like 'Tears, Idle Tears'; and, second, in the way it challenges the entire project of an ahistorical criticism, and implicitly exposes the ideological limitations and biases of such a critical method.

These limitations appear with special clarity in the recent commentary, such of it as exists, on 'The Charge of the Light Brigade'. The only reader who has anything good to say about the poem is Christopher Ricks, and he confines his remarks to stylistic matters. Like everyone else, Ricks goes out of his way to avoid discussing the poem's subject-matter—both the historical events and their ideological significance. The Crimean War, the famous charge at Balaclava, and Tennyson's own attitudes toward these matters are universally recognized by the critics, but only because they are universally regarded as embarrassments, both in themselves and to the poem.[13] My own view, however, is that such a critical stance has misunderstood the relation which exists between poems and their historical formats, and that the significance of 'The Charge of the Light Brigade', its achievement as a poem, can only appear now through a critical elucidation of the work's historical aspects.

The topical character of the poem is established by its first printing, which was in *The Examiner* (9 Dec. 1854) one week after Tennyson read of the events at Balaclava and wrote the poem. But the poem is not so much a commentary on the war and British foreign policy in the Crimea as it is a eulogy of the British character. As such, its specific location in time and place focuses the poem's choice of a certain ideological point of view, and that point of view in turn focuses the historical and

[13] See Christopher Ricks, *Tennyson*, New York, 1972, pp. 244-5. The best contextual discussion of the poem to date is in Michael C.C. Adams, 'Tennyson's Crimean War Poetry: A Cross-Cultural Approach', *Journal of the History of Ideas*, XL (July-Sept. 1979), pp. 4005-22.

human drama which the poem embodies and represents. Let us begin to elucidate that drama, to clear away the vaguenesses which have gathered about the poem and permit it to recover its aesthetic resources.

As we have seen, the poem was from the outset a 'popular' work—it took its origin in a newspaper report, and it first appeared in the popular press. Indeed, the poem in many respects is a distilled interpretation of the popular reaction to the charge as that reaction was expressed in the newspapers. *The Times* leader of 13 November 1854 carried the first reasonably complete report of the event, and it began as follows.

We now know the details of the attack on Balaclava . . . We have . . . in the despatches before us nearly the whole of the loss, which it would be vain to conceal is most lamentable, and all the more so because it seems to have arisen from some misunderstanding . . . The disaster . . . is not more, but it is not much less, than the annihilation of the Light Cavalry Brigade. . . . Even accident would have made it more tolerable. But it was a mere mistake—evidently a mistake, and perceived to be such.

The note of puzzlement in this passage will be picked up and repeated throughout the many press rehearsals of the events at Balaclava. The question put in *The Times* leader on the next day, 14 November, brings into clear focus the central concern expressed in the public reaction: 'What is the meaning of a spectacle so strange, so terrific, so disastrous, and yet so grand?' The press reports themselves were to work out their explanations, and these had a profound influence on Tennyson's poem, as we shall see. But the press influence reached Tennyson, first, in the request for an explanation, the demand for a meaning. 'The Charge of the Light Brigade' is in great measure a response to the question set out in *The Times*.

We may begin to elucidate Tennyson's answer by looking at the newspaper text of the poem, which was its first printing. *The Examiner* prints a version of lines 5-6 which contain an interesting variation on the received reading.[14] The latter has:

> 'Forward, the Light Brigade!
> Charge for the guns! he said:

[14] My texts of the poems here will be cited from *The Poems of Tennyson*, ed. Christopher Ricks, London, 1969.

In the first printing, however, these lines read:

> 'Forward, the Light Brigade!
> Take the guns,' Nolan said:

The Examiner's reference to Capt. Lewis Nolan is a concrete detail which would have focused contemporary audience response to the poem in a particular way. Nolan was not just another cavalry officer, but a highly respected and even celebrated figure, and a recognized authority on the management and tactics of cavalry units. In 1853 he published two books 'which created a sensation in military circles—*Cavalry, Its History And Tactics* and *Nolan's System for Training Cavalry Horses*.[15] That he took part in the charge of the Light Brigade, indeed, that he was killed in that charge, was of course common knowledge by the time of Tennyson's poem. Indeed, the detail is only there in the text because Nolan's career and his death *were* common knowledge.

In the reports which reached England immediately after the charge, Capt. Nolan's name was linked with the infamous 'blunder' which sent the brigade to its fate. Controversy boiled around the degree of his responsibility for the disaster, and he characteristically was made the focus of all the explanations. This happened because Nolan epitomized in the public mind 'a cavalry enthusiast, who had but lately published his opinion that cavalry could do everything in war', as *The Times* leader put it. Part of the explanation for the charge at Balaclava, then, lay in the rash enthusiasms of what *The Times* called 'a proud Dragoon officer'.

When Thoreau commented on the events at Balaclava from his alien American vantage, he took them to demonstrate 'what a perfect machine the soldier is', and in particular what a thoughtless and rather brutish character was the typical British recruit.[16] But Thoreau's view of the poem and its recorded events is based upon a gross misreading not only of the objective facts of the situation, but of the British response to those events. Once again we have to exercise our historical imaginations if we are to see the human drama of this poem as in itself it really is. As we do this, we must at all times remember that

---

[15] Cecil Woodham-Smith, *The Reason Why*, New York, 1943, p. 167.

[16] *H. D. Thoreau. Reform Papers*, ed. Wendell Glick, Princeton, 1973, p. 119.

the narrative I am reconstituting here is one that was common knowledge at the time.

Tennyson, like so many others in England, first read a full account of the charge in *The Times* leader of 13 November, and his poem in fact follows this narrative in a number of details, and even uses some of its exact phrasing. The famous lines 'What though the soldier knew/ Some one had blundered' rework a passage in the newspaper report which says that the cavalry officers 'knew well what they were about' when they made their charge, were fully aware that 'some hideous blunder' had occurred. Indeed, this is the passage which also supplied Tennyson with the phrase 'the valley of Death'. 'With nothing to lose but themselves, and no inducements out of their profession', the Light Brigade

risked on that day all the enjoyments that rank, wealth, good social position, and many fortunate circumstances can offer . . . Splendid as the event was on the Alma, yet that rugged ascent . . . was scarcely so glorious as the progress of the cavalry through and through that valley of death, with a murderous fire, not only in front, but on both sides, above, and even in the rear.

The last part of this passage clearly anticipates some of the most well-known lines in Tennyson's poem. Furthermore, the newspaper account draws attention to a crucial aspect of the poem which will not be found in it *literatim*, but which is none the less present and important: the social standing of the cavalry officers, and the image which the public at the time had of the light cavalry, and especially of the particular units which had been sent to the Crimea. The newspaper's reference to the battle of the Alma, only recently fought, highlights these matters in a way that would have been unmistakable to any contemporary of Tennyson's, but which is necessarily obscure to us now. We must clarify that obscurity.

The charge of the Light Brigade was carried out in three lines. The first was made up of the 13th Light Dragoons and the 17th Lancers; the second of the 11th Hussars; and the third of the 4th Light Dragoons and the principal body of 8th Hussars. This body of light cavalry was in all respects like the rest of the regiments sent to the Crimea; that is to say, they were all the most socially élite units in the British army, spit-and-polish, dashing, and notoriously affected groups which had never seen a battlefield. The units had not been in action since Waterloo, and when they were chosen for the Crimean campaign over the experienced field-tested troops from the Indian frontier, the decision caught the public notice and generated some controversy. Questions were raised whether these 'wasp-waisted, dandified army officers, whom the comic magazines loved to caricature, [would] prove to have any of the mettle of the Peninsular or Waterloo' combatants.[17] This question is implicit in the conclusion of *Maud* when the hero of Tennyson's poem declares: 'Let it flame or fade, and the war roll down like a wind,/ We have proved we have hearts in a cause, we are noble still' (iii. 54-5). 'The Charge of the Light Brigade' is Tennyson's attempt to show not merely that the English aristocracy has not lost its leadership qualities, but in what respect this historically threatened class still exercises its leadership.

This aspect of Tennyson's meaning emerges when we recall that the battle of the Alma was regarded by the English as a noble victory of the English infantry forces; and furthermore, that traditionally, and in the English mind as well, the infantry and the cavalry were distinguished along class lines; and finally, that the cavalry sent to the Crimea was a special object of public concern, and even at times contempt. The charge of the Light Brigade took place in the context of these facts and attitudes, and the popular explanation of the charge which finally emerged (in its first complete form in *The Times* leader on 14 November) took account of them—as Thoreau's remarks did (and perhaps could) not do.

The cavalry in our service is supposed to have always claimed a species of rank over the infantry. Its frequent attendance on the person of Royalty, its splendid uniforms, and the exemption from colonial service, have made it the favourite resort of the aristocracy, and infected it with the weakness of caste. This has long been so notorious as to be the subject of caricature, which would not have been understood had it not appealed to popular estimate. With these feelings on the two sides, it is no wonder if the cavalry have acted during this campaign with a dignity that rather interfered with their use, and if, on the other hand, the infantry thought the cavalry were saving

---

[17] Michael C.C. Adams, p. 419; and see as well Cecil Woodham-Smith's discussion of these and related matters, pp. 134-5.

themselves somewhat too carefully. We believe that this feeling arose much more from the want of a good understanding and a sort of jealousy between the services than from any particular facts; yet, so it is, that from one reason or another the cavalry did little at the Alma, where it was much wanted, and had no other opportunity of distinction during the campaign. We may presume that feelings of this sort would be rather aggravated by the hardships and dangers of the siege, in which, of course, the cavalry could do but little, and by the general want of occasion for its service. Such suspicions and insinuations, unfounded as we believe them to have been, would not be long in finding their way; nor is it likely that such sensitive, high-spirited men, as Lords CARDIGAN and LUCAN would be wholly proof against them. Nothing is more natural than that every feat of daring done by any other branch of the service would be felt as a new summons to do something worthy of the rank assumed by the cavalry. Let us suppose the Light Brigade in view of the enemy on the 25th with such feelings, and spectators of the victorious charge of the Heavy Brigade. Let us further imagine them receiving a written order, in terms that seemed to leave no discretion, to advance and recapture the guns in the hands of the enemy. Let the order be borne, interpreted, and enforced by a cavalry enthusiast, who had but lately published his opinion that cavalry could do everything in war, storm any battery, break any square, whether supported or not. Let the order be passed from officer to officer, each one more jealous of the other, and adding, possibly, personal feelings to a wounded *esprit de corps*. There you have in the proud Dragoon officer, in the stimulating example, in the grand occasion, the crowd of spectators, the absolute order, the enthusiastic messenger, and peremptory interpreter, too ample explanation of a noble but disastrous deed—a fatal display of courage which all must admire while they lament.

Tennyson's poem grounds itself in the feelings and attitudes which this passage has adopted. The six-hundred dead cavaliers are 'noble' still, not merely by virtue of their actual class position, but by reason of their deeds, and the spiritual 'nobility' which their deaths have shown. They have not merely equalled, at Balaclava, the victory achieved at Alma by 'the lower orders', they have surpassed them altogether, and regained their rightful place in society: not its political leaders, but its spiritual models.

Tennyson's poem sets out to make the same kind of statement. This is partly why it does not always attract a later middle-class audience, which may find it difficult to generate a sympathetic attitude toward a patently aristocratic poem. Originally the work was able to cross class lines because the event itself exerted a national impact, because in the context of a foreign war class differences and conflicts tended to dissolve in national sympathies. In such a context it would be well for all the social orders if the 'superior orders' were not in fact effete and socially ineffectual.

One of the principal technical means which secured this meaning for Tennyson—which in fact enabled his poem to cross class lines and speak to the nation at large—is hidden in the iconography of the poem. The images in 'The Charge of the Light Brigade' are drawn from the newspaper accounts of the day, but the form of those images is based upon an iconography of heroism which Tennyson appropriated. His sources are French, bourgeois, and painterly, and his use of them in his English, aristocratic, and verbal work represents another struggle with foreigners which the entire English nation could sympathize with. In this struggle Tennyson means to settle an old score with the French, and to complete, as it were, Wellington's victory at Waterloo: to complete it at the level of ideology.

The key fact about the charge, for Tennyson, is that it took place despite the fact that the cavalry officers understood a blunder had been made somewhere, that the charge was, from the point of view of military tactics, a terrible mistake. The inexorable rhythm of Tennyson's poem:

> Half a league, half a league,
> Half a league onward,

perfectly mirrors the cavalry's implacable movement, and both of these correspondent motions reveal the human elements in the situation that Tennyson wishes to emphasize: the men's steadiness of purpose, as well as their entire understanding of what is involved in their action. 'They went with their eyes open', *The Times* reported, 'as if under a spell'.

> Cannon to right of them,
> Cannon to left of them,
> Cannon in front of them
>   Volleyed and thundered;
> Stormed at with shot and shell,
> Boldly they rode and well.

The reports which came back to England from the battlefield repeatedly emphasized the orderliness of the charge, its steadiness and fearfully determined resolution: 'in perfect order', said *The Times*, 'to certain destruction'. The English cavalry was generally acknowledged to be manned by the best horsemen in Europe, though it was also widely recognized as a cavalry which had not achieved the successes commensurate with its equestrian talent. Balaclava came to seem what *The Times* called the 'glorious doom' of the Light Brigade, their mission and their fate.

They went as fanatics seek the death that is to save them, and as heroes have sought death in the thick of the fight, when they could no longer hope to conquer . . . There was organization and discipline; there was even experience and military skill, at least enough to enable the chiefs to know the terrible nature of the deed . . . this was not war, as the French General said; it was a spectacle, and one worthy of the 'cloud of witnesses' that encompassed the performers. (*The Times*, 14 Nov.)

All these attitudes were to be gathered up into Tennyson's poem, where the Light Brigade's suicide mission becomes, paradoxically, its crowning glory.

> When can their glory fade?
> O the wild charge they made!
> All the world wondered.

These lines refer specifically to the newspapers' widespread reports of the astonishment which the charge produced in those who observed it—in particular, in the allied French soldiers. The words of the *Morning Chronicle* typify the accounts in all the newspapers. 'French officers, who saw with dismay the madness of the act and the certainty of destruction, express themselves amazed by the invincible spirit of our men.' The remark of the French general Bosquet was reported everywhere and perfectly captures Tennyson's own understanding of the event: '*C'est magnifique, mais ce n'est pas la guerre.*'

But Tennyson's poem gives an altogether new meaning to Bosquet's famous remark. Tennyson insisted that he was not a person who favoured or delighted in war, and of course later ages have had little difficulty seeing through his ideological confusions on this matter. If we shift the overtones of Bosquet's observation just a little I think we may see past the evident confusions of Tennyson's mind to its (perhaps) not so evident clarities. For 'The Charge of the Light Brigade' describes a cruel and stupid military event as if it were a spiritual, even an aesthetic, triumph. *But of course* this isn't war, it is magnificence, it is glory. The poem's images present the cavaliers as if they were cast in a tableau, or in a heroic painting—and in one case at least, as if they were statues. The Light Brigade comes before us in Tennyson's poem as an aesthetic object, as we see very clearly in the fourth stanza, where the riders are made to assume the classic pose of the equestrian hero in action. Such a figure lived in the nineteenth-century's eye in a whole array of paintings and statues, some great (e.g., in the work of David, Gros, Géricault, and Delacroix), some merely ordinary (e.g., in the statuary familiar throughout the cities of Europe).

> Flashed all their sabres bare
> Flashed as they turned in air.

The fact that the military gestures in 'The Charge of the Light Brigade' are modelled upon a certain tradition of heroic military art is extremely important to see. For that artistic tradition is almost entirely French and it emerges out of the Romantic styles which were connected with Napoleon, the First Empire, and the exploits of the *Grande Armée*. One has merely to compare, say, David's famous portrait of Napoleon with any of the portraits of Wellington, or even of Nelson, in order to perceive the gulf which separates their ideological points of view. Like Gros's portrait of Murat at the Battle of Aboukir, or Géricault's famous picture of the *chasseur* of the Imperial Guard, David's picture is charged throughout with various signs of Romantic motion, force, and energy. English painting of the same period never triumphed in this style. Consequently, in the immediately subsequent history the French *chasseurs* of the Napoleonic wars became heroic models throughout European art and culture, whereas the English cavaliers are either models of equestrian decorum, or objects of broad ridicule—in the last instance, mere aristocratic dandies. Besides, the fact that the heroic French *chasseur* did not come from the well-born and élite classes of society was an important element in his ideological significance. In this respect he came to stand for the human meaning of the historical events which tore Europe apart at the end of the eighteenth century. Napoleon's world-historical import was epitomized in the figure of the French *chasseur*, whose exploits in battle over-shadowed and surpassed in glory the military acts of Europe's congregated élite forces:

Wellington had won the battle of Waterloo, but England had lost to France the ideological struggle which followed. Indeed, the ancestors of Tennyson's Light Brigade had been present at Waterloo, but their presence was hardly noted and not decis-ive. Out of the defeat of Napoleon's grand army, artists like Gros and Géricault snatched a brilliant aesthetic triumph. Tennyson's poem deliberately, if perhaps only half-consciously, enters into this complex historical network in order, as it were, to gain for the English cavalry the emblems of the heroism they deserved, but had never had. Thus it is opportune that it should have been the French who stood by at Balaclava to comment upon the English cavalry's charge. 'All the world won-dered' at this charge, but that worldwide wonder was appro-priately registered in a French accent. More than anyone else they would have understood the meaning of the charge for it was carried out in a famous French manner: the measured, deliberate pace of the Light Brigade's advance had been the won-der of Europe since the grand army invented and defined it.

Tennyson's poem, then, represents an effort to appropriate for an English consciousness those images of heroism which had been defined in another, antithetical culture. The poem conceals an act of revisionist historical criticism, an 'English-ing', as it were, of certain French possessions. This revisionist act emphasizes the predominant motive of the entire poem, however, which is to institute through the art of poetry a change of meaning analogous to the one which Gros and Géricault instituted earlier through their painting. The world's wonder at Waterloo had been focused on Napoleon and his armies, despite the fact that England and Wellington had won the military encounter. But the Light Brigade's act at Bala-clava offered to Tennyson the chance to change the outcome of England's spiritual and ideological defeat.

Tennyson's method, therefore, is grounded in a set of para-doxes, the most fundamental of which is that his model should

have been French and Romantic rather than English and Victorian. Out of this basic paradox Tennyson constructs a series
of new and changed views on certain matters of real cultural
importance. Most clearly he wants to show that the charge was
not a military disaster but a spiritual triumph, and that the
men of the English cavalry are not dandified and enervated
aristocrats—that they are not merely 'noble still', they are the
deathless spiritual leaders of their country. These changes of
meaning are epitomized in the poem's most notable linguistic
transformation, whereby Tennyson manages to suggest that
the name of the 'Light Brigade' bears a meaning which transcends its technical military significance. The pun on the word
'Light' points to the quasi-religious identity and mission of this
small brigade of cavalry. Indeed, in that pun we observe
Tennyson moving his poem out of its secular and non-verbal
French models into a Victorian set of attitudes which are
peculiarly his own.

III

This historical reading of Tennyson's poem is an attempt to
restore it to our consciousness in something that approximates
to its own original terms. The purpose of such a reading, however, is not to make us sympathize with the poem on its own
terms—to submit to the poem's peculiar mid-Victorian ideological attitudes. On the contrary, the aim of the analysis is to
make us aware of the ideological gulf which separates us from
the human world evoked through Tennyson's poem. 'The
Charge of the Light Brigade' embodies certain specific ideological formations, and it attaches these attitudes and feelings
to certain specific events. Everything about this poem—everything about every poem that has ever been written—is time-
and place-specific. This we sometimes forget. But we also tend
to forget, when considering the employment of an historical
criticism, that every reader of every poem is equally time- and
place-specific. The function of an historical criticism, properly
executed and understood, is to clarify the historical particularities of the entire aesthetic event, whether observed from the
vantage of the original work, on the one hand, or of the later
reader(s) of that work on the other. A collision of ideologies and

consciousness will necessarily take place when such a criticism is set in motion.

Out of that conflict—which *is* one way of undergoing the aesthetic experience—emerges the sort of light and understanding which poetry was meant to bring: what I would have to call critical sympathy. In the case of 'The Charge of the Light Brigade', we re-experience the original Victorian response to that most pitiful of all events: a blundered tragic action. Some of Tennyson's contemporaries, and a large part of Tennyson himself, saw the charge at Balaclava as a kind of heroic tragedy—in the words of one correspondent, '*a grand national sacrifice*'. But another part of the population, and another part of Tennyson, understood that it was only a *kind* of heroic tragedy, and that its blundered and failed aspects gave it a different quality altogether. For in the end the poem rests in an evident, a simple, yet a profound contradiction which is the basis of all its related sets of contradictions. The Light Brigade achieved, in its famous assault, an immortality, a final spiritual triumph. In the event it suffered as well, in the words of *The Times*, a human 'catastrophe', an 'annihilation'. This triumph is also 'The disaster . . . of which the mere shadow has darkened so many a household among us.' Tennyson's poetry is in the pity even as it is also in the glory.

The poem, in other words, embodies an original set of contradictions which can be of use to us as its inheritors, as its subsequent readers. For we too, like Tennyson and his contemporaries, intersect with our own age and experience—including our experience with this poem—in certain specific and ideologically determined ways. 'The Charge of the Light Brigade' is important for us precisely because of the differential which it necessarily represents. Indeed, I should even venture to say that its importance as a cultural resource, for us today, will be a function of our immediate lack of interest in it or hostility toward it. Time and human experience—which are the measures of all future experience—have sanctioned the achievement of this work. Whatever immediate or practical usefulness it may have rests with us, and particularly with those of us (or that part of ourselves) who feel most alienated from the (piteous, not tragic) human experience enacted in this poem.

Thirty-five years ago a book was published which has since

been seen to have defined the subsequent period of academic criticism in its attitude toward art objects (as verbal constructions, or 'texts'), as well as in its attitude toward the criticism of art objects (anti-historical). The position taken by Cleanth Brooks in *The Well-Wrought Urn* is epitomized in the following passage.

I insist that to treat . . . poems . . . primarily as poems is a proper emphasis, and very much worth doing. For we have gone to school to the anthropologists and the cultural historians assiduously, and we have learned their lesson almost too well. We have learned it so well that the danger now, it seems to me, is not that we will forget the differences between poems of different historical periods, but that we will forget those qualities which they have in common.[18]

This is a farewell salute to the nineteenth-century tradition of philological studies and a manifesto of a new anti-historical criticism. Its limitations as a critical method are now, two generations later, quite clear to everyone who reflects upon these matters. Brooks's words, once the veritable epigraph of a new tradition of academic readers, now appear as its inevitable epitaph. For the danger which Brooks then saw is now less apparent, whereas the one he dismissed—'that we will forget the differences between poems of different historical periods,' as well as the aesthetic significance of those differences—is only too clear.

Being a part of history we must follow Brooks in time, and so we also mean to follow him in thought. 'We too may want to treat . . . poems . . . primarily as poems', but when we do so it will be in the light of another tradition of thought that we also must follow. For it is philology which shows us that to treat poems *as* poems means that we must encounter them in the full range of their concrete particularity. This entails that we must grasp them in their historical uniqueness. Like Ahab, every poem has its special humanities. It is the business of literary criticism to reveal the human histories of its subjects, a task which will—which must—include an acknowledgement of literary criticism's own historical limits. Both of these subjects together constitute the field in which literary criticism undertakes to read and study the works of the poets.

(1981-2)

18 Brooks, p. 197.

IV

Problems of Canon and Periodization: the Case of Christina Rossetti

1. Christina Rossetti's Poems:
a New Edition and a Revaluation

I

The first volume of Rebecca Crump's edition of *The Complete Poems of Christina Rossetti*[1] comes at an opportune moment. In the last fifteen years, we have seen a remarkable scholarly effort to recover our contacts with the lost generations of Victorian poets. Many of these efforts have been unsatisfactory, but the equivocal results can be traced directly to the critical heritage which still lies behind so much of Anglo-American criticism. Recent efforts to correct certain erroneous academic commonplaces about Victorian poetry are notable and praiseworthy, and they have had much to do with the publication—after many vicissitudes[2]—of the present edition.

This work is also opportune because of the present state of Rossetti criticism. The last good study of Rossetti's work was published in 1931 by Eleanor Thomas, and although recent scholars have produced some fine material, criticism continues to lag.[3] One would have thought that feminist critics would have scrutinized her work *on principle*, but so far this has not been the case.[4] Of course, Rossetti's special ideological positions

[1] Christina Rossetti, *The Complete Poems of Christina Rossetti*, ed. Rebecca Crump, Baton Rouge, 1979.

[2] The edition was refused by several university presses, not on the grounds of its quality—which was not called into question—but on the grounds of its subject. Christina Rossetti's poetry was not considered important enough to justify such a project.

[3] Eleanor Thomas, *Christina Georgina Rossetti*, New York, 1931.

[4] Since the completion of the present essay in 1979 a number of feminist readings of Rossetti have appeared. See e.g. Dolores Rosenblum, 'Christina Rossetti: The Inward Pose', in *Shakespeare's Sisters*, ed. Sandra Gilbert and Susan Gubar, Bloomington, 1979, pp. 82-98; Miriam Sagan, 'Christina Rossetti's "Goblin Market"', *The Pre-Raphaelite Review* iii (May 1980), pp. 66-76; Helena Michie, 'The Battle for Sisterhood', *The Journal of Pre-Raphaelite Studies* III (May 1983), pp. 38-55; and several essays by Diane D'Amico, including ' "To another land": An Analysis of C. Rossetti's "Moonshine"', *The Pre-Raphaelite Review* iii (Nov. 1979), pp. 54-62; 'Christina Rossetti's *Maude*: A Reconsideration', *U. of Dayton Review* xv (Spring 1981), pp. 129-42; 'Christina Rossetti: The Maturin Poems', *Victorian Poetry* xix (Summer 1981), pp. 117-37.

can easily put one out of sympathy with her, particularly when one compares her reactionary ideas on the Woman Question with those of, say, Elizabeth Barrett Browning. In this context, one is dismayed (though not surprised) to find so intelligent a person as Germaine Greer producing an essay on Rossetti which could scarcely have been more misguided in its psychoanalytic speculations.[5] Fortunately, the essay seems to have had little or no influence. Its existence and special approach, however, testify to the continuing power of that most treacherous of all 'schools' of Rossetti criticism: I mean, of course, the tradition which seeks to explain her work in relation to her putative 'lost love'. Lona Mosk Packer's speculative psychobiography carries this line of criticism to its self-destructive limits,[6] and although informed scholars recognize the worthlessness of Packer's critical imaginations, the book seems to have diverted scholarly attention from its main tasks.

II

In this general context, a new edition of Christina Rossetti's poetry has a salutary, restorative effect. This is particularly true of Crump's edition, which is a purely textual one. The preface and introduction offer concise descriptions of the context and plan of this edition, on the one hand, and the printing history of past editions, on the other. The edition contains as well a table of manuscript locations and two bibliographical appendices. All the notes are textual.

Crump plans a three-volume edition. The initial volume prints the contents of Rossetti's first three published works: *Goblin Market and Other Poems* (1862), *The Prince's Progress and Other Poems* (1866), and *Goblin Market, The Prince's Progress and Other Poems* (1875), the last an augmented edition of the first two books. The plan is to include her three other published works of poetry in volume two—that is, *Sing-Song* (1872), *A Pageant and Other Poems* (1881), and *Verses* (1893), 'as well as the poems with which she expanded these volumes after their initial publication' (p. xi). Volume three is to contain a miscel-

---

[5] Germaine Greer, Introduction to Christina Rossetti, *Goblin Market*, New York, 1975.

[6] Lona Mosk Packer, *Christina Rossetti*, Berkeley and Los Angeles, 1963.

laneous collection of (*a*) poems 'published individually but never included in one of her collections' (p. xii); (*b*) privately printed works, and in particular the early *Verses* (1847); and (*c*) 'poems that Christina did not publish' (p. xii). The general principle underlying this entire scheme is stated thus: 'This organization distinguishes the poems that Christina deemed suitable for publication from those which she chose to withhold from the public eye' (p. xii).

This new edition has several distinct virtues. First, the completed work will print *all* of Rossetti's poetry, which is principally to say that it will add to the standard collections several hundred unpublished poems. Second, as an announced 'variorum edition' (in the modern, vulgarized sense), the work presents a generous *apparatus criticus* in the textual notes. Third, the editing and proof-reading have been carried out with meticulous care. Finally, printing the poems in a volume-by-volume arrangement has certain obvious benefits. In effect, this plan puts at our disposal a complete set of Rossetti's works in their initially published forms.

Anyone who has studied Christina Rossetti knows the maddening frustration of working with the hitherto 'standard' collection of her poems edited by her brother William Michael Rossetti.[7] His edition is beset with problems, not the least of which is the carelessness and high-handed behaviour of the editor. He prints posthumously published works incompletely and incorrectly in numerous cases: lines and stanzas are dropped, punctuation is altered or mishandled, and titles are changed.[8] The more careful editorial habits of Crump, shown in her first volume, are a fair surety that her third volume, where the posthumous works are to be printed, will not carry these sorts of error.

William Michael Rossetti's edition is still extremely useful for the wealth of information in his notes and prefatory material. But his edition has no apparatus, and it provides little

[7] Christina Rossetti, *The Poetical Works of Christina Georgina Rossetti*, ed. William Michael Rossetti, London, 1904.

[8] The problems with William Michael Rossetti's edition are graphically analysed by Gwynneth Hatton in *An Edition of the Unpublished Poems of Christina Rossetti, with a Critical Introduction and Interpretative Notes to All the Posthumous Poems*, PhD dissertation, St. Hilda's College, Oxford, 1955. The introduction and notes are extremely useful, and, in fact, the thesis is probably the single most important piece of work done on Christina Rossetti between Thomas's book and Crump's edition.

data illustrating Rossetti's habits of composition and revision. He suggests that his sister did not rework her manuscript poems very much,[9] and while it is true that her manuscripts do not resemble Keats's or even Byron's, her habits of revision are extremely interesting. Crump's edition shows, for example, that Rossetti not infrequently established her final texts by cutting away the original openings and conclusions. The word-by-word changes are not especially remarkable, but these more severe prunings are unusual and very important. Whole stanzas and stanza sequences are lopped away from the poems' original beginnings and endings, and equally large passages are sometimes also removed from other parts of the poems. The lean and often enigmatic beauty and power of her work is certainly related to such revisionary practices.

In these respects, Crump's edition supplies what is missing from its predecessor. But her work supersedes William Michael Rossetti's in other ways as well. One of the most annoying faults of his collection lies in its arrangement of the poems under six headings (The Longer Poems; Juvenilia; Devotional Poems; General Poems; Poems for Children, and Minor Verse; and Italian Poems). Some of these categories are chronologically ordered; others are not, and there are various sub-categories. The result is that one has no sense of the structure of the original volumes, no clear view of chronological relationships, and no easy way to locate even very familiar poems.

Crump's edition is better planned, though I suspect it will be censured for not printing the poems in a strict chronological arrangement. Indeed, because her edition will be brought out in volumes to be issued separately over a number of years, a reader of this first volume cannot help feeling a certain disappointment. For many of the unpublished poems are early works, and, in fact, most of Rossetti's greatest verse was written before 1865.

Still, we will have, soon enough, the complete poems, and we can surely count on a clear and dependable text. In this alone, Crump is performing an enormous scholarly and cultural service. Nevertheless, Crump must still face the problem of a useful arrangement of the material that will appear in her third volume. I would, therefore, strongly urge the editor to print the poems in volume three in a strict chronological arrangement.

9 See William Michael Rossetti, pp. lxviii-lxix.

Such a procedure will supply readers with a means of relating these works to the poems published by Rossetti in book form. Failure to do this will, I think, merely perpetuate, in another form, the sort of textual situation which Rossetti's brother created in his edition. Crump would also do well to include at least two appendices in the final volume: a table of the contents of the 1847 *Verses* and, most important of all, a complete list of Rossetti's poems in chronological order. I assume that indices of titles and first lines will be provided.

The principal object of Rossetti studies at this time is to see that her works are put into print (complete editions of the letters and prose writings are imperative). Because a scrupulous textual edition of all the poems answers our most immediate needs, Crump's work is an important event. Nevertheless, the appearance of a good text calls attention to other critical needs. A widespread notion prevails (it runs parallel to the psychological speculations) that Rossetti's poetry is transparent to itself, that its power comes from its 'universal' themes and its simple, passionate forms. Rossetti was a great craftswoman, so that her work does often cultivate the manner (and hence the poetic illusion) of a clear, simple surface; but we must not think from this that her works can do without glosses and commentary. Indeed, an advanced criticism of her poetry might well begin with an intelligent set of notes elucidating those deceptively simple poetic surfaces. Readers of her work have to be supplied with a floral dictionary, for example, if they are to deal with one of her most elementary, and pervasive, symbolic structures. Similarly, nearly all of her poems contain important allusions to and quotations from *The Book of Common Prayer* and the Bible, not to mention the network of references to more recondite spiritual works like the *Imitatio Christi* (a book that enjoyed an enormous popularity in the period, for reasons which have never been explored). Finally, her own prose works—esecially *Maude, The Face of the Deep*, and *Time Flies*—contain manifest commentaries on some of her most important poems.[10] A reading edition of her poetry ought to put these passages in its notes just as it

---

[10] Crump has a good edition of *Maude*, with an introduction and notes, Hamden, Connecticut, 1976. *The Face of the Deep: A Devotional Commentary on the Apocalypse*, London, 1892, is quoted below and cited in the text as *Deep*. Quotations from Christina Rossetti's verse are taken from Crump's edition, where possible, and from William Michael Rossetti's otherwise.

ought to avail itself of the important material contained in the
notes of William Michael Rossetti's edition.

III

The strictly religious poetry aside (which I will return to later),
Christina Rossetti's work is dominated by a powerful mixture
of certain specific social themes, on the one hand, and a set of
characteristic symbolic modes, on the other. These themes,
announced in her earliest work during the 1840s (and well
before she met William Bell Scott),[11] focus on the psychological
tensions recognized by a single woman experiencing and studying human love under specific social circumstances. Her all but
obsessive studies of women in love have sanctioned, and helped
to perpetuate, the largely misguided biographical searches for
her own lost love. But what is important about Rossetti's work
will not be elucidated by searching for that hypothetical man-
she-loved-in-vain; rather, it will be revealed when we understand better the patterns of frustrated love as they appear in the
works and the social and historical formations which those patterns dramatize.

Indeed, Rossetti's understanding did not have to depend
upon a personal experience of the failure of love. Her sensibility
was larger than that, and she clearly recognized that the patterns
of such failure surrounded her everywhere, in art as well as in
life: in society at large, as the notorious life and death of Letitia
Elizabeth Landon (for example) revealed,[12] and near at hand,
in her early home life as well as in the later, disastrous love
experiences which centred on her brother Dante Gabriel. The
great value of Christina Rossetti's work—and in this she is like
no other woman writer of the period—lies in its pitiless sense that
the world is a scene of betrayal and that the betrayal appears
most clearly, and most terribly, in the relations between men
and women. Only Dante Gabriel Rossetti's vision of the world as
the hell of love produces a comparable body of work (A. C. Swinburne's is different and much more benevolent). In Christina

---

[11] Scott is, according to Packer, Rossetti's 'lost love'.

[12] That Christina Rossetti understood Landon's cultural significance is plain from
her poem 'L.E.L.' (Crump. p. 153), which was written in response to Elizabeth
Barrett Browning's earlier important poem on Landon.

Rossetti's case, the poetry seizes the advantage of its alienation—that it was written by a single women, a fact emphasized
by her work and never to be forgotten by the reader—and it
explores, more self-consciously than her brother had done (if
no more passionately), the root patterns of betrayal.

Before we look more closely at these thematic aspects of her
poetry, however, we have to examine, at least briefly, some of
Rossetti's typical stylistic procedures. Deeply read, and even
schooled, in Christian typology, Rossetti possessed a sophisticated symbolic method and apparatus which she used repeatedly
and self-consciously (see *The Face of the Deep*, for example, where
she has some important discussions of these symbolic modes of
expression).[13]

The central moral problem in a symbolically ordered world
involves distinguishing between what seems and what is. For an
artist, however, this moral problem can locate a set of expressive
powers since it offers the artist opportunities for constructing
multiple levels of statement. For a morally committed artist like
Rossetti, these multiple levels form part of a structure which
exercises and puts to the test the reader's powers of apprehension. Her poetic characters are themselves typically placed in
situations where they are asked to distinguish the real from the
illusory. This technique is so widespread that one need only
cite a few of her most famous works—'Sleep at Sea', 'The
Lowest Room', 'The Hour and the Ghost', or 'Memory'—to
see how fundamental the procedure is.

Let me give two examples of Rossetti's typical method. The
first poem was called 'Two Choices' by Christina Rossetti (it is
not in Crump's first volume, and William Michael Rossetti
retitled it 'Listening'):[14]

> She listened like a cushat dove
>   That listens to its mate alone:
> She listened like a cushat dove
>   That loves but only one.
>
> Not fair as men would reckon fair,
>   Nor noble as they count the line:

---

[13] *Deep*, pp. 195-6, 215, and 217-18. Hatton has an excellent discussion of this subject on pp. lxxxii-lxxxvii.

[14] The poem offers a good instance of Christina Rossetti's method of pruning her
original version; see Hatton, p. 233.

Only as graceful as a bough,
    And tendrils of the vine:
Only as noble as sweet Eve
    Your ancestress and mine.

And downcast were her dovelike eyes
And downcast was her tender cheek;
Her pulses fluttered like a dove
    To hear him speak.

The sinister quality of this poem depends upon several ambiguous elements which radiate into a general problematic pattern. The scene presents, schematically, the figures of a man and a woman to whom he is speaking, obviously of his love. The event shows the woman being drawn into a state of thrilling trepidation and innocent dependency. The sinister overtones emerge because of the ambiguous nature of the poetic comparisons. The association of the woman with Eve is pivotal, for with that reference one begins to question the figural value of the scene's apparent innocence. Yet the verbal surface does not urge an inversion of the poem's appearances; on the contrary, it sustains these appearances even as it suggests the melancholy ambiguousness of the emblem.[15] Precisely in that tension does the poem achieve its principal effects. The female figure listens to the man, and her posture offers the reader a procedural sign for reading the poem: we too listen and try to detect the meaning of the words we encounter. Is the man in the poem Adam to the woman's Eve or is he Satan, the serpent who, in traditional typology, is frequently represented as exercising a fatal fascination over the innocent dove?[16]

The poem gradually develops that sort of problematic question. The figure of the dove is associated with innocence, and the Holy Spirit takes the form of a dove; but the dove is also associated with the pagan Aphrodite and represents, in that figural love context, sensual beauty and pleasure. So we also come to wonder if the woman's eyes are 'downcast' in an emblematic pose of modesty or if they are 'cast down' as a sign

[15] For a good discussion of Christina Rossetti's characteristic treatment of the figure of Eve, see Hatton, p. 237.

[16] The woman in the poem has 'two choices', acceptance or refusal, but the poem presents a network of alternative choices which reflect and elaborate upon the elementary narrative choice.

of her unhappiness (or of her future betrayal?). In a similar way, we are brought to worry over the meaning of her fluttering pulses and what they tell us about this relationship.

Finally, one notices the pronoun 'your' in line 10. At first it seems to refer, simply, to the entire human race, whose mother Eve is. But the love context works a subtle shift in our attention as one begins to suspect that 'your' refers to women only. When that happens, the critical edge of the poem makes itself very plain, for such an idea insists upon the special insight and experience of a dependent group or class. Indeed, for the poem to address itself directly to women only, and hence to exclude men from its innermost levels of discourse, is to emphasize the alienation of women from men and their lack of true intercourse. An apparently benevolent love ideology is represented at the poem's level of immediate appearance—which is the level of stylistic 'dominance'—but the subversive insights of an estranged feminine experience reveal the deceptiveness of those appearances at more oblique levels. For people who do not normally question the 'truth' of the mischievous social structure and set of ideas represented at the dominant levels—and these may be women as well as men—the poem offers the opportunity of a new freedom via critical understanding. Christina Rossetti defines herself as an individual even as she speaks directly to others as individuals ('Your . . . and mine'), and the form of this address dramatizes a relationship radically different from what is represented in the poem's non-dialectical structures (and via the poem's focusing symbol of those non-dialectical structures).

Many of Rossetti's poems operate in this way: that is, they test and trouble the reader by manipulating sets of ambiguous symbols and linguistic structures. Here is another example, only in this case we are not dealing so much with ambiguous symbols as with a cunning play with language.

> I cannot tell you how it was;
> But this I know: it came to pass
> Upon a bright and breezy day
> When May was young; ah pleasant May!
> As yet the poppies were not born
> Between the blades of tender corn;
> The last eggs had not hatched as yet,

> Nor any bird foregone its mate.
> I cannot tell you what it was;
> But this I know: it did but pass.
> It passed away with sunny May,
> With all sweet things it passed away,
> And left me old, and cold, and grey.
>   ('May', Crump, p. 51)

Though much could be said about this fine poem, I want to concentrate on two of its elements only. First, the poem is clearly playing for variations upon the biblical phrase 'it came to pass', which is worked to mean both 'something happened' and 'something came only in order to go away again'. This something made its appearance in May, a time traditionally associated with the renewal of life and the coming of love, but the something belied its appearance and turned spring into a spiritual winter. What is most disturbing about these events is the suggestion of purposiveness applied to the actions of the unspecified something ('it').

All of this recapitulates the '*vanitas vanitatum*' theme so prevalent in Rossetti's poetry. But we observe that another ambiguous unit in the poem—the pronoun 'it'—pushes the work into a terrifying level of generality. As a pronoun, 'it' refers here both to May and to a wholly unidentified referent, something unknown and inexplicable both to speaker and reader. This mysterious referent has its invisible character reinforced by the poem's other employment of 'it': that is, as part of an expletive structure in which 'it' serves no pronominal function at all (as in 'it is raining today' or 'it seems all right to do that'). In grammars like these, 'it' stands for an entire conceptual field, but nothing in particular (not even a defined conceptual field itself), so that 'it' finally comes to stand as a sign of total conceptual and experiential possibility. From a Christian point of view, the poem thereby develops the meaning that the world is an illusion, a field of betrayal, an entire vanity; from a more secular point of view, it suggests that understanding the meaning of human events in such a world will always be impossible. Love comes and love goes, but from the point of view of the feminine speaker of this poem, love's movements are arbitrary and beyond her understanding. Her despair arises from the fact that she is purely a relative creature even in those human situations where she is most intimately and deeply involved.

As in all of Christina Rossetti's poetry, the subject-matter in these two works is social and psychological. The poems are also typical in that they deal with love and the idea of beauty from a peculiarly feminine perspective: both poems not only represent the relation of dependency of women to men, they associate that relation with deceptions, fears, and the inability to bring understanding and control into human affairs (for men and women alike). In the memorable words of Swinburne's Althaea: 'Love is one thing, an evil thing, and turns / Choice words and wisdom into fire and air./ And in the end shall no joy come, but grief.'

For Christina Rossetti, love appears as a serious problem when marriage reveals its problematical aspects. In *Maude*, for example, marriage is not entirely rejected, but it is represented as the least attractive possibility available to the women in this book (where only two men appear, and they only in a nominal way). The author makes perfectly clear, through the character of Mary and especially through Maude's sonnet 'Some ladies dress in muslin full and white', that marriage will seem unattractive to any woman (*a*) who has a sense of, and belief in, her own personal worth and integrity, and (*b*) who cares for something other than the things of this world, and especially its material comforts and luxuries. Well before Christina Rossetti became one of what Dora Greenwell was to call 'Our Single Women', this poet had a deeply personal view of her world and a profound sense of her own integrity. The spectacle of the Victorian marriage market appalled her. Wives, she says in 'A Triad' (Crump, p. 29), are 'fattened bees' who 'Grow gross in soulless love'. In the end, as we see so frequently in her works (for example, in 'The Iniquity of the Fathers Upon the Children' [Crump, p.164]), her heroines characteristically choose to stand alone, as Agnes does in *Maude*. Those who do not—those who choose either love and marriage or love and romance— almost invariably find either disaster or unhappiness or a relationship marked by a sinister and melancholy ambiguousness.

Thus, if one were to speculate on her biography and on her several 'missed opportunities' in love and marriage, one would probably be closer to the truth to say that Christina Rossetti remained a single woman because she felt deeply ambivalent about love relations with men. One would also, probably, be closer to the truth than Packer was if one agreed that this ambivalence was both natural, explicable, and—finally—justified, both historically and, in terms of her life and career, personally.

The figure which threatens the single woman most directly in Rossetti's work is the spinster, who—in the words of 'A Triad'—'famished died for love'. Her most important poem dealing with the fears of spinsterhood is the remarkable narrative 'The Lowest Room' (Crump, p. 200), but the motif recurs throughout her work. 'A Triad' also shows that if the married women is the spinster's opposite, her dialectical contrary is the fallen women, who 'shamed herself in love' by substituting sensual pleasure for frustration. In Rossetti's myth, these last two figures 'took death for love and won him after strife', but all three fail—'all short of life'—for two principal reasons: first, they are not self-conscious about the meaning of their choices, and second, none of them is truly 'single' since each one's personality only exists in a relation of dependency to something or someone else.

The figures of the spinster and the fallen woman appear throughout her poetry, often in those generic forms but more frequently in slightly altered guises. Both figures appear in various love relationships, sometimes as nuns whose beloved is Jesus (or who leave the world for the convent when they lose a mortal lover), and sometimes as the betrayed woman. Such figures appear most memorably in works like 'The Hour and the Ghost' (Crump, p. 40) as the women who are wailing for their demon lovers. In this mythological territory, the fallen woman is merely another transformational form of the true love or the beloved. This mutation occurs because, in such a (symbolistic) world, love is always appearing in unreal and delusive forms. Marriage is not equivalent to love, but then neither is a romantic relationship. A fierce tension emerges when these two alternatives both reveal their deplorable, threatening aspects, as they do in 'The Hour and the Ghost'. 'The Lowest Room' increases the tension by making two sisters the spokeswomen for each position, thereby forcing the women into a dismal and wrenching conflict with each other.

Rossetti's negation of romantic love appears throughout her early poetry, especially in the many works inspired by Charles

Robert Maturin and in various derivative Metastasian and Byronic scenarios. Among her most moving revelations of the daemonium of such 'love' are to be found in the poems dealing with her brother Dante Gabriel and his works. 'In an Artist's Studio' represents such a love ideology (along with its related structures of artistic expression) as a type of introverted vampirism. 'An Echo from Willow-Wood' goes on to interpret romantic love, along with her brother's great representation of its divine tragedy, *The House of Life*, as a Munch-like drama of inevitable loneliness and identity loss.

Men and women, their 'true loves', their marriages: Christina Rossetti examined these subjects in the life and art of her world and saw the piteous networks of destruction in which they were all, fatally as it were, involved. All of her work, in its secular as well as in its more directly religious forms, represents a protest against these ways of living. Her 'devotional' poems, as she called them, are an integral and important part of her protest and no merely belated form of sentimental piety: the *vanitas* and *contemptus mundi* themes are part of her resistance against her age's worldliness and luxury, along with its subtle forms of exploitation. All are weighed and found wanting. At first her impulse was to try to refuse to have anything to do with the world: thence emerge the 'thresholds' of conventual life and escapist Romanticism which appear so frequently in her work before 1860. But she would not follow either of those paths to the end, though she understood, and used, the critical power of each. Rather, she became, finally, one of nineteenth-century England's greatest 'Odd Women'.

Personal independence is, therefore, one of her central subjects, and it is memorably developed in a poem like 'Winter: My Secret' (Crump, p. 47). This work's effectiveness depends upon the particularity of its experience, that is, on the fact that it is so entirely the expression of a special point of view. And not merely a special point of view: the circumstance dramatized in the poem we necessarily locate in terms of a particular person, place, and period. The teasing and ironic banter is a transformed reflex of a certain type of 'feminine coyness' which social conventions developed and reinforced in women. Of course, the poem uses these conventional patterns of behaviour and usage only to subject them to an implicit critique, but the special character of this critique is that it is carried out in such a decorous and oblique fashion (contrast, for example, Byron's or even Arthur Hugh Clough's handling of similar materials). Rossetti's critique is launched from the vantage, as it were, of the poet's 'secret' place. The indirectness of this subtle poem is part of its strategy for preserving the integrity of its 'secret', and hence for maintaining the very possibility of integrity and truth in speech. Independence and integrity—of which this 'secret' is the symbol—can only be secured by a diplomatic resistance. As in the similar poem 'No, Thank You, John' (Crump, p. 50), the politeness of the refusal veils a differential severity which will not be compromised. In that reserve of purpose lies Rossetti's power, her secret, her very self.

Consequently, her work employs the symbol of the personal secret as a sign of the presence of individuality. Independence is a function of the ability to have a secret which the sanctioned forces of society cannot invade. Maude has her locked book, and Rossetti's poetry is punctuated with a number of secret places and secret choices. That she was well aware of the importance of secrecy in her work is plain not merely from 'Winter: My Secret' but from a variety of other, equally important poems (see 'Memory', for example [Crump, p. 147]).

IV

'Goblin Market' is Rossetti's most famous poem, and certainly one of her masterpieces. The point hardly needs argument, for no one has ever questioned its achievement and mastery. What does need to be shown more clearly is the typicalness of 'Goblin Market' in Rossetti's canon—indeed, its centrality.

Though Rossetti herself declared that the work was not symbolic or allegorical, her disclaimer has never been accepted, and interpretations of its hidden or 'secret' meaning have been made from the earliest reviews. Everyone agrees that the poem contains the story of temptation, fall, and redemption, and some go so far as to say that the work is fundamentally a Christian allegory. Nor is there any question that the machinery of such an allegory is a conscious part of the work. 'Goblin Market' repeatedly alludes to the story of the fall in Eden, and when Lizzie, at the climax, returns home to 'save' her sister, the poem represents the event as a Eucharistic emblem (see especially lines 471-2). Other, less totalizing Christian topoi and references abound. The important 'kernel stone' (line 138) which Laura saves from the fruit she eats, and which she later plants unavailingly (lines 281-92), is a small symbolic item based upon the New Testament parable (see Matthew 7:15-20) about the fruit of bad trees; indeed, the entire symbology of the fruits is Biblical, just as the figures of the merchant men are developed out of texts in the book of Revelation (18:11-17).

Rossetti draws from this passage her poem's controlling ideas of the evil merchants as traffickers in corruption and of their fruits as deceptive and insubstantial. Consequently, an important key for interpreting the poem proves to be her own commentaries on the Revelation text. The commentary on verse 14 has a manifest relevance which can pass without further remark:

14. *And the fruits that thy soul lusted after are departed from thee, and all things which were dainty and goodly are departed from thee, and thou shalt find them no more at all.*

Or according to the Revised Version: 'And the fruits which thy soul lusted after are gone from thee, and all things that were dainty and sumptuous are perished from thee, and men shall find them no more at all':—reminding us of St. Paul's words to the Colossians: '. . . The rudiments of the world . . . (Touch not; taste not; handle not; which all are to perish with the using)'.

As regards the second clause of the doom (*in this verse*), the two Versions suggest each its own sense. The Authorized, as if those objects of desire may have been not destroyed but withdrawn whilst the craving remains insatiable. According to both texts the loss appears absolute, final, irreparable; but (collating the two) that which *departs* instead of *perishing* leaves behind it in addition to the agony of loss the hankering, corroding misery of absence. (*Deep*, 421)

Her commentaries on verses 15-17 are equally pertinent. There the sacred text speaks of the coming desolation of Babylon, the merchant's city; Rossetti says of this event that, though it has not yet come to pass, it 'must one day be seen. Meanwhile we have known preludes, rehearsals, foretastes of such as this', and the thought leads her to her 'lamentation'. In this she cries 'alas' for those traditional political symbols of corruption

(Sodom or Tyre, for example), but her lament builds to an interesting climax: 'Alas England full of luxuries and thronged by stinted poor, whose merchants are princes and whose dealings crooked, whose packed storehouses stand amid bare homes, whose gorgeous array has rags for neighbours!' (*Deep*, 422). Of course, Rossetti was no Christian Socialist (or even a Muscular Christian), and her chief concern here is not with the material plight of the socially exploited. Rather, she focuses on the material condition as a sign, or revelation, of an inward and spiritual corruption. Babylon, Tyre, Sodom, England—as in Tennyson and T.S. Eliot, these are all, spiritally, *one* city ('Unreal city'), the passing historical agencies of the recurrent reality of a spiritual corruption.

The Bible, both the Old and New Testaments, characteristically associates these 'Babylonian' corruptions with sensuality and sexual indulgence, and Rossetti uses this association in her poem. The goblin merchants tempt the two sisters with fruits that offer unknown pleasures, more particularly, with fruits that promise to satisfy their unfulfilled desires. The figure of Jenny is introduced into the poem partly to make plain the specifically sexual nature of the temptation and partly to show that the issues are intimately related to the middle-class ideology of love and marriage. Jenny's is the story of the fallen woman.

In this context, the final (married) state of the sisters might easily be seen as sanctioning the institution of marriage as the good woman's just reward. To a degree this is indeed the case; but 'Goblin Market' presents the marriages of Laura and Lizzie in such an oblique and peripheral way that the ideology of the marriage-as-reward is hardly noticed and is conspicuously de-emphasized by the poem. The only men present in the story are the goblins, and Laura and Lizzie's emotional investments are positively directed toward women and children only. In fact, the poem's conclusion suggests that the sisters have made (as it were) 'marriages of convenience', only, in 'Goblin Market', that concept has been completely feminized. It is as if all men had been banished from this world so that the iniquity of the fathers might not be passed on to the children. Hence we see why the only men in the story are goblin men: the narrative means to suggest, indirectly, that the men of the world have become these merchants and are appropriately represented as goblins.

The ultimate evil of the goblin merchants is that they tempt to betray, promise but do not fulfil. Indeed, they do not merely fail in their promises, they punish the women who accept these promises as true. Yet the power of their temptations does not come from the inherent resources of the goblins; it comes from the frustration of the women, which is represented in Laura's (and Jenny's) longings and curiosity. The goblins, therefore, tempt the women at their most vulnerable point, which turns out to be, however, the place of their greatest strength as well.

Here we approach the centre of the poem's meaning, the core of its paradoxical symbolism. The temptation of the goblins always turns to ashes and emptiness because it does not satisfy the women's fundamental desires (see Rossetti's commentary on Revelation 18:14 above). But in terms of the Christian allegory, this simply means that the goblins offer 'passing shows' to match what in the women are 'immortal longings'. Notice how tenderly Laura and Lizzie are presented together immediately after Laura's 'fall'; how she finally emerges from her experience completely unstained; how the poem turns aside, at all points, any negative moral judgement of her character; and how it does not read Laura's condition as a sign of her evil. Rather, Laura's suffering and unhappiness become, in the poem, a stimulus for feelings of sympathy (in the reader) and for acts of love (by Lizzie). These aspects of the poem show that, for Rossetti, the 'temptation and fall' do not reveal Laura's corruption but rather the nature of her ultimate commitments and desires, which are not—despite appearances, and were she herself only aware of it—truly directed toward goblin merchants and their fruits.

Laura's desires (they are 'Promethean' in the Romantic sense and tradition) are fulfilled in the poem twice. The first fulfilment is in the notorious passage at 464-74, which is as patently erotic and sensual in content as it is Eucharistic in form. The significance of this elemental tension becomes clear when we understand that the scene introduces a negative fulfilment into the work: Laura is released from the spell of erotic illusions ('That juice was wormwood to her tongue, / She loathed the feast' [lines 494-5]) and permitted to glimpse, self-consciously, the truth which she pursued in its illusive form:

> Laura started from her chair,
> Flung her arms up in the air,
> Clutched her hair:
> 'Lizzie, Lizzie, have you tasted
> For my sake the fruit forbidden?
> Must your light like mine be hidden,
> Your young life like mine be wasted,
> Undone in mine undoing
> And ruined in my ruin,
> Thirsty, cankered, goblin-ridden?'—
> She clung about her sister,
> Kissed and kissed and kissed her:
> Tears once again
> Refreshed her shrunken eyes,
> Dropping like rain
> After long sultry drouth;
> Shaking with anguish, fear, and pain,
> She kissed and kissed her with a hungry mouth.
>
> ('Goblin Market', lines 475-92)

This passage anticipates the poem's conclusion—the second, positive scene of fulfilment—where Laura tells the children the story of a sisterly love and bids them follow its example: 'Then joining hands to little hands / Would bid them *cling* together,—/ For there is no friend like a sister' (lines 560-2, my emphasis). For passion and erotics are substituted feeling and sympathy, and for men are substitued women and children, the 'little' ones of the earth.

Thus we see how the Christian and Biblical materials—the images and concepts—serve as the metaphoric vehicles for understanding a complex statement about certain institutionalized patterns of social destructiveness operating in nineteenth-century England. As in so many of her poems, 'Goblin Market' passes a negative judgement upon the illusions of love and marriage. But the poem is unusual in Rossetti's canon in that it has developed a convincing positive symbol for an alternative, uncorrupted mode of social relations—the love of sisters.

This situation requires some further explanatory comment. In the story of Laura and Lizzie, we can observe patterns of conceptualization familiar from Rossetti's other works. One notes,

for, example, that the goblins' power over women comes ultimately from the women's (erroneous) belief that the goblins
have something which the women need, that the women are
incomplete. Part of the meaning of 'Goblin Market' is the
importance of independence, including an independence from
that erroneous belief. Lizzie's heroic adventure on her sister's
behalf dramatizes her integrity, her freedom from dependency
on the goblins: she is not a relative creature but is wholly herself, and capable of maintaining herself even in the face of great
danger.

Nevertheless, the premium which Rossetti placed upon personal integrity was always threatened by the demon of loneliness ('And left me old, and cold, and grey'). 'Goblin Market'
turns this threat aside, principally via the symbol of sisterly
love and the alternative socializing structures which that symbol
is able to suggest and foster. An important formal aspect of the
poem's resolution depends upon our awareness that Lizzie is
not Laura's 'saviour', for this would simply represent a variant
type of a dependency relationship. The true beneficiaries of the
grace issuing from the events are 'the children', or society at
large in its future tense.

So far as 'Goblin Market' tells a story of 'redemption', the
process is carried out in the dialectic of the acts of both Laura
and Lizzie. Laura behaves rashly, of course, but without her
precipitous act the women would have remained forever in a
condition of childlike innocence. Lizzie's timidity is by no means
condemned, but its limitations are very clear. Laura's disturbed
restlessness and curiosity suggest, in relation to Lizzie, an
impulse to transcend arbitrary limits. But Laura's behaviour is
the sign of her (and her sister's) ignorance and, therefore, of
their inability to control and direct their own actions. When
Laura 'falls', then, her situation reveals, symbolically, the problem of innocence in a world which already possesses the knowledge of good and evil. Where ravening wolves prowl about in
sheep's clothing, the righteous must be at once innocent as the
dove and cunning as the serpent. Lizzie's function in the poem,
then, is to repeat Laura's history, only at so self-conscious a
level that she becomes the master of that history rather than its
victim. Still, as the story makes very clear, her knowledge and
mastery are a function, and reflex, of Laura's ignorance and

weakness. The definitive sign of their dialectical relationship appears in the simple fact that Laura is not finally victimized. She is only a victim as Jesus is a victim; she is a suffering servant. In a very real sense, therefore, the poem represents Laura as the moral begetter of Lizzie (on the pattern of 'The child is father of the man'). Lizzie does not 'save' Laura. Both together enact a drama which displays what moral forces have to be exerted in order, not to be saved from evil, but simply to grow up.

Laura and Lizzie, then, share equally in the moral outcome of the poem's events. The fact that their names echo each other is no accident—and who has not sometimes confused the two when trying to distinguish them at some memorable distance? Still, it makes a difference if one locates the poem's principal moral centre in Lizzie alone, as readers have always done. In fact, to have read the poem this way is to have read it accurately (if also incompletely); for Rossetti, as a morally self-conscious Christian writer, encouraged such a reading, as she wanted to do—for both personal and polemical reasons. She encouraged it because *that* way of reading the poem supports a Christian rather than a secular interpretation of the theme of independence. All readers of the poem will recognize its polemic against the women's dependence upon the lures of the goblin men; but from a Christian viewpoint, this polemic is based upon the idea that people should not put their trust in mortal things or persons, that only God and the ways of God are true, real, and dependable. Therefore, in the affairs of this world, the Christian must learn to be independent of the quotidian— translate, *contemptus mundi*—and come to trust in the eternal. So far as Lizzie seems a 'Christ figure'—a Eucharistic agent— 'Goblin Market' argues for a severe Christian attitude of this sort.

But, of course, Lizzie seems something much more—and much less—than a Eucharistic emblem, as Christina Rossetti well knew: she never placed 'Goblin Market' among her 'Devotional Poems'. Consequently, because Lizzie is primarily a 'friend' and a 'sister' rather than a 'saviour', the poem finally takes its stand on more secular grounds. Nevertheless, it uses the Christian material in a most subtle and effective way: to mediate for the audience the poem's primary arguments about love, marriage, sisterhood, and friendship.

In much the same way does the poem use the disarming formal appearance of a children's fairy story. This choice was a stroke of real genius, for no conceivable model available to her could have represented so well a less 'serious' and 'manly' poetic mode. When her publisher Alexander Macmillan first read the poem to a group of people from the Cambridge Working Men's Society, 'they seemed at first to wonder whether I was making fun of them; by degrees they got as still as death, and when I finished there was a tremendous burst of applause.'[17] All three phases of their response were acute. 'Goblin Market' cultivates the appearance of inconsequence partly to conceal its own pretensions to a consequence far greater than most of the poetry then being produced in more 'serious', customary, and recognized quarters.

Lizzie triumphs over the goblins (lines 329-463) by outplaying them at their own games, but one should notice that her victory is gained in and through her correct formal behaviour. It is the goblins who are violent, disorganized, out of control— and impolite. She addresses them as 'good folk' (line 362) and says 'thank you' (line 383) to their insidious offers. The goblins smirk and giggle at her apparent simple-mindedness, yet the poem clearly represents her as enjoying an unexpressed, superior laughter at their expense. Lizzie's behaviour is the equivalent, in 'Goblin Market', of what we spoke of earlier in relation to 'Winter: My Secret' and 'No, Thank You, John'.

Lizzie's behaviour is also a stylistic metaphor standing for Rossetti's poetry, whose correct beauty judges, particularly through its modest address, all that is pretentious and illusory. The fruits, the language, the behaviour of the goblin merchants are all metaphors for what Keats had earlier called 'careless hectorers in proud, bad verse'. The issues here are nicely suggested in a brief passage immediately following Lizzie's victory over the goblins: 'Lizzie went her way . . ./ Threaded copse and dingle,/ And heard her penny jingle/ Bouncing in her purse,—/ Its bounce was music to her ear' (lines 448, 451-4). This is Rossetti's sign of a true poetic power—a mere penny

[17] Alexander Macmillan to D.G.Rossetti, 28 Oct. 1861, quoted in *The Rossetti-Macmillan Letters*, ed. Lona Mosk Packer, Berkeley and Los Angeles, 1963, p. 7.

which jingles like the surface of the verse. Nonsense (the original title of 'Winter: My Secret') and childishness—Edward Lear, Lewis Carroll, 'Goblin Market'—come into a great inheritance amid the fat and arid formulas of so much High Victorian 'seriousness'.

But 'Goblin Market' gains its results in the most obliging and diplomatic fashion. Christina Rossetti was a severe woman, and her ironic intelligence and quick tongue were observed, and respected, by all of her contemporaries who knew her. But so were her modest and retiring ways. She did not cultivate the weapons, or methods, of George Sand or even of Elizabeth Barrett Browning. Lizzie's behaviour with the goblins is Rossetti's poetic equivalent for her own life and work. What Lizzie does—what Rossetti does in her verse generally—is not to make a frontal assault upon her enemy, but quietly to secure his defeat by bringing righteousness out of evil, beauty out of ugliness. Rossetti's model for her revisionist project appears explicitly in her Revelation commentary cited above:

> Yet on the same principle that we are bidden redeem the time because the days are evil, Christians find ways to redeem these other creatures despite their evil tendency. Gold and silver they lend unto the Lord: He will pay them again. Precious stones and pearls they dedicate to the service of His Altar. With fine linen, purple, silk, scarlet, they invest His Sanctuary; and fragrant 'thyine' wood they carve delicately for its further adornment . . . Whoso has the spirit of Elijah, though his horse and chariot have come up out of Egypt, yet shall they receive virtue as 'of fire' to forward him on his heavenward course. And this despite a horse being but a vain thing to save a man. (*Deep*, 420)

Out of these convictions develop, naturally, the charming catalogues of the goblins as well as their own temptation speeches; but we recognize this habit of mind most clearly in the unspeakably beautiful litanies praising the poem's loving sisters:

>   Golden head by golden head,
>   Like two pigeons in one nest
>   Folded in each other's wings,
>   They lay down in their curtained bed:
>   Like two blossoms on one stem,
>   Like two flakes of new-fall'n snow,

> Like two wands of ivory
> Tipped with gold for awful kings.
> Moon and stars gazed in at them,
> Wind sang to them lullaby,
> Lumbering owls forbore to fly,
> Not a bat flapped to and fro
> Round their rest:
> Cheek to cheek and breast to breast
> Locked together in one nest.
> ('Goblin Market', lines 184-98)

Thematically this passage is important because of its position in the poem. Although the lines describe the evening rest of the sisters *after* Laura's encounter with the goblins, the passage does not draw any moral distinctions between Laura and Lizzie. In the perspective of Christina Rossetti's poem, Laura remains fundamentally uncorrupted. By goblin standards, she is now a fallen woman, but the poem intervenes to prevent the reader from accepting such a judgement.

This moral intervention occurs at the level of poetic form and verse style. As such, it does not merely tell us of the need for a new moral awareness, it suggests that this new awareness cannot be an abstract idea. On the contrary, it must operate in a concrete form appropriate to the circumstances—in this case, within the immediate literary event of the poem itself. The poem's general social critique (which is abstract) appears in the verse as a series of particular stylistic events (which are concrete). In a wholly non-Keatsian sense then, Beauty becomes Truth: not because the beauty of art represents a purified alternative to worldly corruptions, but because art's beauty is itself a worldly event, an operating (and, in this case, a critical) presence which argues that human acts will always escape, and dominate, what is corrupt.

In this sense one can and ought to say that 'Goblin Market' is *about* poetry. For the poem's critique of the symbolic goblins is itself a symbolic mode of statement comprehending all that is suggested by, and hidden in, the symbol; and part of what is hidden in the symbol of the goblins is the particular corruption of the age's literature. 'Goblin Market' develops its general social indictment by passing a special judgement upon poetry. For the corruption of the goblins operates in all quarters of society, as the poem's generalizing form (symbolic fairy story) necessarily implies: in the infrastructural regions ('the market'), of course, but also in all of the related superstructural institutions, including that of literature. Fundamentally the corruption originates in the 'marketplace' where women 'have no place' and 'do not belong'. But Rossetti wittily inverts the meaning of this alienated condition by suggesting why women must not seek positions in the capitalized market if they want to preserve their integrity and, thereby, to deliver a prophetic message to the future—the need of an alternative social order. Her argument is an outrageously subtle revision of the age's notorious attitude toward women expressed, for example, in John Ruskin's 'Of Queens' Gardens'.

In this respect, Christina Rossetti's poetry takes up an ideological position which is far more radical than the middle-class feminist positions current in her epoch. The principal factor which enabled her to overleap those positions was her severe Christianity, as a close study of her religious verse would clearly show. Space does not permit me to develop that demonstration here, though I hope I have shown, in the course of this essay, how such a demonstration might be carried out. Christina Rossetti's notorious obsession with the theme of the world's vanity lies at the root of her refusal to compromise with her age or to adopt reformist positions. Like Giacomo Leopardi's pessimism,[18] Christina Rossetti's *contemptus mundi* is the basis of her critical freedom and poetic illumination.

Unlike the atheist Leopardi, however, Christina Rossetti did not set himself in open revolt against her age. Yet her conservative posture once again proved an asset to her work, for in accepting the traditional view of 'a woman's place', she uncovered a (secret) position from which to cast a clear eye upon the ways of her world. Lizzie, 'Goblin Market', and Christina Rossetti, then, all act in similar ways. All are radically critical, yet they are modest and oblique at the same time; they are independent; they preserve the idea of the importance of beauty in a dark time; and they cherish the secret of their work. 'Goblin Market' specifically is a serious critique of its age and of the age's cultural institutions which supported and defined

[18] See Sebastiano Timpanaro, 'Alcune Osservatione Sul Pensiero Del Leopardi', in *Classicismo e illuminismo nel' Ottrocento italiano*, Pisa, 1965, pp. 133-82.

what was to be possible in love, social relations, and art. When Swinburne spoke of Christina Rossetti as the Jael who led their hosts to victory, he said more than he knew, but he did not say too much.

(1979-80)

2. The Religious Poetry of Christina Rossetti

I

One of the difficulties which an explicitly Christian poetry or art presents for criticism is its appearance of thematic uniformity. Readers of such work (even critics of such work) frequently seem to think not merely that religious ideas are in themselves eternal truths which wake to perish never, but that these ideas are traditionary, self-consistent, and unchanging—in brief, that the ideas are transcendent rather than historically particular (whatever the scale of their historical particularity may be). Of course, one recognizes that certain doctrinal positions will or may produce divergent religious emphases in different poets—as, for example, the ideological differences between the Christian poems of Donne, Herbert, Crashaw and Dryden. But if the specifically controversial poems are set aside (like certain of the Holy Sonnets and *The Hind and the Panther*), the doctrinal variances, we often think, tend to disappear into a basically congruent economy of Christian thought. Christian poetry from the Middle Ages to the present thus comes to us as a body of work which, despite shifting emphases and interests, expresses a uniform world-view or ideological focus.[1]

In one sense, of course, this general conception is quite correct: Christian poetry, whether sixteenth or nineteenth century, whether Calvinist or Catholic, Evangelical or Anglican, English or French, rests in a tradition of such length and continuity that all its divergent expressions trade in certain common shares of

[1] Because the ideological arguments within Christianity were so central during the Renaissance, contemporary writers of various persuasions tended to emphasize the differences between their doctrinal positions. During the Enlightenment a secular challenge began to be raised against Christianity in general, and the consequence of this was the emergence, within the various Christian sects, of a consolidating movement. Broad Church protestantism gained its ascendancy during the nineteenth and twentieth centuries, a period in which we have also observed, particularly during the last fifty years, several strains of ecumenism. These developments within Christianity follow upon the challenge of humanism and secularism, and they can be seen quite clearly in the world of literary criticism and scholarship as well. M. H. Abrams's *Natural Supernaturalism*, New York, 1971, is an obvious instance, and the entire corpus of Northrop Frye's work is paradigmatic.

feeling and thought.[2] Nevertheless, if Christian poetry exhibits many common elements, the individual work of different poets is marked by distinctive qualities. Scholars will try to mark out these distinctive features by restoring the work of the religious poets to their special local habitations. If you map the verse of Donne or Herbert on the grids of an historical or biographical analysis, the peculiar features of their work are forced to yield themselves up. This result is especially important in the case of religious poetry read in a culture which maintains and (to a large extent) still propagates the ideological self-representations of such poetry. For in such a culture we are continually tempted to attribute some sort of inherent value to the content of religious verse.

But suppose for a moment you wanted to convince a non-Christian Japanese friend of the power of Christina Rossetti's poetry, or—perhaps better—a humanist scholar from the Soviet Union—or simply any non-believer. What line would you take? What would you say?

Christina Rossetti's poetry might be usefully approached in terms of such a problem. That is to say, it might be usefully studied in this way by western scholars and readers like ourselves, who have been brought up within the ideological apparatuses of a Christian culture, precisely because her poetry has been largely judged inferior, or at most only of incidental interest, by the chief twentieth-century spokesmen of that culture's values. The enormous revival of interest in Christian and even Catholic poetry which began in the Modern Period and which flourished with the New Criticism did not take any serious account of the work of Christina Rossetti. Hopkins yes, Rossetti, no.[3]

[2] The root of the matter probably hinges upon that famous Pauline *sine qua non*: 'if Christ be not risen, then is our faith in vain' (I Cor. 15:13-14). This text contains certain essential features of the Christian economy in all its variant forms: of faith in Jesus as the saviour of mankind and of the nature of Christian hope in the individual's own salvation through resurrection. The other key features of Christianity involve the eucharistic feast and its practical/doctrinal concomitant, the ideal of Christian love (cf. especially the gospel of John 15:12-13 and Matthew 5:43-4; the last should be compared with what is said at Matthew 22:36-40).

[3] See R. W. Crump's *Christina Rossetti. A Reference Guide*, Boston, 1976, where the history of Rossetti's critical reception is schematically presented in a good annotated bibliography. The neglect of Rossetti is especially remarkable when one considers the (often noted) similarity between much of her verse and the work of Herbert. The latter is, we know, one of the favourite subjects of New Critical and contemporary formalist exegesis.

Why this choice should have been made by those who celebrated the virtues of so many seventeenth-century religious
poets is not a subject to be dealt with in a short essay such as
this, for the topic involves the whole dehistoricizing program of
Modernism and the New Criticism. But we must pause to consider the roots of this choice, if only in a brief way. Why is it
that not a single critic associated with the New Critical movement ever wrote anything about Christina Rossetti? And what
does that lack of interest mean?

II

Let me begin with a few commonplaces. The poetry of the
English Metaphysicals, particularly their religious poetry, was
one of the touchstones by which the New Critics would measure
a poet's value. This criterion was itself allied to a more general
one which prized verse that exhibited a high degree of surface
tension, ambiguity, and complexity. Such qualities were
associated with the presence of a central conflict or paradox
which seemed to define the very nature of the poet and poetry
itself: a struggle to reconcile opposite and discordant qualities
such as tradition and individual talent, reason and feeling,
religion and the secular world. Furthermore, immediately
behind the work of the New Critics lay the example of the early
Modern poets, who seemed to exhibit many of these qualities
in their own verse. Most dramatically, the work of the early
Modern poets sought and found a way to break the spell and
authority of Tennyson, Swinburne, and Pre-Raphaelitism,
where the poetic surface tended to disguise or sublimate all
forms of disjunction and irregularity.

The cultural vantage of Modernism and New Criticism,
then, stood in a hostile relation to much of what they understood as 'the Victorian frame of mind' as it manifested itself in
a poetic medium. The model of Donne seemed more useful as a
point of departure, for poet and critic alike, than the model of
Tennyson. Yet the religious and moral critique of science and
the secular modern world, so vigorously maintained (and in
certain respects initiated) by the Victorians, was a cultural
resource which was far from being abandoned or repudiated.
What would greatly benefit the polemic of the New Criticism

would be a Victorian religious poet who stood in some clear antithetical relation to his own age—whose verse seemed to stand closer to Donne or Dante than to *The Christian Year* and the Society for the Promotion of Christian Knowledge.[4]

From various points of view, therefore, Hopkins was just the sort of person whom 'the (new) age demanded'. He was Victorian but he didn't sound like Tennyson or Swinburne, his verse displayed an extraordinarily high degree of surface tension (unusual rhythms, obscurity, disjointed syntaxes, startling images and conceits), and—not least of all—he was a religious poet who went virtually unrecognized in his own time. Hopkins was a very epitome of the sort of poet whom Eliot had set up as a model in his 1921 essay 'The Metaphysical Poets'. The fact that he was a Catholic poet writing in an age dominated by sentimental late protestant religious verse only underlined his significance. In Hopkins one discovered an example of resistance to that dissociation of sensibility which had been exerting such an evil effect upon poetry since the seventeenth century. In Hopkins one could discern as it were a proof case that the touchstone event of the Metaphysicals might arise at any time and anywhere—might arise as an obscure Jesuit writing agonized verse in what was widely regarded as the most bland and enervated period of English literary history.

If Gerard Manley Hopkins had never existed, the New Criticism would have had to invent him (and, to the degree that they elevated him above the master-poets of the late Victorian period, this is precisely what they did). It is highly significant that Hopkins only exploded on the literary scene in 1930, with the publication of the second edition of his *Poems*. The first edition, published in 1918 in a print run of 750 copies, sold slowly over the next twelve years, though the critical notices were favourable and often written by significant critical figures. The first edition was compiled and introduced by Hopkins's friend Robert Bridges, the elegant, learned, and ageing Poet Laureate. Bridges died in 1929, however, so the second edition, when called for, had a new editor—the young Anglo-Catholic Charles Williams. It is with the publication of this second edition that Hopkins's reputation as a major poet begins.[5]

[4] I choose the second example because several of Rossetti's later books were published under the auspices of that society.

[5] For a survey of Hopkins's critical reception see the first two chapters of Todd K.

In many ways the early 1930s represented the watershed moment for the next forty years of literary and cultural criticism.[6] John Crowe Ransom's *God Without Thunder. An Unorthodox Defense of Orthodoxy* was published in 1930, Eliot's *Selected Essays* and *After Strange Gods* appeared in 1932 and 1934, and Tate's *Reactionary Essays* came out in 1936. The religious and anti-historical focus which was so to dominate the New Criticism is rooted in this period. It is the period of Hopkins's astonishing academic ascendancy; it is also the period which marks the virtual disappearance of Christina Rossetti from our cultural consciousness.[7]

Why Rossetti, whom Hopkins admired to a fault, should have thus fallen out of fashion may seem at first rather odd—or at least it may seem odd that the Christian, Anglican, and Anglo-Catholic polemicists should not have maintained her reputation. She was a Dantist, she was Anglican and severely orthodox in her public profession, she was impeccably conservative. Later critics who found a rich mine of ore in the drama of Hopkins's spiritual and psychic life were not interested in these aspects of Rossetti, whose personal life, like her poetry, remained virtually a closed book until the theme of sexual frustration offered itself to certain readers.[8]

But Rossetti's orthodoxy is not sufficiently 'unorthodox', at least by New Critical standards. When Ifor Evans says of her work that it 'is removed from the Elizabethan tradition by an infrequency of conceit, and by an increased earnestness',[9] he indicates three of the more apparent (and related) reasons for her lack of favour with the new apologists for poetry. The style of her verse is simple, chaste, and severe, but it is also recognizably in a Victorian stylistic tradition, and in that respect

Bender's *Gerald Manley Hopkins*, Baltimore, 1966.

6 For some survey critical views of the New Criticism see Murray Krieger, *The New Apologists for Poetry*, Minneapolis, 1956; Richard Foster, *The New Romantics*, Bloomington, 1962; and chaps. 2 and 5 of Gerald Graff's *Literature Against Itself*, Chicago, 1979.

7 See Crump's *Reference Guide*. A number of books about Rossetti appeared in the early 1930s, several quite good, but after that she virtually disappeared from the academic scene for almost three decades; and even then she remained a marginal interest for another ten years or more.

8 This line is epitomized in Lona Mosk Packer's *Christina Rossetti*, Berkeley, 1963.

9 B. Ifor Evans, *English Poetry in the Later Nineteenth Century*, London, 1933, rev. and repr. New York, 1966, pp. 100-1.

it is 'orthodox' precisely where Modern poets and New Critics looked for the 'unorthodox'. Her poetry does not get worked up at the surface.

More crucial, perhaps, is an ideological deviance between Rossetti and certain less explicit aspects of New Critical theory. Consider the conclusion to Ransom's influential *God Without Thunder*:

> With whatever religious institution a modern man may be connected, let him try to turn it back towards orthodoxy.
> Let him insist on a virile and concrete God, and accept no Principle as a substitute.
> Let him restore to God the thunder.
> Let him resist the usurpation of the Godhead by the soft modern version of the Christ, and try to keep the Christ for what he professed to be: the Demigod who came to do honor to the God.[10]

For Rossetti, some of this will do, but some of it will not do; and the final exhortation about Christ will never do. Worst of all, for a poet such as she, is the aggressive *maleness* of all this in the sense that Ransom simply takes his patriarchialism for granted. Serious issues are at stake for Ransom, which is to say that the issues will be conceived in a patriarchal mode such as this. What Ransom has most in mind is the historical transformations which Christianity had been undergoing since the early nineteenth century: the persistent tendency toward Broad Church and liberal doctrinal positions with their correspondingly innovative interpretations of the Christian experience. Because religion for Ransom is an original matter, a God without thunder is seen as a latter-day perversion of Christianity, and a dangerous apparition. This is the burden of his attack upon the religious ideologies which spill out from various nineteenth-century forms of protestant thought.[11]

---

[10] *God Without Thunder*, New York, 1930, pp. 327-8.

[11] See ibid., chap. 1. In literary/critical terms, Ransom sets his face against ideological models which were developed out of Romanticism and Victorianism, including their characteristic tendency to define volatile and problematic issues via historicist and symbolical methods. In England this tendency is epitomized in the work and programme initiated by S.T. Coleridge. Early twentieth-century reactionary criticism from Irving Babbitt to Eliot, Tate, and Brooks deplored this tendency and its methods; the well-known catch-phrase 'spilt religion' accurately describes the double nature of their criticism of Romantic and post-Romantic poetry: that it represented equally a debasement of the proper objects of poetic discourse and the appropriate character of religious experience.

Related to these issues of poetic style and religious idea is the conviction that the practice of poetry is a serious intellectual and moral event. Indeed, it is an event of such moment that it leaves no room for the sentiment of pathetic or (good) intentional fallacies. Its object is no less than the Truth, and its function is to seize and define the Truth in times of crisis (whether personal or cultural). Rossetti's poetry, even among those critics who profess to admire it, seems to lack the intellectual rigour which alone can sustain its (evident) moral seriousness. As Lionel Stevenson has put it: 'Christina Rossetti's poetry comes closer to the pure lyric mode than that of any other Victorian, male or female, for the obvious reason that it contains a minimum of intellectual substance. Though she was equipped with a normally keen mind, it was firmly suppressed by several forces.'[12] One might argue with this passage on a number of counts. Here I want only to call attention to Stevenson's idea that Rossetti's poetry lacks 'intellectual substance'. As we shall see shortly, this idea is profoundly mistaken—*profoundly* not simply because it is not in fact true, but becase the error arises out of a lapse in historical awareness.[13]

Indeed, all of the reasons just given might count for little against Rossetti had the New Criticism not set out, deliberately, to 'revolt against historical scholarship'.[14] These words are Tate's own characterization of the New Critical programme, and they go far to explain why and how Rossetti disappeared so long from our critical consciousness. The restoration of an historical perspective to the critical task will therefore help us to understand Rossetti not only in her own terms—from an historicist pespective—but in terms that are important for readers and educators of this later day.

III

To survey the line of commentary that has preserved the name of Christina Rossetti in twentieth-century literary culture is to

---

[12] Lionel Stevenson, *The Pre-Raphaelite Poets*, Chapel Hill, 1972, p. 88.

[13] I should point out that Stevenson is a distinguished historical scholar. His failure, in this case, to grasp the historical issues at stake in reading Rossetti's poetry is not typical of his work, and least of all is it a function of any New Critical anti-historicism.

[14] Cf. 'The New Criticism', a discussion involving Tate and several others, in *The American Scholar* xx (1950-1), p. 218.

discover, first, that the New Criticism ignored her work, and second, that those who praised her did so in terms which were bound to prove largely ineffectual: she is a pure craftswoman, she is the best woman lyricist of the nineteenth century, she is an impassioned mystical poet, she is the poetess of the Tractarian Movement; her verse is 'spontaneous', 'ascetic', 'unblemished', and 'sweet'.[15] There are a few important commentaries on Rossetti in the fifty or sixty years following her death, but they are—in contrast to the critical work on Hopkins—exceptional in every sense.

The consequence of this situation, it seems to me, is that Rossetti has reaped the benefits of what Trotsky once called 'The Privilege of Historical Backwardness.'[16] Those who gathered the strength of writers like Donne, Herbert, and Hopkins found Rossetti's work variously 'morbid', 'sterile', 'sweet'—in any case, from a Christian perspective, far inferior to the 'virile' work of those religious poets of our Great Tradition. This neglect of her verse kept her safe from the critical presuppositions and approaches of Modernism and New Criticism. As a consequence, her work is once again being read seriously only in recent years, and her best readers now have nearly all been more or less strongly marked by other critical vantages and presuppositions, not the least of which are those we associate with Feminist Criticism and its natural ally, historical method.[17]

I want to argue, therefore, that to read Rossetti's religious poetry with understanding (and therefore with profit and appreciation) requires a more or less conscious investment in the *peculiarities* of its Christian orientation, in the social and historical particulars which feed and shape the distinctive features of her work. Because John O. Waller's recent essay on Rossetti focuses

[15] These terms and ideas (as well as 'morbid' and 'sterile', cited below) tend to occur repeatedly in the critical literature on Rossetti.

[16] See Trotsky's *The Russian Revolution*, selections edited from his *History* by F. W. Dupee, New York, 1959, p. 3.

[17] For recent Feminist and Feminist-influenced essays on Rossetti see the previous chapter, n. 4. Besides the work of R. W. Crump and Gwynneth Hatton (cited above and in the previous chapter), other significant historical scholarship includes John O. Waller, 'Christ's Second Coming: Christina Rossetti and the Premillenarianist William Dodsworth', *Bulletin of the New York Public Library* lxxiii (1969), pp. 465-82 and Joe K. Law's 'William Dyce's *George Herbert at Bemerton*: Its Background and Meaning', *Journal of Pre-Raphaelite Studies* iii (1982), pp. 45-55.

on some of the most important of these particulars, it seems to me one of the most useful pieces of scholarship ever written on the poet. The essay locates the special ground of Rossetti's religious poetry in that peculiar Adventist and Pre-millenarian context which flourished for about fifty years in mid nineteenth-century culture. In point of historical fact—and it is an historical fact which has enormous significance for the aesthetic character of Rossetti's poetry—her religious verse is intimately meshed with a number of particular, even peculiar, religious ideas.[18] From the vantage of her strongest poetry, the most important of these ideas (along with the associated images and symbols they helped to generate) were allied to a once powerful religious movement which later—toward the end of the century—slipped to a marginal position in English culture.

The whole question [of Premillenarianism] was overshadowed first and last by the Tractarian Movement, Anglo-Catholicism, and the resulting Protestant reaction. And we can see in retrospect that all through the years [1820-75] the theological future actually belonged to liberal, or Broad Church, principles. By the middle 1870s, apparently, [the issues raised through the Premillenarian Movement] were no longer very alive.[19]

In this context we may begin to understand the decline of Rossetti's reputation after the late nineteenth century, when she was still regarded as one of the most powerful and important contemporary English poets. Her reputation was established in the 1860s and 1870s, when Adventism reached the apogee of its brief but influential career. Thereafter, the availability of religious poetry was mediated either through the Broad Church line (which stretches from Coleridge and the Cambridge Apostles and Arnold, to figures like Trilling and

___

[18] It is a commonplace of Rossetti criticism that her poetry is the best expression we have of the ideas and attitudes of Tractarianism. But this is a most misleading view (though not entirely wrong); one might rather turn to a work such as *The Christian Year* for an epitome of Tractarian ideology. Rossetti's evangelical sympathies kept her protestantism resolute, as one can readily see in her lifelong hostility to the revival of Marianism. Waller's observation is very much to the point: '[Rossetti's] spiritual adviser [i.e. William Dodsworth] during her impressionable adolescence [was an] improbable combination of High Church activist and premillenialist preacher that would mold the peculiar configuration of her religious sensibility' (p. 466).

[19] Waller, p. 477. For a general discussion of millenarianism in the early nineteenth century see J. E. Harrison, *The Second Coming, Popular Millenarianism 1780-1850*, London, 1979.

Abrams in our own day), or through the High Church and Anglo-Catholic line (which was defined backwards from certain influential twentieth century figures like Eliot to include the Noetics, Hopkins, and various seventeenth-century religious writers). The premillenarian and evangelist enthusiasm which supported Rossetti's religious poetry had been moved to the periphery of English culture when the canon of such verse began to be formed in the Modern Period.

To read Rossetti's religious poetry, then, we have to willingly suspend not only our disbelief in her convictions and ideas, but also our *belief* in those expectations and presuppositions about religious poetry which we have inherited from those two dominant ideological lines. Waller has drawn our attention to the general premillenarian content of her work, and I should like to follow his lead by emphasizing another crucial and even more particular doctrinal feature of her poetry.

IV

The well-known lyric 'Up-Hill' is a useful place to start. In certain obvious ways, this moving poem follows a traditional model, and its all but explicit forebears are two of Herbert's most familiar pieces, 'The Pilgrimage' and the last poem in *The Temple*, 'Love (III)'. When we set Rossetti's poem beside the two by Herbert we will perhaps be initially struck by the difference in tone: Rossetti's poem is melancholy (one might even say 'morbid') whereas Herbert's two lyrics discover and disclose their religious confidence in their respective conclusions:

> My hill was further; so I flung away,
> > Yet heard a crie,
> Just as I went, 'None goes that way
> And lives.' 'If that be all,' said I,
> After so foul a journey death is fair,
> > And but a chair.'
> > > ('The Pilgrimage')

> 'You must sit down,' says Love, 'and taste my meat.'
> So I did sit and eat.
> > ('Love (III)')

If Herbert's pilgrimage has been long and weary, and if his soul—conscious that it is 'Guilty of dust and sin'—at first hesitates to accept Love's invitation, in the end all comes to confidence, content, and even joy. For at the end of his life the Christian (this Christian) comes to the feast of the blessed, and a place in the house of God.

In Rossetti it is different, and the difference is signalled in the startling last two lines of her poem. The speaker questions her divine interlocutor about the pilgrimage but the answers she gets are strange and mysteriously portentous through the first twelve lines. Finally, however, Rossetti is told, in a disturbingly ambiguous phrase, that her laborious journey will be complete: 'Of labour you shall find the sum.' The poem then concludes:

> Will there be beds for me and all who seek?
> Yea, beds for all who come.

Surely this seems a peculiar way to end a poem which seems to describe the pilgrimage of the Christian soul to its final reward. No 'feast' opens before her final eyes, nor does she seem to believe that the dying Christian should expect to receive anything other than a bed, presumably to sleep in. The image is almost grotesque in its lowliness, and not far from a parody of such exalted Christian ideas that at death we go to our eternal rest, or to sleep in the bosom of God. Does Rossetti imagine that when we go to heaven we shall sleep away our paradise, or is she simply a weak-minded poet, sentimentally attached to certain traditional phrases and ideas which she has not really thought through?

The conclusion of 'Up-Hill' would not have been written as it was if Rossetti had not subscribed to, and thoroughly pondered the artistic possibilities of, the peculiar millenarian and Anabaptist doctrine known popularly as 'Soul Sleep'.[20] This idea,

---

[20] The technical term for this doctrine is psychopannychism; the *OED* defines psychopannychy as 'the state in which (according to some) the soul sleeps between death and the day of judgment'. For discussion see O. Cullmann, *Immortality of the Soul or Resurrection of the Dead?*, New York, 1958, and two papers by J. Héring, 'Entre la mort et la résurrection', *Review of the History of Philosophy and Religion* xl (1960), pp. 338-48 and 'Eschatologie biblique et idéalisme platonicien', in *The Background of the New Testament and Its Eschatology*, ed. W. D. Davies and D. Daube, Cambridge, 1956, pp. 443-63.

in a richly dispersed and elaborated variety of poetic forms, pervades the work of her greatest years as a poet, i.e., the period of 1848-75. It takes its origin from the time of Luther (whose position on the matter was unsettled), and it means to deal with the problem of the so-called 'waiting time', i.e. the period between a person's death and the Great Advent (or Second Coming). The orthodox view distinguishes between the Particular Judgement, which the soul undergoes at death, and the General Judgement, which takes place at the end of the world. According to traditional doctrine (epitomized in Episcopalian and Roman Catholic theology), the soul at death passes to its final reward (I leave aside here the possibility of a purgatorial period) and suffers no 'waiting time'. The body corrupts in the grave and is reunited with the emparadised soul on the Last Day.

According to Adventist doctrine of Soul Sleep, however, death initiates the period during which the soul is placed in a state of 'sleeping' or suspension. Only at the Millennium, on the Last Day, is that sleep broken and the soul confronted with its final reward.

There is no question that Rossetti adhered to the doctrine of Soul Sleep, for it can be found at all levels of tenor and vehicle in her work. From her earliest to her latest poems—from works like 'Dream-Land' composed in 1849 (and placed third in her first published volume) to the famous culminant lyric 'Sleeping at Last', written in 1893 or early 1894—this premillenarian concept is the single most important enabling principle in Rossetti's religious poetry. By this I mean that no other idea generated such a network of poetic possibilities for her verse, that no other idea contributed so much to the concrete and specific character of her work.

Most obviously, the doctrine provides a ground from which Rossetti can both understand and judge her sense of the insufficiency of a mortal existence. The pervasive theme of *vanitas vanitatum* is generated and maintained through the energy of an emotional weariness, through a sense that living in the world is scarcely worth the effort it requires, since what the world has to offer is, in any case, mere vanity, empty promises, betrayal. Soul Sleep is precisely what would appear to be the first and greatest need of the weary pilgrim under such circumstances; in a word, it answers to the most fundamental emotional demand which

Rossetti's poetry sets forth. In addition, however, the doctrine validates Rossetti's peculiarly passive stance toward the world's evil. Rossetti's negative judgements of the world do not take the form of a resistance but of a withdrawal—a strategic withdrawal carried out under the premillenarian consciousness that any commitment to the world is suicidal. It is highly significant that one of the principal sections of her 1893 volume of devotional poems, *Verses*, should have been headed 'The World. Self-Destruction'.

From the doctrine of Soul Sleep also emerges Rossetti's special employment of the traditional topos of the dream-vision. Several of Rossetti's poems set forth paradisal visions, and in each case these proceed from a condition in which the soul, laid asleep, as it were, in the body, is permitted to glimpse the millennial world. In fact, the logic of Rossetti's verse only allows her access to that world through the dream-visions that are themselves only enabled by the concept (and the resultant poetic reality) of Soul Sleep. How that logic operates can be readily seen by studying the relations between a group of poems like 'Paradise (Once in a dream I saw the flowers)', 'Mother Country (Oh what is that country)', 'I Will Lift Up Mine Eyes Unto the Hills', 'Advent (This Advent moon shines cold and clear)', 'Sound Sleep (Some are laughing, some are weeping)', 'Rest (O Earth, lie heavily upon her eyes)', and even the exquisite 'Song (When I am dead, my dearest)'. The sleeping soul is surrounded by a 'stillness that is *almost* Paradise' ('Rest' 8; my italics), a condition of virtually complete stasis that is also (and paradoxically) premonitory: 'Until the morning of Eternity/Her rest shall not begin nor end, but be' (lines 12-13). And in that sleep which is not death what dreams may come? Rossetti says that 'Night and morning, noon and even,/ Their sound fills her dreams with Heaven' ('Sound Sleep' 17-18). Soul Sleep permits the visions and dream-glimpses of paradise which is the object of those who desire a better country (cf. 'They Desire a Better Country').

> As I lie dreaming
>   It rises, that land;
> There rises before me,
>   Its green golden strand,
> With the bowing cedars
>   And the shining sand;

> It sparkles and flashes
> Like a shaken brand.
>
> ('Mother Country', lines 9-16)

The initial rule in Rossetti's ideology is that only the dreams of Soul Sleep give one access to the real details of the Christian paradise (cf. 'I Will Lift Up Mine Eyes Unto the Hills'). The poetic imagination of what such dreams must be produces, in turn, the actual verse descriptions of paradise which we find in Rossetti's poetry. In all cases, however, the importance of the initial rule is emphasized by a secondary (operating) rule: that Rossetti's poetry will only venture upon a description of paradise through the rite of passage initially defined in the doctrine of Soul Sleep (with its accompanying poetic imagination of the 'dreams' and visions which must accompany such a state). So, in the poem 'Paradise' Rossetti gives a detailed description of the heaven she saw 'Once in a dream', a concrete representation which she draws from various traditionary Christian sources not the least of which is the New Testament, and in particular the Book of Revelation. The catalogue of details which make up her picture of heaven concludes in an 'o altitudo', however, which means to emphasize the secondary nature of the poetic representation. For the poem records as it were a dream of the sleeping soul's more final dream, and as such it stands at three removes from paradise. The dream *version* of the sleeping soul's *dream-vision* is itself beyond any possibility of an accurate concrete rendering. The closest approximation one can arrive at in this world to the vision that can be expected after death in Soul Sleep is a description not of paradise itself, but of the emotional effect which results from the actual desire for such a vision. Thus it is that the poem's description of paradise concludes (indeed, culminates) in the utter defeat of all concrete imaginative detail:

> Oh harps, oh crowns of plenteous stars,
>   Oh green palm branches many-leaved—
> Eye hath not seen, nor ear hath heard,
>   Nor heart conceived.
>
> ('Paradise', lines 37-40)

The premonitory dreams of the sleeping soul take place in a region set far apart from the ordinary, 'self-destructive' world;

and that world is thereby submitted to the negative judgement implicit in the invocation of such a visionary place.

But that is only one function of the machinery of Soul Sleep as used by Rossetti. Its other principal function is to provide Rossetti with a rationale capable of explaining, and even justifying, her existence in the late Victorian world of getting and spending which she judged so severely. That is to say, Rossetti consistently used the grammar of the doctrine of Soul Sleep as an analogue for the condition of the contemporary Christian. Rossetti's poems take their model from the visions of Soul Sleep, and the latter state is itself used repeatedly as a model for the state of the Christian soul in the premillenial period of late Victorian England. By thus manipulating the machinery of the doctrine of Soul Sleep Rossetti was able to produce such famous and beautiful poems as the 'Song' (When I am dead, my dearest), for in that and so many similar works she elaborated an analogy between the (physical) 'resting place' of the body and the (spiritual) place in which the sleeping soul was to be suspended.

This last result has a widespread and profound effect upon the character of Rossetti's poetry. In the first place, it tends to blur any clear distinction between her secular and her religious poetry, since almost all of her best work is generated through a poetic grammar that is fundamentally religious in origin and character. We must, of course, distinguish between her 'Devotional' and her non-devotional poetry, partly because *she* made such a distinction, and partly because it is an important distinction *in fact*.[21] But if a large part of her work is not specifically *devotional*, it is virtually all 'religious' in its orientation.

In the second place, when we begin to see that a specific religious orientation has had a signal impact on all aspects of her verse, we are unexpectedly (and almost paradoxically) provided with a means for gathering the power of her work outside

[21] The distinction is marked in her volumes of poetry, where specially 'devotional' poems are marked off in a separate section at the end. Her 1893 *Verses* is a volume exclusively containing devotional poems. While almost all of her poetry could be called 'religious', the 'devotional' poems are those which deal with specific liturgical topics and occasions. To a strict sabbatarian like Rossetti (and many of her readers were sabbatarians as well), only devotional verse would be suitable for perusal on Sunday. Moreover, the devotional verse is always conceived with an audience in mind which understands and actively practises devotional exercises of various kinds.

of its own religious self-representations. That is to say, we begin to see how the Christian and Adventist machinery in her work is an historically specific set of images which do not so much describe actual spiritual realities (like paradise and so forth) as they indicate, by poetic obliquity, how difficult it seemed to imagine, least of all actually to live, a fully human life in the real world of her place and time.

This non-religious, this *human*, view of her poetry is implicit in the following shrewd set of remarks made about Rossetti's work in 1895 by Arthur Benson in *The National Review*:

> Some writers have the power of creating a species of aërial land-scape in the minds of their readers, often vague and shadowy, not obtruding itself strongly upon the consciousness, but forming a quiet background, like the scenery of portraits, in which the action of the lyric or the sonnet seems to lie. I am not now speaking of pictorial writing, which definitely aims at producing, with more or less vividness, a house, a park, a valley, but lyrics and poems of pure thought and feeling, which have none the less a haunting sense of locality in which the mood dreams itself out.
>
> Christina Rossetti's *mise-en-scène* is a place of gardens, orchards, wooded dingles, with a churchyard in the distance. The scene shifts a little, but the spirit never wanders far afield; and it is certainly singular that one who lived out almost the whole of her life in a city so majestic, sober, and inspiring as London, should never bring the consciousness of streets and thoroughfares and populous murmur into her writings. She, whose heart was so with birds and fruits, cornfields and farm-yard sounds, never even revolts against or despairs of the huge desolation, the laborious monotony of a great town. She does not sing to the caged bird, with exotic memories of freedom stirred by the flashing water, the hanging groundsel of her wired prison, but with a wild voice, with visions only limited by the rustic conventionalities of toil and tillage. The dewy English woodland, the sharp silences of winter, the gloom of low-hung clouds, and the sigh of weeping rains are her backgrounds.[22]

Benson has indeed located the primal scene, as it were, of all of Rossetti's poetry. It is a scene which stands in an antithetical relation to the life of Rossetti's immediate experience, to the life and 'the way we live now'. Secondly, this scene elaborates a set of images which are, as we have already noted, analogous

---

[22] A. C. Benson, 'Christina Rossetti', *National Review* xxiv (Feb. 1895), pp. 753-63; quoted from Mackenzie Bell's *Christina Rossetti*, London, 1898, pp. 330-1.

to those which were generated through Rossetti's use of the doctrine of Soul Sleep. In each case, however, we may come to understand that such 'poetical' places and scenes constitute Rossetti's imaginative transportations—poetic idealizations— of actual places and scenes which she either knew and recoiled from (the Babylon that she saw as the world of London), or that she recollected, dreamed of, and yearned toward. It is beyond question that the charming *mise-en-scène* to which Benson draws our attention is a fantasy delineation of the rural environs of Holmer Green in Buckinghamshire, where Rossetti's grand- father Gaetano Polidori had a cottage and small garden. Rossetti's childhood visits to this place (they ended when she was nine years old) were later to become, by her own ac- knowledgement, the source of the ideal forms which she asso- ciated with the natural world.[23] As such, they allow us to reconceptualize her 'religious' idealizations, which are struc- turally congruent with the 'natural' idealizations. In each case we are dealing with symbol structures that express, and re- present, a network of socially and psychologically specific ten- sions and contradictions. In a word, Rossetti's poetry is not 'about' that fantasy scene pointed out by Benson, nor is it about the equally abstract 'religious' scenes offered to us at the surface of her poetry. Her poetry is an oblique glimpse into the heaven and the hell of late Victorian England as that world was mediated through the particular experiences of Christina Rossetti.

As I have argued in the previous chapter, Rossetti's heaven and hell are conceptualized in terms of personal love relations: true and real love as opposed to the various illusions of happi- ness, pleasure, and fulfilment. Indeed, hell for Rossetti is merely the culminant experience of any life which has been lived in a 'worldly', which is to say in a self-destructive, way. Heaven, conversely, is the achievement of a complete and final escape from such an existence. The importance of the doctrine of Soul Sleep is that it postulates a condition or state which mediates between the finalities of heaven and hell. In that state, according to the doctrinal position adopted by Rossetti's poetry, one achieves an initial release from the wearying con-

---

[23] See Bell, pp. 9-11 and anon., 'Rossetti Family in Bucks', *Notes and Queries* clix (6 Sept. 1930), p. 176.

fusions of the world as well as one's first visionary glimpses of a paradisal (or non-worldly) existence.

Carried over into her verse, the doctrine of Soul Sleep provides Rossetti with an analogue for poetic vision itself—more specifically, for a poetic vision conceived in certain religious terms which are broadly grounded in the general ideology of Christian ideas. It is as if Rossetti were postulating a doctrinal foundation for Wordsworth's famous Romantic formulation of the state of poetic vision, when one is laid asleep in body to become a living soul, and when one may finally begin to 'see into the life of things'. This poetic employment of the doctrine of Soul Sleep provides Rossetti, as we have already seen, with the means for generating 'paradisal images' which answer to her emotional needs: images which at once sustain her deepest and most frustrate desires, and which also help to reveal the circumstances which are responsible for experiences of misery and betrayal.

The doctrine also helped Rossetti to develop a complex theory of dream-vision which can be most graphically seen in poems like 'Sleep at Sea' and in particular the great 'From House to Home'. 'Sleep at Sea' narrates the voyage of a ship of fools who are called 'the sleepers' and whose ominous fate is specifically connected to the sleep in which they are caught up.[24] In this state they have certain dreams that recall the premonitory dreams of paradise we have already noted in the poems written out of the doctrine of Soul Sleep; but in this case the dreams are represented as perilous illusions, just as the sleep is only a parodic version of a true Soul Sleep:

> Oh soft the streams drop music
>   Between the hills,
> And musical the birds' nests
>   Beside those rills:
> The nests are types of home
>   Love-hidden from ills,
> The nests are types of spirits
>   Love music fills.

---

[24] I do not know that critics have yet pointed out a signal aspect of this poem: that it is in crucial ways a meditation on, and interpretation of, Coleridge's 'Rime of the Ancient Mariner', and especially the (later) parts of the poem which treat of the dead mariners and the visiting troupe of animating spirits.

> So dream the sleepers,
>   Each man in his place;
> The lightning shows the smile
>   Upon each face:
> The ship is driving, driving
>   It drives apace:
> And sleepers smile, and spirits
>   Bewail their case.
>
> (lines 17-32)

The original manuscript title of the poem, 'Something Like Truth',[25] indicates the purposefulness with which Rossetti constructed this demonic version of Soul Sleep and dream-vision. The doctrinal message of the poem is, of course, quite clear: that the Christian must be watchful on all occasions, that the structures and images of the spiritual life are themselves liable to an evil inversion. Particularly treacherous are the paradisal temptations which are generated out of the desire for rest, comfort, and the eternal life:

> No voice to call the sleepers,
>   No hand to raise:
> They sleep to death in dreaming
>   Of length of days.
> Vanity of vanities,
>   The Preacher says:
> Vanity is the end
>   Of all their ways.
>
> (lines 81-8)

In 'From House to Home' the contrast between illusory dreams and paradisal vision is even more elaborately developed. The first 75 lines of the poem construct the dream of 'An earthly paradise supremely fair/That lured me from the goal' (lines 7-8). But the central love-object in that paradise eventually flees from it and the speaker is left empty and devastated (lines 77 ff.). The second part of the poem develops an alternative dream-sequence in which the goal of a paradisal vision is associated with a nightmare rite of passage. The importance of this association, from a technical (rather than a doctrinal) point of view, is that it forces Rossetti to subject all aspects of her own poetical machinery to a critical examination at all points; and

[25] See Crump's edition, p. 262.

this in its turn frees her to exploit in unusual ways the imagistic, tonal, and symbolic materials which are generated out of that machinery. Specifically, any image, mood, or symbol is laid open to sudden and arbitrary inversions of their apparent poetic value. Indeed, it seems to me that the often-noted melancholia which pervades so much of Rossetti's poetry is a direct function of its openness to such arbitrary inversions—as if she were herself aware of the treacherousness of her own most cherished dreams and ideals, as if she were also aware that all that she might say might just as well have been unsaid, or been said rather differently, or might not even have been said at all. This is the burden that hangs about the touching and plangent lines of a song like 'When I am dead, my dearest', where the poetry is haunted by the vanity and inconsequence which it reveals and appears to triumph over, but by which it too is at least partially victimized.

V

Thus, the ultimate marginality of Rossetti's particular Christian stance was to become the source of its final strength, the privilege of its historical backwardness. The ideological triumph of Broad Church Christianity and Anglo-Catholicism in the early twentieth century—in the academy at any rate—drove Rossetti out of the Great Tradition and its attendant anthologies. To us, however, her work seems peculiarly alive, *as poetry*, to her age's cultural contradictions because it is able to reveal how those contradictions are replicated at the heart of her own deepest beliefs and commitments. Moreover, that those commitments should have been located within the tradition of Christianity proves to be the conclusive source of her poetry's importance and power. On the one hand, her poetry contains a forcible and persistent reminder that the themes of Christian poetry—even the greatest of such themes, like those of guilt and redemption, of resurrection, of incarnation—are time- and place-specific, that they have had a beginning, and a middle, and that they will finally have an end as well. To imagine otherwise is a vanity and an illusion, a peculiar blindness from which only those who recognize their own historical backwardness will be exempt. On the other hand, her poetry also demonstrates, through the self-destruction of its own special worldliness (that is, through the self-destruction of its own religious certainties), the true ground of poetic transcendence. Poetry does not triumph over its times by arriving at a 'vision' or idea of the Truth, whether religious or otherwise; it triumphs when it reveals, once again, the local and human origin of all particular and historical events. Hence it is that poetry only maintains its life in later ages and cultures when it preserves its integrity, when it confronts those later ages and cultures with a human world which is important to other human worlds precisely because it is different, local, limited. The survival of that which is specific and therefore obsolete—in particular, the survival of those things which are most conscious of their own limitedness— is the ground of all we can mean by 'transcendence'. It is the reciprocal, indeed, the dialectical gift which past and present give to each other in order to secure the future.

(1982-3)

V

Literature and the Critique
of History

1. The Book of Byron and the Book of a World

Thought is no longer theoretical. As soon as it functions it offends or reconciles, attacks or repels, breaks, dissociates, unites or reunites; it cannot help but liberate or enslave.

(Michel Foucault)

I

Byron's popularity—the fact that he was a bestseller and 'famous in [his] time'—has always focused certain literary problems not least of all at the outset for Byron himself. 'Lord Byron cuts a figure—but he is not figurative,'[1] Keats waspishly observed in a letter to the George Keatses. This is an envious and illuminating remark which reveals as much about Keats and his ambitions for a successful career as it does about the character of Byron's verse, the phenomenon of Byronism, and the changing structure of the institution of letters at the beginning of the nineteenth century. Later writers have sometimes condescended to Byron, particularly to the Byron of the pre-exilic period, as a factitious writer who had merely seized the main chance during the Years of Fame. Of course it is true that he was himself largely responsible for creating the enormous popularity of the Oriental and Byronic Tales. Nevertheless—so the story goes—he cranked out verse between 1812-15 to various formulas and audience expectations. In this activity he was not so much a poet as he was a pander and whore to public taste. It passes without saying that those tastes were corrupt. (The non-malicious version of this general view is that Byron invented the myth of himself as The Romantic Poet, thereby creating a new structure of authorship which answered to the changing conditions that were rapidly transforming the English literary institution.)

Byron himself was well aware of these events and social formations. His letters and his poetry alike reflect on these matters

[1] *The Letters of John Keats*, ed. H. E. Rollins, Cambridge, Mass., 1958, ii. 67.

often. In May, 1813, for example, at the peak of his London years, Byron writes to Thomas Moore about projects in poetry: 'Stick to the East;—the oracle, Staël, told me it was the only poetical policy . . . The little I have done in that way is merely a "voice in the wilderness" for you; and, if it has had any success, that also will prove that the public are orientalizing, and pave the path for you.'[2] Later, of course, he came to speak more critically, even disparagingly, of this kind of careerist calculation. In January 1822 he tells Douglas Kinnaird that '*my* object is not *immediate* popularity in my present productions which are written on a different system from the rage of the day'; and in another letter three days later: 'Now once and for all about publication—I [n]*ever courted the* public—and I will never yield to it.—As long as I can find a *single* reader I will publish my Mind . . . and write while I feel the impetus'.[3]

Byron arrived at this changed position largely because of the Separation Controversy and its aftermath, which exposed to critical analysis a whole train of Byron's most cherished ideas and illusions. The idea which dominates his 'Epistle to Augusta'—that 'I have been cunning in mine overthrow,/ The careful pilot of my proper woe' (lines 23-4)—has its deepest filiations with Byron's public life and poetical career between 1807 and 1816:

> With false Ambition what had I to do?
> Little with Love, and least of all with Fame;
> And yet they came unsought; and with me grew;
> And made me all which they can make—a Name.
> Yet this was not the end I did pursue;
> Surely I once beheld a nobler aim.
> ('Epistle to Augusta', lines 97-102)[4]

This critical examination of himself, his public life, and his poetical/moral goals will dominate most of his later years and will affect all aspects of his work in the most profound ways.

I have sketched this brief history in order to recollect the

---

[2] *Byron's Letters and Journals*, ed. Leslie A. Marchand, Cambridge, Mass., 1973-82, iii. 101 (cited below as *BLJ*).

[3] *BLJ* ix. 92, 94.

[4] The texts of Byron's poems which were printed after 1816—with the exception of the last two cantos of *Childe Harold* and all of *Don Juan*—are here taken from *Byron's Works. Poetry*, ed. E. H. Coleridge, London, 1898-1904. For the other texts, see below.

most salient aspect of Byron's work: that he wrote about *himself*, and that his books, like God's human creatures, are all made in his image and likeness. The most dramatic example of this biographical/historical imperative in his work is perhaps to be found in the amusing stanzas 51-2 of *Beppo*.[5]

> Oh! that I had the art of easy writing,
>   What should be easy reading! could I scale
> Parnassus, where the Muses sit inditing
>   Those pretty poems never known to fail,
> How quickly would I print (the World delighting)
>   A Grecian, Syrian, or *As*syrian tale;
> And sell you, mixed with western Sentimentalism,
> Some samples of the *finest Orientalism*.
>
> But I am but a nameless sort of person,
>   (A broken Dandy lately on my travels) . . .

Part of the genius of this passage is that it manages to be at once critical and sympathetic toward Byron's career, his own earlier work, and the audience which found (and which continues to find) an interest and profit in such things. This poetry institutes a benevolent critique of itself and its World, on the one hand, and on the other of the verse which fashion will cultivate at various times, as well as the very concept and event of 'the fashionable'.

This pointed and personal quality in Byron's work is apparent from the beginning. His first book, *Fugitive Pieces*, was privately printed in 1806 for an audience of friends and acquaintances who were privy to its local references and biographical connections—many of which were connections with themselves. *Hours of Idleness*, his first published work, appeared the following year, and it sought to extend the range of Byron's intimacies to a somewhat larger book-purchasing audience. Here, Byron projected himself before his English audience as a recognizable figure whom, he trusted, they would be happy to take to their breasts. Here, the English world at large met, for the first time, not the Man but the Lord of Feeling, a carefully constructed self-image which was fashioned to launch him on his public

---

[5] Similar autobiographical references abound in *Don Juan* (see e.g. Canto XI sts. 55-85). Quotations from *Don Juan* below are taken from the *Variorum* edition of T. G. Steffan and W. W. Pratt, Austin, Tex., 1957 (cited here as *DJV*).

career. This was not conceived, at the time, as a literary career.[6]

Byron succeeded in his effort, though not precisely as he had expected. Certain hostile reviews—most notoriously Brougham's in the highly visible and influential *Edinburgh Review*—interrupted Byron's initial, unruffled expectations. Had he reflected more critically on the hostile reception which *Fugitive Pieces* had provoked in certain narrow quarters of its local (Southwell) society, he might have foreseen some trouble for his next book.[7] But he did not, apparently, and seems only to have realized later that he was destined to be both the darling and the demon of his age.

The attack on *Hours of Idleness* was another opportunity for Byron to produce yet a third Book of Himself: this time, *English Bards and Scotch Reviewers*, the fiery counter-attack on his persecutors and the culture which supported such beings.[8] If it is true that Byron was 'born for opposition', this book revealed that fact, for the first time unmistakably.

And so it went on. In 1809 Byron left benighted England to chew over the high rhetoric of his last book, and he plunged into Europe and the Levant, where his next productions began to accumulate their materials in the much larger context of European affairs. He wrote a continuation, or sequel, to *English Bards and Scotch Reviewers* called *Hints from Horace*, which was not published in his lifetime, and he composed the first two cantos of that unsurpassed act of literary self-creation, *Childe Harold's Pilgrimage. A Romaunt*.[9]

This book is worth pausing over—not the poem, but the book.[10] It is a handsome and rather expensive (30s.) quarto

---

6 For a discussion of these matters see my *Fiery Dust. Byron's Poetic Development*, Chicago, 1968, chap. 1, and *Lord Byron. Complete Poetical Works*, ed. Jerome J. McGann, Oxford, 1980- , i. 360-3. The latter work is hereafter referred to as *CPW*. The best single piece of work on the biographical dimensions of Byron's poetry—it is one of the most important essays on Byron ever written, as well as a crucial work on the methodology of biographical studies—is 'Narcissus Jilted', by Cecil Lang, first given in an abbreviated version as a lecture at the 1984 Caltech/Weingart Conference in Humanities.

7 See *CPW*, ibid. and poems 24, 25, 28 in *CPW*.

8 *CPW* i. 398-9.

9 *CPW* i. 426-7 and ii. 268-71.

10 For complete bibliographical details see *Byron's Works. Poetry*, ed. E. H. Coleridge, London, 1901-4, vii. 180-4 and T.J. Wise, *Byron. A Bibliography* . . ., London,

volume beautifully printed on heavy paper. It comprises four distinct parts: 1. The title poem in two cantos (pp. iii-109); 2. The extensive notes to these cantos (pp. 111-61); 3. A section headed 'Poems' which included fourteen short pieces (pp. 163-200); 4. An Appendix containing bibliographical materials, translations, Romaic transcriptions and one facsimile manuscript, all having to do with the current state of the literary culture of modern Greece (pp. 201-[27]). Its publisher conceived its audience to be a wealthy one, people interested in travel books and topographical poems, people with a classical education and with a taste for antiquarian lore and the philosophical musings of a young English lord. As it turned out, all of England and Europe were to be snared by this book's imaginations. It went through a dozen (cheaper) editions in three years and established all of the principal features of that imaginative (but not imaginary) world-historical figure known as Byron. Later circumstances would only provide the public with slightly different perspectives on this figure.

The book of *Childe Harold* published in 1812 picks up the autobiographical myth which Byron had left *in medias res* when he left England in 1809.[11] The notes specifically recall the controversy surrounding *English Bards and Scotch Reviewers*, the section of 'Poems' is so arranged as to mirror the personal tale narrated through the title poem, and the latter presents a dramatic picture of a young lord who leaves his local home and friends, as well as his country, in a condition of psychic and cultural alienation. Simply, he is disgusted with himself and the world as he has thus far seen it. He finds, when he flees to other lands and in particular to the fabulous Levantine seat of western culture, that his own personal *anomie*, experienced in the tight little island of Britain, mirrors the condition of Europe (or, in Byron's startling and important variation on this ancient topos, that Europe and the entire world mirrors *his* personal condition). Thus does Byron force himself—and the individual person through himself—to the centre of attention. What his book

---

1932-3, i. 50-4. The history of the book's publication is discussed in *CPW* ii. 268-9. The prose quotations below from *Childe Harold's Pilgrimage. A Romaunt* are taken from the first edition, and page nos. are given in the text.

11 For a more detailed discussion of the context and meaning of the poem see *CPW* ii, ibid. and *Fiery Dust*, Part II.

says is not simply that we should deplore the condition of western culture in this critical time, but that we should deplore it because its debasement has poisoned its chief, indeed, its only, value: the individual human life. In particular, Byron's life.

Byron inserts his personal history into the latest phase of the European crisis which began in 1789. The outbreak of the Peninsular War in 1809 initiated the last act in the drama of the Napoleonic Wars, which would end in the defeat of Napoleon and the restoration of the European monarchies under the hegemony of England. In *Childe Harold* (1812) Byron's itinerary takes him first to the very heart of the Peninsular events, where his initial mood of disgust at his English existence acquires its European dimension. When he moves to the East and the dominions of the Turkish Empire, including Greece, his cynicism is confirmed: Greece, the very symbol of the west's highest ideals and self-conceptions, lies in thrall not merely to the military rule of the Porte, but to the contest of self-serving political interests of the English, French, and Russians.

This is the context which explains Byron's peculiar Appendix, with its heterogenous body of Romaic materials. *Childe Harold* (1812) is obsessed with the idea of the renewal of human culture in the west at a moment of its deepest darkness. This means for Byron the renewal of the value of the individual person, and the renewal of Greece as an independent political entity becomes Byron's 'objective correlative' for this idea. *Childe Harold* (1812) is thus, on one hand, a critique of present European society and politics, and, on the other, a pronouncement of the crucial need, throughout Europe, for the independence of Greece. As Byron would later say: 'There is *no* freedom—even for *Masters*—in the midst of slaves.'[12] The question of Greece thus becomes for Byron a way of focusing the central questions which bear upon the present European epoch. The Europeans normally date this epoch from 1789, and rightly so, but in this book (as well as in his next two books, *The Giaour* and *The Bride of Abydos*) Byron argues that the conflict of European self-interests can be best and most clearly understood in terms of the recent history of Greece, whose abortive efforts for independence in the late eighteenth century

[12] *BLJ* ix. 41.

were either neglected by the European powers or actively betrayed.

Thus, in *Childe Harold* (1812) Byron enlarged his personal myth, which he had already begun to develop in his earlier books, by inserting it into the wider context of the European political theatre as it appeared to him in 1809-12; and the central ideological focus of the entire myth involves the question of personal and political freedom in the oppressive and contradictory circumstances which Byron observed in the world of his experience. More than anything else this book says that the most personal and intimate aspects of an individual's life are closely involved with, and affected by, the social and political context in which the individual is placed. Byron goes further to say that such a context is more complex and extensive than one ordinarily thinks, that each person is more deeply affected by (as it were) invisible people, places, and events than we customarily imagine. Ali Pacha and his Albanians may appear far removed from England and the Napoleonic Wars, but to the perspicacious European they will have more than a merely exotic interest. Similarly, Byron's use of antiquarian and classical materials, though ostentatious, is not merely a clumsy display of learning and artistic pendantry. On the contrary, he invokes the classical world and the later history of Europe's investment in that world because this complex ideological and political network exerts a powerful effect upon current European affairs, and hence on the experience of each single person living in Europe. A powerful and illuminating irony runs through Byron's flight from contemporary England and Europe and his pursuit of ancient Greek ideals:

> Of the ancient Greeks we know more than enough; at least the younger men of Europe devote much of their time to the study of Greek writers and history, which would be more usefully spent in mastering their own. Of the moderns, we are perhaps more neglectful than they deserve; and while every man of any pretensions to learning is tiring out his youth, and often his age, in the study of the language and the harangues of the Athenian demogogues in favour of freedom, the real or supposed descendants of these sturdy republicans are left to the actual tyranny of their masters . . . (*Childe Harold's Pilgrimage. A Romaunt* (1812), p. 173)

Byron's proposal in his book is to look at England, Europe, and

Greece not as these political entities appear in their ideological self-representations, but 'as they are' (p. 174) in fact. The reality reveals an Islam and a modern Greece very different from what they are commonly represented to be in English and European commentaries; it also reveals the hypocritical fault lines which run through the high-minded and Greek-derived ideologies of liberty to which the major European powers give lip-service. In Byron's book, the image of the young European gentleman acquiring a classical education is contradictory and deeply satiric. Such a person's mind is filled with self-serving and self-deluding ideas which permit him to identify with the dream of ancient Greece even as they also allow him to remain blind to certain important actualities: that the Russians 'have twice . . . deceived and abandoned' the Greeks, that the French seek 'the deliverance of continental Greece' as part of their policy for 'the subjugation of the rest of Europe', and that the English, in addition to the pursuit of their economic self-interests, profess to seek the freedom of Greece even as they subjugate the rights of 'our Irish Helots' (p. 201) and 'Catholic brethren' (p. 172).

In Byron's books—*Childe Harold* (1812) is merely prototypical in this respect—the variety of materials often conveys an image of heterogeneity, but in fact this image is no more than the sign of intrinsic connections which are not normally perceived, of connections between 'opposite and discordant' matters which only *appear* to be separated, but which are in fact fundamentally related. The soon-to-be published Oriental Tales are not merely a set of exotic adventure stories. They constitute a series of symbolic historical and political meditations on current European ideology and politics in the context of the relations between East and West after the break-up of the Roman Empire and the emergence of Islam.[13] That later readers and critics have often taken Byron's Levantine materials as a sign of a (presumptively shallow) poetic interest in local colour and oriental ornamentation merely testifies to a failure of critical intelligence and historical consciousness. Byron was deeply interested in these social and political questions and he used his poetry to probe their meaning and their roots. Later criticism has too often

---

[13] See the commentaries to the Oriental Tales in *CPW* iii.

translated *its* lack of interest into a myth of the intellectual poverty of Byron's verse.

Byron's skill at manipulating his publications produced some of the strangest and most interesting books of poetry ever printed in England. *The Giaour* may stand as one example out of many.[14] Like the other tales which were soon to follow, this poem is a political allegory told from the point of view of those 'younger men of Europe' whom Byron described in the notes to *Childe Harold* (1812). The subject of the poem, at the plot level, is the state of modern Greece around 1780. At the narrative level, the poem is a contemporary (1809-13) meditation on the meaning of the European (and especially the English) understanding of Levantine politics between 1780 and 1813. The poem's story (its plot level) is a nihilistic tragedy in which all parties are involved, and destroyed. The meditation on the story is carried most dramatically in the introductory (167) lines, which appear as the 'original' work of the poem's redactor (Byron himself), as well as in the poem's 'Advertisement' and its many prose notes, also represented in *The Giaour* as the 'original' work of the editor/redactor Byron. The entire significance of this excellent work does not appear unless one responds to the interplay between the poem's two 'levels'. Briefly, the 'original' work of the editor/redactor comprises a set of deeply contradictory materials: on one hand, a complete romantic sympathy with the characters and events as well as an absorption in the heroic ideology which they exhibit; on the other, a mordant series of comical remarks on Eastern mores and commonplace European ideas about such matters. This radical split in the poem's attitude at its meditative level reflects, and interprets, the European understanding of the Levant between 1780-1813. The interpretation which Byron produces is a critical one: the European understanding is self-deluded and helpless, and Byron's own exposure to this failed understanding is represented as the vision of the one-eyed man in the kingdom of the blind. The comedy of the poem's notes, apparently so urbane, is in fact a flinching away, the laughter,

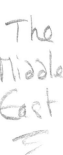

---

[14] *CPW* iii. 406-15. For an excellent discussion of the political aspects of two of the books of Byron's tales see Peter Manning, 'Tales and Politics: *The Corsair, Lara, The White Doe of Rylstone*', in *Byron. Poetry and Politics . . .*, ed. E. A. Stürzl and James Hogg, Salzburg, 1981, pp. 204-30.

spoken of in *Don Juan*, which serves to hold back weeping and bleaker realities.

All of Byron's works, and especially his published books, exhibit intersections of these kinds. Thus, his bibliography is more than a scholar's guide and resource, it is also a graphic display of his life in books, and of the extension of his life through books. The piracies, the huge number of translations, the numerous printings all attest and perpetuate the poetic explorations of reality which he initially set in motion. And it is the 'books', rather than the 'poems' (or least of all the 'texts'), which draw attention to the central quality of Byron's poetical work; for when we study the works through their material existences we are thereby helped to see and understand the social and historical ground which defines their human meanings.

II

Nowhere is this fact about Byron's work more clear than in the case of his masterwork, *Don Juan*. We respond to its name as if it were one thing, as indeed it is; but it is also, like the world which it expresses and represents, incredibly various and heterogeneous. Readers have of course always responded to that variety, but we must do so even as we also bear in mind that the variety is of a determinate and specifiable sort. *Don Juan* is, formally, a romantic fragment poem comprising six authorized and published volumes, along with a body of material published only after Byron's death, at different times and with various justifications. The first two volumes were published by John Murray in a certain way, and the next four volumes were published by John Hunt in a very different way. Important aspects of the meaning of the poem are bound up with these interesting events in the work's publication history.[15]

Most important to see is that when Byron began publishing the poem with John Hunt he was released from certain constraints which he had to struggle against when he was publishing with the conservative house of Murray. *Don Juan*'s (rejected) Preface and (suppressed) Dedication emphasize the political and social critique which is finally so fundamental to the

---

[15] For a discussion of the history of the poem's publication see *DJV* i. 25-52.

poem.[16] But Murray and his allies forced Byron to revise the published version of the first five cantos so as to *de*-emphasize this aspect of the epic. As a consequence, the original Cantos I-V (the first two published volumes of the poem) preserve the poem's social and political critique as a peripheral and subsidiary matter, an incidental topic that seems to appear and disappear in the poem in a random way. The suppressed Dedication was not published until 1832, and the rejected Preface did not appear until 1901.

With the appearance of Cantos VI-VIII, published by Hunt, the situation changes radically. These cantos are introduced with a prose Preface where the social and political issues are finally raised to great, even to a dominant, position; and the poetic materials as well undergo a shift in emphasis toward more explicitly social and political matters. This change in the poem has been recognized for some time and critics have described the differences between the earlier and the later cantos in various (often useful) ways. What has not been seen, however, is the structural change brought about in the poem as a whole when Byron began his epic 'again' (as it were) with Cantos VI-VIII and John Hunt.

We can begin to see what is involved here by looking briefly at the original Preface to Cantos I-II. Byron never completed this Preface, which descends to us in his fragmentary draft manuscript. Nevertheless, what he completed gives us some interesting information about his initial conception of the work. In the course of satirizing Wordsworth Byron tells his readers that 'the following epic Narrative' is to be regarded as the work of a certain 'Story-teller' who is living, and delivering his narrative, at a certain place and time: specifically, 'in a village in the Sierra Morena on the road between Monasterio and Seville' sometime during the Peninsular War (the reference to the village in the Sierra Morena is autobiographical and

---

[16] See *DJV* ii. 3-20 and iv. 4-15. The Preface is placed at the beginning of the text of *Don Juan* in *DJV* as well as its sequel, the Penguin modernized edition. Leslie A. Marchand's school edition also places it at the poem's beginning. Such a placement is seriously misleading, however, for Byron not only left this Preface in an uncompleted state, he discarded it and meant originally to replace it with the verse Dedication. The latter he reluctantly removed from Cantos I-II under pressure from his publisher and friends. The conjecture of *DJV* (see ibid.), that the fragmentary Preface was written after the verse Dedication and then abandoned, is almost certainly not right.

specifies the date as 1809). As for the narrator himself, 'The Reader is . . . requested to suppose him . . . either an Englishman settled in Spain—or a Spaniard who had travelled in England—perhaps one of the Liberals who have subsequently been so liberally rewarded by Ferdinand of grateful memory—for his restoration.'[17] This passage establishes a second point of view on the events treated in the poem: that is, one subsequent to 1814 and the early years of the period of European restoration following the fall of Napoleon. As it turns out, the reader inevitably places this historical vantage-point at that moment of contemporaneity which attaches to the poem's date of composition and/or publication (in this case, 1818-19).

Byron finally dropped his Preface with its specific historical perspectives, and he did not fully exploit the structural advantages of his poem's double perspectivism until he began to reconceive the project of *Don Juan* in 1822-3. Before considering that act of reconception, however, we should reflect upon the double historical perspective in terms of which the work was initially conceived and set in motion. Like the later cantos, Cantos I-V organize their materials in two dialectically functioning historical frames of reference: on the one hand, the frame of the poem's plot or 'story', which contains the narrated events of Juan's life; and, on the other hand, the frame of the poem's narrating voice, which comprises Byron speaking to his world between 1818-24 via the six published volumes of *Don Juan*. Byron's rejected and incomplete Preface to Cantos I-II reminds us that he initially had some idea of using the plot and the narrative to comment on each other, and that he thought of Juan's life in specific historical terms. As it turned out, he rejected the idea of setting the poem's narrative frame in the complicated way suggested by the initial Preface, where it is unclear whether the narrator speaks from the vantage of 1809 or 1818, or both. In Cantos I-V Byron also neglected to specify clearly the historical frame in which Juan's career is placed. When he published Cantos VI-VIII with John Hunt, however, he finally let his contemporary readers see very clearly the exact relation between the history of Juan's career and the history of the poem's narrator, Byron *in propria persona*.

---

17 *DJV* ii. 4-5.

We can date Byron's reconception of his epic with some precision: in January and February 1822, which is the period when Byron resumed his composition of *Don Juan* (he left off his poem when he finished Canto V at the end of 1820). Byron wrote to Murray on 16 Feb. 1821 and outlined a projected plot for Juan's adventures.[18] This outline, however, only corresponds in a loose and general way to the episodes of the poem that he was soon to write, and hence shows that Byron had not yet fixed on a definite plan. Byron first articulated this plan to Medwin between December 1821 and March 1822:

I left him [Juan] in the seraglio. There I shall make one of the favourites, a Sultana . . . fall in love with him, and carry him off from Constantinople . . . Well, they make good their escape to Russia; where, if Juan's passion cools, and I don't know what to do with the lady, I shall make her die of the plague . . . As our hero can't do without a mistress, he shall next become man-mistress to Catherine the Great . . . I shall . . . send him, when he is *hors de combat*, to England as her ambassador. In his suite he shall have a girl whom he shall have rescued during one of his northern campaigns, who shall be in love with him, and he not with her . . . I shall next draw a town and country life at home . . . He shall get into all sorts of scrapes, and at length end his career in France. Poor Juan shall be guillotined in the French Revolution! What do you think of my plot? It shall have twenty-four books too . . .[19]

This scheme corresponds fairly closely to the poem as we now have it, and it holds to the general plan which Byron gave to Murray at the beginning of 1821 (though not to the particular details of the episodes). The most important episode missing from Byron's outline is the siege of Ismail, though it is clear from this and Byron's immediately preceding discussion that he planned to send Juan into war. But in the first few months of 1822 Byron seems not yet to have decided on the Ismail episode, as he had not yet worked out how to separate Juan and Gulbeyaz. These decisions would be made in the next few months. The idea of having Juan die on the guillotine in the French Revolution was certainly fundamental to the plot of the poem from the earliest stages of its conception as a plotted sequence.

[18] *BLJ* viii. 78.
[19] *Medwin's Conversations of Lord Byron*, ed. Ernest J. Lovell Jr., Princeton, 1966, pp. 164-5.

The Preface to Cantos VI-VIII, written in September 1822, calls attention, on one hand, to the historical immediacy of the poem as Byron's act of discourse with his world, and, on the other, to the specific (past) historical nexus in which Byron's story of Juan's career is imbedded. The second part of the Preface is a bitter diatribe against Castlereagh, who had recently taken his own life, against the present condition of Europe under the restored thrones and their allied policies, and against those like Southey who were at once supporters of these institutions and detractors of Byron's recent work. The opening sentences of the Preface, however, tell us that the material in Cantos VII and VIII is based upon an actual event: the siege of Ismail by the Russians in Nov.-Dec. 1790. The latter was the chief episode in the (latest) Russo-Turkish War, which had been renewed in 1787. The Preface tells the reader, in other words, that Juan's career in Byron's poem is unfolding within real historical time, and—specifically—that we are to map his career in terms of specific places, dates, and events. When Juan goes to Catherine's court after the siege of Ismail the date is early 1791. Shortly afterwards he goes to England.

Clearly, then, Byron's projected scheme for the plot of Juan's career was actually being implemented when Byron renewed the poem's composition at the beginning of 1822. That he was preparing Juan for a trip to Paris and death on the guillotine in 1793 at the end of the poem is borne out by the fulfilment of the other details which he gave to Medwin, as well as by the chronology of Juan's exploits established in the siege of Ismail episode.[20] We should note that this precise dating of Juan's life in the poem accommodates the events of Cantos I-VI. Before the Preface to Cantos VI-VIII, Byron had not forced his audience to read the events of Cantos I-VI within a specific historical frame of reference. After the Preface, however, those events are drawn into the poem's newly defined historical scheme. Juan's career in Byron's poem begins in Seville just as the French Revolution has broken out, or is about to break out. He is then sixteen years old. His life will

---

[20] Some of Byron's marginal jottings in Canto XIV schematize two of the poem's episodes, including the death of Juan. These marginalia appear on a scrap of manuscript (not known to the *DJV* editors) now in the Murray archives. The notations occur on a MS carrying a variant version of lines 479-80.

end at the end of Byron's poem, and the date for him will be 1793.

Lacking the precise historical frame which Byron established for his poem in 1822, Juan's career would appear episodic, the verse equivalent of the fictional careers of characters in Smollett, Sterne, and Fielding.[21] The exact historical placement changes the situation radically. Juan at first appears to move through Byron's poem in a picaresque fashion, but as the poem develops and his life is brought into ever closer relations with the great and epochal events shaking Europe in the early 1790s, the reader begins to glimpse an order, or perhaps a fate, which was not at first evident or even suspected. Having Juan die in the Reign of Terror at the end of Byron's poem is a daring conception: on the one hand, it seems a surprising, even an arbitrary, end for Byron's inoffensive hero, but on the other it calls attention to a hidden constellation of forces drawing together far-flung and apparently unrelated people and events. History proceeds 'according to the mighty working' of forces which gather up the odd and the disparate, and historical explanation, in Byron, proceeds according to the mighty working of a poem which *reveals* these odd and unapparent connections.

Not least of all does it reveal the connections which hold between the pan-European world of 1787-93 and its counterpart in 1818-24. The revolutionary epoch in which Juan's career begins and ends is explicitly examined from the vantage of the period of Europe's restoration. Juxtaposing these two worlds allows each to comment on the other. More crucially for the poem, however, the juxtaposition gives Byron the opportunity to expose certain congruences between these periods, and to suggest that the second period is a variant repetition of the first. These congruences are established via the third historical frame which gives a structure to *Don Juan*: the period in which the Book of Byron was initally composed, and more especially the central years of that period, 1809-17/18.

---

[21] Critics have frequently drawn attention to *Don Juan*'s parallels with eighteenth-century picaresque novels. See Elizabeth Boyd, *Byron's 'Don Juan'*, New Brunswick, NJ, 1945, esp. chaps. 4-7; Andras Horn, *Byron's 'Don Juan' and the 18th Century Novel*, Bern, 1962, and A. B. England, *Byron's 'Don Juan' and Eighteenth Century Literature*, Lewisburg, Pa., 1975, esp. chap. 3. In fact, however, Scott's example in the Waverley novels was perhaps even more important for *Don Juan*. For it was Scott who showed Byron how to incorporate historical events into a fictional narrative in a significant and illuminating way.

The congruences appear most dramatically as a series of related and repeating sequences of gain and loss, rise and fall, triumph and disaster. Juan's career illustrates this pattern both in its particular episodes and in the larger scheme which Byron projected for his hero. Adversative forces of various kinds interrupt and thwart Juan's plans and hopes. Some of these are represented as his responsibility while others originate in external circumstances over which he can have no control. In both cases, the pattern of an early promise which later fails or is betrayed appears in Juan's life as well as in the course of the French Revolution. Juan's life follows the moral arc of the revolution even as his career follows its early chronological development. But what is most important, so far as Byron's poem is concerned, is that both of these sequences recur in the next generation. The second phase of the revolution is dominated by the rise and fall of Napoleon, whose professed aim (at any rate) was to establish the revolution on a secure European footing. The consequence of his career was, on the contrary, the final defeat of the revolution's historic agenda. This repetition, in Napoleon's life, of the historical course of the early years of the revolution appears in Byron's poem through its autobiographical analogue: the meteoric rise and subsequent fall of Lord Byron, a series of events which we—following Byron—associate with the years 1809-17/18. In Byron's and Napoleon's careers the reader of *Don Juan* observes, once again, the pattern established in Juan's life and in the course of the early revolution.

Following his self-exile from England in 1816 Byron meditated on the meaning of this pattern in his life and on its relation to similar patterns in past and contemporary history. The most important of the meditations comes down to us as *Childe Harold's Pilgrimage*, Canto IV, which Byron completed shortly before he began *Don Juan*. Here Byron decides that all history, when judged by meliorist or revolutionary standards, is a story of disaster and unsuccess. What he also decides, however, is that against this fatal and repeating story may be, and has been, placed the deed of the opposing mind and will, the individual voice which, while it recognizes the evil pattern, refuses to accept or assent to it.

Yet, Freedom! yet thy banner, torn, but flying,
  Streams like the thunder-storm *against* the wind;
Thy trumpet voice, though broken now and dying,
  The loudest still the tempest leaves behind . . .
                              (*CHP* iv, stanza 98)
Yet let us ponder boldly—'tis a base
  Abandonment of reason to resign
Our right of thought—our last and only place
  Of refuge . . .
                              (*CHP* iv, stanza 127)

These attitudes establish the ground on which *Don Juan*
comes to judge the patterns of historical repetition. Byron
begins the poem from the vantage of 1818, a point in European
history when time appears to have rolled back upon itself.
Thirty years have passed, yet the enormous upheavals which
marked those years seem to have returned the European world
virtually to the same political position that it occupied in 1788.
Furthermore, Byron observes in this period a series of repetitions which suggest that the cycle of revolutionary disappointment is a general pattern which is found in many historical
periods and which is replicated for the individual as well as for
society. In terms of the narrator's historical frame (1818-24),
Don Juan is yet another revolutionary undertaking begun in a
period of darkness. As such, the bleak patterns of repetition
over which the Byron of 1818-24 will brood—the pattern of
Juan's career and the early phase of the revolution, the pattern
of Byron's career and the Napoleonic wars—threaten the narrative project of 1818-24 with a fearful end.

III

The early cantos of *Don Juan* represent this threat most
dramatically, perhaps, in connection with the 'Isles of Greece'
lyric in Canto III. Within the Juan/Haidée/Lambro cantos this
passage focuses the most self-conscious episode from an
historical and political standpoint. The passage involves a complex act of poetic ventriloquism through which Byron is able to
develop, simultaneously, a polemical analysis of recent European history and a self-conscious critique of his own character
and professed social ideals. To understand how this is managed

we will have to recall briefly Byron's famous ideas about poetic 'mobility'.

The discussion of this concept comes up in Canto XVI when Byron is describing Lady Adeline Amundeville. Her mobility, Byron says, is a characteristic of a certain type of person, and in particular of artists.

> This makes your actors, artists, and romancers,
>   Heroes sometimes, though seldom—sages never;
> But speakers, bards, diplomatists, and dancers,
>   Little that's great, but much of what is clever;
> Most orators, but very few financiers . . .
>   (stanza 98, lines 1—5)

In other words, people whose work or life demands that they treat with others in a broadly public or spectacular field.

In a note to this passage Byron defines mobility as follows: 'an excessive susceptibility of immediate impressions—at the same time without *losing* the past; and is, though sometimes apparently useful to the possessor, a most painful and unhappy attribute.' Lady Adeline Amundeville shows that she possesses this equivocal virtue when she is observed dealing with her guests at Norman Abbey.

95

> But Adeline was occupied by fame
>   This day; and watching, witching, condescending
> To the consumers of fish, fowl and game,
>   And dignity with courtesy so blending,
> As all must blend whose part it is to aim
>   (Especially as the sixth year is ending)
> At their lord's son's, or similar connection's
> Safe conduct through the rocks of re-elections.

96

> Though this was most expedient on the whole,
>   And usual—Juan, when he cast a glance
> On Adeline while playing her grand role,
>   Which she went through as though it were a dance,
> (Betraying only now and then her soul
>   By a look scarce perceptibly askance
> Of weariness or scorn) began to feel
> Some doubt how much of Adeline was *real*;

97

So well she acted, all and every part
 By turns—with that vivacious versatility,
Which many people take for want of heart.
 They err—'tis merely what is called mobility,
A thing of temperament and not of art,
 Though seeming so, from its supposed facility;
And false—though true; for surely they're sincerest,
Who are strongly acted on by what is nearest.

These lines deserve some attention. If mobility is 'an excessive susceptibility to immediate impressions', the passage also suggests that it is not *simply* a psychological attribute. Lady Adeline is at home in this social world; indeed, her entire life in the poem shows that she is governed by a *social* 'susceptibility' to this kind of structure. She has at once a taste and a gift for managing social affairs of these kinds with brilliance. In the end, however, the passage shows that the psychological attribute and the social formation call out to each other, that they are, indeed, symbiotic and interdependent.

When Byron says that such mobility is 'a most painful and unhappy attribute' we will understand what he means when we meditate on Lady Adeline's barely perceptible 'look . . . Of weariness or scorn'. Juan glimpses an important aspect of her character and its social determinants when he observes her 'now and then'—in the very midst of her social brilliance— 'Betraying . . . her soul' in those looks of scorn and weariness. 'Playing her grand role' involves, within a Romantic Ideology, a reciprocal danger: lack of authenticity. Thus Lady Adeline 'betrays' her soul in at least two senses when she inadvertently reveals her mobility to Juan and ourselves.

What is crucial to see in all this is that mobility involves a structure of social relations and not simply a psychological characteristic. Byron *interprets* mobility in psychological terms, but his verse exposes this interpretation as a special (ultimately, a Romantic) view of what is clearly a much more complex state of affairs. Scarcely less important is an interesting paradox which Byron calls attention to. Mobility appears as a set of social graces, a capacity to charm and to be all things to all men. But it arises, apparently, from a ground of 'sincerity' in those kinds of people 'Who are strongly acted on by what is nearest'. Yet it *appears* the very height of insincerity and calculation. Which is it: 'a thing of' one's spontaneous 'temperament', or of one's role-playing and 'art'? Is it 'false' or is it 'true'?

This set of paradoxes and contradictions gets registered for us in Lady Adeline's looks of weariness and scorn, and in Byron's remark that mobility is painful and a source of unhappiness. Lady Adeline's 'soul' is rent by these paradoxes which her situation reflects but which her consciousness does not appear to understand (or even try to understand). When Byron reflects upon her situation he gains a clearer knowledge of the contradictions, but he too remains incapable of producing anything more than a demonstrative and aesthetic explanation (which is itself supplemented by the psychological explanation of his note). Reading Byron's verse we *see* it all much more clearly than Lady Adeline does, for we are provided with a much more comprehensive vantage of the field of relations being played out.

The connection of social mobility to the Romantic artist's ideal of spontaneity and sincerity has often been noted by scholars, most trenchantly, perhaps, by George Ridenour.[22] Thus we now commonly equate the 'conversational facility' (xv, stanza 20) of *Don Juan*, or the 'strain of passionate improvisation' in Byron's High Romantic mode,[23] with the mobility of Lady Adeline and the 'actors, artists, and romancers' who are her equivalents. What is less often noted is the negative dimension which Byron sees in the artist of mobility. It is mildly shocking, but quite necessary, to understand that the dark shadow cast by the mobility of the spontaneous Romantic poet is called (in *Don Juan*) Robert Southey, and sometimes William Wordsworth. Byron calls Southey an 'Epic Renegade' at the very outset of the poem ('Dedication', stanza 1) and he links the recent laureate with Wordsworth as instances of poets who apostasized their early republican principles in their later years. Southey's 'conversion' ('Dedication', stanza 6) 'has lately been a common case' ('Dedication', stanza 1), Byron says, but if such 'Apostasy's . . . fashionable' now ('Dedica-

[22] George Ridenour, *The Style of Don Juan*, New Haven, 1960.

[23] H.J.C. Grierson, 'Lord Byron: Arnold and Swinburne', *Wharton Lecture on English Poetry* no. 11 (1920), p. 11.

tion', stanza 17), it was not always so. Milton rises up in Byron's 'Dedication' as one who 'deigned not to belie his soul in songs' ('Dedication', stanza 10) which swerved from his initial ground and principles. Byron, of course, justifies himself with such an ideal of poetic and ideological behaviour: 'And, if in flattering strains I do not predicate,/ 'Tis that I still retain my "buff and blue"' ('Dedication', stanza 17).

In Byron's 'Vision of Judgment' Southey's political apostasy is elaborated into a general 'literary character', a Grub Street avatar formed in the image of his own time.

96

He said—(I only give the heads)—he said,
  He meant no harm in scribbling; 'twas his
    way
Upon all topics; 'twas, besides, his bread,
  Of which he buttered both sides; 'twould
    delay
Too long the assembly (he was pleased to
    dread),
  And take up rather more time than a day,
To name his works—he would but cite a
    few—
'Wat Tyler'—'Rhymes on Blenheim'—
  'Waterloo.'

97

He had written praises of a Regicide;
  He had written praises of all kings what-
    ever;
He had written for republics far and wide,
  And then against them bitterer than ever;
For pantisocracy he once had cried
  Aloud, a scheme less moral than 'twas
    clever;
Then grew a heavy anti-jacobin—
Had turned his coat—and would have turned
    his skin.

98

He had sung against all battles, and again
  In their high praise and glory; he had
    called
Reviewing 'the ungentle craft,' and then

Became as base a critic as e'er crawled—
Fed, paid, and pampered by the very men
    By whom his muse and morals had been
        mauled;
He had written much blank verse, and
        blanker prose,
And more of both than any body knows.

99

He had written Wesley's life:—here turning
        round
To Satan, 'Sir, I'm ready to write yours,
In two octavo volumes, nicely bound,
    With notes and preface, all that most
        allures
The pious purchaser; and there's no ground
    For fear, for I can choose my own
        reviewers:
So let me have the proper documents,
That I may add you to my other saints.'

Like Lady Adeline when she is 'occupied by fame' (xvi, stanza 95), Southey too is ever 'watching, witching, condescending' with those who might advance his literary career and projects. He will write on any topic, from any point of view, in any style or medium. He is, besides, keenly aware of all that is most current, and anxious to be borne along by that current. Finally, he understands how the institutions of literary production operate in his day. In his own summing up, Southey's is 'a pen of all work' (stanza 100) and he is a poet of skill and industry, without malice (or conscience), good-natured (and culpably unscrupulous). He has all of Lady Adeline's (and by extension Byron's) gifts, and would be an exact literary reflection but for one thing: his looks never betray that telltale glance 'Of weariness or scorn'. His mobility is complete but, in the end, un-Byronic, for Southey does not feel it as a 'most painful and unhappy attribute'.[24]

---

[24] I suppose it does not need to be remarked that this representation of the laureate is a travesty of his actual character. In fact, the worst truth one might say of Southey would be the opposite—that he was self-righteous and absolutist (Byron of course accused him of these vices as well). For a good assessment of his character see Geoffrey Carnall, *Southey and His Age*, Oxford, 1960.

IV

Byron's most profound presentation of his idea of Romantic mobility comes, as we might expect, when he draws himself and his own practice into the analysis. 'Changeable too—yet somehow "*idem semper*"' (xvii, stanza 11): thus Byron sought to describe both himself and his poem in his last, fragmentary canto. The characterization intersects with the entire constellation of ideas related to the concept of mobility, and thereby also gestures toward the similarities and differences which link Byron to his dark double Robert Southey. In Canto III these similarities and differences are fully elaborated in the figure of the poet who comes to sing at Juan and Haidée's lavish banquet and festival.

Byron's introductory stanzas (78-86) describe the character of this poet as 'a sad trimmer' (stanza 82). This passage distinctly recalls what Byron had said earlier about Southey in the (abandoned) 'Preface' to *Don Juan* and the (reluctantly cancelled) 'Dedication'. There the tone is much more savage, however, resembling in this respect the satiric passage cited earlier from 'Vision of Judgment'. All the (by now) familiar charges are brought forward—for example, in stanzas 80 and 85.

80

He was a man who had seen many changes,
    And always changed as true as any needle,
His polar star being one which rather ranges,
    And not the fix'd—he knew the way to wheedle:
So vile he 'scaped the doom which oft avenges;
    And being fluent (save indeed when fee'd ill),
He lied with such a fervour of intention—
There was no doubt he earn'd his laureate pension.

85

Thus, usually, when he was ask'd to sing,
    He gave the different nations something national;
'Twas all the same to him—'God save the king,'
    Or '*Ca ira*', according to the fashion all;
His muse made increment of any thing,
    From the high lyric down to the low rational:
If Pindar sang horse-races, what should hinder
Himself from being as pliable as Pindar?

These stanzas epitomize Byron's usual critique of the poet as renegade and unscrupulous time-server, and they sum up the general tone of Byron's presentation in the passage as a whole. But two other stanzas in the sequence disturb the proprieties which customarily govern Byron's satire in these situations. In stanza 84 Byron tells us that this poet

> had travell'd 'mongst the Arabs, Turks, and Franks,
> And knew the self-loves of the different nations;
> And having lived with people of all ranks,
>   Had something ready upon most occasions—
> Which got him a few presents and some thanks.
>   He varied with some skill his adulations;
> To 'do at Rome as Romans do,' a piece
> Of conduct was which he observed in Greece.

These lines recall nothing so much as Byron himself: first, as the Levantine cruiser of 1809-11, and second, as the poet and social lion of 1812-14. Byron had fun at Southey's laureate expense, and while he sometimes protested that he never courted his immense popularity or flattered his adulators, he knew that he had in fact 'filed [his] mind' (*Childe Harold* iii, stanza 113) during his Years of Fame. For Byron himself, those years were far from innocent of the 'adulations' for which he denounced Southey. Of himself he could say, with far more certainty than he could of Southey, that he had written verse to foster his image and advance his career. Like Lady Adeline, however, such work was produced side by side with those self-revelatory looks (or poems) 'Of weariness or scorn' which reflected critically on the 'adulations'. Indeed, the 'adulations' themselves frequently displayed their own internal self-contradictions.

In the 'sad trimmer' poet, then, we glimpse the face of Robert Southey, and this is no great surprise; but in the allusion to Southey the outlines of another, unexpected face are also glimpsed. This palimpsest produces an unstable and apparently self-contradicted text whose true biographical subject— Byron himself—emerges from beneath the layers of his own normal satiric displacements.

83

> But now being lifted into high society,
>   And having picked up several odds and ends

Of free thoughts in his travels, for variety,
  He deem'd, being in a lone isle, among friends,
That without any danger of a riot, he
  Might for long lying make himself amends;
And singing as he sung in his warm youth,
Agree to a short armistice with truth.

This could be, and is in part, an oblique thrust at Southey's renegado turn from his youthful republicanism to his later apostasy. It is also, however, an even more oblique glimpse of Byron's political and poetical career up to 1816, which was marked by its own definite, if much less apparent, forms of ideological backsliding and dishonesty. Byron was much more 'cunning in [his] own overthrow' than Southey was, but that he had pursued 'False Ambition' and betrayed his soul's 'nobler aim' he could not, and would not, deny (see 'Epistle to Augusta' lines 97, 102). And so 'for long lying' he aimed, in this passage, to 'make himself amends' in the form of an imitation revolutionary Greek ballad, the famous 'Isles of Greece'.[25]

The poem is at once an admonishment, or call, and a fulfilment of his highest poetical ideals. And the fulfilment lies precisely in this: that when he *now* sings 'as he sung in his warm youth' he reveals, self-consciously and deliberately, both his utopian goals (to which he rededicates himself) as well as his understanding that he has been the worst betrayer of those goals. He is the worst because he appeared, to himself and to others, as one of their staunchest supporters.

The ballad's subtle mastery emerges when this network of allusions, intertexts, and subtexts is fully comprehended. In general, Byron's fiction is that the ballad is sung by a Romaic poet in the late 1780s to an audience of his fellows who live quiescently under Turkish rule. It calls them from their lives of pleasure and political degeneracy to take up a more strenuous and principled course of action. At this level, it is a poem determined to raise the Greek national consciousness. Consequently, though its fictive date is the late 1780s, and though it recalls the Greek patriotic songs of the late eighteenth century (like Rhiga's War Song), its 1820 context is equally operative. In

---

[25] For an excellent discussion of the poem's Greek context, both classical and modern, see Kiriakoula Solomou, *Byron and Greek Poetry*, PhD Thesis, U. of Aberdeen, 1980, pp. 294-9.

fact, the Greek war for independence was to commence in 1821, and Byron's early attachment to that cause would draw him in 1823 from Italy to western Greece and his famous death in 1824.

Don Juan's fictive level—that is, the plot of Juan's career in the poem's imagined time-scheme stretching from about 1787 to its (unreached) conclusion in 1793—is always calling attention to its narrative (or 'real') level: that is, to the poem as a continuing historical event which unfolds before its European audience between 1818 and 1824, and which makes that context part of its subject. This interplay between a fictive and a narrative time-scheme throws into relief a dominant fact about *Don Juan*: that it is fundamentally an autobiographical poem which comments upon and interprets the course of European history between 1787 and 1824. In the case of 'The Isles of Greece', Byron's fictional Greek poet masks only to reveal more clearly the poem's true author. As always in *Don Juan*, Byron reveals and thereby manipulates his poetical machinery in a self-conscious drama of his own mind. We therefore observe this ballad as a vehicle for satirizing Southey and all other republican turncoats, for satirizing generally those who have betrayed the cause of the European political ideal of liberty which had its origin in ancient Greece and which appeared once again in various revolutionary movements during the late eighteenth and early nineteenth centuries (paradigmatically in America and France). So, when we read 'The Isles of Greece' we are also to *see* Lord Byron satirizing Robert Southey in 1820.

At the poem's most complex level, we also *see through* Lord Byron's satire of Southey into the innermost drama of his own mind. Consider the ballad's fifth stanza.

> And where are they? and where art thou,
>   My country? On thy voiceless shore
> The heroic lay is tuneless now—
>   The heroic bosom beats no more!
> And must thy lyre, so long divine,
> Degenerate into hands like mine?

An act of poetic ventriloquism multiplies the pronominal references in these lines. The Romaic poet sings here of himself and of Greece, but the English poet sings of England and Lord Byron. The ideal of Greece calls out to Byron's, and England's, identification with the ideal, just as the degeneracy of present-day Greece (whether conceived in the context of 1787 or 1820) reflects upon England's, and Byron's, betrayals of their most cherished, and Greek-derived, ideals.

Two fictive voices sing 'The Isles of Greece'—the imaginary Romaic poet of 1787 and the imaginative Robert Southey of 1820; and they sing of the ideals and betrayals of themselves and their respective countries. In the end, however, the two voices are incorporated as the poetically 'actual' voice of Lord Byron, who sings of his own immediate psychic and political situation and the context in which it had developed.

> 'Tis something, in the dearth of fame,
>   Though link'd among a fetter'd race,
> To feel at least a patriot's shame,
>   Even as I sing, suffuse my face;
> For what is left the poet here!
> For Greeks a blush, for Greece a tear.

A passage like this dramatically reveals the complex voicing techniques of the ballad, along with the related and equally complex network of references and levels of statement. In these lines the 'Fame' is Greece's, England's, and Byron's; the 'fettered race' is Greek, but also Italian (Byron is writing his poem in the Italian dominions of the Austrian Empire), and—even more generally—European ('There is *no* freedom—even for *Masters*—in the midst of slaves'). Thus, when Byron gestures to 'the poet here', his words resonate in the widest European context of 1787-1824.

The ballad plays itself out as a contest between the rival claims of 'The Scian and the Teian muse,/ The hero's harp, the lover's lute.' Representing a poetical career and its goals as a dialectic between the shifting claims of heroic and amatory verse—here, specifically, between Homer and Anacreon—is a pre-eminently Byronic structure of thought.[26] His entire life's work as a poet develops as a self-lacerating experience of their rival claims. Whenever Byron moves too definitively toward one of these poetical and political ideals he will call upon the

---

[26] We should recall Byron's many early translations of Anacreontic verse.

other to limit, criticize, and judge its illusions and appeals. Byron's great lyric 'On This Day I Complete My Thirty-Sixth Year' culminates this conflict by representing it as (by itself) a hopeless one. 'On This Day' calls for its cessation by invoking the option of suicide.

This is also the option toward which 'The Isles of Greece' makes its final gesture.

> Place me on Sunium's marbled steep,
>   Where nothing, save the waves and I,
> May hear our mutual murmurs sweep;
>   There, swan-like, let me sing and die:
> A land of slaves shall ne'er be mine—
> Dash down yon cup of Samian wine.
>   (stanza 16)

As in the later lyric, when the poet here chooses death to break the impasse of his life, his choice involves a decision for the claims of heroism. What is important to see is that this is an historical choice, one demanded by time, place, and circumstance. The voice of the Scian muse plays through 'The Isles of Greece' to remind us of the essential virtues of a truly civilized life, which would not include war and violence. But no such life is possible when the social structure is degenerate at its ground.

> Fill high the bowl with Samian wine!
>   Our virgins dance beneath the shade—
> I see their glorious black eyes shine;
>   But gazing on each glowing maid,
> My own the burning tear-drop laves,
> To think such breasts must suckle slaves.
>   (stanza 15)

In such times the image of love itself becomes an occasion for swerving toward heroic values. Nevertheless, we have to see that the move toward the heroic is now regarded as deeply equivocal, a fate or doom embraced by those who are willing to sacrifice themselves by choosing an heroic life in order to secure, at some future date, the restoration of a civilized order.

Thus the ideological structures of 'On This Day' and 'The Isles of Greece' are all but exact equivalents. However, 'On This Day' is a much more interiorized poem, and that difference is crucial. The fact that Byron's voice in 'The Isles of Greece' is explicitly mixed with the voices of Southey and the modern Greek patriot, and implicitly with the entire Anacreontic and Homeric traditions, socializes the lyric in a number of important and specific ways. The history imbedded in 'On This Day' is Byron's personal history and the drama is fundamentally psychic. In 'The Isles of Greece', on the other hand, the complex voicing extends the world of which and for which the poem is speaking. 'On This Day' is set in 1824, in Greece, and in Byron's mind—finally, in the relations which the poem establishes between these three *loci* and all that each implicitly involves. The layered voices in 'The Isles of Greece' dramatically enlarge the poem's network of references, forcing the reader to consider the complex *relations* of those references. In the end—like *Don Juan* itself—the lyric implies that European history between 1787 and 1820 is all of a piece, and that the condition of Greece during the period is the very symbol of the condition of Europe. At the end of the eighteenth century Greece looked for freedom from Turkish rule as Europe looked for a revolutionary emancipation from inherited and archaic political orders; in 1820, despite the intervening years of turmoil and promise, the *status quo* has been (at least formally and materially) preserved. Even more telling, however, is the poem's revelation of all of Europe's—including England's—complicity in this state of affairs. In 1809-11 Byron began to fear the truth of such complicity and he expressed his fears in *Childe Harold's Pilgrimage* I-II.[27] In 1820 his fears have been fully realized. 'The Isles of Greece' exposes, analyses, and judges this complicity. The English Lord speaks as and for the failed Greek patriot and the turncoat jacobin Southey. In *Don Juan's* 'Dedication' and elsewhere Byron will separate himself from Southey, Castlereagh, Metternich, and the forgers of Europe's spiritual slavery. Here, by contrast, he speaks with their voices

---

[27] The whole of this book comprises a commentary on Greece and Europe's relation to Greece's political condition under Turkish rule. Byron was deeply critical of the hypocrisy of English, French, and Russian philhellenism, as we see most clearly in that book's notes and appendices. Most telling of all—and almost never remarked upon—is Byron's reference to, and partial translation of, the Romaic satire on Greece, England, Russia, and France: the so-called 'Rossanglogallos'. See Solomou's discussion, pp. 186-90, 218-21, 310-318; and see also *CPW* ii. 213-15.

and says, of himself and for all those who have judged themselves innocent: '*Hypocrite lecteur, mon semblable, mon frère.*'

In 'The Isles of Greece' Byron's voice does, however, gain a
certain frail integrity through its aspiration toward the whole
truth, toward complete freedom from cant. The ballad reveals
and denounces the canting life of its age by constructing a poem
which gives lip-service to the traditional western ideas of love
and honour. Its honesty appears as a double understanding:
first, that these ideals, in their inherited forms at any rate, are
conflicted and self-contradictory; and second, that lip-service,
in Byron's age, is the most which history could expect. Byron
everywhere speaks of the degeneracy of his period, a condition
he deplored in the cant political, poetical, and moral which was
being delivered by contemporary ideologues like Southey.
These are the voices who speak with authority of what is right
and wrong, good and evil, angelic and satanic. Byron's voice,
by contrast, undercuts and ironizes every voice which pretends
to assume this kind of authority. The shock and even the genius
of this procedure lies in the poetry's final level of irony, where
Byron deliberately assumes the *rhetoric* of a total and dependable
authority. Byron's high style—which appears once again in
this famous ballad—projects the ideal of the poet and hero
manqué, the figure who alone (in both senses) can speak in an
unbetrayed voice of his age's persistent betrayals:

> Thus sung, or would, or could, or should have sung,
>   The modern Greek, in tolerable verse;
> If not like Orpheus quite, when Greece was young,
>   Yet in these times he might have done much worse:
> His strain display'd some feeling—right or wrong;
>   And feeling, in a poet, is the source
> Of others' feeling; but they are such liars,
> And take all colours—like the hands of dyers.
>
> (III, stanza 87)

Thus Byron sums up the significance of the ballad he has just
presented. The statement displays the ironic equivocalness
engineered in 'these times', but it equally and forthrightly says
that a poet 'might have done much worse' than this. The
remark recalls Southey's laureate performances as well as
Byron's earlier work in which the truth he is fundamentally

committed to had been subtly, cunningly betrayed. Like the several stanzas which follow, this one concludes in that typical Byronic gesture of resolute irresolution: an equivocal affirmation of the power of poetry, on the one hand, and an equally equivocal pronouncement upon its unreliability.

The Shakespeare echo at the end of the stanza recalls Byron's views on poetic mobility. The cynical tone in which the echo is made, however—so unlike the original passage—reminds us, in this case, that Byron's ventriloquism, or mobility, is everywhere marked by the 'weariness or scorn' which Juan glimpsed in Adeline's accommodating looks. Paradoxically, Byron's cynicism is a liberating rather than a defeatist move because Byron is aware that the past—its deeds, its voices, its ideas—cannot be appropriated to the present through simple gestures of mobility or chameleonic acts. Byron turns a mordant eye on the inheritance of greatness (especially poetic greatness) because he knows that its ideal apparitions conceal human, equivocal truths. Indeed, when those equivocal human forms do not appear, the ideals enter the world as monsters.

In the ballad, the temptation to accept an idealized view of the voices and deeds of the past appears most clearly in the call to heroic action—for example, in stanza eight:

> What, silent still? and silent all?
>   Ah! no;—the voices of the dead
> Sound like a distant torrent's fall,
>   And answer, 'Let one living head,
> But one arise,—we come, we come!'
> 'Tis but the living who are dumb.

But the fact is that these martial voices from the dead may (and have) issued calls to freedom *and* to tyranny. The 'Turkish hordes' of stanza nine have answered that call as surely as did the three hundred who fell at Thermopylae. If 'the living . . . are dumb' now to that call, their silence may be the honesty of Keats's aesthetic escapism, or the critical judgement of the sybarite Sardanapalus. Besides, Byron has seen the call answered too often and too well by the poets and ideologues of European imperialism: by a Southey in his Waterloo hymns, and by a Wordsworth who could proclaim that the carnage of battle is the daughter of God.

So in the ballad the voice of the Scian muse repeatedly undercuts the voice of the Teian—but not definitively. Anacreon's
role, in this respect, is to introduce the note of 'weariness or
scorn' into the poem's act of heroic ventriloquism. In this way
Byron tries to insure that he will raise up from the past a human
rather than a demonic figure; and in this way he also manages
to compose, in 1820, a song on behalf of human freedom which
escapes incorporation by the Age of Cant. The crowning wit of
the poem is that the song is offered to the reader as a familiar
Byronic *tour de force* in which his identity is submerged in a network of competing voices. Byron appears, in the end, as the
self-conscious creator and observer of his own verse: the man
who finds his identity and freedom when he acknowledges the
constellation of his own social determinants, the man who discovers his voice in a conscious and dialectical act of poetic ventriloquism.

V

The episode which incorporates the 'Isles of Greece' displays
the continuities which hold between Byron's past life and
career and his present concerns as they are revealed and acti-
vated in *Don Juan*. The episode also shows the place which his
life and career occupy within the larger social and political
framework of European affairs between 1788 and 1820. Finally,
the mordant critical view which he takes toward himself and this
period of European history involves an important set of revolutionary ideological judgements which comprise an integrated
and comprehensive interpretation of his age.

Byron begins *Don Juan* already knowing that individual and
social history, from a revolutionary point of view, always
follows a curve of disappointment or disaster. In this sense (but
only in this sense) is the poem 'nihilistic'. In every other respect
the poem is a great work of hope, for it insists that projects of
change and renewal must continue to be raised up despite the
fact of absolute adversity. The Byron who set *Don Juan* in motion
understands that the eye begins to see only in a dark time, and—
more crucially—that there never is a time which is or was not
dark. Those who seek not merely to understand the world, but
to change it, strive toward an ideal of human life which will

have to be 'anywhere out of the world'. This is the strife of *Don Juan*'s hope, the deed of its mind—the fact of its books. The poem begins its quest for renewal under its own prophecy of failure, and it seeks to persuade its readers that one begins in this way simply because there is no other place *to* begin, that the renewal arrives with the event, not in the end. For in the end you lose, always.

Thus Byron begins his poem in 1818 by calling for a new hero to take the place of all the failed heroes of the past, and in particular of all the failed heroes of the preceding revolutionary epoch. Byron catalogues their names in Canto I only to toss them aside in favour of 'our friend, Don Juan', whose history he purposes to tell. As we have seen, however, and as every reader of the poem has always recognized, that fictive history recollects and alludes, at every point, to the actual history of Lord Byron, who is the poem's true 'hero' and central figure. Juan's progress from Seville to the Levant, and thence via Russia to England and (prospectively) to Paris and his death, is shadowed by the actual career of Byron. In fact, Juan's career is no more than a displaced re-presentation of Byron's, a coded fiction through which the reader may glimpse the friends, enemies, and the incidents of Byron's life, as well as the patterns and epochs of that life. The English Cantos, at the level of the poem's plot, should be located in the summer and early autumn of 1791; at the level of the poem's recollective autobiographical structure, as everyone knows, these cantos reflect Byron's life in England during his Years of Fame.

When Byron reinitiated his *Don Juan* project at the beginning of 1822, therefore, he did so with two objects clearly in his mind. The first of these involved structural matters: specifying a precise chronology for Juan's life in the poem. This move entailed, as a consequence, a dramatic refocusing of the poem's materials. Because of the move readers would be better able to see the tripartite organization of the poem's historical vision. *Don Juan* examines the period 1789-1824 in terms of its three dominant phases: the early years of the French Revolution (the poem's displaced fiction); the epoch of the Napoleonic Wars (viewed through Byron's analogous and contemporary experience of those years); and the epoch of the European restoration (dramatically fashioned and presented at the poem's immediate narrative level).

Byron's second object, which is related to the first, aimed at reasserting in an unmistakeable way the socio-political character of his work. When he began *Don Juan* he spoke of it as 'bitter in politics',[28] but as he struggled to get Murray to publish his cantos he was gradually led to de-emphasize both the bitterness and the politics. The de-emphasis appeared in the published work itself—the removal of the 'Dedication', the decision not to print the Wellington stanzas in Canto III, and so forth—as well as in Byron's letters back to England in which he raised his defence of the poem against his publisher's and his friends' objections.[29] During 1819-21 these letters take a conciliating and mollifying line. Byron tried to get his poem accepted by assuring his friends that it was actually a harmless thing, an elaborate *jeu d'esprit* conceived more in a comic than a satiric mode, 'to giggle and make giggle'.[30] In 1822 the structural changes are accompanied by an uncompromising and candid political stance. In his resumed poem, he told Moore in July, 1822, he meant to 'throw away the scabbard' and make open ideological war with the new reactionary spirit of the age. By December he was equally clear on the subject in a letter to Murray: *Don Juan* 'is intended [as] a *satire* on *abuses* of the present *states* of Society'.[31] Cantos VI-VIII, issued by the liberal Hunt rather than the conservative Murray, are prefaced with Byron's prose declaration of mental war, and the next volume—Cantos IX-XI—begins with the diatribe against war and Wellington which Byron, in 1819, had withdrawn from Canto III.

Byron's purposes with his poem, then, are accompanied by important changes in his aesthetic and political consciousness. Not the least of these was his new and clearer understanding of the *wholeness* of the period 1789-1824, of the intimate relations which held between the three major phases of this period, and of the connections between people and events which might appear, at first, to have little do do with each other. No episode in the poem reveals more clearly Byron's increased understand-

---

[28] *BLJ* vi. 76-7.

[29] See *DJV* i. 13-24; Samuel C. Chew, *Byron in England*, London, 1924, chap. 4; and J.J. McGann, *Don Juan in Context*, Chicago, 1976, pp. 51-67.

[30] See *BLJ* vi. 208; see also vi. 67.

[31] *BLJ* ix. 191 and x. 68.

ing of these historical repetitions and relations than the Siege of Ismail, the episode in which Byron initially focused the historical and political restructuring of his epic.

The siege is, at least in part, what it appears to be: a satire on war and its violence. Byron was not a pacifist, however. He supported patriotic struggles and wars of liberation, and he eventually went to serve in the Greek effort to break free of the Turkish Empire. We have to specify, therefore, the ground of Byron's satire. This ground begins to emerge when we reflect upon Byron's chief source for his details. He used the account in Marquis Gabriel de Castelnau's *Essai sur l'Histoire ancienne et moderne de la nouvelle Russie* (3 vols., Paris, 1800).[32] The ideology of this book is reactionary and monarchist, and its narrative of the siege is largely based on the first-hand details supplied to Castelnau from the diary of Armand Emmanuel du Plessis, Duc de Richelieu (1767-1822). Byron mentions Castelnau's *Essai* in the Preface to Cantos VI-VIII, where he also speaks of the Duc de Richelieu as 'a young volunteer in the Russian service, and afterwards the founder and benefactor of Odessa'.[33] The irony and satire implicit in these remarks arises from Byron's negative approach to Castelnau's glorifying account of the siege, as well as from his ironic sense of the young Richelieu's benefactions.

Reading Castelnau Byron saw that many of the officers in Catherine's army at the siege of Ismail were 'distinguished strangers' (Canto VII, line 254), a wickedly oblique phrase calling attention to the fact that these men, like the young Duc de Richelieu, were *émigrés* from France and the revolution. Richelieu and the other distinguished strangers are not patriots fighting for their country, they are military adventurers. That Byron intended this line of attack on the French *émigrés* at Ismail is perfectly plain from the letter to Moore in which he said that his new cantos (the siege cantos, that is) constitute an attack upon 'those butchers in large business, your mercenary soldiery'.[34] Lying behind the satire of this battle and the entire Russian episode in the poem is the idea, commonly found in liberal thought of the period, that monarchists like Richelieu

---

[32] See Boyd, pp. 148-50 and Nina Diakonova, 'The Russian Episode in Byron's "Don Juan"' *The Ariel* iii (1972), pp. 51-7.

[33] *DJV* iii. 3.   [34] *BLJ* ix. 191.

have no other business in life except to fight in wars (any wars will do) and intrigue at court. The fact that Juan's rescue of Leila is based upon an actual incident in Richelieu's life only underscores Byron's mordant comments on the indiscriminate militarism of aristocratic ideology:

> If here and there some transient trait of pity
>   Was shown, and some more noble heart broke through
> Its bloody bond, and saved perhaps some pretty
>   Child, or an aged, helpless man or two—
> What's this in one annihilated city . . .?
>
>   (VIII, stanza 124)

These lines, and the larger passage from which they are drawn, cut back against Castelnau's account of the war, on one hand, and the supposed 'noble heart' of the young duke. The man celebrated by reactionaries like Castelnau as 'the founder and benefactor of Odessa' is as well one of those who destroyed a city in which he had no personal or political interest whatsoever, who fled his own country at a moment of crisis, and who later—after the fall of Napoleon—returned to France to become minister for foreign affairs in the restored monarchy.[35]

Richelieu merely epitomizes what Byron wishes to attack in his narrative of the siege and in the Russian cantos generally: the character of monarchist régimes. He is even more important in Byron's poem, however, as a focus for the political filiations which connect, on one hand, such apparently separated events as the siege of Ismail and the events in France in 1789-90, and, on the other, the strange twists and eventualities of European history between 1789 and 1818. Richelieu and the other distinguished strangers do not find their way into Catherine's army merely by chance, nor is it chance that brings him back, at the Bourbon restoration, to serve as an important functionary in the reactionary alliance. Neither is it chance which leads Byron in 1822 to expose this pattern of relations through his narrative of the siege. Byron had been well aware, at least since 1809, of the imperialist stake which various European powers had in Balkan and Levantine affairs. The narrative of the siege

---

[35] Byron's critique of the contemporary world of the restoration operates as well in his treatment of 'Suwarrow' in the Russian cantos. For a good discussion see Philip W. Martin, *Byron. A Poet Before His Public*, Cambridge, 1982, pp. 213-17.

of Ismail forces the reader to recall to mind that network of political and economic interests, as well as to see that the power and self-interests of the monarchies has not been broken by the revolutionary and Napoleonic years. When Byron looks at the siege from the vantage of the restoration, then, he integrates it into the pattern of pan-European affairs of 1789-93 (that is to say, the event is integrated into the order and fate of Juan's fictional-historical career), and he also uses it to comment upon current European conditions. In effect, Byron's employment of his sources involves him in a massive critical-revolutionary reinterpretation of the history of Europe from the outbreak of the French Revolution to the early years of the restoration.

VI

Thus, in 1822 Byron transforms *Don Juan* into a book of the European world, a comprehensive survey and explanation of the principal phases of the epoch 1789-1824. The period is dominated by repetitions, by the violence which has accompanied them, and by the ignorance and indifferences which have abetted these repetitions and their violences. Against these things Byron sets the project of *Don Juan*, which is itself finally recognized to be involved in, to be a part of, the epoch and its repetitions. *Don Juan* becomes a book of the European world by becoming, finally, the Book of Byron, an integrated meditation and commentary upon his own life as it is and was and continues to be a revelation of the meaning of his age.

Don Juan is the Book of Byron because he is its hero, because the poem gives the reader a history of 1789-1824 which is set and framed, at all points, in terms of Byron's history. Juan's fictional movements retraverse actual places and scenes which Byron once passed through, and their details recollect persons and events in his past. In addition, the digressive narration often ruminates Byron's career to comment on and finally to judge it. In short, the poem repeatedly gives the reader views of Byron's past life in the coded sequence of its fictional level as well as in the memorial sequence of its narrative level. All this is widely recognized, as is the related fact that the history of an entire epoch is to be glimpsed in the reflective details of the poem.

Less apparent is the significance of the narrative as it is an *immediate* rather than a recollective event. Cantos I-V constitute the fictional level and the narrative level through two volumes of verse issued by John Murray in 1819 and 1821, and the remaining cantos constitute themselves through the four succeeding volumes issued by Hunt in 1823 and 1824. In addition, however, the last four volumes reconstitute what was originally printed in the first two volumes (*a*) by forcing the reader to place the whole of the fictional level in a specified historical frame of reference, and (*b*) by making this important interpretive shift a part of the poem's developing structure, a part of its own self-criticism. Byron begins the Hunt volumes of his poem, Cantos VI-XVI, with a Preface announcing his ideological purposes, and describing the key elements in the historical restructuring of the poem. Cantos VI-XVI then carry out these changes of direction, and thereby force Cantos I-V to accommodate the changes. The structural accommodations we have already discussed. The ideological changes appear as a more comprehensive understanding of the subjects taken up by the project of *Don Juan*. Most noticeable here is Byron's effort to present a totalized interpretation and critique of his age: to compel his readers to understand how the several phases of the period 1789-1824 hang together, and to persuade them that his critical-revolutionary reading of the period is the correct one. Related to this polemic is the poem's vision of self-judgement, its critical-revolutionary reading of the limits and blindnesses of Cantos I-V. Byron's revisionary turn on the first five cantos is not, of course, a repudiation of them. Though an act of self-criticism, the change of direction in Cantos VI-XVI assumes—indeed, it demonstrates—a dialectical continuity with its objects of criticism. The advances and the retreats of Cantos I-V, their boldness and timidity, accumulate a set of dynamic contradictions which eventually generate Cantos VI-XVI.

In this way *Don Juan* represents not merely a comprehensive interpretation of the period 1789-1824 but a comprehensive critical interpretation which incorporates its own acts of consciousness in its critique as part of a developing and changing act of interpretation. All readers have recognized this quality of the poem's digressive and shifting style, but it is important to see that this stylistic feature is grounded in the work's ideological structure. Even more important to see, however, is that the ground of this ideological structure is not in some definable form of critical interpretation which we may educe from the work. Rather, it lies in the act of the poem, the social and historical deeds of its consciousness which appear to us, most immediately, as a set of specific acts of publication. Of course, the fragmentary character of the work has heretofore obscured somewhat the comprehensiveness of its historical argument. Scholarship helps to bring that argument into sharper focus, to lift it from the sphere of a reader's intuition into a more explicit and defined frame of reference.

Late in the poem, we recall, Byron said of himself that like his own work *Don Juan* he is 'Changeable too—yet somehow *"Idem semper"* ' (xvii, stanza 11). Readers have not found it easy to say what exactly in the poem is 'changeable' and what exactly stands resistant to change. I think we can now make an attempt to isolate these factors. What changes in the poem are its ideas; these are continually subjected to qualification, revision, even repudiation. What remains the same is the perpetual dialectic of the individual mind in its social world, the active deed of its committed intelligence. Fichte called this ground of permanence '*Tat*', Schopenhauer '*Wille*'. These are of course nothing more than conceptual markers for an act of social consciousness which can only be *carried out* in words but which cannot be defined in them. The act of the poem's mind, then, is an understanding that changes and brings about change. In *Don Juan*—to adapt a contemporary formulation of a fragment from Herakleitos—'What does not change/ is the will to change.'[36]

(1982-3)

---

[36] This is Charles Olson's translation of Herakleitos, frag. 23, which appears as the first line of Olson's poem 'The Kingfishers'.

2. The Anachronism of George Crabbe

I

Hazlitt's revulsion from Crabbe's poetry epitomizes the attitude of most English Romantics—Byron only, as usual, excepted. Leavis said later, correctly, that 'Crabbe . . . was hardly at the fine point of consciousness of his time', and we see what he meant when we read remarks like the following from Coleridge and Wordsworth:

. . . in Crabbe there is an absolute defect of the high imagination.

I am happy to find that we coincide in opinion about Crabbe's *verses*; for *poetry* in no sense can they be called . . . After all, if the Picture [given in his work] were true to nature, what claim would it have to be called Poetry? . . . The sum of all is, that nineteen out of twenty of Crabbe's Pictures are mere matters of fact . . .[1]

These Romantic judgements upon Crabbe eventually became normative, not merely for those who agreed with their assessment of Crabbe's *value*, but even for those who—like Leavis himself—saw Crabbe as 'a living classic'. It is a commonplace of criticism to say of Crabbe that he was 'the last of the Augustans'. Leavis himself reproduced such a view when he said that Crabbe's 'sensibility belongs to an order that those who were most alive to the age . . . had ceased to find sympathetic'. In short, Crabbe was an anachronism, and was recognized as such by the most advanced of his contemporaries.[2]

We may obtain a sharper understanding of these critical judgements, however, if we place them in a more generous

---

[1] See Hazlitt's *Spirit of the Age*, London, World's Classics, 1960, pp. 270-7; F. R. Leavis, *Revaluation*, London, 1936, p. 128; S. T. Coleridge, *Table-Talk and Omniana*, ed. T. Ashe, London, 1884, p. 276; Wordsworth's letter to Samuel Rogers, 29 Sept. 1808, in *The Letters of William and Dorothy Wordsworth*, ed. Ernest de Selincourt, 2nd edition, rev. by Mary Moorman, Oxford, 1969, II. i. 268.

[2] For good summaries of the critical history of Crabbe's work see *Crabbe: The Critical Heritage*, ed. Arthur Pollard, London, 1972, and *Romantic Perspectives*, ed. Patricia Hodgart and Theodore Redpath, New York, 1964, pp. 85-124 *passim*. See also Walter E. Broman, 'Factors in Crabbe's Eminence in the Early Nineteenth Century', *MP*, li (1953), pp. 42-9.

historical context. We must see, first of all, that the Romantic judgement was part of a more general ideological struggle in which various parties engaged. Coleridge's and Wordsworth's views corresponded to those set forth in, for example, the *Quarterly Review*, but they were vigorously contested by many others—most notably in the series of articles on Crabbe written for the *Edinburgh Review* by Jeffrey. Indeed, Jeffrey's hostility to Wordsworth and the Lake School, and his approbation of Crabbe, constitute one of the most important local manifestations of the various cultural struggles which marked the entire period. We may glimpse the complexity of these struggles if we simply recall that Hazlitt—no champion of Crabbe's work—had reluctantly to grant not only his artistic power, but his surpassing originality among the poets of the early nineteenth century.

Coleridge's and Wordsworth's judgements, then, must be seen for what they are: part of a polemic on behalf of certain poetical criteria. The fact that their programmes largely prevailed—we now call the period which nurtured Jane Austen and Crabbe 'The Romantic Age'—establishes the proper measure of the truth of their judgements: that is to say, they measure a relative truth, a partisan view.

From our present perspective, however, the Romantic judgement upon Crabbe's poetry must be forced to yield up its specific historical shape. We may begin to define precisely what the Romantics took their stand upon by turning to Crabbe himself, who contested, in a most illuminating way, the very issues which his own work has raised into view.

In his 'Preface' to the *Tales* (1812) Crabbe shows himself well aware of the charges brought against his work (its matter-of-fact and anti-imaginative qualities, its gloomy and even depressing effect). More than this, Crabbe understands that these specific issues represent a more fundamental argument over the nature of poetry. 'Nevertheless, it must be granted that the pretensions of any composition to be regarded as poetry will depend upon that definition of the poetic character which he who undertakes to determine the question has considered as decisive.'[3] Crabbe then begins his counter-argument with an

---

[3] *The Poetical Works of George Crabbe*, ed. A.J. Carlyle and R.M. Carlyle, Oxford, 1908, p. 216. All subsequent quotations from Crabbe's prose and poetry will be taken from this edition, and page-number citation will be made in the text. For a good

ironic attack upon Romantic premisses and authorities. His antagonists found their 'definition of the poetic character' upon 'the words which the greatest of poets, not divinely inspired, has given to the most noble and valiant Duke of Athens'. Crabbe quotes the relevant passage from *A Midsummer Night's Dream* (V.i) and explicates the Romantic concept of Imagination. The visionary poet captivates

the imagination of his readers, he elevates them above the grossness of actual being, into the soothing and pleasant atmosphere of supra-mundane existence: there he obtains for his visionary inhabitants the interest that engages a reader's attention without ruffling his feelings, and excites that modern kind of sympathy which the realities of nature oftentimes fail to produce, either because they are so familiar and insignificant that they excite no determinate emotion, or are so harsh and powerful that the feelings excited are grating and distasteful. (p. 217)

Crabbe's argument is empirical and quietly ironic. In the first place, he attacks the Romantic 'definition' by exposing its lack of inclusiveness. The received facts of the matter belie the definition, which necessarily excludes 'a vast deal of what has been hitherto received as genuine poetry'. Chaucer, Dryden, and Pope are Crabbe's most prominent instances, but his most trenchant and subtle is Shakespeare himself. Indeed, Crabbe's use of Shakespeare constitutes a brilliant piece of ironical argumentation. Though the author of one of the famous statements on behalf of the inspirational theory of poetry, Shakespeare is 'not divinely inspired'. Far from being a visionary poet, Shakespeare is the creator of an array of human creatures some of whom—like Duke Theseus—believe that poets are 'of imagination all compact'. But Crabbe's Shakespeare overlooks the opinions of his various fictional creatures.

Crabbe's ironic point, then, is not merely that the world displays many different sorts of poets and poetry—some of them 'divinely inspired' in the Romantic sense—but that the *measure* of what constitutes poetry is human, social, and historical rather than divine, inspired, and transcendent. Crabbe's

discussion of Crabbe's aesthetic see Peter New, *George Crabbe's Poetry*, New York, 1967, pp. 3-9. The best book on Crabbe's verse in general is probably still Lilian Haddakin's *The Poetry of Crabbe*, London, 1955.

prime exemplar of the 'poetic character' is Shakespeare, who is at once 'the greatest of poets' (as all agree), but who is also 'not divinely inspired', and who does not measure poetry in inspirational terms. Shakespeare's fictional Duke proposes such a measure, and in so doing he aligns himself with a particular theoretical tradition; but Crabbe, following Shakespeare, argues the limited nature of such a view.

Crabbe's position follows upon his different 'definition of the poetic character'. According to Coleridge, for example, the immediate object of poetry is 'pleasure, not truth', but its ultimate object is 'a species of Revelation' akin to a religious experience. In its balance and reconciliation of opposite and discordant qualities, poetry elevates the human mind into contact with the whole truth of existence: with the transcendent Idea, the Truth of the One Life.[4] This definition of poetry derives from the general tradition of Christian Humanism epitomized earlier in Sidney. It ultimately connects with the classical idea that poetry should teach and delight, but it changes the pragmatic and operational character of those ancient concepts into philosophic categories (pleasure and truth). This alteration follows directly on the method of Kantian aesthetics as it was set forth in the third *Critique*.

Rather than dealing with poetry in terms of pleasure and truth, however, Crabbe's definition is based upon functional notions much more akin to the ancient classical concepts. In the 'Preface' to *Tales of the Hall* (1819) he speaks of 'the entertainment or the instruction' which poetry produces, and of the author's obligation 'to please or to instruct' the audience (p. 338). This formulation in fact supports Crabbe's own poetic practice, which does not aim for Kantian/Coleridgean aesthesis, and does not aspire to the revelation of a final Truth. Rather, Crabbe's field of poetic 'pleasure' contains a variety of less totalizing pleasures: it gratifies, entertains, and pleases (in many different local and particular ways). As for its 'truth' content, once again Crabbe takes a human, non-transcendent approach. Crabbe wants to teach and to instruct, not to deliver a new (or old) revelation.

---

[4] For a convenient summary of Coleridge's aesthetic views see John Spencer Hill, *Coleridge on Imagination*, Totowa, N.J., 1978; see especially pp. 83, 169.

In all these respects Crabbe obviously differs sharply from Coleridge, but the ways he differs from Wordsworth are perhaps even more instructive. The clearest *locus* of their differences will be found in Wordsworth's 1802 'Preface' to *Lyrical Ballads*, in the famous discussion of the relative prerogatives of science and poetry. When Wordsworth says that poetry's 'object is truth, not individual and local, but general, and operative', he specifically means to separate the scientist and historian— those dealers in mere 'matters-of-fact', in Wordsworth's view —from the poet, whose commitment to the expression of 'passion' allows him a direct and 'natural' contact with the universal human truth that Wordsworth called 'sympathy'. Because poetry's object is to reveal, directly, that primary truth of a universal sympathy among persons and peoples and between mankind and nature (Coleridge's One Life), it differs from the seriatim and processive truths of empirical science (whether history or natural philosophy):

To this knowledge [of universal sympathy] which all men carry about with them, and to these sympathies in which without any other discipline than that of our daily life we are fitted to take delight, the Poet principally directs his attention. He considers man and nature as essentially adapted to each other, and the mind of man as naturally the mirror of the fairest and most interesting qualities of nature. And thus the Poet, prompted by this feeling of pleasure which accompanies him through the whole course of his studies, converses with general nature with affections akin to those, which, through labour and length of time, the Man of Science has raised up in himself, by conversing with those particular parts of nature which are the objects of his studies. The knowledge both of the Poet and the Man of Science is pleasure; but the knowledge of the one cleaves to us as a necessary part of our existence, our natural and unalienable inheritance; the other is a personal and individual acquisition, slow to come to us, and by no habitual and direct sympathy connecting us with our fellow-beings.[5]

When Wordsworth speaks, later, of the 'primal sympathy/ Which having been must ever be', and when he avers that 'Nature never did betray/The heart that loved her',[6] he asserts

[5] *Wordsworth and Coleridge: Lyrical Ballads*, ed. R.L. Brett and A.R. Jones, New York, 1963, pp. 252-3.

[6] In the 'Intimations Ode', lines 182-3, and 'Tintern Abbey', lines 123-4. Well-known passages from various Wordsworth poems are quoted throughout the discussion without specific citation.

his faith in the One Life and the ultimate benevolence of history in a natural world. For Crabbe, however, though God may be—is—in his heaven, all may not be—rarely is—right with the world. Crabbe's nature and history are fields of betrayal, places where one can and must expect adversity, disaster, even malevolence. Crabbe, Wordsworth, and Coleridge all agree that 'man and the objects that surround him [are] acting and reacting on each other', but whereas this systematic complex is a benevolent One Life to the Romantics, it is a circumstantial field to Crabbe, who sees in it endless eventual possibilities, most of which will be hurtful and destructive rather than benevolent precisely because the eventualities—being unforeseeable—will rudely interrupt our projects and plans.

The difference between Wordsworth and Crabbe is interesting since both men wrote a number of narratives which deal with similar subjects. What Wordsworth represents in, for example, 'The Brothers' or 'Michael' or 'The Ruined Cottage' has much in common with the typical Crabbe narrative. 'The Ruined Cottage' is especially pertinent here, first, because the grim features of the story are so comparable to Crabbe's tales of woe; and second, because those very similarities serve to highlight the final and decisive differences. The fact that Wordsworth's is a framed narrative—with the author presenting himself as a dramatic figure in the story, and the reader's surrogate for the poem's moral lesson—reveals an important difference between a typical Wordsworthian narrative and Crabbe's characteristically non-subjective method of tale-telling. Wordsworth wants, and proposes to deliver, a solution to the problem of evil in the world. Armytage, a man tried and schooled in adversity, delivers that moral lesson to Wordsworth; and Wordsworth, in re-presenting that consolatory narrative, turns the lesson he received into an instruction of the poem's reader:

> That what we felt of sorrow and despair
> From ruin and from change, and all the grief
> The passing shews of being leave behind,
> Appeared an idle dream that could not live
> Where meditation was. I turned away,
> And walked along my road in happiness.
>   (lines 520-5)[7]

[7] 'The Ruined Cottage', in *The Ruined Cottage and The Pedlar*, ed. James Butler, Ithaca, N.Y., 1979, pp. 41-76.

Such a lesson emerges from 'a sense sublime/Of something far more deeply interfused' into the life of things than 'sorrow and despair . . . ruin and . . . change'. Wordsworth's characteristic view is that such a sense emerges from a person's meditative interchange with 'natural forms'. So it is at the end of 'The Ruined Cottage', where Armytage and Wordsworth are left sitting together in silence 'beneath the trees . . . on that low bench':

> And now we felt,
> Admonished thus, the sweet hour coming on:
> A linnet warbled from those lofty elms,
> A thrush sang loud, and other melodies
> At distance heard, peopled the milder air.
> (lines 529-33)

When the two men leave their field of desolation and travel on, consoled, to a place of comfort ('A rustic inn, our evening resting-place'), they move in the 'milder air' of Wordsworth's benevolent Nature.

That Nature never betrays the loving heart because such a heart necessarily—by very definition—participates in its 'primal sympathy'; and the latter is a permanent and universal reality, an ineradicable Idea to which we assent by virtue of actual experience ('having been must ever be'). Thus Wordsworth's Nature 'upholds and cherishes' suffering humanity 'first and last and midst and without end'. Ecological nature is Wordsworth's fundamental sign and symbol of his transcendent Nature because the objective natural world—the field of chemistry, physics, biology—contains for human beings, whose immediate lives are lived in social and historical fields, the images of permanence which they need. Like Coleridge, however, Wordsworth translates those ecological forms into theological realities: nature as Nature, the Active Universe and manifest form of the One Life. When Wordsworth writes framed tales, then—his famous retrospective narratives—he uses a poetic form which itself represents the prevenient existence of that something far more deeply interfused. Benevolence and consolation arrive when they are discovered, when we see that their authority has always been present, though unseen. When M.H. Abrams describes the 'Natural Supernaturalism' of Romanticism, with its characteristic 'circuitous journeys', this is the pattern he details for us.

The pattern is not Crabbe's, whose orderly couplets mar-
shall, paradoxically, a world 'Sad as realities, and wild as
dreams' ('The Parting Hour', p. 230). Whereas Wordsworth's
symbolical method constantly offers the reader an anticipatory
narrative—a tale whose benevolent ending is hidden in its
beginning—Crabbe's method is to move inexorably from point
to point, couplet to couplet, building its features of grimness as
'sorrow takes new sadness from surprise' ('The Parting Hour',
p. 225). Like Wordsworth, Crabbe knows that human beings
are subject to unforseeable events and circumstances; unlike
Wordsworth, Crabbe does not see that a system of divine benevolence—to which both men gave official assent—provided
anything more than an ideological solution to problems which
were fundamentally social, psychological, and economic.
Crabbe's tale of Ellen Orford—so comparable to Wordsworth's
tale of Margaret—gives us a woman who has undergone intolerable sufferings, and who has yet remained in the end 'true' to
her religion and the social structures she was born to.

> And as my mind looks cheerful to my end,
> I love mankind and call my GOD my friend.
>
> (p. 191)

These final lines in the poem, which in Wordsworth would be
consoling, are in Crabbe perfectly shocking because nothing in
the narrative justifies them. Ellen Orford's final testament of
faith comes to us as one last item in an empirical and seriatim
narrative. God and mankind have not protected Ellen Orford
from her miseries—on the contrary, in fact—but then she,
quite rightly, does not look for such protection. Wordsworth
too does not look directly to God or society for protection from
misery, but tells us to trust to the 'humanized' (Wordsworthian)
imagination, which can generate tales and poetic devices which
themselves create the consolations and the solutions which
human beings need. 'The Ruined Cottage' is itself the answer
to the problems the poem raises up for us out of the world
beyond the poem's tale.

Crabbe's story of Ellen Orford, however, vigorously forbids
any solution that is grounded in the Romantic Imagination.
Indeed, the poem is largely an indictment of such solutions via
its attack upon those popular romantic narratives of Crabbe's

day which built up tales of woe only to afford a final deliverance from their machineries of terror:

> Till some strange means afford a sudden view
> Of some vile plot, and every wo adieu!

(p. 189)

Wordsworth's stories do not reveal 'some vile plot'; they involve, as it were, the apocalypse of 'some kind scheme' which displaces the misery in a benevolent spiritual field. Crabbe's tales, however, involve neither vile plot nor benevolent scheme; they simply demonstrate what he called 'realities'. Ellen Orford is both subject to and aware of such 'realities', but in terms of a functional knowledge she remains in darkest ignorance. Indeed, when Crabbe presents her, in the end, as helpless and literally blind, he gives the reader an objective correlative for the state of her human understanding. What 'Ellen Orford knows'—*all* that she knows—is 'That we should humbly take what Heaven bestows' (p. 189). Though he honours such piety, Crabbe is well aware how sadly inadequate it is to the whole of her case. Still, his sympathetic presentation of such piteous and fragile creatures contains the secret to the appalling power of his narratives, which are at once full of pity, yet (finally) pitiless.

When Ellen Orford calmly narrates her terrible story she calls her life 'A common case' (p. 189) because it is, as she unprotestingly knows, typical of people who live in certain social and economic circumstances. Readers of her story, then as well as now, find her narrative peculiarly shocking for this very reason: she records a detailed history which the more comfortable reader, alienated from her social 'realities', must acknowledge to be a generic story rather than a special case. In Crabbe's handling of such realities, no adequate preventions can be expected from God or society or imagination, which at best can promise to displace them within various ideological transformations. But the method of a Crabbe narrative resists a final displacement, and especially disallows that famous Romantic displacement we recognize in the Wordsworthian mode. Crabbe's couplets serve at once to fix our attention on specific matters, on a series of particular facts and ideas and events, and at the same time to accumulate their data in an additive scheme.

This additive method results in a poetry of truths rather than a poetry of Truth. Crabbe's work takes up its traditional human materials but delivers them to us under the sign not of Imagination but of Science. He accumulates his material, he distinguishes it into various parts, he particularizes. Furthermore, he adds that last, crucial scientific dimension by historicizing his materials at all points. Finality, in the philosophic sense, does not govern Crabbe's tales, which emphasize relative creatures, human time, and a continuous movement of accumulation that marks out not a Romantic form of process but a scientific form of addition.

Thus Crabbe's is a poetry of science in a very particular sense: his work illustrates a modern scientific method not in its synthetic or theoretical phase, but at its fundamental inductive and critical stage, when the necessary data are being collected. 'The Muses have just about as much to do [with Crabbe's poetry] as they have with a Collection of medical reports, or of Law cases', said Wordsworth when he dismissed Crabbe's 'verse'.[8] The critique accurately reports the method of many of Crabbe's poems; what may be disputed, then as now, is the comparative value of Crabbe's method.

Crabbe and his contemporary defenders represented his 'value' under two principal headings. First, his work dealt with the 'truth' of certain important human 'realities' which poetry did not normally examine. It was therefore important not merely for the *facts* of its content but for the originality of its subject-matter. Second, Crabbe's poetry offers the reader the pleasure of coming to such knowledge—the pleasure of learning new 'realities'—rather than the pleasure of an imaginative aesthesis.

Because this last distinction is crucial for understanding Crabbe's work, I must expand upon it in some detail. The Romantic—prototypically Coleridgean—concept of poetic pleasure is a philosophic category of human Being. Though a subjective experience, it is metaphysically transcendent; indeed, the individual's experience of such an aesthetic pleasure is a felt apprehension (rather than an understood cognition) of the persistent reality of that transcendent Form of Being. Poetry is a vehicle which induces the experience of such pleasure, thereby

8 See n. 1 above.

reaffirming the reality of the ultimate Form of Pleasure in the act of reading the poem. What Crabbe called, in the 'Preface' to the *Tales* (1812), the 'painful realities' of existence are revealed, through Romantic Imagination, to be 'passing shows' and temporal illusions. Romantic Imagination creates a 'world elsewhere' which corresponds to whatever the heart desires; it substitutes an Eden of Imagination for the lost Edens of the past.

Crabbe does not undertake to offer such acts of final substitution. His poetic pleasures deal with more limited values in a world which, to Crabbe's experience, seems more various, complex, and unknown than is often realized by himself or his middle and upper class readers. He is especially interested in the 'painful realities of actual existence' among which he includes—indeed, emphasizes—the realities of the Romantic Imagination. His work endeavours to create, via the illusion of art, a peculiar place of disinterested 'repose by substituting [for our "perpetually-occurring vexations" of life] objects in their place which [the mind] may contemplate with some degree of interest and satisfaction':

for when it is admitted that they have no particular relation to him, but are the troubles and anxieties of other men, they excite and interest his feelings as the imaginary exploits, adventures, and perils of romance;—they soothe his mind, and keep his curiosity pleasantly awake; they appear to have enough of reality to engage his sympathy, but possess not interest sufficient to create painful sensations. Fiction itself, we know, and every work of fancy, must for a time have the effect of realities. (p. 218)

What is important about Crabbe's proposal is that the 'pleasant effect upon the mind of the reader' which his poetry offers is conceived in very limited terms ('some degree of interest and satisfaction'). Crabbe's pleasure is a moment of repose whose local and particular character is defined by the systems of 'painful realities' which his poetry uncovers. Crabbe speaks of 'those every-day concerns . . . and vexations' of life, but he treats poetry in precisely similar terms, as if it too were an everyday matter, only a pleasant one. The pleasure we are to derive from his poems, then, is not conceived as 'moments in the being of the eternal silence' so much as moments in the being of a recurrent bedlam.

To understand this interesting (and unromantic) theory of poetic pleasure we must grasp the importance which Crabbe attaches to his particularities. The 'every-day concerns . . . and vexations' may nevertheless 'lift the mind [of the reader] from the painful realities of actual existence' because the stories are 'not [in literal fact] the very concerns and distresses of the reader'. We sympathize with the characters and their stories because they detail commonplaces with which we are familiar; but we are distanced from the stories because the experiences are not, *in their particulars*, our own (something, as Crabbe says, 'hardly to be supposed'). This apparently pedantic and fussy distinction points toward the crucial importance which matters-of-fact play in Crabbe's work. Indeed, it shows us the fundamentally scientific (rather than metaphysical) bent of Crabbe's mind. Distinctions for him can be made both categorically and empirically. Furthermore, empirical distinctions—the fact that Edward Shore's best friend was a certain age, or the fact that Dinah's aunt (in 'Procrastination') lived longer than expected—may focus differences which, from a human (social and psychological) point of view, are every bit as important as any 'fundamental' distinction in metaphysics, ethics, or epistemology. In the world of human experience it may be just these 'insignificant' empirical differences which make *all* the difference in the lives of individuals, social groups, even kingdoms. Ultimately, then, Crabbe's method subjects all higher-order syntheses, whether cognitive (philosophic) or non-cognitive (poetic), to an existential critique.

The empirical distinction Crabbe draws in the passage I have been discussing represents no small matter for him. The entire issue of poetic distance and sympathy for Crabbe rests on the differences that poems draw between particular readers and particular subject-matters. These are, literally, differences in fact which signal important differences in (subsequent) poetic effects. By establishing the separation of the reader from the poem on this empirical basis, Crabbe emphasizes the very terms under which a reading of his work will take place. The 'pleasure' of a Crabbe poem is not a matter of 'seeing into the life of things', of experiencing a sense of the One Life or the 'One Spirit's plastic stress'; it is rather the pleasure of a particular experience wherein the mind becomes an observer within a manifold of fascinating, highly specified details and differentials. Crabbe's reader is lifted above the poetic materials the way an observer gains distance on the objects brought before his view.

From this elevated vantage Crabbe fashions his critique of the Idealistic traditions of poetry and criticism. This argument is explicitly made not only in the 'Preface' to the 1812 *Tales*; it appears in earlier works as well. *The Village* (1783) is famous for its attack upon idealized representations of country life, but a similar assault is mounted in the opening Letter of *The Borough* (1810). The basis for the attack lies in Crabbe's insistence upon factual accuracy in verse, a criterion which demands that poetic details be presented in contexts that are time- and place-specific. Such contexts, because they are empirically structured and elaborated, deliver poetry from the grip of abstract and idealized modes of perception.[9]

In addition to this critique, however, Crabbe's method opens up an entirely new poetic world. His verse is at once critique and revelation, for its novel subject-matter represents the discovery that no subject lies outside the province of verse. This definitive break with a traditional (and increasingly threatened) rule of poetic decorum represents a far more important theoretical advance than has often been realized. In his new subject-matter Crabbe defined the significance of his new aesthetic: that his was a poetry of discovery and investigation, of empirical research whose initial limits would be set in scientific terms.[10]

[9] I trust that my use of terms like 'fact', 'particulars', 'empirical details', etc., will not be taken in some crudely positivist sense. 'Facts' and 'details' and the like may refer to physical objects and conditions, but they may equally refer to social or psychological events (e.g. the *fact* of a person's class). Furthermore, 'facts' are by no means static quantities, though humanists often misunderstand the term and its referents in this positivist way. Within their own defining heuristic systems—e.g. chemical facts or social facts postulated and gathered within the respective systems of a chemistry or a sociology—they are conceptually fixed. But such 'facts' are systematically fixed for specific investigative purposes; the dynamism in the field of reality is not altered, and is always recognized. Indeed, the scientific act of defining and fixing 'facts' is a research performance which is itself dynamic in character. Crabbe's 'matters-of-fact' are precisely of this sort, for they function in his work as highly critical materials. Crabbe uses them to demystify, to explain, and, finally, to raise up serious human problems which lie hidden in the situations he wishes to investigate.

[10] The symmetry between Crabbe's poetry and certain scientific attitudes and practices is important, in the history of poetics, because this symmetry—when considered

Crabbe's method, then, is to train his readers in critical and exploratory observation. A concrete and 'material' vantage is adopted because it alone provides an escape from received conceptions (and hence perceptions) of the world. Empiricism is, for Crabbe and his epoch, a sharp critical differential from received methods and.categories of religious and philosophic thought. This materialist differential operates in *The Village*, as we know, but it loses none of its force or relevance in the later poetry, where it undermines that latest appearance of Idealistic ideology, Romantic displacement.

Crabbe's poetic 'originality', then, which was universally acknowledged by his contemporaries (and which is generally forgotten by us), is a function of an aesthetic that made a fundamental break with traditional approaches. When twentieth-century scholars classify him as an Augustan or Neo-Classical throwback, a reactionary figure who somehow lived on to write verse in the proto-modern Romantic Age, some crucial distortions are being allowed to enter the analysis. *The Village* is a critique of Neo-Classical poetic standards as they were embodied in the traditional method of pastoral verse. But the poetry which Crabbe wrote after *Lyrical Ballads*, precisely because it was published *when it was* (1807-19), has shifted the focus of Crabbe's attack from Neo-Classical ideas to the new Romantic ones. Crabbe's 'Preface' to the 1812 *Tales* shows us quite clearly that he was aware of his new set of opponents; indeed, the remarks on Crabbe made by so many of the period's leading Romantic figures, like Wordsworth, Coleridge, and Hazlitt, reinforce our sense of the gulf which divides Crabbe's work from theirs.

The symmetry between the attack launched in *The Village* and the critique of Romanticism to be found in the later verse highlights an interesting, and neglected, aspect of Romanticism: that its ideologies share important attitudes with the ideologies of Neo-Classicism. Romantic aesthetics are based upon

in its precise historical situation—contains an implicit critique of current poetic practice, both the traditional kind as well as the new modes being initiated by Wordsworth and Coleridge. Crabbe's poetry aims to establish itself upon models developed in the traditions of science, and especially of modern (Baconian) science. Because it does this, Crabbe's poetry finds itself compelled to struggle with the ideologies of traditional poetic practice since, in Crabbe's day, the principal ideological state apparatuses—i.e. the Church, the schools, and the artistic media—operated in terms of the humanism of non-scientific disciplines.

processive and historicist models, and these contrast sharply with, for example, the doctrines of Pope's *Essay on Criticism* and *Essay on Man*. Furthermore, Romanticism espouses an interior geography which is far removed from the social parameters of Neo-Classical verse. Nevertheless, despite these (and other) important differences, Neo-Classicism and Romanticism emerge as symmetrical ideologies when we compare them with the antithetical position adopted by Crabbe. The latter's empiricism—praised and, in some respects, elaborated by Byron—exposes the common Idealism which Pope's aesthetic shares with Wordsworth and Coleridge. The famous conclusion to the first Epistle of Pope's *Essay on Man* might well be set out as an epigraph to *The Prelude*, or *The Rime of the Ancient Mariner*:

> All Nature is but art, unknown to thee;
> All chance, direction, which thou canst not see;
> All discord, harmony not understood;
> All partial evil, universal good:
> And, spite of pride, in erring reason's spite,
> One truth is clear: Whatever is, is RIGHT.

The instance of Crabbe, then, brings an important fact about the early nineteenth century into sharp relief: that is has been denominated 'The Romantic Age' not because all its significant art products are Romantic, but because the ideology of Romanticism came to dominate the period. The age's actual field of human productive activity incorporated a diversity of work far richer than what we know as the Romantic. The lesson that Crabbe teaches could as well be learned by studying, in their historical contexts, those other antithetical positions marked out by Austen, Scott, and Peacock.[11]

I began this paper by contrasting Wordsworth's and Crabbe's poetical theories in order to illuminate the special character of Crabbe's work, and to revise our estimate of the significance and value of what he did. I want to conclude with another set of comparisons and contrasts in order to clarify certain aspects of Wordsworth's poetry which bear re-examination.

---

[11] Some excellent work in these fields has already been done; for example by Marilyn Butler. See in particular her books *Jane Austen and the War of Ideas*, Oxford, 1975 and *Peacock Displayed*, London, 1979.

Crabbe's attack upon Romantic ideas in *The Borough* (especially Letters I, XXIII, and XXIV), in his 1812 'Preface', and
in any number of the tales (like 'Delay Has Danger'), focuses
on what he sees as the illusionary character of Romantic attitudes. His exemplary argument is functional rather than theoretical or aesthetic in its method. When individual desires or
perceptions or feelings are made standards of judgement, false
views and perilous circumstances ensue.

Wordsworth himself developed a similar (though more subjectively based) argument in his great poem on Peele Castle, a
work widely regarded as—in one influential critic's term—a
'palinode' [12] to Wordsworth's early Romantic faith. This view
responds to Wordsworth's explicit rejection of what he calls
'the fond illusion of my heart', his sense that Nature is ruled by
'A steadfast peace':

> I could have fancied that the mighty Deep
> Was even the gentlest of all gentle Things.   (lines 11-12)

But 'A deep distress' forces Wordsworth to confess how 'blind'
such a view is; and George Beaumont's 'Picture of Peele Castle,
in a storm' provides him with the vehicle for expressing his
revisionary statement:

> O 'tis a passionate Work!—yet wise and well,
> Well chosen is the spirit that is here;
> That Hulk which labours in the deadly swell,
> This rueful sky, this pageantry of fear!
>
> And this huge Castle, standing here sublime,
> I love to see the look with which it braves,
> Cased in the unfeeling armour of old time,
> The lightning, the fierce wind, and trampling waves.
> (lines 45-52)

Because Wordsworth can 'commend/This sea in anger, and
that distant shore', these great lines measure the distance between Crabbe's grim and fearful pageantries, and Wordsworth's
way of dealing with similar matters. Both men chasten 'the
fond illusion' of the benevolent heart, but whereas Wordsworth
can say that he 'loves to see' 'Such sights, or worse, as are

[12] See Harold Bloom, *The Visionary Company*, New York, 1961. p. 179.

before me here', Crabbe narrates his tales of woe with no will or pleasure or hope. Nothing in Crabbe's ideology can offer a deliverance from the evils he portrays once the characters and events of the stories are set into their circumstantial courses. Edward Shore, Abel Keene, Allen Booth, Benbow, Grimes, Ellen Orford: the disasters of these lives take place in this world, where they lie so far beyond a material redemption that Crabbe will not even raise—is too humane to argue—the issue of a compensatory (spiritual or imaginative) redemption.

For Wordsworth, however, 'The feeling of my loss' generates a demand for some compensatory justice, and produces those patterns of Romantic displacement for which his work is so justly celebrated. Whereas Crabbe must force himself to tell, and us to hear, his fearful stories, Wordsworth's celebration of disaster is the certain sign of his Romanticism, the 'fond illusion' of Wordsworth's heart that some uncertain hope presides over all disastered things. Wordsworth finally rejects the illusion of 'A steadfast peace', but he embraces another: that the awful 'Characters of the great Apocalypse' are in fact the benevolent and redemptive 'types and symbols of Eternity' (*Prelude* (1850) vi, lines 638, 639).

Displaced hope—interiorized justice, an Ideal of hope, spiritual and imaginative redemption—these are the certain marks of a Romantic sensibility. This fact explains why 'Peele Castle' is no palinode to Wordsworth's original Romantic faith, for the argument in the poem is the same as the argument in 'Michael' and 'The Ruined Cottage'. Wordsworth's grim Romantic pleasure in seeing the fearful picture of Peele Castle is analogous to his melancholy Romantic thankfulness in hearing Armytage's terrible story of Margaret:

> The old Man ceased: he saw that I was moved.
> From that low bench rising instinctively,
> I turned aside in weakness, nor had power
> To thank him for the tale which he had told.
> I stood, and leaning o'er the garden gate
> Reviewed that Woman's sufferings; and it seemed
> To comfort me while with a brother's love
> I blessed her in the impotence of grief.   (lines 493-500)

This symmetry between 'Peele Castle' and 'The Ruined Cottage' helps to explain the apparent discrepancy between the two poems. The 'fond illusion' in the former is called 'A steadfast peace', whereas in the latter, when Wordsworth rejects an 'idle dream', he seems to embrace a position that is antithetical to 'Peele Castle': for it is 'ruin and . . . change, and all the grief' which is declared to be an illusion. Reality is interior, the geography of the meditative mind; and the imagination's re-creations of the world (i.e. poetical works) are themselves what compensate for the losses we sustain in our everyday lives.

This Romantic displacement, this interiorized standard of reality, is very different from Crabbe's. The latter defines poetry as a recreation, not a re-creation. Furthermore, poetry and meditation in Crabbe are not acts of spiritual displacement but of materialistic and socialized revision. His religious ideology remains completely and explicitly socialized just as his critical presentation of the world refuses to accept transcendental compensations. The consequence of his procedures, from a twentieth-century vantage, is that his fearful stories escape what must inevitably seem to us the pitfalls and compromises of Romantic ideological resolutions.

In the historical triumph of Romantic ideology, later commentators found it convenient to treat Crabbe as a Neo-Classical anachronism in a Romantic age. Anti-Romantic Modernists, like Pound and Leavis, sought to 'save' Crabbe from his age by calling him an Augustan, whereas Neo-Romantic critics merely ignored Crabbe as an insignificant glacial deposit. Both of these views, however, are seriously inadequate, as we may now begin to see. More than that, however, we may also begin to see how later historical imperatives transform our sense of the place of certain writers. A critical view of Romantic ideology in our day inevitably makes Crabbe seem not an Augustan throwback but a writer whose true historical period has yet to arrive.

In contrast to Wordsworth's and Coleridge's efforts to reformulate the traditional view that poetry deals with 'general' and 'universal' Truth, Crabbe's work everywhere insists that it must be time- and place-specific: in Wordsworth's terms 'individual and local'. Each of Crabbe's characters focuses, as it were, a case-history of some important sort. Ellen Orford, Peter Grimes, Edward Shore: they are all what Lukács would later call 'typical' characters, and their stories are illustrative instances. Most emphatically are they not 'types and symbols' in either the Neo-platonic or the Romantic sense. The problems they illuminate are social, psychological, and historical, which is why a Crabbe narrative must operate with individual and local matters—with specific details and highly particularized representations of time, place, circumstance.

For the Romantics, Crabbe's was a peculiarly depressing form of art. Formulated to deal with the same severe realities which Crabbe saw, the Romantic programme stipulated a final (spiritual) solution to the recurrent problems of human change and suffering. Reading Crabbe, however, we clearly see that the Romantic solution—which Wordsworth and Coleridge call Imagination—ought to be taken as no more than yet another final solution; indeed, under the circumstances, ought to be regarded as something even more desperate, as a sort of final grand illusion. This quality in the work of the Romantics—this conceptual blindness—supplies them, paradoxically, with their special artistic insight. Romantic texts, that is to say, inscribe their own *Genealogy of Morals*; and Crabbe's work can help us to see this fact. The emotional sign under which the Romantic Imagination operates is Melancholia, or even Agony. In Crabbe, however, this mood is shifted out of the Imagination and into the stories, the subjects, the people and their places: into what Crabbe calls his 'figures of imagination'. These are characteristically desperate and incapable figures, lost souls whose final place of refuge is with phantasms, pathetic dreams and memories, or mere nightmare visions.

The Romantic revulsion from Crabbe's poetry is entirely understandable, then, since the truths to which he is devoted institute a critique of the Truth which Romanticism sought to sustain: that 'ruin and . . . change, and all the grief' are transitory and epiphenomenal, and that Imagination inaugurates an absolute triumph over sublunary evil. The Romantic Agony ought to have reminded us that such a Truth is, even in the experience of the Romantic poets themselves, a terrible and pathetic illusion. Reading Crabbe we cannot fail to see that illusion. His poetry takes up its traditional human materials, but it delivers them to us as a desire and pursuit of the truth rather than a Desire and Pursuit of the Whole. In Crabbe we are forced to move in a world of relative creatures, human time.

(1980-1)

3.   Rome and its Romantic Significance

I

Why should the subject of Romantic Rome have anything more than a passing interest for criticism and scholarship? Imagination, Nature, the Self: these are the crucial elements of the Romantic experience. Rome is not. Wherein lies its scholarly significance?

The answer to this question begins to emerge when we recall certain facts about the Romantic experience. First, most Romantics did not like cities, which seemed to them the emblems of a debased social life. In this respect cities represent a defining limit of the Romantic experience in its own predominant self-conception. How Victorian ideology separates from Romanticism can be seen, in part, through the deliberate interest which Victorian writers took in cities and the urban experience.

Only one city escaped the judgement of Romanticism, and that was Rome. The obsession of Napoleon and Chateaubriand, the grave of Keats, Rome attracted to herself—to the idea of herself, perhaps we should say—nearly all the great figures of the Romantic Movement. Body or soul, she came to possess most of these people. Even Wordsworth would eventually visit Rome and memorialize his experiences and thoughts in verse we are spared from having to remember.[1]

The Rome which focused Romantic attention was a far different place from either Renaissance or Counter-Reformation Rome, which together comprise what we now call Papal Rome in the age of its vigour, or Rome between the reigns of Martin V (1417-31) and Clement XIII (1758-69). The end of this great period in the history of Rome should probably be dated from 1773, the year in which Clement XIV agreed, under pressure from Paris and Madrid, to suppress the power of the Jesuits. But the decline and fall of Counter-Reformation Rome signalled the emergence of Romantic Rome, and it was the great art

---

[1] *Memorials of a Tour in Italy*, London, 1842.

historian Winckelmann who presided over its birth. Winckelmann went to Rome in 1755 and entered the circle of scholars who gathered around Cardinal Albani.[2] The recent excavations at Herculaneum and Pompeii were the impetus of a renewed interest in the ancient world. Rome was a museum in which historical scholarship could inaugurate systematic investigations into the antiquities of the west.

As the city of ruins, then, Rome would receive the investments of Romantic ideology to an extent that was not possible for any other city, not even Venice. This historical fact is a peculiar gift to subsequent critical scholarship, since in it we shall find an opportunity for tracing a special and important history: the history whereby Romanticism came to discover the limits of its own ideological experience.

We may begin with one of the most famous Romantic passages dealing with the Roman experience, Chateaubriand's short piece of poetic prose called 'Promenade dans Rome au clair de lune'.

Rome is asleep in the midst of her ruins. This orb of the night, this sphere which is supposed to be extinguished and unpeopled, moves through her pale solitudes, above the solitude of Rome. She shines upon the streets without inhabitants, upon enclosed spaces, open squares, and gardens in which no one walks, upon monasteries where the voices of monks are no longer heard, upon cloisters which are as deserted as the arches of the Colosseum.[3]

This solitude is an emblem that a living culture has departed; the people whom Chateaubriand cannot see are not the actual inhabitants of early nineteenth-century Rome—they are there, of course, but they do not engage his feelings. The inhabitants he looks for in vain are those who once gave life to the empty places and ruins of the present.

What is crucially Romantic about this scene, however, that which sets it apart from a Renaissance, or Baroque, or even a Neo-classical view of Roman ruins, is its melancholy sense that time has not only borne down the Rome of the ancients, it has

---

[2] For details on the circle of Cardinal Alessandro Albani see Lesley Lewis, *Connoisseurs and Secret Agents in 18th Century Rome*, London, 1961.

[3] From *Voyages et mélanges littéraires*, in *Œuvres Complètes*, Paris, 1872, ix. pp. 253-4. See also the letter to A. M. de Fontanes, Rome le 10 janvier 1804 (ibid., pp. 269-85) as well as Books IV-V of *Les Martyrs*. (My translation.)

also overcome the Rome of the popes, the greatness of the Church. Traces alone remain of what Chateaubriand calls 'the two Italies' with their 'two glories'. In this night of Rome Chateaubriand can see, by the light of the Romantic imagination, that 'pagan Rome is plunging deeper and deeper into her tombs, and Christian Rome once again descends, little by little, into the catacombs whence she originally came.'[4]

Chateaubriand's Romantic vision of Rome is born not merely of a sense that time overcomes the works of human greatness, but that its power can be seen to move even in the midst of this very life, in the works and days of one's own world and culture. The passage is dominated by an historical sense which scholarship like Winckelmann's had helped to create; but Chateaubriand's sense of the triumph of time has moved beyond Winckelmann to a consciousness that his own culture was as historically fragile as that of pagan Rome.

The picture of a Rome dominated by ruins and monuments but deserted of people is typically Romantic, and is often delivered to the reader (or viewer) under that most explicit of Romantic signs, the moonlight. The greatest English text offering such a scene is of course *Childe Harold* Canto IV.[5] This Byron text is as central as it is, in the iconography of Romanticism, because its emblems belong to more than one form of Romantic consciousness. Before we can understand the peculiar arrangements that Byron's poetry makes with Rome, however, we must retreat to a period before Chateaubriand wrote his prose poem—specifically, to a moment between the time when Winckelmann came to Rome and the outbreak of the French Revolution.

II

Late in September, 1786, having just turned his thirty-seventh birthday, Goethe left behind the bourgeois life he had been leading for the previous ten years—left behind Frau Von Stein, his state duties in Weimar, his friend the Duke—and entered Rome. He would spend fifteen months in the city (until June, 1788) and he would be utterly changed by this, the single most

---

[4] Quoted from the 'Promenades', in the *Œuvres*.
[5] See also the prose fragment by Shelley commonly known as 'The Colosseum'.

important experience of his life. 'I reckon my second life, a very rebirth, from the day I entered Rome,' he wrote at the time in his *Italian Journey*.[6] The record of his first months at Rome shows that he deliberately took Winckelmann as his mediator and guide. Soon after he arrived he bought the new edition of Winckelmann's *History* translated by Carlo Fea, he read Winckelmann's letters from Italy, and he recurred to the great scholar's experiences as to a model for his own rebirth.[7]

This morning I came by chance on the letters which Winckelmann wrote from Italy, and you can imagine with what emotion I have started to read them. Thirty-one years ago, at the same time of year, he arrived here, an even greater fool than I was. But, with true German seriousness, he set himself to make a thorough and accurate study of antiquity and its arts. How bravely he worked his way through! And, in this city, what it means to me to remember him! (p. 137)

The intellectual legacy bequeathed by Winckelmann to Goethe was that, in the study of antiquity and the arts in general, 'judgment is impossible without a knowledge of historical development' (p. 156). But Winckelmann's work also taught Goethe how such historical knowledge could offer to the contemporary European a programme of spiritual liberation. Because Winckelmann showed how to trace 'the history of styles in their gradual growth and decadence' (pp. 155-6), he opened an avenue back to what Goethe called 'the Everlasting Rome, not the Rome which is replaced by another every decade' (p. 142).

Winckelmann helped Goethe explain to himself why he felt, when he came to Rome, that 'The noble objects with which I am surrounded never lose their freshness for me' (p. 135). Again and again Goethe is struck by the apparent perfection in the arts of the Greeks, the Romans, and even of the more recent artists of the Italian Renaissance. And this experience leads him to his true, immediate interest, his personal need: 'But can we, petty as we are and accustomed to pettiness, ever become equal to such noble perfection?' (p. 135)—The answer

[6] J. W. Goethe, *Italian Journey (1786-1788)*, trans. with an Introduction by W. H. Auden and Elizabeth Mayer, New York, 1968, p. 136. Subsequent references are given in the text.
[7] *Storia della arti del disegno presso gli antichi* . . . aumentata dall' abate C. Fea, Rome, 1783-4.

emerges from Goethe's meditations on Winckelmann's historiography. To understand the cycles of art's growth and decay in Greece, in Rome, and finally in the Italian Renaissance—to understand, even more, the relations in which these cycles stand to each other—is to place one's self at the beginning of yet another cycle. The German scholar and poet come to Rome to initiate again the birth of art's 'noble perfection'. 'At sight of the immense wealth of this city, even though it consists of scattered fragments, one is inevitably led to ask when it came into being' (p. 155). Goethe's conclusion is that 'Everlasting Rome' comes into being in a cycle of rebirths, and that her latest rebirth is even now taking place at the end of the eighteenth century through the agency of people like Cardinal Albani, Winckelmann, and, of course, Goethe himself.

This insight, or conviction, informs the entire cycle of the *Roman Elegies*,[8] and it appears explicitly in Elegy xv when Goethe invokes the sun and its everlasting knowledge of perpetual cyclic renewal: 'And out of the ruins once more an even greater world!' This general theme will eventually be linked to the power of poetry itself ('Ünd ihr, wächset und blüht, geliebte Lieder,' Elegy xx), and specifically to Goethe's own love elegies as these incarnate the living freshness of antiquity.

In his *Roman Elegies* Goethe deliberately sets out to enshrine in his own verse vital spirit immortalized in the Latin love elegy, especially in the elegies of Propertius. The peculiar character of these great poems appears most forcibly when we compare the Faustina of Goethe's work with Propertius' cruel and imperious mistress. Indeed, Goethe's poetic mistress could scarcely be more unlike any of the famous women whose names and characters appear through the agency of Catullus, Propertius, and Tibullus—the three 'Triumvirs' who are explicitly acknowledged in Goethe's elegies.

That Propertius' Cynthia should not resemble the voluptuous and compliant innocent of Goethe's cycle is of course exactly what we should expect. For if Faustina corresponds to any Roman girl whom Goethe knew, or to Christiane Vulpius, or perhaps if she is an imaginative creature drawn from several

---

[8] The present translations of the *Elegies* are taken from the excellent bilingual edition *J. W. von Goethe's Roman Elegies and Venetian Epigrams*, trans. with an Introduction, Notes, and Commentaries by L. R. Lind, Lawrence, Kansas, 1974.

life originals, that fact is ideologically subordinated in the poems.[9] Faustina is not a woman, a fictive representation of a particular human being, she is the embodiment of Goethe's idea of Rome: that is to say, of human life as perpetually fresh, perpetually young, perpetually being reborn. As Amor says to Goethe in Elegy xiii: 'I, your teacher, am always young, and I'm fond of young people. I don't like you when you're precocious. Awake! Understand me! Antiquity also was new when those blessed ones lived! Happily live your life so the past may live in you!'

Being a god, Amor speaks of such matters with an ease born of a certain distance—as it were, in a 'naïve' rather than in a 'sentimental' mode of discourse. This tone corresponds to Goethe's not only in the *Italian Journey*, so notable for its lack of self-absorption, but in the *Roman Elegies* as well. The famous Elegy v epitomizes what being 'in love' means in this cycle of poems: that is, it means being young in the antique manner, being 'naïve'. 'Inspired on classical ground', Goethe means to reincarnate the classical spirit. His success in this effort is achieved in the manner of Winckelmann rather than in the manner of Propertius. Like the Roman relics and ruins lying open to Winckelmann's passionate interest, Faustina lies in bed next to Goethe, and as his hands 'glide down her hips' he thinks: 'at last I can understand sculpture.' More than this, however, through her he rediscovers the youthful spirit of the ancient world. Self-conscious without also being self-absorbed, Goethe recovers the spirit of the ancients as it were by art rather than by nature or cirumstance. Nothing reveals this aspect of the elegies so well as the scholarly mind which works through them; and perhaps no detail reveals the presence of that scholarly mind better than the unexpected appearance of the word 'Quiriten' at the end of Elegy xviii; 'Grant me, O Romans ["o Quiriten"], my happiness.' Before this passage the inhabitants of Rome are always referred to in the usual form 'die Römer', as to those who visibly inhabit the actual city of Goethe's sojourn. In the final elegies he resorts to the verbal form which calls up the idea of a primitive and (as it were) absolute Rome, the city and people which he called 'Everlasting' in his *Italian Journey*.

9 See Lind's discussion, pp. 12-15, 219-22.

Because Goethe imagined that he and his world stood at the beginning of a new historical cycle, that an Everlasting Human Life was actually in process of being born again, his Roman experience constitutes a challenge and a call, rather than, as with Chateaubriand, a mood of melancholy nostalgia. This difference is nicely displayed when we compare Chateaubriand's meditation among the Roman ruins with the corresponding meditations in Goethe's *Italian Journey*. For Goethe, 'each day [is] spent in distractions mingled with sadness,' but when he walks out 'quite alone' in the moonlight to the Capitol the experience is like entering 'an enchanted palace in a desert' (p. 496). Goethe is transported out of the present by the great Roman presences from the past, is transported with the sense that he is now at last moving 'into another simpler and greater world', that a splendid vision of futurity can be glimpsed in the noble remains of this past. He describes the experience as 'awe-inspiring', he narrates the fear which this past greatness induces, and he even confesses to a failed effort to match the greatness of the ancients. 'Aroused' to 'a mood I might call heroic-elegiac', Goethe recalls an elegy from the third book of Ovid's *Tristia*, but when he tries to compose his own elegy he cannot do it. The book therefore closes with a quotation from Ovid rather than from Goethe, but the effect of this, paradoxically, is to reveal not the failure of Goethe's poetic powers, but their desire, their energy, and their promise. At the end of the *Italian Journey* Goethe has placed himself at the beginning of a world-historical cycle, a young man whose future is beginning to unfold as he 'ventures upon something unusual'.

III

To explain the different effects of the experience of Rome on Goethe and Chateaubriand is beyond the scope of this essay and my own competence. Nevertheless, the intervention of the years 1789-1803 is manifestly significant. Both men were deeply influenced by the recently developed theories of historical periodicity, and in *Le Génie du Christianisme* Chateaubriand had offered a theory of the Christian religion which challenged the views of the *philosophes*. Bonaparte's accession to power had opened a space in France for the development of conservative ideology. The Concordat was signed in 1801, Chateaubriand's celebrated book appeared in 1802, and in 1803 the event which Chateaubriand had hoped and even angled for finally came about. He was sent to Rome as the secretary to the legation. He intially saw Bonaparte as the engine which would bring about the renascence of the Christian world. Only a few months would pass, after he arrived in Rome so full of hopes and plans, before his vision of a reborn era of Christianity would collapse, before he would write passages like the one quoted above, as well as its famous companion-piece, the letter to Fontanes on the Roman *campagna* (10 January 1804). We do not need to rehearse the well-known events of late 1803, when Chateaubriand revealed a sort of sublimity in political incompetence, to realize that his vision of a new Christian era did not collapse because of a mismanagement of his worldly affairs, or because Bonaparte was unequal to such a glorious mission. Christianity was a once and future kingdom and as such it stood outside the cycles of historical change and repetition. Similarly, the two Romes— pagan and Papal—were once but not future kingdoms, and so Chateaubriand's historical sense finally returned him to the essential truth of his imagination: that Papal Rome, like the city of the Republic and the Empire, was born to perish, and that Chateaubriand, for his part, was born to minister at her going. This is the central message of the *Memoires*, just as it is the inspiration of his prose-poetic moonlight meditations on the ruins of Rome. 'Grief is my element,' he said at the time; 'it is only when I am unhappy that I really find myself.' [10]

For the liberal and jacobin consciousness, the course of the French Revolution from 1789-1802 taught another, if equally disheartening, lesson. Goethe's sense that a new day was dawning has its English counterpart in Blake's *Marriage of Heaven and Hell*, but the confidence and exuberant hope of the *Elegies* and the *Marriage* was to succeed, following the Terror and Bonaparte, to the melancholy of works like *The Prelude*. When, in 1818, Byron sets forth his great, extended meditation on Rome and her ruins, he explains what the Revolution meant to those who identified with it:

[10] Quoted in André Maurois, *Chateaubriand*, trans. Vera Fraser, New York, 1940, p. 121.

> There is the moral of all human tales;
> 'Tis but the same rehearsal of the past,
> First Freedom, and then Glory—when that fails,
> Wealth, Vice, Corruption,—barbarism at last.
> And History, with all her volumes vast,
> Hath but *one* page,—'tis . . . written here . . .
>   (*CHP* iv, stanza 108)

Set against the background of his Roman reflections on the Revolution in France (stanzas 89-98), the '*one* page' to which Byron refers involves a dismal interpretation of Goethe's cyclic vision. The interpretation is typical of the post-Revolutionary Romantic consciousness.

The liberal and humanist Romantics will not, however, use this interpretation to fashion an ideology of reaction based upon a Christian or transcendental historical renunciation. Their problem was—to adapt a phrase from Blake—to keep the human vision in a time of trouble, to preserve an historical hope, a civilized ideal. The figures who struggled hardest and most successfully in this task were Shelley, Byron, and Stendhal. Of these three I shall here consider only the last two, principally because only Byron and Stendhal used Rome to focus and elaborate their literary programmes. Rome was, for Shelley, the inspiration of *Prometheus Unbound*, but it figured only incidentally in the structure of that work. For Byron and Stendhal, however, Rome is central: to Canto IV of *Childe Harold's Pilgrimage*, on the one hand, and on the other to Stendhal's pair of great Italian travel books, *Rome, Naples, et Florence* (1817, 1826) and *Promenades dans Rome* (1830).[11]

But before we can turn to them we must pause to consider Madame de Staël's *Corinne*, published in 1807; for if Stendhal composes his works in the context of Byron's famous poem, Byron wrote his own work against the background of *Corinne*. And the background of de Staël's novel is her exile from France, her struggle against Napoleon, and her central posi-

---

[11] The first of these books exists in two radically different versions. The 1817 text has not been translated into English; for this I am using the edition *Rome, Naples, et Florence*, Préface et Notes de Victor del Litto, Lausanne, 1961. The 1826 text exists in a good English translation by Richard Coe, *Rome, Naples, and Florence, by Stendhal*, London, 1959. The *Promenades dans Rome* has been well edited and translated by Haakon Chevalier as *A Roman Journal, by Stendhal*, New York, 1957. The last two books supply the English versions here, and page references are given in the text.

tion among the expatriate French ideologues. All this combined to make her perhaps the single most important European liberal of the period, the point of focus for a ragged and disparate band of angels.

IV

In the first book of *Corinne* the novel's heroine conducts Lord Nelvil on a tour of the Capitol in Rome. This is his first view of 'the vestiges of ancient Rome' and it inspires him to the following meditations.

> The reading of history, and the reflections to which it gives rise, operate less forcibly on our minds, than these stones in disorder, than these ruins interspersed with new habitations . . . Without doubt we are annoyed by all the modern buildings, which interfere with the ancient ruins . . . Everything is common, everything is prosaic in the exterior of most of our European cities, and Rome more than any other presents the mournful appearance of misery and degradation; but all at once, a broken column, a half-destroyed basrelief, stones united by the indestructible means of the ancient architects, remind us, that there is in man an eternal power, a spark of divinity, and that we must not omit to excite it in ourselves, and to re-animate it in others. (pp. 186-7)[12]

The conceptual basis of this passage is very close to the ideas we have already seen in Goethe's *Roman Elegies*, but the tone is entirely different. That de Staël's awareness of Winckelmann is no less acute than Goethe's is apparent throughout the novel— as we see, for example, at the end of Nelvil's and Corinne's tour of the Capitol. 'In Rome', Nelvil observes, 'there are many distinguished men whose sole occupation is to discover a new connection between history and the ruins.' He praises the 'animating' powers of this scholarly activity: 'We might say, that we gave a second life to all that we discovered, and that the past re-appeared from under the dust where it had been buried' (p. 212). Though Nelvil here invokes the theme of rebirth through an historical consciousness, his remarks betray a divergence from Goethe's thought which helps to explain the melancholy nostalgia of de Staël's novel. In this book, the greatness

---

[12] Quotations from Vol. i of the three-volume London edition of 1807; page references given in the text.

of the past does not live again in the present, does not appear incarnate in the novel and its characters. Corinne is not the ancient Tanagran poetess *redivivus*; she possesses that name as a memorial to one splendid but scarcely remembered 'spark of divinity' from the past. Corinne's function—her novel's function—is to reanimate that spark in others, which is to say that her life's purpose is oriented toward the past and the future. The present—and we must remember that the action of the novel is set between the years 1794 and 1807—is seen as a time of darkness and loss, a time when the spark of divinity is cherished for a new birth of freedom that is to come. The novel's promise falls not to Nelvil or to Corinne, whose love is star-crossed, but to Nelvil's daughter, born of another woman but, at the novel's conclusion, educated by Corinne.

Corinne is a very brainy book (possibly too brainy, but quite befitting so resolute an intellectual as de Staël was). Indeed, it is an allegory part at least of which we now easily decode. The heroine is Italy epitomized as the imaginative spirit of Rome, and she focuses the attention of the two chief male figures in the book, Lord Nelvil (a Scotsman who stands for Britain) and the Count d'Erfeuil (who represents the interests of France). A fervent admirer of British political institutions and democracy, de Staël presents Nelvil as Corinne's natural mate and lover; d'Erfeuil is, beside Nelvil, too self-centred, too deficient in moral seriousness, to be worthy of Corinne. In the end, neither man will enjoy or be truly worthy of Corinne's love, and the promise of civilized life which she holds out will remain unrealized.

Like Chateaubriand, de Staël saw the historical promise embodied in the French revolution collapse in the actual historical events which that revolution unfolded. Chateaubriand's reaction against Napoleon was to the right and out of time, a not untypical Romantic move into religion and the ultramontane. For her part, de Staël refused the illusory promises of a Napoleonic present in favour of a future hope, when the historical ideal of the revolution would achieve the actuality it could not live without.

The liberal, humanist future embodied in de Staël's picture of Rome in the European context of 1807 carries over to Byron's treatment of Rome in 1817-18. Byron's Roman meditations culminate the fourth canto of *Childe Harold* (stanzas 78-175), and de Staël's book guides much of Byron's thought. Central to both texts is the conviction that Rome's is a tragic history of lost promises and betrayed greatness, so that in her melancholy precincts we too, contemporary sufferers, 'may be consoled even for the sorrows of the heart' (p. 86). This theme—along with the related one of the revivifying power of art—dominates Corinne's famous improvised poem in Book I, chap. 3, the 'Extempore Effusion of Corinne in the Capitol'. Byron's Roman stanzas are written in conscious recollection of this text, as we can see even in the opening passage of Byron's Roman stanzas.

> Oh Rome! my country! city of the soul!
>   The orphans of the heart must turn to thee,
> Lone mother of dead empires! and controul
>   In their shut breasts their petty misery.
> What are our woes and sufferance?
>
> (stanza 78)

In following this theme, however, Byron necessarily introduces a profound mutation of its form. De Staël's Rome provides the sorrowful and melancholy soul, such as Lord Nelvil's, with a model of suffering which should lead him to see that his own happiness depends upon the depth of his love and commitment to Corinne and to Rome (who are the psychological and the political forms of a single ideal). Rome and Corinne, for de Staël, have an objective existence toward which one can move. In Byron's poem, however, Rome is a private and interiorized locale: '*my country*', Byron calls the great city, a metropolis of 'the soul'. Like everything else in Byron's poem, Rome is an expression and extension of himself, a model which Byron receives from de Staël only to appropriate in a gesture of Romantic, even Napoleonic, imperialism. Byron ridicules the 'petty misery' of the ordinary person, but he does not enter Rome to discover that his own miseries are of this sort. On the contrary, to his initial, ambiguous question—'What are our woes and sufferance?'—Byron will eventually answer, at least for himself, that they are so great, so terrible, so barely to be borne, that the history of Rome becomes an emblem of his heart.

In this respect Byron has returned to the stylistic posture which we observed initally in Goethe. The future perfect tense which dominates and gives such a sentimental nobility (if the oxymoron be permitted) to de Staël's novel appears in Byron's poem, as it does in Goethe's elegies, merely to establish a limitless range of experience, a something evermore to be. Goethe and Byron both establish their works at the outset of an historical cycle whose end they cannot foresee, but whereas Goethe's is a cycle of new and exuberant life, Byron's is a cycle of high-energy trials and suffering. And, unlike de Staël, what Byron anticipates for the future is not the eventual realization of a civilized and human way of life, it is a perpetuity of energetic struggle: 'Then let the winds howl on! their harmony/ Shall henceforth be my music' (stanza 106).

Like Goethe, then, Byron comes to incarnate in himself an idea of Rome which—to adapt a line from Wordsworth—'having been must ever be'. But the mode of both his Romanticism and his Romanism is tragic and desperate rather than comic and hopeful because—unlike Goethe's—the history he has inherited includes the crucial years of 1789-1817, when western civilization suffered what he brilliantly called 'man's worst, his second fall'. A promise given twice and lost twice means for Byron a history in which the promise will never fail to be given and will never succeed in being realized. Byron believes in what de Staël calls 'the long dream' of the civilized imagination (p. 88), but it is a faith bereft of any correspondent hope: 'A faith', in short, 'whose martyrs are the broken heart' (stanza 121).

V

With Stendhal the Romantic morphology of Rome achieves a final, ironic shift. Byron's work is Stendhal's immediate precursor, but Stendhal is a Byron with no faith at all in the political ideal of intellectuals like de Staël. Again and again Stendhal heaps ridicule on 'the North' and its 'metaphysical' predispositions. 'The South', and pre-eminently Italy, guides its life by feeling and passion rather than by brain and superego. It is a Tom Wolfe of Restoration France who declares: 'I almost think that one can say that the North feels only by thinking: to such people one must speak of sculpture only by borrowing the forms of philosophy.' As far as Stendhal is concerned, Byron's admiration for the intellectual idealist de Staël is thoroughly misguided and Stendhal can think of nothing truer (or more devastating) to say of his French compatriots than this: 'to bring the general public in France to a feeling for the arts it would be necessary to give to language the poetic bombast of Madame de Staël's *Corinne*'[13] (p. 187). So much for de Staël's sentimental brainstorming along with its correspondent breeze, that peculiarly French form of sublimation called the life of the mind.

Like Byron, Stendhal transforms Italy into a geo-political myth through which he can criticize the deficiencies of contemporary Europe, on the one hand, and intimate more generous and vital forms of human civilization on the other. Moreover, he too associates different Italian cities with variant specific forms of a central Italian ideal. The two most important books in which Stendhal represents his idea of Rome are, as I have already noted, his *Promenades* and *Rome, Naples, and Florence*. The latter is a drastic reworking of a text he had published earlier as *Rome, Naples, et Florence en 1817* and in which he first presented his theory of Italy, as it were. The 1817 book is a thinly veiled *cri de cœur* over what he saw as the tragedy of the restoration of the thrones following Waterloo and the Congress of Vienna. Stendhal journeys to Italy in 1817 as to the shrine of a lost ideal embodied in Napoleon. This is the ideal of the energetic, spontaneous, and passionate life.

We shall find it useful to keep in mind the 1817 text of *Rome, Naples, and Florence* because it is so different from the 1826 text that they illuminate each other brilliantly. For my present purpose the 1826 version is the important one, since that book not only elaborates the theory of Italy set forth in the early work, it proposes as well—something not possible in the 1817 text— what has been aptly called 'a hope for the future as well as a message of solidarity addressed to the victims of police repression'.[14]

The book's title is as misleading as its travelogue form. Stendhal organizes his book as a traveller's journal for 1816-17,

---

[13] Stendhal, *Rome, Naples et Florence* (1826), p. 187.
[14] Quoted from the del Litto edition, p. 16.

but of course the series of entries correspond in no way to any journey Stendhal actually took. Furthermore, the itinerary does not move Rome-Naples-Florence, nor are Naples and Florence nearly so important in the book as Milan. Stendhal's travelogue begins in Milan as in the city which, for him, most perfectly exhibits his theory of Italian spontaneity. It ends—or rather, it culminates—in Rome, as in the city where the promise of the future is most appropriately located. Indeed, the most significant formal change made between the texts of 1817 and 1826 involves the reconstitution of Stendhal's view of Rome, which also involves, necessarily, a reconstitution of his view of himself. In the 1817 text Rome is Stendhal's initial Italian subject, and as such she is made to illustrate the peculiarly degraded condition into which Italy—and with her, all of Europe—has fallen. In 1826, on the other hand, the travelogue reaches its climax and conclusion in Rome, just as Byron's pilgrimage had done earlier.

Both versions of Stendhal's work are as personally constructed as Byron's poem had been, but the 1826 work has these additional affiliations with Byron's poem: it too associates a European renascence with an Italian *risorgimento*, it too presents Rome as the key to Italy's future promise, and—most important of all—it relates these political changes to a renovation that takes place within the author himself. In Byron this is largely a psychological renovation, whereas in Stendhal it involves so drastic a shift in his political opinions that his entire character and fundamental self-conception are altered as well.

This change begins, according to the narrative of 1826, in the three hours which Stendhal spends in Rome on 6 February [1817] as he journeys from Florence to Naples. His initial impression of the city is not at all favourable, and when his progress is interrupted by a military procession honouring the appointment of the Minister of War to 'the dignity of Archbishop'. Stendhal's liberal, republican, and anti-clerical contempt erupts into a short prose invective. But as he is leaving the city via the *Campagna*, the ancient ruins induce in him a profound sense of awe which 'left [him] all on edge' and force him to reflect seriously upon some of his most cherished ideas. He suddenly realizes that his liberalism, his republicanism, and even his anti-clericalism are all compromised by other, conflicting tendencies: 'aristocratic leanings' and 'a certain predilection for . . . the Christian Establishment'. In fact, Stendhal's burst of contempt was a piece of self-delusion generated by his near-sighted view of Rome's present condition. The truth is that Rome is as much his dream and ideal as it was the dream of Napoleon.

> And yet, in spite of so many grievances, my heart still sides with Rome . . . [I]n every page of history, I behold the deeds and see the life of Rome; and what the eye cannot see, the heart cannot love. Thus do I account to myself for my obsession with those vestiges of Roman grandeur, those ruins, those inscriptions. Nor is this the limit of my weakness: for I even detect in certain churches of remote antiquity the pale reflection of still older pagan temples. Christianity, triumphant at the last after so many years of persecution, would fall with implacable rage upon a shrine of Jupiter, and rend it stone from stone; yet hard beside the old foundations, there would arise a new Church of St. Paul. (P. 346)

Here Stendhal observes the scene with an eye schooled by Winckelmann, in a prose that recalls the passage from *Corinne* quoted above, and in a frame of mind exactly analogous to Byron's in the famous Colosseum stanzas (Canto IV, stanzas 138-147) when he is forced to reconsider his call for revenge against the bloody tyrants of Imperial Rome.

In the final pages of his book Stendhal accepts the contradictions of Rome. From the first, Stendhal's Romanticism had been tied up with his irony, just as Byron's Romanticism reached its culmination and apotheosis in irony. But Stendhal moves past the final form of Byronic (and Stendhalian) Romanticism by de-subliming that mode of Romantic irony— specifically, by reducing the size and pretensions of his own most cherished illusions, the ideal of Romantic Irony. This event comes at the end of his book when Romantic Irony is revealed in its true significance and its purest form. Stendhal's entry for 10 October is an enthusiastic report of an 'evening spent in the company of the marionettes of the *Palazzo Fiano*'; as such, it is also a literal representation of the importance, as well as the triviality, of his Romantic Irony—indeed, of the importance *of* that triviality.

The very fact that he could produce such a narrative is significant, for in Stendhal's initial, contemptuous remarks about

Rome (journal entry for 6 February) he had singled out 'the wooden limbed marionettes' (p. 343) of Rome as an especially notable example of the debased condition of the city and its culture. Such remarks were, of course, made out of ignorance and self-satisfied prejudice. Stendhal's encounter with Rome and the Romans has cleared his mind of some of its worst cant, so that now, at the conclusion of his trip, he can not only appreciate the puppet-theatre of Rome, he can understand its cultural and political significance.

I doubt whether there be any race in Europe with a greater fondness for the bite and ingenuity of satire than the worthy citizens of Rome; so acute and subtle are their minds, that they will pounce with eager delight even upon the remotest of allusions. The element which raises the level of their happiness so infinitely far above that which prevails, say, in London, is their acquaintance with *despair*. Accustomed now for three whole centuries to regard the evils which it endures as inevitable and eternal, the Roman *bourgeoisie* feels no desire to pour forth the seething rage within its heart against the Minister; it has no wish to bring about his death; it knows full well that *this* particular incarnation of authority will merely be replaced by another, not a whit less evil-minded. Consequently, what the people of Rome desire above all else is to show their strong contempt for the powers that control their destiny, and to laugh at their expense; hence the dialogues between *Pasquino* and *Marforio* . . . [I]n Rome, the censorship is more meticulous than in Paris, [so that] comedy in the live theatre is nothing but a string of unspeakable platitudes. True laughter has sought refuge among the marionettes. (Pp. 472-3)

The puppet-theatre of Rome produces its satiric political allegories in so miniaturized and trivial a form that its work escapes the censor's power. Furthermore, the puppet-theatre is a model of artistic integrity. The chief target of its satire is the 'oligarchic Court . . . [where] power tends to accumulate in the hands of old age' (p. 474). Nevertheless, the form in which the satire is delivered tells an equally profound truth about the critical elements of Roman culture in 1826—a truth which does not spare to be very clear about the critical limits to which this truth-telling, in these circumstances, is subject. As Stendhal observes, this is a comedy born of despair.

For all its limits, however, this Roman culture seems to Stendhal, in the larger European context, one of the few places where one can still find a society which prizes truth and exhibits vitality and energy. Stendhal's myth of Italy and Rome is produced in relation to his contempt for the convention-bound and hypocritical societies of France, England, and Germany in 1826.

The imaginary travelogue which Stendal published in 1826 would be succeeded three years later by an equally extraordinary book, the *Promenades dans Rome* (published in two volumes). This work appears to be the diary of a visit to Rome undertaken between August 1827 and April 1829. In fact, it was written in a hotel room in Paris in 1828-9 partly from Beyle's recollections (his last visit to Rome was in 1824), but largely from books and notes supplied to him.[15] The *Promenades* represents itself to be an on-the-spot report of immediate experiences and spontaneous reactions; it is, in reality, an imaginary voyage to a Rome constructed in Stendhal's brain out of a heterogeneous collection of second-hand materials.

What is especially interesting about the Rome of Stendhal's *Promenades* is the manner in which he has incorporated, and finally transformed, the earlier Romantic imaginations of the city—including his own earlier presentation set forth in 1826. The *Promenades* resumes the images, attitudes, and forms we have already seen, but with the heroic element definitively removed. The contrast with his book of 1826 is especially notable. There, his final eulogium of the Roman character included the following prophetic declaration: 'Do but grant him [the Roman citizen] a Napoleon for the space of twenty years, and you will see him rise, beyond question, to be the foremost race in Europe' (p. 472). In 1829, however, Stendhal takes a much more problematic view of the matter. When he discusses the disappearance of banditry in the Papal states, he not only associates the phenomenon with a general decline in the level of Italian 'energy', he connects this deplorable loss of the Italian national character with the emergence of Napoleon as a force in Italian culture (pp. 282-3, 287). By a supreme sort of paradox, Stendhal's Romantic model of the energetic hero becomes the instrument which is destroying his Romantic model of the energetic society, the society defined by erotic

---

[15] See the discussion in Chevalier's 'Introduction' to *A Roman Journal*, xxix-xx.

love, an appreciation of the fine arts, and fierce independence.

The cannon of the bridge of Lodi (May, 1796) began the awakening of Italy. Generous souls were able to forget love and the fine arts; something newer was offered to their imaginations.

I repeat: in 1829 there are no more organized bandits between Rome and Naples; they have entirely disappeared. (p. 283)

But this new thing offered to the imagination of the generous soul would itself be taken away, from Stendhal as well as from Italy, and in the remaining void would appear the volatile and ironic consciousness which we associate with Stendhal and which he associated with Rome.

Stendhal's Rome, then, locates the same kind of nostalgia epitomized in Chateaubriand, except that Stendhal's presentation is not itself nostalgic. Stendhal also exhibits the despair which Byron made immortal, as well as the future perfect promise defined by de Staël; but Stendhal's is a despair without a sense of desperation, and a hope for the future which need not take itself seriously. He is, in fact, precisely like those he represents at the Roman puppet-theatre: a man who sees the evils of his society as 'inevitable and eternal', and who responds to his situation with irony and contempt. But he is also a man with 'no wish to bring about' practical changes because he has no belief that change can mean anything but superficial alteration. For Stendhal, change is repetition in disguise.

VI

Goethe wished to experience a spiritual rebirth at Rome, a change that would transform his immediate historical life into a deathless form correspondent to the Eternal City he identified with. The same pursuit dominates the Romanism of Chateaubriand, de Staël, and Byron, as we have seen, and in Stendhal it achieves its ironic conclusion. When Alberto Moravia, himself a Roman, praises Stendhal's work for its modernity, he helps to explain the significance of Stendhal's attitude toward Rome.

[N]o more than in Stendhal's time has novelty in modern Rome succeeded in transforming, or making an impression on, or in any way modifying, the unalterable core of Roman 'indifference.' As in 1827, so today, everything that is done and happens in Rome, happens and is done without any real participation on the part of the people . . . With the people of Rome, participation is conditioned and restricted by a deep, yet at the same time discouraging (at least as regards political effects), sense of eternity; hence the all-embracing unreality of life in Rome, which is like a magnificent stage for performing tragedy, comedy, farce, or plain drama, without it making any difference.[16]

Here is a revelation of the 'eternity' of the Eternal City which will not be found in Goethe or the Romantic writers we have considered. Here is an 'eternity' generated when social life is consciously pursued and maintained under retrograde and inveterate circumstances. Change takes place but makes no difference in Stendhalian Rome; and that famous Roman 'energy' which Stendhal celebrates is actually, Moravia says, 'a sort of irritation or exasperation' (p. 162) which erupts, like heat lightning, in an oppressive climate.

Moravia will not implicate Stendhal in the reactionary world he represented: 'it was the Italy he described with so much enjoyment that was reactionary, not the man who described it' (p. 163). This is generous, but misleading. Stendhal's Rome is as much a project of his own imagination as it is a fictional model or representation of an actual human world. The contradictions which appear in Stendhal's representation of the Rome he knew reflect the Roman culture of the period as well as Stendhal's own ideological contradictions; they do so, however, because the subject of Stendhal's books is neither the one nor the other of these particular sets of contradictions, but the meaning—the significance—of their nexus. Stendhal the writer was a political liberal with a host of embedded reactionary commitments; Rome, on the other hand, was a centre of ultramontane and conservative power which exhibited as well various contrary impulses and ideologies. The works which Stendhal produced are important because they have opened an engagement between these two worlds, and because, in doing so, they have illuminated each of these worlds in a critical way, as well as the larger European world which they shared.

[16] Alberto Moravia, 'Roman Walks', in *Man as an End*, trans. Bernard Wall, New York, 1966, p. 161; further page references are given in the text.

With Stendhal the Romantic experience of Rome, as well as the Romantic understanding of itself through that experience, achieves its most profound level—which is to say that Romanticism here encounters and acknowledges the limits of its own ideology. Not even the Byron of *Childe Harold* Canto IV was able to drive through his Romantic agony to this kind of objectivity and cool self-knowledge. What we distinguish here are the Romantic *experience* of itself and the Romantic *understanding* of itself. Byron's is perhaps the supreme example of the Romantic experience in a Roman mode, though one might also recall Shelley's *Adonais*, whose desperate heart breaks in a Rome symbolized by the grave of Keats. At Rome Shelley and Byron lament that their highest hopes have departed from all things here. In this gesture they demonstrate a refusal to part with their most cherished forms of Romantic illusion and displacement.

With Stendhal it is different, which is why Stendhal, like Heine, should be so important to later scholars and critics of Romanticism. For in Stendhal—and pre-eminently in Stendhal's experience of Rome—the Romantic Movement has summed itself up: has weighed itself in the balances of love and desire, and has found itself, as it had found all other things, finally wanting.

(1982)

Conclusion:
Imaginative Belief and Critical Commitment

I

In *The Romantic Ideology* I tried to graph the characteristic patterns of Romantic displacement in poetry. The object of this exercise was twofold: first, to expose the tragic and/or self-critical aspects of Romantic poetry, and especially of Romantic poetry carried out under utopian or transcendental signs; and second, to persuade scholars that criticism ought to be trying not to reify, or recuperate, or repeat Romantic interests and experience, but to use them for clarifying and criticizing our own immediate interests and experiences. In both cases— whether I was facing the past or the present—the project might fairly be called, as it has since in fact been called by a demurring colleague, a 'project in radical unbelief'.[1]

The book explicitly presents itself as one part of a much larger programme in historical method. Other parts will be found elsewhere, and some have yet to be undertaken. One important topic which remains to be addressed is the positive (as opposed to the critical) aspects of poetry and criticism. What, if any, are the utopian elements in the acts of Romantic displacement? Or are such displacements simply ideological illusions which call out to be demystified? Correlatively for criticism itself, is it to be no more than a set of deconstructive operations, with the past set adrift in a relativistic sea, and the present sent to wander off in a world of critical speculation and free play? According to some, the work I have been doing these past five years, and in particular the work in *The Romantic Ideology*, seems to deny poetry and criticism its positive utopian functions. After such work things of beauty cannot be joys for ever, and criticism has lost its sweetness and light. 'Whither is fled the visionary gleam?/ Where is it now, the glory and the dream?'

---

[1] This is Charles Altieri's formulation, made during the 1983 Humanities Institute Conference at University of Southern California; see his similar strictures in 'An Idea and Ideal of a Literary Canon', *Critical Inquiry* x (Sept. 1983), pp. 38-9.

We may begin by recalling a fundamental aspect of all utopian literature: that its transcendental impulses are deeply allied to satiric and critical strategies. 'We normally think of utopia as associated with the ideal, satire with the actual,' observes Robert C. Elliott. 'In fact, . . . the two modes—utopia and satire—are linked in a complex network of genetic, historical, and formal relationships.'[2] The essential dialectic is crucial to keep in mind when we read either poetry or the criticism of poetry. In the case of Romantic poetry, as we know, the impulse to transcendence is always allied to critical moves against the phenomenal and the given, including those things which the poets give and represent to themselves. Blake, Shelley, and Byron exemplify this aspect of Romantic poetry most clearly, I suppose, because all three often resort to traditional satiric and critical strategies. But the critical and self-critical aspects of Romantic poetry are present in all its forms, as scholars, especially more recent scholars, have regularly observed.

This relationship of utopia and satire, of 'the ideal . . . with the actual', bears further investigation, particularly in the context of Romantic poetry. In a purely critical or negative sense, Romantic poetry can be shown to re-enact the internal contradictions of its own expressed ideal attachments. Romantic melancholy and Romantic irony are the manifestations of the presence of such re-enactments, the felt truths of those longed-for lies which the poets were sometimes compelled to defend. The exposure of this special dynamism in Romantic poetry is one of the principal topics of *The Romantic Ideology*. It is the well-known dynamic of Romantic displacement.

The question then obtrudes: does this dynamic have a positive dimension? The answer is what readers and critics of Romantic poetry have always believed, that it does.[3] We may begin to glimpse the presence of this positive utopianism by considering for a moment a famous passage in Wordsworth's 'Prospectus' to *The Recluse*. I choose this as my point of departure for purely tactical reasons; that is to say, I choose it because in *The Romantic Ideology* I used Wordsworth as my paradigm example of the dynamism of Romantic displacement.

[2] Robert C. Elliott, *The Shape of Utopia*, Chicago, 1970, p. 3.
[3] See, for example, the recently published *English Romanticism. The Grounds of Belief*, by John Clubbe and Ernest J. Lovell, Jr., DeKalb, Illinois, 1983.

After telling us that 'the Mind of Man' will be 'the main region of my song' (lines 40-1), Wordsworth asks his famous question about

> Paradise, and groves
> Elysian, Fortunate fields—like those of old
> Sought in the Atlantic Main—why should they be
> A history only of departed things,
> Or a mere fiction of what never was?
>
> (lines 47-51)[4]

Human desire, in Wordsworth's view, insists upon the actuality of these things, and Wordsworth's scheme in which the 'discerning intellect of man' is 'wedded to this goodly universe' (lines 52-3) is the mechanism for grounding the reality of paradise in the earth and mortal world.

As we know, Wordsworth gradually moved to interiorize this mortal utopia, to situate it in that Christian space we call the 'paradise within'. This is his act of displacement carried out under the emotional signs of sorrow and nostalgia. A critical intelligence sees the act as the locus of contradictions which Wordsworth's own expressed interests serve to reveal. For if this inward paradise is actual, human, and situated in time, it is marked by 'a deep distress' as well. And yet Wordsworth had said, in the 'Prospectus', that his new human paradise would be marked by no contradictions or signs of conflict, that it would be a place of celebration, a 'spousal', a 'great consummation'.

We understand the structure of this contradiction when we turn to Book XI of *The Prelude*, where Wordsworth again speaks about paradise and utopia in an equally famous passage and in entirely analogous ways. In the dawning of the French revolution when it was bliss to be alive, all those who had 'fed their childhood on dreams' of a new human world 'Now . . . found' a social structure in which to realize them (lines 125-39 *passim*):

> Not in Utopia,—subterranean fields,—
> Or some secreted island, Heaven knows where,
> But in the very world which is the world

---

[4] My texts from Wordsworth here are taken from *William Wordsworth. The Poems*, ed. John O. Hayden, Harmondsworth, 1977.

Of all of us,—the place where, in the end,
We find our happiness, or not at all.

(lines 140-4)

But when Wordsworth found his hopes raised with the rising of
France defrauded, he turned them inward, substituting a
psychological space and process for the failure of his social
hopes. Once again, however, the crucial element to see in this
process of displacement is the sign of contradiction: the 'deep
distress', or what he calls in *The Prelude* 'the anxiety of hope'
(xii. 313). Milton's paradise within is the fulfilment of hope
and a place of happiness far exceeding the primal paradise. In
Wordsworth the inner paradise of imagination is only 'Not
without hope', a place filled by 'the still sad music of humanity'
and the 'soothing thoughts that spring/ Out of human suffering'. The 'joy' and the 'bliss' which announced Wordsworth's
new paradise, in his childhood and again in France, have
departed.

It would be easy enough, nor entirely wrong, to take Wordsworth's melancholy imagination of a human paradise as proof
that his greatest ethical and poetic aspirations had failed of
achievement. This 'failure' arrives, however, because Wordsworth was trapped by the contradictions which arose from his
own demand for a utopia that would not be situated beyond the
social world of human beings. He never gave over that demand.
The nostalgia that marks his presentation of the paradise within shows us that he (quite literally) could not *imagine* (though he
could *conceive*) the 'Perfect contentment, Unity entire' of which
he spoke in *The Recluse* (lines 142-51) and which he laboriously
sketched in *The Excursion*, particularly in Book IX. We conclude, therefore, that the figures which represent the final
accomplishment of 'unity of being' are the figures of ideology:
of the wishes and interests which lay behind Wordsworth's
actual poetic productions. We honour Wordsworth's poetic
achievements, however, not for these figures of unity and accomplishment, but for the resistances he brought against these
figures, and for the dissatisfactions and yearnings he drew out
of them.

Therefore, if we reflect upon the structure of Wordsworth's
poetic displacements we will see something besides the failure

of an accomplishment. To the Wordsworth who desired in this world a state of 'Perfect contentment, Unity entire,' the apparent failure of this hope was first consciously experienced in the fiercely conflicted social world of France and Europe, as he tells us in *The Prelude*. The second failure—which Geoffrey Hartman was the first to describe in clearest terms—took place in the psychic space of Wordsworth's mind and his mind's imaginary projection, the 'England' of *The Excursion*. For according to Wordsworth's poetic representations of these failures, each is distinguished by various signs of division, conflict, contradiction. These disruptions in Wordsworth's imagination of an accomplishment gained in the political and social order are replaced—or displaced—as a scheme of psychic struggles and disruptions. In the latter case Wordsworth finds himself able to accommodate both his need for 'contentment' and peace, and his demand that this peace be achieved in a state of perpetual tension and dynamism which is characteristic of a mortal existence in history and society. Sometimes his poetry represents this accommodation in flat and non-dynamic terms, but his best work—which Hartman concentrates upon—represents the accommodation as always taking place under the emotional signs of fear, sorrow, dissatisfaction, longing. In these poems and passages—they do not need citation, they are familiar to us all—we encounter Wordsworth's experience of a dynamic world which tears at and drives itself on its own energies of frustration and desire. And Wordsworth's perfect contentment with this dynamic world appears in his poetry as a sense of wonder, or surprise, in which his personal desires seem to have been transcended by a glimpse into a dynamic so vast as to be all but incomprehensible: 'Of first and last and midst and without end.'

What I want to argue is that the full meaning of this dynamism —the model in which it originates and the completion in which it ends—lies in that one crucial something which is always evermore about to be in Wordsworth's scheme of psychic displacements, but which never actually arrives because it has been radically or consciously displaced. Wordsworth's dynamic of human process and hope is grounded in his losses, and the greatest of these losses is the unachieved reality of the human order glimpsed and promised at the time of the French Revolution. For it was then that Wordsworth first saw the dialectic operating in its ultimate human form, in the social and political struggles not merely in France but throughout Europe—in, that this is to say, 'the very world which is the world/ Of all of us'.

We are accustomed, after Hartman, to observe Wordsworth recoiling from the furthest reach of his imagination in order to naturalize his greatest longings. And we are, in addition, accustomed to locate this act of recoil in purely psychic space, in the field of Wordsworth's displacements. What we ought to see, however, is that the recoil is encompassed by political and social space, and the experiences recorded in the revolutionary books of *The Prelude*. Wordsworth naturalized and psychologized his highest imaginations, and he then set these displacements under the truth-sign of his Romantic melancholy. The utopian dimension of his work lies precisely in that love which cannot speak its name, in his longing for the highest world his imagination could conceive: the world of a dynamic social order which he first hypothesized, as a child, as an order of natural feelings, and which he first experienced, self-consciously, in the revolutionary social upheavals of the 1790s. It is this human world toward which his poetry points and longs, the world that he lost and, having lost, that he then banished and denounced. But it is the world to which his poetry finally remains true. Not all of Wordsworth's reactionary political ideas could cure him of his sorrow and sense of loss, or convince him of his contentment, or—finally—cause him to break faith with his socialized and dynamic idea of utopia.

So we conclude that this central stylistic device of Romantic poetry, the act of displacement, also locates the radically utopian element of the Romantic ideology. The act of displacement at once perpetuates the condition of desire and calls attention to the lost object of desire. More than this, however, it defines—at a defended remove—the special character of Wordsworth's imagination of what the human world should be: a dynamic society composed of various elements whose dialectics and collisions provide the ground for a constant process of self-critical development. This is the invisibilized imaginative faith of the entire *Prelude*, and not least of the famous central passage in Book VI which culminates in the Gorge of Gondo. In fact,

Wordsworth's displacement of his social vision permits him to define through a poetic enactment the radically new element in his social vision: the idea of a society which actively criticizes and alters itself as the need arises. Wordsworth's interiorized displacement is a critique of the social world of his period in England, France, and Europe generally, a statement that what *is* nowhere corresponds to what *should be*. Displacement is therefore Wordsworth's poetical version of the act of social criticism which his newly imagined form of social order demands of society. To read that critique, at this point in time, as an invitation to substitute interiorized spiritual values for social ones is, in my view, a travesty of Wordsworth's work.

In this respect Wordsworth's case is paradigmatic for Romantic work as a whole, which is everywhere characterized by similar patterns of displacement. Displacement is one process by which people have preserved the divine vision in a time of trouble. The word 'divine' here, Blake's word, is itself a displacement. It means in fact 'human', as Blake always insisted; and it means 'human' in the fullest sense, in the sense that to be human is to live not in the heart or the imagination alone, but in a political and social world of shared and conflicting values and commitments.

As the characteristic move in a Romantic programme, then, displacement re-enacts the experiences and processes of loss. Later clerics of the Romantic experience have often made haste to tell us, however, that Romantic melancholy and Romantic agony find their compensations, that they do not stand or end in loss and sorrow. Wordsworth himself can seem to license such a view in many of his greatest poetic moments—for example, in the famous conclusion to the 'Intimations Ode' where he says that for the loss of 'the radiance'

> We will grieve not, rather find
> Strength in what remains behind.
> (Lines 180-1)

Yet this is clearly a problematic statement, for whatever the ideas may *seem* to say, we know that the poem keeps its sorrow to the end. Abundant recompense does not unmake the experience of loss, it only sharpens Wordsworth's sense of what will never be unbroken and what will never again return. We should cherish the ambiguity in the phrase 'what remains behind', where Wordsworth looks before and after, to the lost past and the unarrived future, and where he finds his strength in despair and hope at once. This paradox is one of the chief features of Wordsworth's and Romanticism's human, secular faith.

'Not without hope we suffer and we mourn.' It is a difficult banner to enlist under, a sign in which you may be certain *not* to conquer. Wordsworth gave up for lost his political faith and commitments, but they stayed to haunt him by their absence, the ghosts of a past and future promise that would not be kept. They are what darkens the spousal and consummation of all his verse; they are also what drives it to persist in its quest for a world raised up in imagination by need and desire. Reading Wordsworth, and the Romantics in general, one is constantly reminded of Benjamin's 'Theses on the Philosophy of History' and of the utopian social projects advanced by Horkheimer and the Frankfurt School:

ever since the transition from religious longing to conscious social practice, there continues to exist an illusion which can be exposed but never entirely banished. It is the image of a perfect social justice.
  It is impossible that such justice should ever become a reality within history. For, even if a better society develops and eliminates the present disorder, there will be no compensation for the wretchedness of past ages and no end to the distress in nature.[5]

From this hopelessness comes, however, 'not the refusal of the idea [of perfect social justice] but the understanding of the limits set to its fulfillment'.[6] Wordsworth's understanding of those limits is, of course, different from Horkheimer's because Wordsworth worked at a far different historical point in 'the transition from religious longing to conscious social practice'. None the less, both men, in Benjamin's phrase, 'brush history against the grain'[7] and measure their work by its commitments to the lost and the victimized, in whose ranks they are numbered as well. Consequently, we understand that Wordsworth's call

---

[5] Max Horkheimer, 'Thoughts on Religion', in *Critical Theory. Selected Essays*, trans. by Matthew J. O'Connell and Others, New York, 1972, pp. 129-30.
  [6] Ibid., p. 130.
  [7] Walter Benjamin, 'Theses on the Philosophy of History', in *Illuminations*, ed. with an Introduction by Hannah Arendt, New York, 1969, p. 257.

for a 'Perfect contentment, Unity entire' is just the ideology of his imaginative beliefs, the kind of dreamy and inhuman idea which is exorcised in a poem like 'Peele Castle'. Wordsworth's true voice of feeling is much closer to Horkheimer's, with its brave and terrible human demands. Like Horkheimer's, Wordsworth's truth is darker, more intransigent, more *faithful*.

The particular historical locus of Wordsworth and the other Romantics, however, give to their work a uniquely personal slant. Like Byron and Shelley, Wordsworth reflected the networks and tensions of an undesired human world as a psychic drama—social distress represented as an outrage on the person, injustice at an egotistical sublime. Horkheimer, on the other hand, dismissed every inclination to internalize such problems. A theory of social justice, he maintained, does not

bring salvation to those who hold it. Inseparable from drive and will, it preaches no psychic condition, as does the Stoa or Christianity. The martyrs of freedom have not sought their own peace of soul. Their philosophy was politics, and if their souls remained calm in the face of terror, this was not their goal. Nor could the dread they experienced bear witness against them.[8]

This is a severity that recalls Trotsky's characterization of the makers of the Russian Revolution.[9] Perhaps it is too impersonal, but then perhaps the Romantic salient is sensitized to excess. The social and historical circumstances, in each instance, help to explain these divergent moods of address. All we might want to say, at this present vantage, is that the absence of either position would alone seem truly intolerable.

(1983)

---

[8] 'Traditional and Critical Theory. Postscript', ibid., p. 252.
[9] See Leon Trotsky, *The Russian Revolution*, selected and edited by F. W. Dupee, New York, 1959, pp. 250-1.

Theses on the Philosophy of Criticism

I. Poetry is, from the individual's point of view, a particular type of human *experience*; from a social point of view, however, it is an *event*. Criticism studies these experiences and events in their successive and interrelated apparitions. A work of poetry is not a thing or an object, nor should criticism conceive it as such; it is the result of an interactive network of productive people and forces.

II. A work of poetry always enters the horizon of an experience as a unique ordering of unique appearances. The uniqueness of any current experience becomes clear when we can observe, for that experience, the history of its differentials and continuities with other unique experiences.

III. A work of poetry produces 'a shock of recognition'. Criticism ought to make it equally clear why the experience seemed both a shock and a recognition.

IV. Any current interpretation of a work of poetry issues from the previous history of the work's meanings. One of the functions of criticism is to elucidate those meanings on their own terms. To do this is to hypothesize a structure of differentials and continuities (periodization) in the history of the meanings. This hypothesis is commonly called 'historicism'. It is a heuristic methodology for setting in motion a critical point of view into the immediate act of interpretation.

V. What is called 'beauty' in poetry is that which elicits our (human) interest at an emotional/intuitive level. Another function of criticism is to produce an equivalent discourse which demonstrates, in an immediate act of reflection (in both senses), that emotional/intuitive response.

VI. Interpretation may be critical or uncritical. Uncritical interpretation produces those meanings for the poetic experience which are generated out of an immediate set of particular human interests. Those meanings may be either historicist or otherwise. Critical interpretation installs a set of interpretive differentials by which the 'original' meanings of the artistic experience can be known and judged. It develops a set of correlative and antithetical meanings of the meanings.

VII. In the pursuit of these meanings of the meanings, if the initial interpretation is not an historicist one, then the antithetical interpretation must be grounded in the historicist hypothesis.

VIII. The historicist hypothesis, in the human sciences, is the necessary (but not sufficient) ground of any critical activity. Without it, the dialectic of investigation must remain purely intersystemic.

(1984)

Index